THE EC PUBLIC
PROCUREMENT RULES

THE EC PUBLIC PROCUREMENT RULES:
A Critical Analysis

JOSÉ M. FERNÁNDEZ MARTÍN

CLARENDON PRESS · OXFORD
1996

Oxford University Press, Walton Street, Oxford OX2 6DP
Oxford New York
Athens Auckland Bangkok Bombay
Calcutta Cape Town Dar es Salaam Delhi
Florence Hong Kong Istanbul Karachi
Kuala Lumpur Madras Madrid Melbourne
Mexico City Nairobi Paris Singapore
Taipei Tokyo Toronto
and associated companies in
Berlin Ibadan

Oxford is a trade mark of Oxford University Press

Published in the United States
by Oxford University Press Inc., New York

British Library Cataloguing in Publication Data
Data available

Library of Congress Cataloging in Publication Data
Fernández Martín, José María.
The EC public procurement rules / José María Fernández Martín.
p. cm.
Includes bibliographical references.
1. *Government purchasing—Law and legislation—European Economic*
Community countries. 2. *Public contracts—European Economic*
Community countries. I. Title.
KJE5632.F47 1995
346.4'023—dc20
[344.0623] 95–46835
ISBN 0–19–826017–2

1 3 5 7 9 10 8 6 4 2

Typeset by Graphicraft Typesetters Ltd, Hong Kong
Printed in Great Britain
on acid-free paper by
Bookcraft Ltd., Midsomer Norton, Avon

A una castellana de sólidos principios y a un gallego sabio.
Por todo.

'Dend-aqui vexo un caminho que non sei a donde vai,
po-lo mismo que non sei, quixera o poder andar'

Rosalía de Castro, 1958.

Foreword

Francis Snyder*

Public procurement has long been (and remains) among the most controversial areas of law and policy in the European Union. It raises two sets of intractable practical and theoretical issues. The first set concerns the nature of decision-making: the level of decision-making, decision procedures, the legitimacy of decisions, the relation of procedures and outcomes to their political and economic context, and the distribution of power between the European Community and the Member States. The second set refers to the role of the state in the economy: for example, to what extent, and how, should the state be involved in macro- and micro-economic processes, either directly, for example by means of public ownership, or indirectly, for example by means of public procurement; what are the differences between the public sphere and the private sphere; and what is the meaning of the 'public interest' in the contemporary world and how may it best be advanced and safeguarded. These sets of issues are interwoven in European Community public procurement law. It thus constitutes a formidable challenge to any observer or policy-maker.

In this innovative book, Dr José María Fernández Martín proves himself more than equal to this challenge. The book not only deals skillfully with a highly technical area of law; it is also very ambitious in its theoretical scope. By design, it departs considerably from most legal analysis of the topic. The bulk of legal scholarship in this field—regardless of its many merits—begins and ends with legal doctrine, the 'black-letter' law consisting of Treaty articles, legislation and judicial decisions. In contrast, Dr Fernández invites us also to try to understand the law as it operates in its social, political and economic context. Of course he analyses the law as it has evolved. But he also identifies the implicit assumptions of the lawmakers, the basic structural features of public procurement as a 'sector' of the economy, and the enduring features of the European Community legal system. In this respect this book exemplifies the best work of the European University Institute in Florence, where an earlier draft was awarded the PhD degree with Distinction.

Dr Fernández' book deserves our attention also because it is a detailed and highly acute analysis of a legislative failure. Such an analytical task

* Professor of European Community Law, European University Institute, Florence; Professor of Law, College of Europe, Bruges; Honorary Visiting Professor of Law, University College London.

may seem unusual in the world of legal scholarship. It is, however, well known and highly considered in the fields of public policy and sociology of law, even though these fields, like legal scholarship itself, usually focus on the impact of law rather than the law's lack of impact. As if inspired by these sister subdisciplines, this book seeks to explain why European Community law has had so little success in achieving its main aim of opening public procurement markets. In other words, why has the legislation been so ineffective? Dr Fernández' answer is that we must look at the context in which the law operates. By this, he means the structural features of public procurement, together with those of the supranational system of European Community law. He argues, in my view convincingly, that these factors explain the ineffectiveness of law. His study of legislative failure thus is highly productive, fully justifying its choice of subject, analytic strategy and emphasis on certain explanatory factors. It deserves serious attention from both academic observers and policy-makers.

Let me mention some of the features of this work which struck me the most. The book forces us to ask—and to answer—the question as to what 'failure' means with regard to a legislative programme. Can we measure it? How do we evaluate it? Indeed, what does it mean to 'measure' or to 'evaluate' failure, to mention only two of the socio-legal processes with which this book deals? What are its implications for the legal and political system and for other legal and political processes? Reflection on these questions should stimulate us to integrate the study of legislative processes and the implementation of law with the study of organisations. We need to understand how organisations learn, and in this particular context how the European Union institutions learn.

Dr Fernández' explanation of the lack of legal impact emphasises several factors: the inadequacy of prior research, the lack of a cost-benefit analysis, a failure to appreciate economic structures, and a belief in the power of law. The last factor is of special interest to European Union lawyers. The symbolic and substantive importance of law to European integration has very often been stressed, sometimes at the risk of over-emphasis and to the detriment of a real understanding of the ideology of law. By focusing on a counter-example, this book points us in the direction of a more adequate appraisal of the role and limits of law as an instrument of social change. It offers a perspective which is surely needed in the contextual study of European Union law.

European Community public procurement legislation, in Dr Fernández' view, led to substantial changes in national legislation but few changes in national practice. This observation calls upon us to ask, once again, how law and society fit together, whether they are best conceived as separate but related spheres or as integral to each other. The reader of this fascinating study might ask whether practice has affected the law, even if the law appears not to have affected practice. If prophets fail, how are they affected by the fact that the predicted end of the world does not occur? The perspective presented in this book challenges us to reflect on the context of law. The context may not only blunt the impact of law but also, in a later phase, be integrated into the elaboration and implementation of legislation.

Dr Fernández shows us that the field of public procurement is a veritable laboratory for the study of law and social change. In the European Union this inevitably involves the relation between several levels of government, particularly the European Community and its Member States. As this book indicates, the relationship is not at all uni-directional. The impact of European Community law is not to be presumed: legislation and judicial decisions are not unerring guides to practice. This book invites us to reflect on how European Community law operates in practice, and why. It must be admitted that there are many ways to study the law in its social, political, economic and cultural context. Dr Fernández's work should serve as an inspiring and stimulating example for his colleagues and for students of the study of European Community law in context.

Acknowledgements

The author would like to express his gratitude to the following:

Prof. Francis Snyder for his invaluable help and advice while supervising my work.

Prof. Sue Arrowsmith. Many parts of the argument have greatly benefited from long discussions with her.

Prof. Christian Joerges, who together with Prof. Snyder, encouraged me and my fellow research colleagues at the EUI always to look at things from the other side of the fence.

Profs. Lucía Millán Moro and Diego Javier Liñan Nogueras for being members of the jury at my thesis defence.

All my colleagues at Leicester University Law Faculty and University of Cádiz Law Faculty at Jerez for their support and friendship.

Manolo, Sesé, Carmen, Alvarito, Pepe, Marcos y Alvaro, my family, for putting up with me during all these years (and hopefully putting up with me in the future).

And, above all, my wife Síofra O'Leary. She knows.

On a personal level, I am grateful to my good friends Edurne, Sara, Declan, Peter K., Kenny, Kath, Dave Black, Niav, Salva, Coro, and to all the members of the International Heroes Football Club, for all those goal passes . . . which I missed.

Without all of them, this book would have never seen the light of day.

On the institutional side, I am grateful to the following institutions:
The Fundación Ramón Areces, whose scholarship allowed me to pursue my research without any financial constraints.

The EUI's academic and administrative staff. Possibly the best place to research, enjoy it and broaden one's intellectual and personal perspectives.

The Publications Committee of the EUI for subsidizing the proof-reading of the final manuscript.

The Bar-Fiasco Association for its invaluable help.

The Spanish Government for financing my stay at the EUI.

This book is based on the PhD thesis defended by the author at the European University Institute, Florence, in November 1993.

Contents

List of Figures

List of Abbreviations

A number of periodicals are referred to in abbreviated form. The abbreviations used are as follows:

Cahiers de Droit Européen	CDE
Common Market Law Review	CMLRev
European Competition Law Review	ECLR
European Law Review	ELRev
Industrial Law Journal	ILJ
International and Comparative Law Quarterly	ICLQ
Journal of Common Market Studies	JCMS
Law Quarterly Review	LQR
Legal Issues of European Integration	LIEI
Modern Law Review	MLR
Public Procurement Law Review	PPLR
Revista de Aministración Pública	RPA
Revista Española de Derecho Administrativo	REDA
Revue du Marché Commun	RMC
Revue Trimestrielle de Droit Européen	RTDE
Yearbook of European Law	YEL

All other periodicals are referred to by their full names.

Table of Cases

SPAIN

UNITED KINGDOM

Table of Legislation

Regulations

Treaties

Agreements

OTHER JURISDICTIONS

France

Germany

Italy

Spain

United States of America

General Introduction

In Western capitalist societies, with the exception of a few key strategic economic sectors where public involvement is greater (such as telecommunications, energy and certain transport sectors), the State very rarely manufactures and produces through State-owned enterprises the goods and services which public authorities require in order to perform their public duties. Public authorities normally resort to the market to purchase and contract their needs. This purchasing is legally articulated through the conclusion of contracts between public authorities and the providers of services and supplies. Due to the wide range of activities covered, public contracting does not easily fit into a dogmatic definition. In general terms, a public contract is any written contract in which a public authority, understood in a broad sense, concludes an agreement with another legal or natural person.[1]

Public contracts constitute, however, a special category of contract. The fact that one of the parties is regarded as representing the public interest determines the specificity of public contracts as compared with contracts entered into by private parties. The way in which public authorities form the will to enter a contract, the budgetary and political constraints on their contracting activities, the public interest usually underlying the contract itself and the need for a strict supervision of the performance of the contract characterize public contracting activities as an autonomous legal category which is subject, to a greater or lesser extent depending on the national legal approach, to particular rules and principles.

This theoretical legal interest is further supplemented by the economic importance attached to public procurement. Due to the level of public spending involved and the sectors in which it takes place, public contracting decisions have unquestionable effects on local, national and, according to some, supranational economies. When, where, what and from whom public authorities buy acquires crucial importance for the profitability, survival or development of certain economic sectors or regions. In brief, public contracts constitute a complex area where economic, political and legal aspects converge.

The interest in public procurement has transcended national boundaries. In the Community context, due to its economic importance and the alleged large quantitative and qualitative economic benefits which would result for the European Communities as a whole, the liberalisation of public procurement markets to European-wide competition has become

---

[1] See Flamme, *Traité Théorique et Pratique des Marchés Publics* (Bruxelles, 1969) at 173.

a priority of supranational regulation. The first positive legal Community measures in the sector date from the early 1970s. However, according to the Commission's findings, they proved ineffective for the achievement of the intended interpenetration of public markets. Thus, many new rules intended to overcome the obstacles experienced were adopted and a stricter monitoring policy was applied after 1985. The main objective was to enhance the effectiveness of the previous rules. As a result, detailed Community rules now cover practically all areas in which national public authorities resort to the private market in order to contract for the goods and services they require.

The main contribution to existing literature intended by this book consists in the analysis of the real causes for the ineffectiveness of the supranational measures in the public procurement sector. In other words, the question we want to answer is, why have the Community rules so far been ineffective and how may they be improved? Delimiting the parameters according to which the 'effectiveness' of legal rules is to be measured is, however, not an easy task.[2] Effectiveness of legal norms may only be achieved through the successful interaction of different factors such as the actual content of the measure, their suitability to the reality they intend to regulate, their correct implementation by the competent authorities and the existence of a set of adequate means of control to ensure compliance. In fact, effectiveness can be measured at two different levels. On a first level, rules can be held to be effective on the basis of a substantive criterion, i.e., whether they are well designed 'to achieve the goals that society regards as desirable'.[3] On a second level, effectiveness is measured in procedural terms: regardless of the social legitimacy of the objectives of the rules, rules can be regarded as effective if they are complied with, that is, when the enforcement mechanism is in itself sufficient to ensure compliance.[4]

In addition, effectiveness of legal rules must necessarily be assessed from a contextual perspective. The legal, political and economic context in which rules are adopted and operate influence, to a large extent, the degree of success in their application. This is particularly the case of Community legal measures.[5] The decision-making process, the objectives to be achieved, the implementation and enforcement mechanisms operating in the Community supranational structure differ quite markedly from those existing in a typical unitary legal system. All these distinctive features influence and

---

[2] Theoretical discussions are not dealt with herein. For a broad definition of the concept of the effectiveness of European Community law see Snyder, 'The Effectiveness of European Community Law: Institutions, Processes, Tools and Techniques' (1993) 56 MLR 19.

[3] Tullock, 'Two Kinds of Legal Efficiency', (1979–80) 8 *Hofstra Law Review* 659. This of course poses the problem of delimiting what objectives are socially desirable.

[4] Ibid. This second test is easier to apply as it merely requires the assessment of the degree of compliance with the norms, without entering into any moral evaluation.

[5] See Weiler, 'The Transformation of Europe' (1991) 100 *Yale Law Journal* 2403 at 2409.

condition the manner in which rules are adopted, applied and enforced, as well as the objectives which may be reasonably achieved by a supranational regulation. In the case of the rules on public procurement, a contextual analysis is even more unavoidable insofar as this area is heavily influenced by political, economic and legal considerations, each of which are of similar importance.

The book attempts to tackle all these aspects of the 'effectiveness' problem of the Community rules on public procurement. Chapter 1 describes the evolution of the public procurement policy of the Community from its origins as well as the measures adopted to bring it into effect. This provides the necessary background on which the substantial analysis is subsequently developed. Public procurement policy in the EC is then placed in its economic and political context in Chapters 2 and 3. The Community policy is assessed on its economic and political merits and is confronted with approaches followed at national level. Any potential conflicts are highlighted. Thereafter, Chapters 4 and 5 discuss the first element of effectiveness, that is, whether the public procurement rules are 'effectively' designed to attain the integration of public procurement markets which the Community seeks to achieve, taking into due consideration the peculiar features of the Community institutional and legal structure. Chapter 4 examines the way in which the Community measures have been implemented at national level. The influence which the implementation measures have had on the application of the Community provisions is assessed. Chapter 5 explores the reasons which may explain the ineffectiveness of the Community rules at the application level. Finally, Chapters 6 to 10 are devoted to the exhaustive analysis of the procedural effectiveness. The supranational measures adopted to combat the lack of procedural effectiveness are thoroughly analysed.

From the examination of each of these stages, the reasons which may explain the lack of success of the Community's public procurement policy are deduced. It is submitted that the failure of the Community policy in the area may be the result of certain structural features peculiar to public procurement markets, rather than to bad will on the part of national contracting authorities. It is believed that these aspects had been overlooked by the Community, and in particular by the Commission, when the policy was originally designed and later revised. In the light of the conclusions reached, the Community public procurement policy is then read in terms of the subsidiarity principle. That is, how this principle, understood in its broadest sense, may or should apply to the EC policy on public procurement. Alternative strategies more in line with the subsidiarity principle are finally proposed.

1

The Evolution of European Community Policy on Public Procurement

INTRODUCTION

Public procurement policy has undergone a remarkable evolution in the European Community. From an uncelebrated origin, it became one of the chosen sons of the 1992 Internal Market project. The object of this chapter is to outline this evolution briefly. The general principles which have inspired Community policy, the changes which occurred after the 1985 'White Paper', the chosen means for its execution and, above all, the alleged reasons explaining its ineffectiveness are analysed in the following pages. This analysis will provide the necessary background against which the critical assessment of European Community (EC) public procurement policy will be developed. A substantial number of works have been devoted to the analysis of the Community rules and their interpretation and application. As a result, this chapter will not embark on a substantial analysis of the legal technicalities and case law which surround these rules. Readers interested in knowing more in this respect may refer to the numerous works which are cited where appropriate.[1]

The chapter is divided into two sections, each of them relating to certain time-periods. First, the original policy applied by the Community institutions is discussed. This involves the examination of the relevant EC Treaty[2] rules and the original secondary legal measures adopted in the area. The second section starts with the analysis of the impact of these original measures on the opening up of public contracts to European-wide competition and the redefintion of the Community's policy in the field after 1985. The main traits of the new policy are set out and the legal instruments intended to give effect to this new policy are considered. For various reasons, public contracts became a priority of the Community's internal market agenda.

---

[1] On the Community rules see generally Trepte, *Public Procurement in the EC* (London, 1993); Weiss, *Public Procurement in European Community Law* (London, 1993). With respect to the Court of Justice's case law see Arrowsmith, *A Guide to the Procurement Cases of the Court of Justice* (Winteringham, 1992) and Michel, 'La jurisprudence de la Cour de Justice sur les marchés publics' (1994) *Revue du Marché Unique Européen* 135.

[2] The EEC Treaty became the EC Treaty after the adoption of the Treaty on European Union. Original provisions of the EEC Treaty will be cited where necessary.

1957–1984: THE EC TREATY AND THE FIRST CO-ORDINATION
DIRECTIVES

The EC Treaty[3]

The Silence of the EC Treaty

Apart from Article 132(4) EC, which is the only provision which explicitly refers to public procurement,[4] and Article 223(1)(b) EC which directly affects public procurement in the defence sector,[5] the original EC Treaty does not contain any specific provision laying down a general Community regime applicable to public contracts. Some commentators have suggested that the economic and strategic importance of public contracts constituted the most serious obstacle for reaching a compromise for their specific regulation in the EC Treaty.[6] Public contracts were regarded as a privileged instrument for intervening in the economy and pursuing a wide range of social, political and economic policy objectives and Member States were reluctant to include such a sensitive issue in the agenda of EC Treaty negotiations.[7]

Other reasons may, however, better explain the original EC Treaty's

[3] On the application of the EC Treaty provisions to public procurement activities and the initial years of the Community's public procurement policy, see Margue, 'L'ouverture des marchés publics dans la Communauté (1ère partie)' (1991) *Revue du Marché Unique Européen* 143 at 149 *ff*; Cartou, 'Les marchés publics dans la Communauté Economique Européenne', in *Mélanges dédiés à Gabriel Marty* (Toulouse, 1979) at 267; Clouet, 'Travaux publics et marché commun' (1969) RMC 83; Hainaut et Joliet, *Les Contrats de Travaux et de Fournitures de l'Administration*, Tome II, (Bruxelles, 1963) 229 *ff*; Weiss, 'Public Procurement in the EEC—Public Supply Contracts' (1988) 13 ELRev 318 at 319 *ff*; Weiss, 'The Law of Public Procurement in EFTA and the EEC: the Legal Framework and its Implementation' (1987) 7 YEL 59; Winter, 'Public Procurement in the EEC' (1991) 28 CMLRev 741 at 743; Ojeda Marín, 'La Comunidad Europea y el GATT en el moderno Sistema de Contratación Pública' (1988) RAP 409 at 413 *ff*; Turpin, 'Public Contracts in the EEC' (1972) 9 CMLRev 411; Benazet, 'Marchés publics de travaux et traité de Rome' (1963) 29 *Revue Internationale des Sciences Administratives* 235; Flamme, *Traité Théorique et Pratique des Marchés Publics* (Brussels, 1969) 269 *ff*; Flamme, 'La libéralisation de la concurrence dans les marchés publics au sein de la CEE' (1965) RMC 277; Rainaud, 'Les marchés publics dans la Communauté Economique Europénne' (1972) RMC 365.

[4] The scope of this provision is limited to the relationships between Member States and the Overseas Countries and Territories. A general Community legal regime applicable to public contracts cannot be deduced from it. On this provision and its relation to public contracts, see generally, Hainaut et Joliet (above, n 3) at 230.

[5] Article 223 EC provides for a general exemption from the applicability of Community legislation for products intended for specifically military purposes. This raises the sensitive issue of defence procurement, which is dealt with in Chapter 5.

[6] See Flamme (1969) (above, n 3) at 272.

[7] Support for this interpretation is found in a 1960 letter from Baron Snoy et d'Oppuers (at that time Belgian Secretary of State for Economic Affairs) to the *Confédération nationale de la Construction*, in which he declared that 'c'est avec sagesse que les auteurs du Traité ont résolu le problème par cette méthode, parce qu'il est à mes yeux certain que l'adoption de règles précises supprimant les discriminations en matière d'adjudication de travaux n'aurait pas été acceptée par les Parlements compétents lors de la ratification du Traité. Les traditions protectionistes de certains pays de la Communauté sont, en effet, beaucoup trop fortes pour que ce-ci ait pu être esperé.'. Cited by Flamme (1969) (above, n 3) at 272.

silence on this point. First of all, contrary to what happens with the ECSC and Euratom Treaties, the EC Treaty was conceived as a *Traité-cadre*. It lays down the general principles to govern the establishment of a common market and provides for an autonomous institutional decision-making structure whose task is to fill in the 'deliberate' regulatory gaps left by the Treaty. Due to their particular nature, public markets were not directly addressed and their eventual regulation was left to the adoption of secondary legal measures.[8] A second reason may be found in the economic context in which the negotiations were pursued. In the 1950s, the main concern of international *fora* dealing with trade liberalisation was the reduction of tariff barriers to trade. Non-tariff barriers were not deemed as significant as they later became in the 1960s and 1970s, especially after the oil crisis. 'Buy national' policies in government procurement were thus not the object of specific studies until the 1960s.[9] The Commission only started to deal with government procurement in the framework of its programme for the creation of a common industrial policy in the 1970s.[10] Furthermore, international competition in the economic sectors where public purchasing is dominant (e.g., telecommunications, energy, transport, defence, high-technological products related to defence programmes) was not as intense as it is nowadays. In these circumstances, the importance of public procurement was bound to be relegated in the negotiations leading to the EC Treaty.

Other EC Treaty Provisions which Apply Indirectly to Public Contracts

This does not mean that national public procurement regulation and policies were not affected by the Community legal regime. Apart from those provisions which gave a general competence to the Community institutions to adopt secondary legislation on matters which came within the scope of the EC Treaty, several other Treaty provisions enabled the Commission to challenge national statutory, regulatory or administrative provisions or administrative acts or practices in the field of public contracts which hindered the completion of an integrated market.

The free movement of goods provisions: Articles 30–37 EC

Member States in general, and contracting authorities in particular, have to observe the limitations imposed on their freedom of contract by the EC

---

[8] Mattera, 'La libéralisation des marchés publics et semi-publics dans la Communauté' (1973) RMC at 206.

[9] In 1970 Baldwin affirmed that: 'What is clearly needed in order to shed more light on the extent and causes of discrimination is a series of careful and thorough statistical studies by the major trading countries designed to obtain reliable data on the direct and indirect import content of government purchases', in *Non-tariff Distortions of International Trade* (Washington DC, 1970) at 78. See also OECD, *Government Purchasing in Europe, North America and Japan* (Paris, 1966).

[10] EC Commission, *Memorandum on Technological and Industrial Policy Programme* (Bruxelles, 1973); see further Hirtris, *European Community Economics* (London, 1988) at 227 *ff*.

Treaty provisions on the free movement of goods. These are mainly relevant for the case of public supply contracts as the main object of the latter is the 'delivery' of goods to contracting authorities.[11] The so-called liberalisation Directive 70/32/EEC, demonstrated how these provisions apply to public purchasing.[12] The Commission's policy in the field of public procurement does not differ substantially from its overall policy with respect to Article 30 EC.

The Court of Justice has directly applied Article 30 EC to national measures on public procurement on various occasions. By way of example, in the *Dundalk* case,[13] the Court held that the requirement that the material to be used in the realisation of certain public works was to be certified as complying with a national technical standard by a national certification institute to the exclusion of equivalent goods was contrary to Article 30 EC. In the *Du Pont de Nemours* and *Laboratorio Bruneau* cases[14] preferential public procurement schemes which reserved a proportion of public supply contracts to undertakings established in a particular region were precluded by Article 30 EC. Article 30 EC was also found to prohibit the inclusion of the so-called 'national origin' clauses whereby all interested firms are invited to present an offer on the condition that, as far as possible, national materials and labour are used.[15]

The free provision of services (Articles 59–66 EC) and right of establishment provisions (Articles 52–58)

The requirements of the free provision of services and the right of establishment apply to public procurement activities of national contracting authorities in a similar manner. The principle which underlies both sets of rules is that of 'national treatment'. No direct or indirect discrimination on the basis of nationality or the original place of establishment is

[11] Articles 30–37 EC may also apply to contracting authorities awarding service or public works contracts as demostrated by the *Dundalk* case, Case 45/87, *Commission* v. *Ireland (Dundalk)* [1988] ECR 4929 at 4963. See comment by Gormley, 'Grandfather clauses in Community Law' (1989) 14 ELRev 157. On Articles 30–37 see generally Oliver, *Free Movement of Goods in the EEC*, 2nd edn. (London, 1988).

[12] Directive 70/32 of 17 December 1969, OJ 1970, L13. In summary terms, these provisions require contracting authorities not to make the supply of foreign goods more difficult or onerous than that of national goods when awarding public supply contracts. At the end of the transitional period, the Directive's provisions have become redundant since the ban on such measures has been directly applicable (Case 78/76, *Steinike und Weinlig* v. *Germany* [1977] ECR 595). For present purposes, the 1969 Directive may be used as an interpretative guide (EC Commission, *Guide to the Community Rules on Open Procurement*, OJ 1987, C358/19 (*Vademecum*) at 10). Discussed by Margue (above, n 3) at 152 *ff*; Mattera, *Le Marché Unique Européen. Ses Règles, son Fonctionnement* (Paris 1990) at 362; Weiss (1988) (above, n 3) at 321; Winter (above, n 3) at 744.

[13] Case 45/87, *Commission* v. *Ireland (Dundalk)* (above, n 11).

[14] Case C-21/88, *Du Pont de Nemours Italiana* v. *Unità Sanitaria Locale No. 2 di Carrara* [1990] ECR I-889, confirmed by Case C-351/88, *Laboratorio Bruneau Srl* v. *Unità Sanitaria Locale RM/24 Monterotondo*, [1991] ECR I-3641. For a complete discussion of these decisions see Chapter 3.   [15] Case C-243/89, *Commission* v. *Denmark*, (the *Storeabaelt* case) [1993] ECR I-3353.

permitted.[16] The scope of these provisions has been extended by the Court of Justice beyond the concept of direct and indirect discrimination in terms parallel to those established in the *Cassis de Dijon* case law as regards the free movement of goods.[17] Thus, any obstacles to the free provision of services or right of establishment arising from domestic regulations, which are either not justified by a general interest or, if they are, do not fulfil the proportionality principle, are equally covered.[18]

These provisions of the Treaty cover both direct and indirect discriminatory or restrictive practices sponsored by Member States in the whole service sector, and are not limited to a particular service.[19] As a result, they apply not only to public works contracts, but to any other contract whose object is the provision of a service. As we shall see, the scope of application of the directly applicable Treaty provisions is broader than that of the original Directives, which were limited to the regulation of public supplies and public works contracts.

The first positive measures relating to the provisions under examination were adopted in 1962, when the Council issued the two General Programmes concerning the abolition of restrictions on freedom to provide services and the abolition of restrictions on freedom of establishment.[20] The requirements of the Programmes were implemented through Council Directives ensuring both the liberalisation and the co-ordination of award procedures for public works contracts. These were the object of a special 'liberalisation plan' in the General Programmes according to which a 'gradual and balanced' removal of restrictions, accompanied by the 'desirable measures of co-ordination of national awarding procedures' was to be applied. The Commission submitted its proposals in 1964 and two Directives were finally adopted by the Council in 1971. The liberalisation Directive 71/304 was concerned with the removal of existing restrictions.[21]

---

[16] See generally Beaumont and Weatherill, *EC Law* 2nd edn. (London, 1994) Chapter 19.

[17] Case 120/78, *Rewe-Zentrale* v. *Bundesmonopolverwaltung für Branntwein (Cassis de Dijon)* [1979] ECR 649. See generally, Beaumont and Weatherill (above, n 16) Chapter 17.

[18] For a recent review of the Court of Justice's case law on general interest exceptions in the area of services see Fernández Martín and O'Leary, 'An Analysis of Judicial Exceptions to the Free Provision of Services' (1995) *European Law Journal.*

[19] Case 71/76, *Thieffry* v. *Conseil de l'Ordre des avocats à la Cour de Paris* [1977] ECR 765.

[20] [1962] OJ at 32 (Spec. Ed. (2nd series) IX. at 3) and [1962] OJ at 36 (Spec. Ed. (2nd series) IX. at 7) respectively. With respect to public procurement activities, Member States were required to abolish restrictions progressively on freedom of establishment and freedom to provide services arising from provisions and practices which, in respect of foreign nationals only, excluded, limited or imposed conditions on the power to submit tenders for, or act directly as a party or as a subcontractor in contracts with the State or with any other legal person governed by public law. See Title III, A, second paragraph (b) of both Programmes. Concerning the General Programmes, see Turpin (above, n 3) at 412; Flamme (1969) (above, n 3) 273 *ff*; Hainaut et Joliet (above, n 3) at 248.

[21] Directive 71/304/EEC, OJ 1971, L185/1. It only applied to restrictions on freedom to provide services in connection with public works and with the award of such contracts to contractors acting through agencies or branches which were in effect at the date of the entry

Directive 71/305 was directed towards the co-ordination of procedures for the placing of such contracts. This is analysed in the next section.

The direct application of the EC Treaty provisions on the freedom to provide services and the right of establishment to public procurement matters is illustrated by several decisions of the Court of Justice. In the *Transporoute* case,[22] the Court of Justice straightforwardly quashed the requirement imposed by a Luxembourg regulation according to which, in order to bid for a public works award in Luxembourg, the tenderer had to be in possession of an establishment permit issued by Luxembourg authorities. Another direct application of the free provision of services provisions to the field of public procurement can be found in the *Rush Portuguesa* case.[23] The Court of Justice upheld the right of contractors to transfer their workforce from their home base in order to perform the contracted work under the same conditions which that State imposed on its own nationals. There was therefore no need to obtain a work permit previously from national authorities.[24] This possibility was made conditional, however, upon the fact that the workers return to their home country once the service is provided, thus preventing them from gaining access to the labour market of the host Member State.[25] Equally, in the *Data-processing* case,[26] the Court of Justice ruled that Italian provisions whereby only companies in which all or the majority of the shares are either directly or indirectly in public or State ownership may conclude agreements with the Italian State for the development of data-processing systems for public authorities, essentially favoured Italian companies and therefore constituted indirect discrimination contrary to Articles 52 and 59 EC.[27] In fact, the Italian government did not hold any shares in data-processing companies from other Member States.[28] Lastly, in *Commission v. Italy*, the Court held that an Italian law which reserved a proportion of public works to sub-contractors whose registered offices were in the region where the works were to be carried out, and which gave preference in the selection of candidates to joint ventures and consortia in which local undertakings were involved was contrary to both Articles 59 and 60 EC. The Italian government claimed that no discrimination on the basis of

---

into force of the EC Treaty. As was the case with Directive 70/32, once the transitory period had expired and since Articles 59 EC and 60 EC became directly applicable (Case 33/74, *Van Binsbergen v. Bestuur van de Berijfsvereniging voor de Metaalnijverheid* [1974] ECR 1299), the Directive only retained interpretative value. See Margue (above, n 3) at 154.

[22] Case 76/81, *SA Transporoute et Travaux v. Minister of Public Works* [1982] ECR 417. Noted by Gormley [1983] *New Law Journal* 533.

[23] Case C-113/89, *Rush Portuguesa v. Office National d'Immigration* [1990] ECR 1417.

[24] [1990] ECR 1417 at 1443.   [25] [1990] ECR 1417 at 1444.

[26] Case 3/88, *Commission v. Italy* [1989] ECR 4035.

[27] [1989] at 4059. See also Case 22/80, *Boussac v. Gerstenmeier* [1980] ECR 3427.

[28] Case 3/88, *Commission v. Italy* [1989] at 4059.

nationality existed, since any foreign company could eventually benefit from the preference. This argument was dismissed by the Court, which found the measures indirectly discriminatory. Italian companies were more likely to fulfil the criteria than foreign ones.[29]

The Insufficiencies of the Treaty Provisions for the Development of a Community Policy on Public Procurement

Public procurement was therefore not totally extraneous to the EC Treaty. However, the Community's scope for developing a policy on the exclusive basis of the provisions examined was limited. First of all, their negative character, prohibiting discriminatory conduct on the part of the State, prevented their use as instruments to solve the obstacles arising from national legal disparities. In the absence of Community harmonisation measures, all provisions and administrative practices which were not of a discriminatory nature were to remain untouched, provided they complied with the proportionality test.[30] As a result, Member States continued to apply their own rules on public contracts, with their different time-limits, procedural requirements, advertising rules, general conditions to be a candidate and so on. An undertaking willing to submit tenders throughout the Community had to face the additional difficulties which such a disparity created. Secondly, and more importantly from the Commission's point of view, no policy initiative could be implemented without the adoption of positive measures. By relying exclusively on the provisions examined, the Commission could only have shaped a policy through political bargaining and, ultimately, through the initiation of infringement actions which would provoke the Court of Justice to adopt decisions. Apart from the obvious drawbacks of such a cumbersome and slow policy-making process, the Commission's role would have been confined to a passive rather than an active shaping of the contents of the policy.

The Commission itself stressed this necessity for a positive policy when stating that '. . . the obligation not to take certain action contained [in the EC Treaty provisions] is, as experience has shown, not sufficient to bring about the desired interpenetration of the public procurement market'.[31] Thus, the enactment of Community measures 'was necessary to make sure

---

[29] Case C-360/89, *Commission* v. *Italy* [1992] ECR I-3415. This case and its relation with the *Du Pont de Nemours* case are discussed at length in Chapter 3.

[30] See Case 120/78, *Cassis de Dijon* (above, n 17) (free movement of goods provisions) and Case 33/74, *Van Binsbergen* (above, n 21) (right of establishment and free provision of services). With respect to the latter EC Treaty provisions, see also the more recent cases discussed in Fernández Martín and O'Leary (above, n 18). See generally Beaumont and Weatherill (above, n 16) Chapters 17 and 19.

[31] EC Commission, *Public Supply Contracts. Conclusions and Perspectives* COM (84) 717 at 4.

that government contracts were open to all nationalities on equal terms and to make tendering procedures more transparent so that compliance with the principles laid down in the treaties could be monitored and enforced'.[32] Once the need for positive measures was established, the Commission was faced with several options as to the content of the policy. It could adopt a minimalist approach and limit its proposals to a simple harmonisation of national award procedures. This would ensure a common minimum set of rules throughout the Community for the benefit of interested firms. Alternatively, it could pursue a more activist stance and propose a more comprehensive policy which would impose the operation of competitive tendering and European-wide advertising of contract notices, together with the increase of its monitoring activities and its involvement in the shaping of national policies in key sectors, where public purchasing was especially relevant. The analysis of the first Directives reveals that the final outcome was half-way between both positions. Some aspects of the co-ordination Directives were intended merely to supplement the shortcomings of the EC Treaty provisions, whereas others showed a broader regulatory intention.

The Co-ordination Directives concerning Public Supplies and Public Works Contracts

In view of the foregoing and building upon the assumption that there was room for greater interpenetration in the public markets at Community level, a positive Community policy in public procurement started to take shape in the 1970s, when two co-ordination Directives for public works and public supplies were adopted by the Council.[33] By explicitly calling for the adoption of a Directive to co-ordinate national award procedures, the two General Programmes paved the way for the adoption of the public works Directive in 1971. Once public works contracts were

---

[32] EC Commission, *Vademecum* (above, n 12) at 15.

[33] Council Directive 71/305 of 21 July 1971 concerning the co-ordination of procedures for the award of public works contracts, OJ 1971, L185 and Council Directive 77/62/EEC of 21 December 1976, co-ordinating procedures for the award of public supply contracts, OJ 1977, L13/1. A substantial amount has been written in relation to these first co-ordination Directives. See, *inter alia*, Margue (above, n 3) at 153 *ff*; Cartou (above, n 3) at 270 *ff*; Weiss (1988) (above, n 3) at 322 *ff*; Winter (above, n 3) at 745; Ojeda Marín (above, n 3) at 418 *ff*; Turpin (above, n 3) at 418; Thys and Henry, 'Government Procurement Regulations of the EEC' (1987) 20 *George Washington Journal of International Law & Economics* 445; Riga, 'Recent Council Directive and Commission Proposals affecting Public Procurement in the European Communities' (1989) 12 *Boston College International & Comparative Law Review* 387 at 390; Laviolette-Vanderpooten, 'Les directives européennes relatives aux marchés publics de travaux' (1972) RMC 474; Janot, 'Les accords internationaux sur les marchés publics: des résultats réels mais limités' (1985) *Revue Française d'Administration Publique* 26; Weiss (1993) (above, n 1) at Chapter 4.

regulated, public supply contracts had to follow suit. The regulations of both Directives respond, in general terms, to the same principles and their content is very similar.[34] The Court of Justice has stated that most of its case law referring to one of the Directives may apply to the provisions of the other.

The main objective of the Directives, which were based on Article 100 EC, is to increase the transparency of the procedure so that foreign contractors are granted a fair chance of winning the contract on the basis of competitive tendering. The market for public works and public supplies was to be opened first of all, by supplementing the prohibition of restrictions on the free movement of goods, the freedom of establishment and the free provision of services contained in the EC Treaty.[35] The insufficiencies of the Treaty were to be overcome by a co-ordination of national award procedures which would level the playing field throughout the Community. The regulation was based on respect, as far as possible, for the procedures and administrative practices regarding public procurement in force in each Member State. National procedures were to remain generally applicable, but were to be adapted to comply with the provisions of the Directives.[36]

The Directives are limited to the regulation of the award procedures and are not concerned with the enforcement stages of a concluded contract. Three procedures are distinguished under the Directives according to the grade of competition they allow. These are the 'open procedure', the 'restricted procedure' and the exceptional 'single tendering procedure'.[37] The former two allow for competition, whereas under single tendering procedure contracting authorities negotiate the terms of a contract directly with a supplier of their choice. Contracts awarded through single tendering procedures are generally excluded from the Directives. However, the use of this procedure is limited to the exhaustive list of cases provided in the Directives.[38] The Court of Justice has consistently applied a very strict interpretation of the conditions under which the Directives allow direct

---

[34] See Mattera (1973) (above, n 8) at 215.

[35] See preambles to Directive 77/62 and Directive 71/305.

[36] See Article 2 of both the public supplies Directive 77/62 and public works Directive 71/305.

[37] In open procedures any interested person can submit a tender. In restricted procedures all interested undertakings may submit their request for participation, proving that they fulfil the economic, financial and technical requirements laid down by the contracting authority. After that, an invitation to tender is sent by the contracting authority to those candidates who are qualified. The actual award of the contract is then decided following the award criteria laid down in the Directives.

[38] These lists strike a balance between the need to constrain the use of this non-competitive procedure and the need to respect public interest considerations which justify recourse to the single tendering procedure. See Article 6(a) to (h) of the public supplies Directive 77/62 and Article 9(a) to (h) of the public works Directive 71/305. See Mattera (1990) (above, n 12) at 365.

contracting to take place, and in all the cases which have come before it, it has never accepted any of the justifications advanced by the defendants.[39]

However, the Directives went further than this by introducing a set of material obligations which provided for the foundations of a Community policy. The additional objectives of ensuring the development of effective competition and bringing about a greater degree of transparency in national award procedures required national contracting authorities to be subject to certain positive obligations. This second set of rules included, principally, the obligation of European-wide advertising and the establishment of compulsory qualitative selection criteria and award criteria which were to favour competitive firms.

The common advertising rules have been described as one of the most valuable features of the Directive.[40] Contracting authorities are required to publish a notice in the Official Journal when they are going to award contracts falling within the scope of application of the Directives. As the case law of the Court of Justice clearly indicates,[41] this publication obligation is a substantial requirement and failure to comply with it represents a violation of Community law imputable to the State.[42]

As regards the participation and award criteria, the Directives lay down the criteria for qualitative selection by which contracting authorities admit or exclude tenderers, and the criteria according to which the award must be decided. The qualitative criteria determine the professional,[43] economic, financial,[44] and technical[45] suitability of the interested candidates, either to present a tender, or to be invited to do so in the restricted procedures. Once a supplier adequately fulfils these criteria, its tender must be assessed pursuant to the two awarding criteria established in the Directives. The criteria for the qualitative selection of candidates respond to a need to protect the public interest so that only those firms capable of adequately

---

[39] See Case 199/85, *Commission* v. *Italy* [1987] ECR 1039 at 1059. See also Order of the President of the Court of 27 September 1988, in Case 194/88-R, *Commission* v. *Italy* [1988] ECR at 5647; Case C-24/91, *Commission* v. *Spain* [1992] ECR I-1989, noted by Fernández Martín in (1992) 1 PPLR 320.   [40] Mattera (1973) (above, n 8) at 208.

[41] See for instance, Case 24/91, *Commission* v. *Spain* [1992] ECR I-1989 and Case 199/85, *Commission* v. *Italy* [1987] ECR 1039.

[42] See especially Case C-359/93, *Commission* v. *The Netherlands*, judgment of 24 January 1995, not yet reported, noted by Fernández Martín in (1995) 4 PPLR CS 74.

[43] See Article 20 of the public supplies Directive 77/62 and Article 23 of the public works Directive 71/305.

[44] See Article 25 of the public works Directive 71/305 and Article 22 of the public supplies Directive 77/62. The Court of Justice has declared that the list contained in the Directives is not exhaustive; see joined Cases 27, 28 and 29/86 *Construction et Entreprises Industrielles (CEI) & others* [1987] ECR 3347.

[45] The list contains different means of proof according to the nature, quantity and purpose of the contract. See Article 26 of the public works Directive 71/305 and Article 23 of the public supplies Directive 77/62. Contrary to what happened with respect to financial and economic standing, the Court regards the lists in the Directives as exhaustive; see Case 76/81, *Transporoute* (above, n 22).

fulfilling the object of the contract are admitted to participate in the procedure. The Court of Justice has held that the competent national authorities are free to determine the level of financial and economic standing and technical knowledge and ability considered sufficient to participate in a given contract and that the Directives' provisions are limited to the regulation of the means of evidence.[46] The case law of the Court of Justice is not above criticism.[47]

Lastly, the criteria for the award of the contract are the same in both Directives: either the lowest price or, when the award is made to the most economically advantageous tender, various criteria depending on the nature of the contract in question: e.g., price, delivery date, running costs, cost-effectiveness, quality, aesthetic and functional characteristics, technical merit, after-sales service and technical assistance.[48] The benefits and disadvantages of these award criteria in the Community context are analysed at length in Chapter two.

The Directives therefore stood midway between a minimalist approach and a more interventionist one. The fact that they claimed to respect national rules to the furthest extent possible is an expression of the former, whereas the detailed regulation of the qualitative selection and award criteria and the imposition of advertising obligations reflects the latter.

Lastly, to fall within the scope of the Directives, the contract had to be for pecuniary consideration and its estimated value had to be not less than 200,000 ECU, net VAT for the case of public supply contracts and not less than 1 million ECU in the case of public works contracts.[49] With respect to the latter threshold it is worth noting that the Preamble to the public works Directive states that, 'in the light of experience', the Commission would submit a new proposal to the Council with the aim of lowering the threshold for the application of co-ordination measures to public works contracts. Finally, the contracts had to be awarded by one of the contracting authorities as defined in the Directives.[50]

The Directives also contained a number of explicit exclusions. The most prominent concerned those economic sectors where public intervention is dominant. Thus, the public supplies Directive did not apply to public

---

[46] Joined Cases 27, 28 and 29/86, *CEI* (above, n 44) at para. 26.

[47] See in particular Case C-362/90, *Commission* v. *Italy* [1992] ECR I-2353, discussed by Arrowsmith and Fernández Martín, (1993) 2 PPLR CS2.

[48] Article 25 (1) of the public supplies Directive 77/62 and Article 29 of the public works Directive 71/305.

[49] Article 5 of the public supplies Directive 77/62 and Article 7 of the public works Directive 71/305.

[50] See Articles 1(b) of both Directives. On the insufficiencies of these provisions see Bréchons-Moulènes, '1988, Année des marchés publics?' (1988) *Revue Française d'Administration Publique* at 591. The notion of contracting authority has been clarified by the case law of the Court of Justice. Its definition has been codified in the latest amendments of the Directives. See Chapter 6.

supply contracts awarded by bodies which administer transport services or which administer production, distribution or transport services for water or energy and telecommunications services.[51] As for the public works Directive, contracts awarded by contracting authorities operating in the field of telecommunications were not excluded from its scope of application. The exclusion, however, operated for the three other sectors.[52] Public contracts having as their object services other than public works were also excluded from the scope of the Directives.

According to the preambles to the Directives, the exemption of these utilities was justified, since bodies administering these sectors enjoyed very diverse legal status in the different Member States, ranging from entities of a public or semi-public nature to entitites governed by private law. In order not to distort competition, since only some of them would have been subject to the provisions of the Directives, while others benefited from total freedom of contract, the Commission decided to postpone the regulation of these sectors until a precise criterion other than that of legal status could be devised. A solution was finally devised 12 years later when the Utilities Directive was approved by the Council. Public supply, public works and public services contracts awarded by contracting authorities operating in the previously excluded sectors are tackled therein.[53] The justification provided in the original Directives only partially explains the exclusions. The insufficiencies of the formal criterion which arose from the divergent legal forms adopted by the contracting authorities in question have now been overcome by the adoption of a material criterion. This definition has by and large been approved by the Court of Justice in a consistent line of case law and has also been codified by the latest amendments of the public procurement Directives.[54]

It is submitted that additional non-legal reasons, of an economic and political nature, underlie the original exclusion of the utilities. When the first Directives were drafted, the issue was not ripe for a political compromise. Due to their economic and strategic importance, these sectors are closely controlled by public authorities which are, moreover, their most important client. The firms operating in these sectors either have close links with public authorities, or are actually under public ownership. The reluctance of Member States to limit their economic discretionary powers by subordinating their contracting freedom in those sectors to Community regulation is not therefore surprising.[55]

---

[51] Article 2(2) of Directive 77/62.

[52] On the interpretation of the scope of these exemptions, see the *Lisbon Airport* case (Case 247/89, *Commission v. Portugal* [1991] ECR I-3659.

[53] EC Council Directive 90/531 on the procurement of entities operating in the water, energy, transport and telecommunications sectors, OJ 1990, L297, substituted three years later by the consolidated Utilities Directive 93/38, OJ 1993, L199/84.

[54] For a full discussion of this point, see Chapter 6.   [55] See Chapter 5.

PUBLIC PROCUREMENT AFTER 1985: THE NEW CONTEXT AND
THE REDEFINITION OF THE POLICY

Introduction

After 1985 a revolution took place in the Commission's public procurement policy. The term 'revolution' may seem exaggerated, but if one compares the Commission's activity in the area with respect to the previous period, the use of the term may be justified. Indeed, after a large period of inactivity,[56] supranational involvement in public procurement acquired sensational vitality after the Commission's Communication in 1984 and the '1992 Internal Market' strategy of the Commission, enshrined in the 'White Paper' of 1985.[57] The new impetus towards European integration represented by the 1992 ideal affected the public procurement area and many other sectors as well. However, the opening up of public procurement markets to European-wide competition became a priority in the Commission's agenda and was regarded as a test case to measure the progress made towards the 1992 Internal Market. Public procurement was transformed from a dormant topic to a highly dynamic one and became the object of abundant academic works, conferences and seminars, supranational legislative measures and a hyperactive Commission policy.

---

[56] After the adoption of the supplies Directive in 1977, the Commission's sole significant action in the public contracts area responded more to the necessity of adapting the Community rules to the international obligations contracted under the GATT than to a will to redesign the applicable rules to improve their efficiency. As a result of the Tokyo Round trade negotiations of the GATT (1973–1979) the EC concluded, inter alia, the Government Procurement Agreement. For present purposes, it will be enough to mention that the Government Procurement Agreement was approved by the Council by Decision 80/271, OJ 1980, L71, and, therefore, became binding on the Community institutions and the Member States as it became part of the Community legal order. Since some of the GATT provisions provide for more favourable conditions for third signatory countries than those laid down in the Directive, the Community institutions deemed it necessary to extend them to the Member States' undertakings. This was done by adopting Directive 80/767 which adapts Directive 77/62 to the GATT regime (OJ 1980, L215 adapting and supplementing Directive 77/62 with respect to certain contracting authorities). See generally, Flory, 'Les marchés de fournitures et les accords du GATT' (1989) RMC 654; Ojeda Marín (above, n 3); Weiss (1993) (above, n 1) Chapter 4. The Uruguay Round Trade negotiations produced a new Government Procurement Agreement which was signed at Marrakesh on 15 April 1994 and will enter into force on 1 January 1996. The Commission is currently drafting some proposals for the amendment of the public procurement Directives in order to bring them into line with the provisions of the new Government Procurement Agreement which binds the Community and its Member States. See generally, Hoekman and Mavroidis, 'The WTO's Agreement on Government Procurement: Expanding Disciplines, Declining Membership?' (1995) 4 PPLR 63. On the Community's proposed amending measures see Trepte, 'The GATT GPA and the Community Procurement Rules: Realignment and Modification' (1995) 4 PPLR CS42.

[57] EC Commission, Completing the Internal Market, COM (85) 310. Schmitt von Sydow, 'The Basic Strategies of the Commission's White Paper' in Bieber, Dehousse, Pinder, Weiler (eds.), *1992: One European Market? A Critical Analysis of the Commission's Internal Market Strategy* (Baden-Baden, 1988) at 82 and 83.

The justification for such a shift in approach was provided both by the findings of the Commission regarding the ineffectiveness of the original measures, which fuelled its determination to act in the area, and by the publication of the Cechinni report on the cost of non-Europe, which furnished the economic arguments for tougher action. This section exposes the Commission's findings regarding the reasons for the ineffectiveness of the original rules. The main changes, both at policy and legislative levels, are then discussed. No critical assessment is undertaken at this stage. The examination of whether the Commission's assumptions are well-founded is left to a later chapter.

The Impact of the Directives

Analysis of the Statistics Provided by the Commission

In 1984, four years later than expected,[58] the Commission issued a Communication to the Council in which the practical results of the Directive on public supplies contracts were analysed.[59] Two years later a second Communication on the same question followed.[60] The degree of compliance by national contracting authorities with the Directives was assessed in these Communications in a two step process. First, the number of notices published in the Official Journal during the years in which the Directives applied was examined. Secondly, the number of contracts awarded to firms established in a Member State other than the awarding State was estimated. Both parameters were to provide the degree of national compliance with the public procurement rules.

The publication of notices in the Official Journal[61]

The data in Table I is self explanatory. The number of notices published every year increases steadily, which suggests that contracting authorities have a tendency to respect their publication obligations. On the basis of

[58] In a Decision of December 1976 (OJ 1977, C11 at 3), the Council invited the Commission to present a report on the functioning of the public supply contracts Directive 77/62 by 1980. The Economic and Social Committee found the reasons for this delay 'not only in the Commission's tardiness', but also in negligence on the part of the Member States in carrying out even the 'apparently rudimentary statistical requirements of Directive 77/62'. ECOSOC, *Opinion on the Communication by the Commission to the Council: Public Supply Contracts-Conclusions and Perspectives*, ESC (86) 399 at 1–2.

[59] EC Commission (above, n 31), COM (84) 717.

[60] EC Commission *Public Procurement in the Community* COM (86) 375. Although the first Communication was only concerned with the implementation of the public supply contracts Directive, according to the Commission the conclusions apply *mutatis mutandis* to the public works contracts Directive. EC Commission COM (86) 375 at 3.

[61] Source: EC Commission COM (84) 717, Table I and EC Commission (86) 375 at 4. The Commission's studies covered the period up to 1986. Data for the years 1986–1994 was kindly provided by Mr P. Shanley, EC Commission. See also Figures 1, 2 and 3 at the end of this chapter.

TABLE 1:   Notices published 1980–1992 Eur 12

Year	Supplies	Works
1980	1,293	n.a.
1981	1,923	n.a.
1982	2,301	n.a
1983	2,583	3,300
1984	n.a.	n.a.
1985	n.a.	4,400
1986	3,709	5,567
1987	4,606	6,677
1988	6,213	8,776
1989	7,818	10,470
1990	9,078	10,480
1991	10,775	7,419[62]
1992	12,830	7,669
1993	14,231	8,796
1994	16,701	9,560

this empirical evidence, even the Commission was satisfied that the observance of the Directives on this particular point had been satisfactory.[63]

The degree of interpenetration of public markets

Did this in turn lead to the achievement of the main goal of the Directive, i.e., the opening up of public markets to European-wide competition? To answer this question the Commission assessed the percentage of contracts awarded under the Directive's provisions which went to firms established in Member States other than the Member State in which the contract was being awarded. The findings were disappointing. The Commission's statistics for 1982 showed that, overall, only 1 per cent of public supplies contracts awarded by central government agencies were won by undertakings established in a different Member State from the one of the contracting authority (in 1981, 93.3 per cent of the contracts were awarded to domestic undertakings and only 4.5 per cent to foreign ones).[64] The general trend has not significantly varied since 1982. The latest data published by the Commission in 1988 showed that imports in public purchasing ranged from 0.3 per cent in the case of Italy to 3.8 per cent in Germany.[65] As regards

[62] The decrease in the public works contract notices published is due to the increase of the threshold from 1 million to 5 million ECU.

[63] EC Commission COM (84) 717 at 15.

[64] Source: EC Commission COM (84) 717.

[65] Source: National Accounts, Eurostat 1985. Atkins 1987. See EC Commission, *Communication from the Commission on a Community Regime for Public Procurement in the excluded Sectors: Water, Energy, Transport and Telecommunications* COM (88) 376.

public works contracts, the same conclusions were drawn by a study carried out by the *Commissariat au Plan* in Paris in 1987. It concluded that for public works contracts in the Community the share given to non-national firms was only 3.2 per cent in France, 2.9 per cent in Germany, 1.8 per cent in Britain, 1.5 per cent in Spain and that it was insignificant in Italy.[66] The same trends have been recently confirmed by the British Department of Trade and Industry in its public procurement review. It found that a very high proportion of contracts have gone to suppliers established in the Member States where the contract was being awarded.[67] Indeed, the data provided in this survey shows that the percentage of awards to domestic firms varies from 70 per cent in Spain and Italy to 90 per cent in Germany, the UK, France and Denmark.

The Commission was aware, however, that these statistics did not take into consideration the origin of the goods purchased, or the fact that some of the winning tenderers may have been local susbsidiaries or agents operating on behalf of firms established in other Member States.[68] Nonetheless, the Commission, after expressing the difficulties involved in tracking down the origin of the goods, concluded that its findings were a fair representation of the failure of the Directives to achieve their objectives, i.e., to enable firms established in one Member State to participate in contract award procedures in another Member State.[69]

Reasons Underlying the Statistical Findings

In view of these statistics, the Commission stated that 'the impact of the Directives has been marginal' and that there was a total absence of 'integration' in the area of public procurement.[70] Two explanations were possible. First, this could have been the result of a deliberate disregard of the rules by national contracting authorities. This interpretation presupposes that there are substantial possibilities for European-wide competition in the areas regulated by the original measures, but that the adopted measures and the policy were misguided. If this was the case, a solution could be provided by means of tougher regulatory and enforcement policy. A second interpretation is that the objective pursued by the measures was unrealistic and that the targeted markets are not susceptible to European-wide competition. The Commission opted for the first of the interpretations and concluded that 'in summary terms, although the dispositions of

---

[66] 'Rapport du Groupe Stratégie Industrielle: Travaux Publics' (1987) *La Documentation Française*, cited by Cox, 'Implementing the 1992 Public Procurement Policy: Public and Private Obstacles to the Creation of the Single European Market' (1992) 1 PPLR 139 at 149.

[67] DTI, *Public Procurement Review* (London, 1994) at paras. 75 *ff.*

[68] The same point is made by the DTI review (above, n 67) at paras. 81 *ff.*

[69] EC Commission COM (84) 717 at 14 and COM (86) 375 at 4.

[70] EC Commission COM (86) 375 at 4.

the Directives in respect of publication are being increasingly observed, it is manifest that the desire of competition is not universally shared by all the participants in the market and that, even the events subsequent to publication are too frequently characterised by a desire to avoid competition . . . Local and national interests often of a short-term character seem to take preference in the decision-making process over the significant benefits which are manifestly to be obtained from an opening of the markets to Community wide competition'.[71] It stated moreover that 'it would not be excessive to state that neither the letter or the spirit of the directives have not been generally respected'.[72] In its two Communications, the Commission therefore investigated the causes for the ineffectiveness of the rules with a view to redefining its overall policy. Hence, the objective pursued continued to be accepted as valid, but the means for its attainment were thought to have been deficient. As the Commission itself concluded, the 'Directives were inadequate to ensure the achievements of their objectives'.[73] What were these alleged inadequacies leading to ineffectiveness?

The exclusions from the Directives's scope

To start with, the narrow scope of the legal measures adopted was considered one of the important reasons for their marginal impact.[74] First, local and regional authorities, which account for 40 per cent of the total public expenditure in the Community, rarely award contracts over the thresholds of the Directives.[75] Secondly, the utilities exclusions included all economic branches where the public sector is a major consumer: telecommunications, transport, energy and water. In these areas, according to the findings of the Commission, public procurement accounted for more than 70 per cent of the total national output for certain related subsectors.[76] Other important exceptions included 'concession contracts', procurement in the defence sector, and, more importantly, all 'public service contracts' other than public works, which is the ever-increasing predominant economic sector in today's western economies. Secondary Community rules simply ignored the regulation of these sectors and were ill-equipped therefore to produce any substantial modification in national procurement policies.

---

[71] EC Commission COM (84) 717 at 15.   [72] EC Commission COM (86) 375 at 4.
[73] Ibid.
[74] Bréchons-Moulènes (1988) (above, n 50) at 756; Flamme M., and Flamme P., 'Vers l'Europe des marchés publics? (à propos de la directive "fournitures" du 22 mars 1988)' (1988) RMC 455 at 457 *ff.*
[75] In 1982 central government agencies awarded public supply contracts to a total value of 12.2 billions ECU. The Commission estimated that 44.4% of these contracts did not exceed the thresholds laid down in the Directive and did not therefore come within its scope.
[76] EC Commission COM (86) 375 at 2. In this sense see also Flamme and Flamme (1988) (above, n 74) at 457.

At the implementation level

The Directives were based on maintenance of national provisions on public procurement. This, together with the nature of the legal instrument chosen, led to a lack of uniformity in the implementation of the Community rules which, in turn, prevented the establishment of equal competition conditions for the undertakings of the different Member States. On top of this, the chosen means for implementing the rules into national law hindered, in some cases, effective operation of the rules. In fact, some Member States transposed the Directives using 'soft' methods of implementation, such as mere administrative rules, which did not favour the binding nature and awaressness of the rules.

At the application level

The situation was particularly unsatisfactory at this level. The rules were simply not followed by contracting authorities. According to the Commission, contracting authorities were generally ignorant of their obligations under the original Directives. The Commission hinted that such a disregard was in most cases due to a deliberate attitude of national contracting authorities. This attitude materialized in various forms. Thus, there was a 'deliberate underestimation of the contract value and overzealous division of projects'[77] in order to avoid the thresholds, notwithstanding the prohibition in the Directives of the division of contracts in lots. An exaggerated use of single tendering procedures,[78] which were of a non-competitive nature, was also to be blamed for the marginal impact. This was in spite of the limitations on their use introduced by the Directives. The Commission believed that contracting authorities interpreted the said cases abusively. This general feeling of distrust was also shared by the Economic and Social Committee, which went further than the Commission and stated that contracting authorities had acted in bad faith, deliberately 'playing around with the rules, i.e., pro-forma going through the open procedure only to declare it null and void on a technicality'.[79] This scenario was worsened, as the Commission recognised, by 'the environment within which [the rules] have had to operate . . . Both Directives were implemented in a period of recession where the purchasing authorities preoccupied by

[77] EC Commission COM (84) at 13.

[78] 28.9% of central Government contracts falling within the scope of Directive 77/62 were awarded following non-competitive single tendering procedures in 1982. EC Commission COM (86) 375. Similar conclusions result from a 1991 survey carried out by the Spanish *Junta de Contratación* on public procurement in Spain. It estimated that 35.83% of the total value of central Government public works contracts was awarded though this procedure. The percentage increased to almost 60% of the total value for supplies contracts. Ministerio de Economía y Hacienda, *Memoria de la Junta Consultiva de Contratación Administrativa* (Madrid, 1994) at 200 and 209.   [79] ECOSOC, ESC (86) 399 at 3.

the economic situation were more sensitive to the pressures of national suppliers.'.[80]

At the enforcement level

Lastly, effective mechanisms for the enforcement of the rules and an operative enforcement policy were lacking. This was, according to the Commission, a particularly serious deficiency of the system given the features of public procurement. These deficiencies appeared both at national and supranational level. At national level, the absence in the Directives of an obligation on Member States to provide for effective redress to frustrated bidders did not help the degree of compliance.[81] As the Commission and others had stressed,[82] this resulted in an utterly unsatisfactory participation of undertakings in the monitoring of contracting authorities through the introduction of judicial actions at national level. Without sufficient guarantees of obtaining adequate compensation, the firms involved simply did not want 'to bite the hand that feeds them' by initiating judicial actions against contracting authorities. This was intimately related to the insufficiencies of the national implementation measures adopted, which, in certain cases, did not provide bidders with judicially enforceable rights at national level. Thus, in some Member States no judicial remedy was available against unlawful award decisions, whereas in others, a well-developed system of judicial protection existed. The Commission understood that this constituted a major obstacle to ensuring equal conditions throughout the Community. Uniform judicial remedies for frustrated bidders had to be introduced by means of Community legislation.

With respect to the supranational enforcement policy, the Commission had administered a laid-back approach which did not put Member States under any pressure to comply with the rules at any level. From 1977 to 1984 only two cases were brought by the Commission before the Court of Justice under Article 169 EC for breach of public procurement rules. This led, as we shall see, to the survival of national measures and practices which were openly in conflict with Community obligations.

Public Procurement Policy as a Top Priority in the Commission's Agenda

The above findings of the Commission were followed by the publication of the Cecchini Report, one section of which was devoted to the analysis

---

[80] EC Commission COM (86) 375 at 3.
[81] Bréchons-Moulènes (1988) (above, n 50) at 756.
[82] Weiss (1988) (above, n 3) at 334.

of the public procurement area.[83] Its findings, which have been subject to strong criticism,[84] provided the necessary economic excuse for the need to enter upon a new supranational policy in the field. Not surprisingly, a common feature of most writings examining the EC regulation of public procurement is to stress the economic significance of the liberalisation of public procurement by referring to the conclusions of the Cecchini Report. Thus, their alleged economic importance, the potential savings which would result from opening up competition and the proved difficulty of attaining their liberalisation made the opening up of public procurement a top priority on the Commission's agenda and resulted in a substantial strengthening of the Commission's policy in the area.[85] It also became a 'test case' to measure the progress made towards the achievement of the 1992 ideal.[86]

In brief, political and economic reasons made public procurement one of the priority topics and the developments in the policy of the Commission bear witness to this. It is true that the policy was carried out by all Community institutions, not just by the Commission. However, this should not conceal the fact that the main actors in the conception, justification, and implementation of the policy were Commission services, who were especially active under the Delors' Presidency. Thus, even though the public procurement policy is formally a Community policy, adopted on the basis of the Community's decision-making process, the Commission bears most responsibility for its conception and implementation, as the following pages will try to demonstrate.

The Restructuring of the Commission Services

The renascence of public procurement policy is first witnessed by the serious restructuring of the Commission's DG III 'Internal Market and Industrial Affairs' services. Until 1984, no division in DG III dealt exclusively with public procurement. The area was treated together with all the other general fields relating to the internal market. In 1984, public procurement was entrusted to a specific Division in DG III. Division 4 of Directorate C was created to deal, although not exclusively, with public

---

[83] EC Commission, 'The Cost of non-Europe in Public Sector Procurement' in the *Cost of non-Europe*, Basic Findings, vol. 5/a and vol. 5/B, study carried out by WS Atkins Management Consultants (Luxembourg, 1988). Further developed in Emerson and others, *The Economics of 1992. The EC Commission's Assessment of the Economic Effects of Completing the Internal Market* (Oxford, 1988). See also Weiss (1993) (above, n 1) at 10 *ff*.   [84] See Chapter 2.

[85] For an overview of the Commission's policy and its practical implementation see Wainwright, 'EC Commission Report to the 14th FIDE Congress' in FIDE, *L'Application dans les États Membres des Directives sur les Marchés Publics* (Madrid, 1990) 13. See also Wainwright, 'Legal Reforms in Public Procurement', (1990) 10 YEL 133.

[86] Hirsch, 'Objectif 1992. Le dossier-test marchés publics' (1988) RMC at 1–2. Bréchons-Moulènes (1988) (above, n 50). See also the White Paper (above, n 57) paras. 81 to 87.

procurement. One year later, this Division became devoted exclusively to public procurement as an autonomous and independent area in the internal administrative structure of DG III.

The most far-reaching restructuring took place in 1988, with the creation of a Directorate specifically charged with the task of opening up public markets to European-wide competition. This Directorate was organised into two Divisions, the first of which was competent to deal with policy matters, that is, the conception and elaboration of the legislative measures required by the White Paper. A second Division was entrusted with all issues relating to implementation and enforcement. This Division handled individual complaints and the initiation of infraction procedures.[87] On top of this, a new Advisory Committee for the opening of public contracts was established alongside the already existing one.[88] Together with this internal modification of the Commission's services, the Commission staff assigned to the area increased substantially by more than 40 per cent throughout this period, through the recruitment of both new Commission officials and national experts.

On the information front, the Commission has equally developed an active policy. It established the Tenders Electronic Daily (TED), a computerised system available to undertakings which gives automatic information on the tenders published in the Official Journal. A similar initiative dealing with the same information front is currently being prepared by the Commission under the name SIMAP (Service Information Marchés Publics), which intends to facilitate access further to contract notices and procurement information through the new developments in information technology. It also intends to overcome the difficulties encountered in the practical operation of the TED. This programme is still in its pilot stages.[89] The Commission also published the 'Vademecum on Government Procurement',[90] a complete guide to public procurement which is of great interpretative value for practitioners and undertakings. It is presently being revised and will be published shortly.[91] In the same vein, the Commission

[87] In September 1990, public procurement disappeared as a separate Directorate, and was integrated into Directorate B 'Horizontal instruments of the internal market' of DG III. Notwithstanding this new restructuring, the basic organizational scheme remained unchanged, with two Divisions devoted to public procurement matters. These Divisions are still in operation in DG XV, which is now the Directorate General in charge of Internal Market affairs.

[88] The Advisory Committee on the Opening-up of Public Procurement was set up by the Commission in 1987 (EC Commission Decision 87/305/EEC, OJ 1987, L152/32 of 26 May 1987) to work alongside the Advisory Committee for Public Procurement, established in 1971 by EC Council Decision 71/306, OJ 1971, L185/15. The Utilities Directive envisages the creation of a similar body to advise the Commission in matters relating to procurement in the Telecommunications sector (Article 31 of Directive 90/531, OJ 1990, L297/1).

[89] See OJ 1994, C189. SIMAP is meant to be fully operative by 1998.

[90] EC Commission, OJ 1987, C358/1.

[91] See Advisory Committee for Public Procurement, *Draft Guide to Public Supply and Works Contracts in the Community: Directives 93/36/EEC and 93/37/EEC*, CCO/94/41 (Brussels, 1994).

has run an awareness campaign aimed at contracting authorities and potentially interested firms. According to one of its officials, more than three
hundred seminars and conferences sponsored by the Commission have
taken place.[92] This new impetus created a parallel interest in academic
and industry circles, which also produced a substantial number of activities
in relation to public procurement matters. Never before had public
procurement been the object of so many academic works, seminars and
conferences.

At the enforcement level, the systematic initiation of Article 169 EC
proceedings against any known alleged violation and the encouragement
of private persons and individuals to address complaints to the Commission's services was also conceived as part of the general policy on public
procurement.[93] The creation of a system of redress which would permit
the Commission, in co-operation with Member States, to ensure respect for
the Directives was also announced. The strategy included the creation of
a 'Public Contracts Committee' within the Commission with far-reaching
monitoring competences which would include a right to intervene in
national award procedures to defend the Community's public interest.[94]
These proposals, however, never materialised.

The Implementation of the Legislative Programme after 1985

The Commission's policy mainly envisaged action at the legislative level,
where it planned a mass of legislative improvements. These constituted,
according to the Commission, 'the starting point for a series of energetic
steps towards the removal of the remaining barriers in the sector of public
procurement',[95] which are now in force.

In the following pages the new legal measures actually adopted as a
result of the drive for 1992, are briefly exposed. I will start with a reference to the innovation of the amendments which the Single European Act
(SEA) introduced as regards the functioning of the internal market, in so
far as they relate to our topic, are discussed.

The Single European Act and public procurement

The SEA represented the legal translation of the political commitment of
Member States to the realisation of the 1992 Internal Market as defined

---

[92] Pinto, 'Contratos Públicos', Paper presented at the Forum Mercados Públicos, organized by the Instituto Superior de Ciencias do Trabalho e da Empresa, Lisbon, June 1995. See
also Wainwright in FIDE (above, n 85) at 31.

[93] Nine Member States are facing Article 169 EC proceedings at different stages at the
time of writing. See Chapter 4 and with respect to the enforcement level, see Chapters 6
and 8.   [94] EC Commission COM (86) 375 at 9.

[95] COM (84) 717 at 3. For an overview see Arrowsmith and Fernández Martín, 'Developments in public procurement in 1992' (1993) 18 ELRev 323.

in Article 8(a) EEC, now Article 7(a). The opening up of public contracts was regarded as an integral part of this programme. However, like the original EEC Treaty, no provision of the SEA specifically tackled the issue of public procurement. Only a marginal explicit reference to public contracts was made in Article 130(f) EC Treaty.[96]

Some authors have regretted this approach.[97] In view of the scarce degree of market interpenetration achieved by the existing Directives, one could have expected more decisive action on the part of the negotiators of the SEA in this sector. In fact, several new powers were attributed to the Community in different policy areas, but none in the field of public procurement. The fact that the main thrust of the SEA was the modification of the decision-making procedure in order to facilitate the adoption of secondary measures may explain the absence of specific rules regulating public purchasing.[98] The negotiators of the SEA considered that any action would be taken by means of secondary legislation and reinforcement of the already available institutional instruments.

Public procurement policy benefited, however, from the improvements made in the decision-making process, in particular from the new Article 100(a) EC which substitutes unanimity under Article 100 EC by qualified majority.[99] The advantages of qualified majority voting are clear in the public contracts area, since all the new Directives have been adopted on the basis of Article 100(a) EC. As a result, the time needed from the first proposal of the Commission to the final adoption by the Council has been considerably reduced. It took less than two years to enact the new public supply Directive and a little over one year in the case of the new public works Directive, whereas their predecessors took over four and five years, respectively. The Utilities Directive was also adopted in two years, although in this case it is true that the Commission's preparatory work was slow.[100] Equally, the provisions adopted in the amending Directives are stricter and more far-reaching than those of the original Directives.

A second major innovation introduced by Article 100(a) EC concerns the procedure to be followed for the adoption of the measures, i.e., the co-operation procedure under Article 149 EC, which provided for a more active, although still insufficient, role for the European Parliament. This materialized in a greater input by Parliament which, in the public procure-

---

[96] For an analysis of the justification and possibilities opened up by this provision in the field of public procurement, see Chapter 5.

[97] See Raux in Reboud (ed.), *L'Achèvement du Marché Intérieur Européen. Signification et Exigences* (Paris, 1987) at 66 and 67.

[98] For a critical analysis of the SEA, see Pescatore, 'Some Critical Remarks on the Single European Act' (1987) 24 CMLRev 7; Ehlermann, 'The internal market following the Single European Act' (1987) 24 CMLRev 361; Reboud (ed.) (above, n 97).

[99] In this connection, see van Voorst tot Voorst and van Dam, 'Europe 1992: Free Movements of Goods in the Wider Context of a Changing Europe' (1988) 25 CMLRev 693.

[100] See later in this chapter at '*The regulation of the excluded sectors: the Utilities Directive*'.

ment field, attained its peak in the debate relating to preferential procurement schemes.[101]

Lastly, Article 100(a) speaks in general terms about 'measures' to be adopted for the approximation of national provisions. Authors have unanimously interpreted the intention of the drafters as including regulations as a possible means for the approximation of laws. However, the Commission added a declaration to the SEA in which it committed itself to giving precedence to the use of Directives if harmonisation involves the amendment of legislative provisions in one or more Member States.[102] In fact, all the Commission's proposals in the field of public procurement have so far been in the form of Directives.[103] Despite it, and in view of the detailed regulation which the Directives establish and the difficulties encountered by some Member States in their implementation, the Commission services are currently studying the convenience of substituting, once again, Regulations for Directives.

The public sector Directives

The amendments of the original public works and public supply Directives
The first task undertaken by the Community institutions was the revision of the first public works and public supplies Directives.[104] It must be stressed that right from the start the process of amending these directives has been unneccesarily complex. It took place in two stages. First, the two original Directives were amended by means of two other Directives, which became applicable and were transposed in several Member States. The amending and the original Directives were not consolidated, however, in a single text and led, as a result, to a confusing set of legal rules spread over several

---

[101]   See Chapter 2.
[102]   Declaration on Article 100(a) annexed to the final Act. As regards the legal value of the declarations, see the radical position of Toth, 'The legal status of the Declarations annexed to the Single European Act' (1986) 23 CMLRev 803.
[103]   For an overview of the adopted measures until 1992, see Arrowsmith and Fernández Martín (1993) (above, n 95).
[104]   New public supplies Directive 88/295 amending Directive 77/62 relating to the co-ordination of procedures on the award of public supply contracts and repealing certain provisions of Directive 80/767, of 22 March 1988, and new public works directive Directive 89/440 amending Directive 71/305, OJ 1989, L210. On these Directives see, *inter alia*, Constantinesco, 'La coordination des procédures de passation des marchés publics de travaux' (1989) RMC 597; Flamme, M. and Flamme, P., 'Enfin l'Europe des marchés publics. La nouvelle directive travaux' (1989) *L'Actualité Juridique-Droit Administratif* 651; Margue, 'L'ouverture des marchés publics dans la Communauté. 2ème partie' (1991) *Revue du Marché Unique Européen* 177; van Bael, 'Public Procurement and the Completion of the Internal Market: Law and Practice' (1989) LIEI 21; Auby and Bronner, 'L'Europe des marchés publics' (1990) *L'Actualité Juridique-Droit Administratif* 258; Sohrab, 'The Single European Market and Public Procurement' (1990) 10 *Oxford Journal of Legal Studies* 522; Hen and Guillermin, 'Les marchés publics de fournitures et l'adaptation de la directive du 21 décembre 1976' (1989) RMC 637; O'Loan, 'An Analysis of the Works and Supplies Directives of the European Communities' (1992) 1 PPLR 40; Bruetschy, 'L'ouverture des marchés publics à la concurrence communautaire' (1989) RMC 593; Weiss (1993) (above, n 1) at Chapter 5.

pieces of legislation. This scenario was further complicated by the fact that the new regulation on public supplies and public works differed in substantial aspects for no apparent reason. In order to solve this bizarre conundrum of legal rules, further modifications followed in 1993. Consolidated versions of both Directives were adopted which substituted the previous individual versions and unified the applicable provisions in one legal text.[105] The consolidated Directives also aligned the provisions in both the public supplies and public works contracts. Fortunately, both Directives now follow similar lines, with the exception of those provisions which have been specifically drafted to take into account the peculiarites of the public supply and public works contracts.[106] Reference is only made to the current regulation for the sake of briefness and clarity. In fact, the consolidated versions represent the culmination of the Commission's policy in the field. The main objective thoughout was to guarantee the development of conditions for effective competition for public contracts by correcting the deficiencies of the previous Directives.

With respect to the entities covered, the consolidated Directives codify the case law of the Court of Justice interpreting what entities or bodies are subject to Community law in general, and public procurement rules in particular.[107] The Directives follow a so-called 'functional approach' to the definition of the concept of public authority, where the degree of financial, political or decisional control which the State or assimilated organs exert over the bodies in question is seen as the determining factor.[108] The inclusion of such a broad definition in the Directive not only ensures the codification of the Court's case law on the matter, but also responds to the need to fight the recurrent practice in public procurement cases, whereby Member States resort to the fiction of declaring the bodies in charge of the management of public services as formally belonging to the private sector and, therefore, excluded from the discipline of the public procurement Directives.[109] The new Directives explicitly preclude such practices by sanctioning the functional definition of the contracting authorities covered.

As far as the thresholds are concerned, there is no substantial modi-

---

[105] Consolidated public supplies Directive 93/36 (OJ 1993, L199/1; consolidated public works Directive 93/37 (OJ 1993, L199/54).

[106] See Trepte, 'Completion of the Internal Market for Procurement: The New Directives on Works, Supplies and Utilities' (1993) 2 PPLR CS118.

[107] This case law adopts the Commission's position in this respect. This issue is discussed in Chapter 6.

[108] See Article 1(b) of the consolidated public supplies Directive 93/36 and Article 4(a) of the consolidated public works Directive 93/37.

[109] For a practical example of this attitude see infraction against Italy No. 88/332. See EC Commission, *1988 Annual Report to the European Parliament on the Implementation and Application of Community Law*, para. 85 and Wainwright (1990) (above, n 85) at 136. Similar arguments were put forward by Portuguese representatives in the context of Case C-247/89, *Commission v. Portugal* (above, n 52), but were not addressed by the Court since no breach of Community law was found to exist.

fication on this point with respect to public supplies contracts.[110] With respect to public works, the threshold above which the Directive's provisions apply has been substantially increased from 1 million ECU to 5 million. According to the preamble of the Directive this increment was necessary 'in view of the rise in the cost of construction work and the interest of small and medium-sized firms in bidding for medium-sized contracts'.[111] By updating the threshold of the 1971 Directive medium and small firms are protected from competition from larger firms. This increment is welcome, since it brings the regulation of public contracts closer to the market structures of public works.[112]

The Directives also intended to increase the transparency of the award of public contracts by making recourse to the open and restricted procedures (i.e., with open competition) the general rule[113] and requiring contracting authorities to produce a justification when they use the non-competitive negotiated procedure,[114] recourse to which is restricted to specific circumstances and subject to certain conditions.[115]

In the same vein, the information obligations of contracting authorities both as regards the Commission's services and with respect to contractors involved in the award procedure, before and after the award of the contract, have been substantially increased. This is probably the most important improvement with respect to the previous regulation. They are, first of all, obliged to inform any unsuccessful firm of the reasons for the rejection if so requested, and, in the case of a tender, the name of the successful tenderer. The new regulation also imposes a *pre-information obligation*, pursuant to which, contracting authorities are required to publish an indicative notice in which they make known the total procurement which they envisage awarding during the following year.[116] Contracting authorities are now also required to provide *post-award information* in which, by means of a notice published in the OJ, they have to indicate the results of the award.[117] This obligation concerns the three types of procedures

[110] The only amendment is the reduction of the threshold from 140,000 to 130,000 ECU as regards Directive 80/767. This reduction was introduced in order to align the new Directive with the amendments resulting from the renegotiation of the GATT Government Procurement Agreement. See *supra* n. 56.   [111] Recital 17 of Preamble Directive 88/295.

[112] It is worth noting, however, that the preamble to the original Directive 71/305 explicitly stated the intention of lowering the 1 million ECU threshold after the operation of the Directive was assessed. See further Chapter 5.

[113] Article 6(4) of the consolidated public supplies Directive 93/36 and Article 7(4) of the consolidated public works Directive 93/37.

[114] The negotiated procedure is the new name that applies to that previously known as single tendering procedure.

[115] Article 7(3) of the consolidated public supplies Directive 93/36 and Article 8(3) of the consolidated public works Directive 93/37.

[116] Article 9 of the consolidated public supplies Directive 93/36 and Article 11 of the consolidated public works Directive 93/37.

[117] Article 9(3) of the consolidated public supplies Directive 93/36 and Article 11(5) of the consolidated public works Directive 93/37.

and the information to be published is not limited to the mere mention of the actual award of a contract but most contain the conditions under which the contract has been awarded, i.e., the criteria applied and the price agreed.[118] This is meant to increase the degree of transparency in the award procedure by providing interested firms with information relating to the merits of the successful tenderer, on the basis of which they may eventually decide to lodge a complaint. Last but not least, contracting authorities are obliged to draw up a written report on each contract award procedure, which is to include various information, such as names of firms admitted and the reasons for their selection, the names of the firms rejected and the reasons for their rejection, the name of the successful tenderer and the reasons for the selection of this tender and the reasons justifying the use of the non-competitive negotiated procedure. This report is to be kept on file and communicated to the Commission if it so requests.[119]

Important amendments have also been introduced in the area of technical specifications. Apart from certain exceptions, these are now to be defined by the contracting authorities with reference to national standards implementing European standards, or with reference to common technical specifications.[120] Thus, from the previous situation in which reference to European standards was left to the discretion of the contracting authority, there is now an explicit obligation to refer to them when these exist. The reason for this change in approach is explained by the different context in which the Directives were adopted.

Finally, more rigorous statistical information concerning all aspects of the award procedure must be supplied to the Commission in order to permit an assessment of the application of the Directives. The Commission may, moreover, determine the nature of any additional statistical information.

The public services Directive

Following the White Paper action programme, a Directive covering the field of services has also been adopted.[121] The intention of this Directive was to close up the regulation of all public contracting activities which

---

[118] Only in the specific cases provided for may the relevant information be omitted, this being limited to that information which could have harmful effects on the winning firm or the public interest.

[119] Article 7(3) of the consolidated public supplies Directive 93/36 and Article 8(3) of the consolidated public works Directive 93/37.

[120] Article 8 of the consolidated public supplies Directive 93/36 and Article 10 of the consolidated public works Directive 93/37. On the judicial application of the previous provisions, see Case 45/87, *Commission* v. *Ireland (Dundalk)* (above, n 11) and Case C-Case C-359/93 *Commission* v. *The Netherlands* (above, n 42).

[121] EC Council Directive 92/50, OJ 1992, L209/1. On the public services Directive, see Trepte, 'Extension of the EC Procurement Regime to Public Services Contracts: an Overview of the Services Directive' (1993) 2 PPLR 1; Arrowsmith and Fernández Martín, 'Developments in public procurement in 1992' (1993) 18 ELRev 323 at 333; Weiss (1993) (above, n 1)

were, in the field of services other than public works, only subject to Treaty provisions. In fact, the scope of application of the Directive is defined in a negative manner: public service contracts mean contracts for pecuniary interest concluded in writing between a service provider and a contracting authority, to the exclusion of those covered by the public supplies contracts, the public works contracts or the Utilities Directives.[122] After the public services Directives, all contracting activities of public authorities are subject to detailed Community rules, with the exception of the particular rules applicable to the utilities sectors.

The main features of the Directive correspond exactly to the current public works and public supplies Directives. Reference is therefore made to the analysis of those measures. The only noticeable peculiarity is that the Directive establishes two different regimes depending on the type of service contracted. Services are subdivided into two categories in the Annexes to the Directive. Annex I A includes those services which, according to the Commission, 'will enable the full potential for increased cross-frontier trade to be realized'. The rules applicable to the public contracting of these services are almost identical to the ones analysed in relation to the public works and public supplies Directives. Services contained in Annex I B are subject however to a more flexible regime. Contracting authorities are only required to apply the common rules on technical specifications when awarding these contracts and, if they wish to do so, send a notice for publication in the Official Journal concerning the results of the award.[123] Annex I B lists those services which seem less susceptible of being subject to European-wide competition. The applicable threshold is the same as the one for the public supplies contracts: 200,000 ECU.[124]

The Remedies Directive
The proposed programme also envisaged the adoption of measures intended to overcome the insufficiencies which had been identified regarding available systems of redress. This was implemented by the adoption of the Remedies Directive. A thorough analysis of its provisions and all related issues is undertaken in Chapters 7 to 10 of this book.

The regulation of the excluded sectors: the Utilities Directive
The sectors which were excluded from the public works and public contracts Directives were also the object of specific Community action. After stating

Chapter 9. As regards the excluded sectors, the Council adopted a Compliance Directive applicable to them: Council Directive 92/13/EEC, OJ 1992, L76/14. For an analysis of its provisions, see Gormley, 'The New System of Remedies in Procurement by the Utilities' (1992) 1 PPLR 259; Weiss (1993) (above, n 1) Chapter 7 at 109 *ff*.

[122] Article 1(a) of public service Directive 92/50.
[123] Article 9 of public service Directive 92/50.
[124] Article 7 of public service Directive 92/50.

the strategic importance of the exclusions, the Commission stressed the need to ensure European-wide competition in those sectors. It also recognized the difficulties which an opening up of those sectors represented, but announced that the measures to be taken were to contain an information system similar to that already applicable to the public supply and public works fields matched with a system of surveillance of these obligations. The Commission thoroughly examined the peculiarities of these sectors and its conclusions were published in a Communication in which its overall strategy was defined.[125] After several proposals by the Commission,[126] the Utilities Directive was finally adopted and came into force on 17 September 1990.[127] This Directive was susbtituted only three years later by a new Directive which included in its scope of application not only public supplies and public works contracts, but also public services contracts awarded by entities operating in the utilities sectors.[128] This Directive incorporated all rules applicable to the excluded sectors in one single text. This Directive was further complemented by a Remedies Directive applicable to contracts passed in the utilities sector which took into account the peculiarities of public contracting in these sectors.[129]

The main concern of the Directive is to identify those situations in the excluded sectors where no real competition exists and where discriminatory contracting practices occur. Even though the Directive must be welcomed,[130] it only imposes some loose obligations on contracting authorities

---

[125] EC Commission, *Communication from the Commission on a Community regime for procurement in the excluded sectors: water, energy, transport and telecommunications*, COM (88) 376.

[126] One for the Telecommunications sector: 'Proposal for a Council Directive on the procurement procedures of entities operating in the Telecommunications sector' COM (88) 378. A second proposal included measures applicable to the transport, energy and water sectors: 'Proposal for a Council Directive on the procurement procedures of entities providing water, energy, and transport services' (COM (88) 377). These two different proposals were finally merged into a single one on the basis of which the Directive was adopted (OJ 1989, C264/22). For a discussion of the proposals, see Riga (above, n 33) at 410.

[127] EC Council Directive 90/351/EEC on the procurement procedures of entities operating in the water, energy, transport and telecommunications sectors, OJ 1990, L297. For a discussion of this Directive see O'Loan 'An Analysis of the Utilities Directive of the European Communities' (1992) 1 PPLR 175; Flamme, M. and Flamme, P., 'La panoplie des directives "marchés publics" se complète: les secteurs hier exclus (eau, énergie, transport et télécommunications) ne le seront plus demain (analyse de la directive 90/531 du 17 september 1990)' (1990) RMC 346; Brown, 'The Extension of Community Public Procurement Rules to Utilities' (1993) 30 CMLRev 721.

[128] Council Directive 93/38 of 14 June 1993 co-ordinating the procurement procedures of entities operating in the water, energy, transport and telecommunications sectors, OJ 1993, L199/84.

[129] Directive 92/13/EEC, OJ 1992, L76/14. On this Directive see Arrowsmith and Fernández Martín (1993) (above, n 121) at 336; Gormley, 'The New System of Remedies in Procurement by the Utilities' (1992) 1 PPLR 259; Trepte, 'Remedies in the utilities sector. The European dimension and application in the UK', paper presented to the *Implementing and Enforcing the EC Procurement Directives* Conference, Birmingham, April 1993.

[130] For a critical assessment see Chapter 5.

when they award supply, works and service contracts in the utilities sectors. The obligations consist principally of the publication of a notice in the Official Journal and informing the Commission of the procedures leading to and the result of, the award of the contract covered. The rules involved are quite flexible.

CONCLUSIONS

This is a brief exposition of the evolution of Community public procurement policy. It became clear during the first period that the Treaty provisions were insufficient to guarantee the adequate opening up of public procurement to European-wide competition and that positive harmonization measures were required. This problem was tackled by the first co-ordination Directives. An examination of the decision-making process which led to the adoption of the original Directives shows that the Directives were peacefully enacted and that no substantial conflict arose between any of the Institutions, or between the supranational and national levels. The Commission's proposals were readily accepted by the Parliament, who did not advise any substantial amendment and also, with minor modifications relating to the use of preferential public procurement, by the Council. No noticeable debate took place in academic or industrial circles with respect to the adoption of the rules, and existing academic works were mainly of a descriptive rather than analytical nature. Furthermore, legal analysis of the public procurement field was mainly by continental commentators of the civil law tradition, since the regulation of public contracts was more advanced in formal terms in these continental Member States. In fact, the Community rules adopted drew susbtantial inspiration from the existing regulation in France. This may explain the greater interest of these authors in dealing with the subject.[131]

At the supranational level, as far as this author is aware, no elaborate survey preceded the adoption of legislation in this area. No Commission service was devoted, on an exclusive basis, to the subject and, according to some Commission officials, the number of persons in charge of the public procurement domain was minimal during these initial stages. The adoption of the rules was the result of the application of the two General Programmes, of which the public works Directive was a direct consequence. The public supplies contract Directive was, in turn, a consequence of the latter. After the adoption of the rules no substantial monitoring activity was noticeable in the Commission. This is evidenced by the fact that between 1971 and 1984 only two cases reached the Court of Justice through

---

[131] Joliet and Hainaut (above, n 3); Flamme (1969) (above, n 3).

169 EC proceedings, despite clear evidence that some Member States had failed to honour their implementation obligations.[132] It seems safe to conclude that no substantial policy existed after the Directives had been enacted. The situation changed dramatically after 1985. The economic importance of public contracts, the expected savings that would allegedly result from their liberalization, the insufficiencies of the first co-ordination Directives and the 1992 Internal Market project fever transformed public procurement into a top priority to which substantial resources and effort was devoted by the Commission services. This new approach brought about the redefinition of its previous attitude and a hyperactive policy at the legislative, enforcement and information levels. This transcended into private circles which readily participated in the Commission's initiatives.

The Treaty on European Union (TEU) did not adopt any specific measures relating to public procurement. It did, however, introduce certain principles, in particular the principle on subsidiarity which, as will be argued, may have a decisive impact on the future shaping of the Community's policy in the area. From a legal point of view, the Directives did not allegedly intend to substitute national regimes with a Community one, but rather to set minimum uniform conditions to foster European competition for public contracts. Although this may be the expressed intention of the legislative action in the field, the truth is that a complete Community code of public procurement which exhaustively regulates the conduct of contracting authorities and defines an autonomous Community policy in the area has developed.[133] This code goes beyond a mere harmonization of existing national approaches. It overcomes national rules by the introduction of Community concepts and detailed award procedures. It also imposes autonomous principles and rules, such as the criteria for the award of the contract, which, moreover, have to be applied with reference to the interpretation given by the Court of Justice. Not only do the modifications introduced after 1985 not change the situation, but they reinforce the autonomous character of the supranational regulation of public procurement and strengthen the independent policy of the Community by imposing further obligations on contracting authorities. Most Member States' public contracts regulations have been greatly influenced by Community rules and one way or another Member States have modified

---

[132] See Chapter 4 on the United Kingdom and Germany.

[133] This is true despite the Court's statement in the *Bellini* and the *Beentjes* cases (Joined cases 27 to 29/86, *CEI and Others* (above, n 44) and Case 31/87, *Gebroeders Beentjes* v. *The Netherlands* [1988] ECR 4635 respectively) that the Directives do not establish a uniform and exhaustive set of rules in the context of public procurement, but leave the Member States free to lay down their own rules in so far as they comply with the specific requirements of Community law. From the wording of the provisions it follows that Member States only remain free to adopt different rules in those aspects not regulated by the Directives. In most matters explicitly covered by the Directives, Member States' discretion is rather limited.

their applicable norms.[134] Since the Community regulation of public procurement is mainly inspired by the continental-Latin tradition, this trend is more noticeable in those Member States where contracts of public authorities were approached from a private law perspective, such as the United Kingdom and Germany. This pre-emption of national competences has been completed by the extension of a public procurement regime to the enforcement level by the adoption of the Remedies Directive.[135]

Even though, from a legal point of view the relevance of Community legislation is unquestionable, if only because of its quantity and scope of application, a different story must be told as regards its practical effectiveness. Essentially, Community rules have proved ineffective to achieve the desired objectives. The Commission assumes that the main cause is the bad disposition of national contracting authorities to abide by the rules. The design of the new and more aggressive legal and general policies after 1985 are influenced by this assumption. The main guidelines are the reinforcement of the Commission's role in monitoring the correct application of the rules and the reduction of the discretion of contracting authorities by the imposition of tighter obligations and more transparency. Since the 1970s, the Community policy has proceeded along the same lines, without anybody questioning the merits of the hypothesis defended therein.

The following chapters analyse whether the ineffectiveness of the adopted legislation is attributable to bad will of national administrations, or whether it relates to the inadequacy of the measures themselves. If the latter is the case, the modifications of the Directives and the large quantity of resources spent will prove equally unsuccessful, since their main thrust has been to strengthen the previous policy of the Commission rather than seeking alternative courses of action.

---

[134] See Chapter 4.
[135] The enforcement level is discussed at length in Chapters 5 to 10 of this book.

PUBLIC AUTHORITIES NOTICES PUBLISHED 1988–94 EUR 12

FIGURE 1:   Works

TYPE	1988	1989	1990	1991	1992	1993	1994
Tenders	8776	10470	10480	7419	7669	8796	9560
Awards	0	626	1145	1525	3507	3948	4428

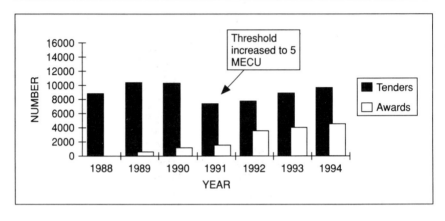

FIGURE 2:   Supplies

TYPE	1988	1989	1990	1991	1992	1993	1994
Tenders	6213	7818	9708	10775	12830	14231	16701
Awards	286	1620	2683	3570	5559	6883	8185

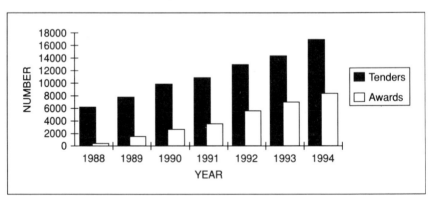

Source: TED database

PUBLIC AUTHORITIES NOTICES PUBLISHED 1992–94 EUR 12

FIGURE 3:   Services

TYPE	1992	1993	1994
Tenders	772	3843	8354
Awards	102	763	3195

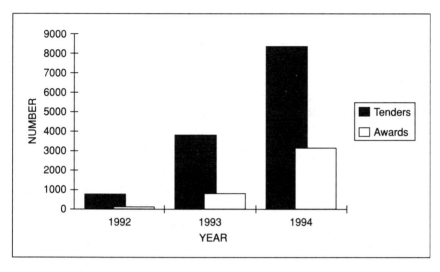

Source: TED database

2

Public Procurement in Context: The Political, Economic and Social Dimensions of Public Procurement in the EC (I)

INTRODUCTION

The main concern of this chapter is to examine public procurement in its political and economic context. The different use to which public authorities have traditionally put their contracting powers and the ideologies which support the different exercise of these powers are discussed. The approaches adopted at supranational and national levels are contrasted against this background in order to highlight potential legal and policy conflicts between them. Reference will be made throughout to the political features peculiar to the Community's constitutional structure. Feasible means for resolution of these conflicts are proposed in the light of the subsidiarity principle, which is applied in a broad sense.

The chapter begins by proposing a theoretical framework against which the policies of the Commission and Member States are assessed. The main conflict between national and supranational approaches, namely the so-called 'instrumental use' of public procurement to achieve regional development and social policy objectives, is examined in detail. The chapter analyses whether this tension has caused an inadequate environment for the implementation of Community policies in the public procurement area.

Even though it is submitted that the first Community Directives struck a fair balance between these two conflicting positions, several decisions of the Court of Justice have tilted the balance in favour of the approach of the Commission to the detriment of any other consideration. Market integration has therefore been preferred to social and regional cohesion. The result has been the withdrawal of a policy instrument such as public procurement from Member States and the imposition of a 'buy efficient' approach as regards public contracting. The general theme underlying the whole analysis is whether, at the present stage of integration and in view of all the relevant issues involved, such a situation is desirable.

THE THEORETICAL FRAMEWORK FOR ANALYSIS

Public procurement can be considered as the innocuous way in which public authorities acquire in the market the goods and services which they need to perform their duties. The activities of contracting authorities could be regarded like that of any other rational consumer, who shops around and assesses the market in order to obtain the best value for money. This perception of contracting authorities as acting as mere private consumers is far too simplistic, however. As will become patent in the following pages, public authorities, in contrast with private consumers, are constrained by the need to perform effectively the public duties imposed on them. They represent the public interest and are entrusted with a responsibility to achieve and promote social welfare. In order to do so, they adopt certain policy choices which are inspired by their political ideology. The way in which they conduct their purchasing activities is, like any other public activity, intended to implement these policy choices.

The role of public procurement as an instrument of policy may be better understood in the context of the conceptual framework developed by Daintith when analysing the role of law in the furtherance of economic policies. First of all, economic policy is defined as 'all purposeful governmental action whose actual or professed primary objective is the improvement of the economic welfare of the whole population for which the government is responsible or of a segment of that population'.[1] In the same sense and supplementing Daintith's definition for our own purposes, social policy could be defined in similar terms as any purposeful governmental action intended to improve the social welfare of the whole or part of the same population. Social welfare can be understood in broad terms as the amelioration of the degree of social integration of the intended beneficiaries of the policy.

On the basis of previous studies,[2] Daintith has distinguished between government aims, objectives, instruments and measures of economic policy. Aims consist of a series of abstract concepts which represent the desirable ends of government action, including economic welfare. Objectives are the economic translations of political aims into concepts which can be given some quantification. These include regional cohesion, improvement of the distribution of income and wealth and so on. Instruments refer to the means by which objectives are pursued. Examples of instruments are money and credit policies, budgetary and fiscal policies, nationalization or privatization of industry, granting of subsidies and so on. Finally, a measure is the use of a particular instrument at a particular time in order to promote one or more objectives. According to Daintith, measures are the acts through which instruments are brought into operation. These normally

---

[1] Daintith, 'Law as a Policy Instrument' in Daintith (ed.) *Law as an Instrument of Economic Policy: Comparative and Critical Approaches* (Berlin, 1988) at 6.

[2] Especially on the basis of the work by Kirschen, *Economic Policy Compared: West and East*, 2 vols., vol. 1 at 17; Daintith, 'Legal Analysis of Economic Policy', *EUI Working Paper*, No. 27, at 7–10. Revised versions of this Working Paper are published in Daintith, 'Legal Analysis of Economic Policy' (1982) 9 *Journal of Law and Society* 191 and Daintith. 'The Executive Power Today: Bargaining and Economic Control' in Jowell and Oliver (eds.), *The Changing Constitution* (Oxford, 1985) 174.

take the form of legal acts. Social policies are also to be defined within the same parameters of government aims and objectives and are also applied by means of instruments and measures. Thus, the abolition of race discrimination in society constitutes an aim of social policy, the equal access of all races to the labour market constitutes an objective, the establishment of equal opportunities policies enters the category of instruments and its specific application by public and private employers amounts to measures.

These concepts materialize in the field of public procurement as follows. Aims and objectives respond to the same characteristics described above, as they are established by government socio-economic programmes in general terms. A positive public purchasing policy applicable to all public authorities falls into the category of instrument. Thus, binding preferential treatment in public contracting of goods produced in a certain region or in an ailing industrial sector may be seen as an instrument of economic policy. Preferential treatment given in public contracts to certain disadvantaged segments of the population constitutes part of the government's social policy. This public purchasing policy materializes in the specific award of a contract to an eligible undertaking fulfilling the pre-established conditions. Contract awards are therefore the 'measures' through which the instrument is implemented.

It follows that public procurement may not be seen as an objective in itself, but as a mere instrument to achieve wider social or economic policy objectives. Its effectiveness is therefore limited, unless it is accompanied by the existence of other instruments and measures.[3] An active public procurement policy certainly does not resolve the problem of unemployment, but may contribute to its attenuation in certain areas. Equally, the effectiveness of a single contract award in achieving wider economic objectives on its own is dubious. Only in those sectors in which the State is the largest consumer of specific goods and services, and therefore enjoys a dominant position on the demand side, may a sectoral policy be implemented through public procurement.[4]

Obviously, it is up to the established economic objectives and the political-economic programme of the elected government to determine the degree, as well as the means, of State intervention in the public economy. In this context Daintith distinguishes between the implementation of policy through the adoption of unilateral binding measures or through bargaining with the social actors by means of contractual measures. The first category, referred to under the generic term of *imperium*, comprises instruments of policy which involve the deployment of force. The second, which Daintith describes as *dominium*, consists of those policy instruments which involve the deployment of wealth by government. The implementation of social

---

[3] Bourcier de Carbon, 'Les marchés publics dans l'économie française' (1961) *Revue Administrative* 435.   [4] With respect to the utilities sectors, see Chapter 5.

or general economic policies by means of public contracting comes within the latter category. Both means of carrying out the action of public authorities are in principle legitimate, as long as their practical implementation complies with general democratic requirements and applicable constitutional constraints.[5] It is the ideology behind the decision-making authorities which determines policy decisions and the means to implement them.[6]

This brings us to the ideological connotations behind the use of public procurement. In general terms, two main ideologies have usually applied in the context of public procurement policies. Since public procurement is primarily an economic activity of public authorities, the applicable policy can follow either a 'free-market' orientation or a more 'interventionist' ideology. The first emphasizes the need to exclusively apply commercial criteria when awarding the contract and, for our purposes, may be called the 'economic rationale' approach. The second regards public procurement as an instrument to realize social and economic objectives wider than mere economic efficiency in the use of public money, and may be called the 'instrumental or redistributory use' approach. There are also intermediate approaches somewhere between these two which try to combine both ideologies by introducing some degree of societal considerations. For the purposes of our theoretical analysis these two general categories should suffice. The question that concerns us now is the analysis of the ideologies behind the policies applied at supranational and national levels and the extent to which they conflict with each other.

THE CONFLICTING VIEWS,

The Commission's Position: the 'Economic Rationale' Use

The aim of the public procurement policy of the Commission has been to ensure effective competition by increasing the transparency of the procedures, restricting the margin of discretion of contracting authorities when awarding contracts and requiring the contracts to be awarded on the basis of strict commercial criteria. This is a position which is favoured by the 'integration of the market', which is the primary objective of the Community. The economic rationale behind this 'buy efficient' approach resides in classical 'economic efficiency' principles. According to various studies, greater competition deriving from compulsory competitive tendering will result in larger economic efficiency through the reduction of costs, which will therefore produce savings for the public exchequer and the maximization of operating efficiency. Thus, the 'fair and equitable' use of taxpayers money is guaranteed.[7] From a strictly economic point of

[5] See Daintith (1985) (above, n 2) at 196.   [6] Daintith (1985) (above, n 2) at 178 *ff*.
[7] Ponssard et de Pouvourville, *Marchés Publics et Politique Industrielle* (Paris, 1982) at 6–7.

view, competitive tendering not only reduces the burden on the public purse but also enhances macro-economic growth, since it promotes restructuring and adjustment.[8]

Savings which could be expected from a competitive regime in the area of public contracts at Community level were assessed at length in the Cecchini Report.[9] The report estimated that savings would amount to a total of 17.2 billion ECU. Competition in the public procurement area would imply savings through the selection of the most competitive suppliers (5.5 billion ECU), savings due to an increase in competition leading to alignment of domestic and external suppliers (2.8 billion ECU) and savings due to the rationalization of production structures (8.9 billion ECU).[10] Given the fact that public procurement overall represents 15 per cent of the Community GNP, the loss in potential growth due to misallocation of resources by a misleading procurement policy should, according to the Report, not be underestimated. The Report reckoned that terminating discriminatory public procurement may increase growth in the EC by about 0.5 per cent.

Before proceeding any further, it must be noted at this stage that these economic forecasts have been the object of sharp criticism. According to several sources, the findings are technically inconsistent, excessively optimistic and disregard the social costs of restructuring.[11] If these criticisms are

---

[8] For theoretical economic analysis of the benefits of competitive tendering see Finsinger, 'Non-Competitive and Protectionist Government Purchasing Behaviour' (1988) 32 *European Economic Review* 69; Parker, 'The 1988 Local Government Act and Compulsory Competitive Tendering' (1990) 5 *Urban Studies* 653 at 659–661; Tovias, 'The Impact of Liberalizing Government Procurement Policies of Individual EC Countries on Trade with Non-members' (1990) *Weltwirtschaftliches Archiv* 722; Baldwin, 'Preferential Government Purchasing Policies' in Jones and Kenen (eds.), *Handbook of International Economics* (Amsterdam, 1987) 602; Mclachlan, 'Discriminatory Public Procurement, Economic Integration and the Role of Bureaucracy' (1985) 23 JCMS 357 and especially Uttley and Harper, 'The Political Economy of Competitive Tendering' in Clarke and Christos (eds.) *The Political Economy of Privatization* (London, 1993) 145 at 147 *ff* where the authors carry out an exhaustive analysis of the arguments in favour of, and against competitive tendering.

[9] EC Commission, 'The Cost of non-Europe in Public Sector Procurement' in the *Cost of non-Europe*, Basic Findings, vol. 5/a and vol. 5/B, study carried out by WS Atkins Management Consultants, (Luxembourg, 1988). Further developed in Emerson and others, *The Economics of 1992. The EC Commission's Assessment of the Economic Effects of Completing the Internal Market* (Oxford, 1988). This latter study reckoned that the savings could amount to 21 billion ECU in 1987. [10] (1988) 35 *European Economy* at 57, Table 3.4.4.

[11] Cox, 'Implementing the 1992 Public Procurement Policy: Public and Private Obstacles to the Creation of the Single European Market' (1992) 1 PPLR 139. Strong criticism is also made by Fiorio who contends that the methodology deployed in such forecasts is criticizable for its microeconomics assumptions, its extrapolations and for its disregard of long-term trends in public procurement. 'Spesa pubblica per investimenti nella CEE e apertura dei mercati indotti dalle pubbliche amministrazioni' *Lezione tenuta presso il Centro Alti Studi Europei dell'Università di Urbino*, 3 May 1989. See also *The Economist*, which criticized the Cecchini Report as a 'breathlessly enthusiastic ramble' and as a concoction of 'dubious guesstimates of the promised frontier-free market . . .' 14 May 1988, cited by Weiss, *Public Procurement in European Community Law* (London, 1993) at 12, n 41.

correct, the economic rationale and legitimacy of the Commission's policy is seriously weakened. From a theoretical economic perspective competitive tendering implies savings and better resource allocation. However, certain conditions need to be met. These include the existence of effective competition on the supply side of the market at a European level, which is not likely to occur for most contracts subject to the Community rules. These considerations will be developed in detail in the following chapter.

Notwithstanding this, most official statements of the Commission refer to the expected benefits which will result from liberalization as the ultimate justification for the Community's policy on public procurement and, in particular, for the need to apply strict commercial criteria when awarding contracts. The Commission's position is summarized in its Communication 'Public Procurement: Regional and Social Aspects', where it is stated that due to its economic importance, the achievement of efficiency in public procurement is of major importance to the economic health of the Community. Accordingly, 'this requires both the fullest possible participation of all potential suppliers in the market place and the allocation of contracts in a way which ensures that goods, services and works required by bodies in the public domain are obtained under the most favourable conditions'.[12] This 'economic rationale' approach is present in the regulation of the award criteria contained in the various Directives. Article 25 of the public supply Directive, Article 29 of the public works Directive, Article 36 of the services Directive and Article 34 of the Utilities Directive require the contracting authority to award the contract on the basis of either the lowest price only or the most economically advantageous tender.

Whereas the lowest price criterion is clear and definitive,[13] the 'most economically advantageous offer' criterion is more ambiguous. To what extent may contracting authorities bring societal considerations into account when awarding their contracts in accordance with this criterion? The Directives provide a list of criteria to determine the most advantageous

---

[12] EC Commission, *Public Procurement: Regional and Social Aspects*, COM (89) 400 at paras. 9 and 10.

[13] See Article 25(5), (6), (7) of the public supplies Directive 77/62 and Article 29(5), (6), (7) of the public works Directive 71/305. The only discretion allowed under this criterion is that contracting authorities may check that the offer is realistic and is not underestimated or 'abnormally low' in the words of the Directives. In this case the contracting authority may reject the tender justifying the rejection and giving the tenderer the possibility of justifying his or her offer. The Court of Justice has interpreted these provisions on several occasions. Case 76/81, *Transporoute* [1982] ECR 417; Case C-103/88, *Fratelli Constanzo* v. *Commune di Milano* [1989] ECR I-1839. For a full discussion of this decision see Fernández Martín and Pellicer Zamora, 'Las ofertas anormalmente bajas en la contratación pública' (1990) *Gaceta Jurídica de la CEE*, serie B, No. 78, 3. See also Case C-295/89, *Impresa Donà Alfonso and Figli* v. *Consorzio per lo sviluppo industriale del Commune di Monafalcone* [1991] ECR I-2967.

offer. Even though this list is not meant to be exhaustive, all the factors referred to are of a commercial nature. A strict interpretation of this provision, therefore, limits the evaluation of tenders to economic or commercial grounds.[14]

Despite the fact that the Commission's position on this issue has been equivocal and sometimes contradictory due to internal discrepancies,[15] its current official interpretation of the Directives' award criteria is that these are intended to establish only objective criteria strictly relevant to the particular procurement decision and uniformly applicable to all bidders.[16] Other non-commercial or price-related considerations should not play a role in the award decision. This becomes apparent in its statements relating to the case of national local labour clauses included as contract conditions, where the Commission held that:

[t]he various criteria [of Article 29 of the public works Directive] given as examples . . . all relate to matters which affect the economic benefit to the contracting entity of the offer in question in the context of the subject matter of a particular works contract. A tenderer's capacity to employ long term unemployed does not normally have any impact on the economic benefit of the contract to the procuring entity. Economic benefits which may result, for example, through the reduction of welfare payments or an increase in spending by those employed, are indirect and quite extraneous to the subject matter of the contract itself. Unless particular circumstances could be shown to exist under which employment of the long term unemployed would improve the economic benefits of the contract to the procuring entity, this criterion would not be compatible with the Directive. The same applies to other criteria which have nothing to do with the subject matter of a particular contract.[17]

It is true nevertheless that, due its sensitive nature, the Commission's position towards social clauses in public procurement cases has been more

---

[14] The Directives refer to various criteria relating to the contract in question which may be taken into account to determine the economically most advantageous tender: e.g., price, delivery date, running costs, cost-effectiveness, quality, aesthetic and functional characteristics, technical merit, after-sales service and technical assistance. If the contracting authority chooses to follow the second criterion, paragraph 2 provides that the relevant criteria must be stated in the contract documents or in the notice.   [15] See below in this chapter.

[16] EC Commission, *Guide to the Community Rules on Public Procurement* (the *Vademecum*), OJ 1987, C358/1 at 26.

[17] EC Commission COM (89) 400 (above, n 12) at para. 48. As a practical example of this position, in 1990 the public procurement services of the Commission opposed procurement practices operated in North-Rhine Westfalia, Germany, whereby firms which employed training apprentices, particularly young female apprentices, were to be accorded preferential treatment. This system was regulated in several circulars from the Minister for Economics, Small and Medium Sized Undertakings of North-Rhine Westfalia. The Commission understood that the only award criteria which a contracting authority could apply were either the lowest price or the economically most advantageous offer. It therefore concluded that the 'social' requirements were not to be taken into consideration as they were in breach of the relevant provisions of the Directives. As a result of the Commission's intervention, the contested system was withdrawn.

flexible than towards regional development schemes operated through public contracting. With respect to the latter, the Commission made its position clear in its observations in the *Du Pont de Nemours* case. These submissions were in line with its general stance on the relationship between Articles 30 and 92 to 94 EC. It argued that such measures were prohibited by Article 30 EC and that they could not be considered as a State aid within the meaning of Article 92 EC. Regional development considerations had to be excluded from any award decision since only a competitive regime should apply.[18]

This 'economic rationale' approach was strengthened after the Court of Justice's rulings on the interpretation of the Directives' award criteria and the subsequent suppression in the Consolidated Directives of all references to preferential procurement for regional objectives. It appears that the Commission is also administering a stricter policy with respect to social clauses and that this has caused controversy at national level. In this vein, it has recently challenged under Article 169 EC certain provisions of an Italian law on social co-operatives[19] which enable contracting authorities, by way of derogation, to favour certain co-operatives employing physically and mentally handicapped and other disadvantaged persons, such as ex-alcoholics and drug addicts. These developments are examined in further detail in the next chapter.

Other Approaches to Public Procurement. The Instrumental Use

Public Procurement as an Instrument of Economic and Social Policy

After the installation of mixed economies in most western societies, State intervention to correct market failures became a general feature. Keynesian doctrines which claimed that an increase in public spending could galvanize a relaunching of the general economy enjoyed widespread support and were generally followed.[20] Public procurement did not escape such a trend and, apart from the most obvious function of providing public authorities with the goods and services they require, it has often been used to further general economic, regional or social policies. The responsibility of public authorities for ensuring harmonious and peaceful economic and social development, together with the volume of government

---

[18] Case C-21/88, *Du Pont de Nemours Italiana* v. *USL No 2 di Carrara* [1990] ECR 889 at 899 *ff.*

[19] *Legge No. 381* of 8 November 1991. The formal letter of notice was sent in August 1994.

[20] Fiorio (above, n 11) at 39 and 64; Keyzer, 'L'importance et la politique des achats publics' (1968) *Hommes et Techniques,* No. 278, 26. Jeanrenaud, 'Marchés publics et politique économique' (1984) 72 *Annales de l'Économie Publique, Sociale et Coopérative,* No. 2, 151 at 154. For a general overview of the role of the State in mixed economies see Lord Roll of Ipsden (ed.) *The Mixed Economy* (London, 1982), especially Hindley in relation to international trade, 'The Mixed Economy in an International Context', ibid. at 187.

procurement, justify this use of public procurement as a socio-economic policy instrument.[21]

The Instrumental Functions of Public Procurement

It is an undisputed fact that public contracting has been consistently used by national authorities as an interventionist tool.[22] Scholars have not questioned the existence of this practice, but have concentrated on how its effectiveness may be improved.[23] Active academic interest in this subject had been dormant, until the Community's policy on public procurement and the debate concerning its approach to these issues contributed to its awakening.

Jeanrenaud has systematised the different functions which public procurement may play as an instrument of economic policy. He describes four instrumental functions, some of which overlap.[24]

(i) First of all, following Keynes' doctrine on budgetary policy, in times of economic recession an increase in public procurement contributes to increasing global demand and to stimulating economic activity.[25] The use of public procurement in this sense was especially patent in the United States from 1935 to 1942.[26] Public procurement was an aspect of this general economic policy based on the increase of public spending. Similarly, in Europe, expansive government budgets were used to fight unemployment through large programmes of public works in the post-war period.

(ii) Secondly, public procurement may be used to protect national industry against foreign competition.[27] The most striking example of this practice is provided by the Buy American Act, still applicable in the United

---

[21] There is widespread agreement on this point. See, *inter alia*, Jeanrenaud (above, n 20) at 153 and Turpin, *Government Contracts* (Harmondsworth, 1972) Chapter 9 at 244 and Turpin, *Government Procurement and Contracts* (Harlow, 1989) at 73 *ff.*

[22] Bourcier de Carbon (above, n 3); Turpin (1989) (above, n 21) Chapter 3; Keyzer (above, n 20); Dilleman, 'Les commandes publiques. Stratégies et politiques', *Notes et Études Documentaires. La Documentation Française*, 1977; Jeanrenaud (above, n 20) 151; see also the contributions in (1984) *Annales de L'Économie Publique, Sociale et Coopérative* (above, n 20); see also Jeanrenaud (ed.), *Regional Impact of Public Procurement* (Saint-Saphorin, 1984); Geroski, 'Public Procurement as an Industrial Policy Tool' (1990) 2 *International Review of Applied Economies*; Batley, 'Allocation of Government contracts in Peru and Venezuela' in Ghai, Luckham, and Snyder (eds.), *The Political Economy of Law. A Third World Reader* (Oxford, 1987) 498; Arrowsmith, 'Public Procurement as an Instrument of Policy and the Impact of Market Liberalisation' (1995) 111 LQR 235.

[23] For a critical view of the effectiveness of a public procurement policy to promote the economy in general, see Bourcier de Carbon (above, n 3) and Keyzer (above, n 20). For a more positive assessment see Arrowsmith (1995) (above, n 22).

[24] Jeanrenaud (above, n 20) at 154–156.   [25] Ibid. at 154.

[26] Keyzer (above, n 20) at 31.

[27] Mclachlan (above, n 8). For a case-study of how this function has been applied in the field of the procurement of medicines by hospitals, see Mougeot and Naegelen, *Les Marchés Hospitaliers. Analyse Théorique et Application aux Achats des Pharmacies Hospitalières* (Paris, 1984).

States, which imposes a binding obligation on contracting authorities to discriminate against foreign goods in favour of goods of American origin.[28] In the context of the European Communities, this second function is explicitly ruled out by the EC Treaty and secondary legislation on the matter with respect to tenderers established within the Community. The Utilities Directive, however, explicitly allows for preferential procurement in favour of goods produced in the Community to the detriment of tenders offering goods originating in third countries when these represent more than 50 per cent of the total value of the tender.[29] This controversial provision has the obvious objective of protecting European production from foreign competition.[30]

(iii) The third instrumental function of public procurement is geared towards the improvement of the competitiveness of certain industrial sectors. It is of more recent origin and takes place mainly in those sectors where public authorities represent by far the largest consumers. It normally involves high technology industrial sectors, such as telecommunications, military equipment, energy and transport. As stated above, due to the fact that these sectors depend on public purchasing to a large extent, sectoral policies can be effectively carried out through specific procurement policies. Furthermore, since these sectors normally provide the technological innovations capable of stimulating the economy as a whole, public procurement acquires fundamental importance in ensuring the competitiveness of national industries. It is, therefore, a usual practice of States to protect their national champions from foreign competition by ensuring a secure market for their production, while linking this protection to the need to invest in Research and Development.[31] Here again, an example of this type of instrumental policy is provided by the abovementioned provision of the Utilities Directive which has institutionalised preferential treatment in favour of European production. European firms, sheltered from foreign competition, can undertake the necessary readjustments to improve

---

[28] For a description of the Buy American Act, see Goodman and Saunders, 'US Federal Regulation of Foreign Involvement in Aviation, Government Procurement and National Security' (1985) *Journal of World Trade Law* 54 and the bibliography cited therein. See also Pomeranz, 'Towards a New International Order in Government Procurement' (1979) 11 *Law and Policy in International Business* 1263.

[29] Article 29 of Council Directive 90/531, OJ 1990, L297/1.

[30] Its application has moreover caused conflicts between Germany and the US since these two States were bound by previous international agreements which were contradicted by the said provision. For an extensive analysis see Grimes, 'Conflicts between EC Law and International Treaty Obligations: A Case Study of the German Telecommunications Dispute' (1994) 35 *Harvard International Law Journal* 535.

[31] Jeanrenaud and Meyer, 'L'incidence à moyen et long terme des commandes de matériel de télécommunication: deux études de cas' (1984) *Annales de L'Économie Publique, Sociale et Coopérative* (above, n 20) 191. For further examples of this use in several Member States, see Savy (ed.), *L'Intervention des Pouvoirs Publics dans la Vie Économique*, 2 vols., Tome 1 (Limoges, 1978) at 110, 469 and 470.

their competitive position, first of all in the Community and then in world markets.[32]

(iv) Finally, Jeanrenaud identifies a fourth instrumental function of public procurement which is to remedy regional disparities and thereby the attainment of redistributory objectives. Different preferential schemes were functioning in some Member States. A brief description of these is provided when commenting on the *Du Pont de Nemours* case.

To these, a fifth instrumental function, which may be called the social function, can be added.[33] This would include the use of public procurement to foster the creation of jobs, favouring marginal sections of the population, or minorities, and the attainment of other legitimate socio-political objectives. Examples of this last category are the blacklisting of companies which do not respect minimum working conditions or standards, preferential schemes for the benefit of ethnic minorities, female workers, the introduction of local labour clauses and so on. This use of public procurement is widespread, not only in the Community but also in the US and Canada.[34] The social function of public procurement is to a certain extent implicit in the previous categories, since all of them have the collateral effect of supporting national employment. It may be considered, however, as a separate instrumental function in itself as it has the specific objective of implementing a social policy.

These functions are operated through 'preferential regimes' pursuant to which certain undertakings benefit from a preferential treatment in the awarding of the public contract provided they fulfil the established criteria. These preferences normally consist either in the total reservation of the public market for their products, or in the automatic award of the contract if the price difference between their tender and the tenders submitted by the other bidders is contained in a band previously determined by national authorities. Usually, 'preferential regimes' are thought to help undertakings that are operating either in sectors which are declining economically or in economically depressed areas.

The two functions which have caused most controversy in the Community have been the regional cohesion and social functions of public procurement. With respect to the latter, the discussion has focused on the compatibility with Community law of local labour clauses and more recently with the so-called 'contract compliance' policies. In the former case, contracting authorities require the successful tenderer to hire local unemployed

---

[32] The economic theory justifying this policy and explaining the market conditions for it to be effective is developed in Tovias (above, n 8) at 731.

[33] See Bourcier de Carbon (above, n 3) at 473.

[34] For an exhaustive analysis of this use of public procurement in the EC, the US and Canada see the detailed study carried out by McCrudden, 'Public Procurement and Equal Opportunities in the European Community. A Study of "Contract Compliance" in the Member States of the European Community and under Community Law' (Brussels, 1994).

labour. In the latter, public procurement is used as an instrument of social policy in order to favour certain disadvantaged sectors of the population and therefore facilitate their full social integration. The analysis of these two functions in the framework of the Community's policy will be discussed later on. It must be noted, however, that the main debate at Community level has so far concentrated on the use of public procurement for regional development purposes.

The British Case. Some Lessons for the Community?

A practical example of an overt conflict between the economic and instrumental approaches to public procurement has occurred in the context of the British debate regarding the powers of local government when awarding contracts. The imposition of compulsory competitive tendering on local government authorities by the 1988 Local Government Act (LGA) has created tensions between the central and local government in relation to the use to be made of their public procurement activities. Since the British experience may shed some light on the supranational debate it is worth analysing it in some detail.

Competitive tendering and the 1988 Local Government Act
After coming into power in 1979, the Conservative Government of Mrs Thatcher introduced a major programme for the privatization and restructuring of the public sector. The general objectives of the programme were to 'cut public expenditure, reduce the size of the public sector and constrain the power of trade-unions'.[35] The 1988 Local Government Act (LGA), adopted after a long debate in Parliament, implemented the general political and economic principles which inspired the Conservative Government's action at local government level.[36] In the field of public procurement, this approach materialized in the introduction of compulsory competitive tendering. This imposed an obligation on local authorities to publicize their contracts, call for tenders, to compete with private firms for the provision of previously defined local services and, subsequently, to assess the different offers on the basis of strict commercial criteria. Until then, services performed by local authorities were mainly operated by

---

[35] Painter, 'CCT in Local Government: the First Round' (1991) 39 *Public Administration* 191 at 192.

[36] Initially, the government was reluctant to adopt binding rules forcing local authorities to adopt competitive tendering. However, the unwillingness of most local authorities to apply competitive tendering *motu proprio* led the government to introduce legislation. Parker (above, n 8) at 653. The LGA was viewed with hostility by most local authorities, Labour or Conservative dominated, as they took the view that it was their exclusive competence to decide how local services should be provided and, as elected bodies, they considered themselves accountable to their electorate for such decisions. Radford, 'Competition rules: The Local Government Act 1988' (1988) 51 MLR 717 at 750.

in-house labour.[37] These provisions aimed to further two major objectives: introducing greater competition and securing greater value for money.[38]

Since 1988, services could only be provided on an in-house basis if this was cheaper than provision by private firms. Section 17(1) of the Act explicitly prohibits authorities from taking into account non-commercial considerations when awarding contracts for the supply of goods, materials and services and for the execution of works.[39] Although the Act does not require local authorities to award the contract to the lowest bidder, they must have good reasons for failing to do so.[40] A parallel can be drawn with the public procurement Directives' awarding criteria as described above.[41]

As a result, public contracting in the UK has been explicitly ruled out as a means of furthering social or regional objectives at the local level. This has meant a substantial change in the general approach to local government contract awards. Local government authorities had traditionally been at the forefront in promoting equal opportunities for ethnic minorities and disabled people and furthering local employment when awarding contracts. As a result, it was generally accepted that when assessing the different offers presented, or when providing for in-house services, local contracting authorities were entitled to take into account matters other than those of a strictly commercial nature as 'it has been felt appropriate that they should demonstrate a degree of social responsibility in conducting their business'.[42] The only limitation was that those matters had to come within the competence of local authorities. Since these are created

[37] At central government level, the same policy is followed, although no statutory provisions have been enacted to implement it (apart from the Regulations adopted to bring the public procurement Directives into force in the UK). See the comprehensive analysis by Turpin (1989) (above, n 21) at Chapter 3, 'Policies, principles and practice of government procurement'.

[38] Secretary of State for the Environment, Nicholas Ridley, HC Deb., vol. 119, col. 79, 6 July 1987. For a detailed analysis of the provisions of the 1988 Local Government Act on this specific issue, see Radford (above, n 36). On the competitive tendering obligations imposed on local authorities see generally Arrowsmith, *Civil Liability of Public Authorities* (Winteringham, 1992) 99 *ff.*

[39] Employees' terms and conditions (including those concerned with training and the use of self-employed labour), association with irrelevant fields of government policy, involvement in industrial disputes, international activities, political and industrial affiliations, are defined as non-commercial matters in s. 17(5). The extent of the duty is comprehensive and applies to all the different procedural stages. Radford (above, n 36) at 751.

[40] In a Department of Environment circular the government explained the latter provision as a means to prevent authorities from discriminating against particular contractors by introducing political or other irrelevant considerations into the contractual process, DoE circular 8/88: 'LGA 1988—Public Supply and Works Contracts: Non-Commercial Matters' at para. 3.

[41] For an analysis of the interrelationship between the public procurement Directives and the CCT provisions of the LGA 1988, see Bennet and Cirell, 'The Interrelationship of EC Public Procurement and Compulsory Competitive Tendering in the United Kingdom' (1992) 1 PPLR 280. On the CCT provisions in general see, by the same authors, *Compulsory Competitive Tendering: Law and Practice* (London, 1990).

[42] Radford (above, n 36) at 757. For an overview of the use made in the UK of public procurement as a tool for socio-economic intervention, see Arrowsmith (1995) (above, n 22).

by statute, they may only exercise those powers explicitly conferred upon them by statute and within the limits therein established.[43] Thus, when awarding contracts, local authorities could use their contracting powers to implement secondary policies for which they were statutorily responsible, as established in *R* v. *Lewisham London Borough Council, ex p. Shell.*[44]

The debate is not new however. Long before the LGA was passed the legality and legitimacy of the use of public procurement in fostering government economic policies was the object of controversy. The debate developed with respect to the Labour Government's programme to fight inflation, which dated from 1975,[45] which led to the blacklisting of firms which had breached the government's pay guidelines.[46] British authors took the view that the award of contracts could be used to achieve more general social or economic policies legally.[47] With respect to the subject-matter of the debate, it was concluded that no respect of the government pay guidelines 'may be justified as a valid consideration ... when [the government exercises] its discretionary power to award contracts'.[48] Thus, non-commercial criteria could be legally taken into account by contracting authorities when awarding contracts.

The implementation of compulsory competitive tendering in practice

The manner in which the different local authorities have abided by the LGA provisions on public purchasing has varied considerably.[49] A comprehensive

---

[43] *Bromley London BC* v. *Greater London Council* [1982] 1 ALL ER 129 at 154.

[44] [1988] 1 All ER 938. Under s. 71 of the Race Relations Act 1976, local authorities were placed under a duty to promote good race relations within their jurisdictions. The defendant in the case, a London Borough where 18% of the residents were black, adopted a policy of boycotting the applicant's products because the company was part of a multinational with economic interests in pro-apartheid South Africa. Neill LJ stated that given the multiracial character of the borough and the duty imposed on the council by s. 71 of the 1976 Act, the council was entitled to decide on the basis of its own experience and perception that trade with a particular company should cease because of the company's links with South Africa. However, the council went further than s. 71 of the 1976 Act permitted, as its objective was to exert pressure on the company to sever all trading links with South Africa. This purpose did not have any relation with the promotion of good race relations and the decision was therefore declared vitiated by an extraneous and impermissible purpose.

[45] White Paper 'The Attack on Inflation', July 1975, at para 23. Cmnd. 6151.

[46] See further Ganz (1978) *Public Law* 333 at 336. This practice caused an intense legal debate in English doctrine regarding the compatibility of such a policy with Constitutional requirements. See Daintith (1985) (above, n 2) and the bibliography cited therein at 195 and Daintith 'Regulation by Contract: the New Prerogative' (1979) 32 *Current Legal Problems* 41.

[47] Turpin (1989) *(above, n 21)* Chapter 3. In *Holliday Hall Ltd* v. *Chapple and others*, the Attorney General argued that the government had a right to place its contracts in the manner which in its view will best serve the national interest, and hence to take into account among other relevant factors, whether an employer is, or is not observing the White Paper guidelines for the purposes of controlling inflation. Therefore, the Court did not consider the question of legality of the use of public purchasing as a means to foster social or economic policies. Cited by Ganz (above, n 46) at 339.   [48] Ganz (above, n 46) at 345.

[49] Before the 1988 LGA was passed, no local authority dominated by the Labour party followed the government's indications as regards compulsory competitive tendering. Previous practices were upheld and services were still provided on an in-house basis.

survey of the initial impact of the LGA provisions was carried out by the Centre of Local Economic Strategies.[50] It covered 229 local authorities of various political ideologies and it assessed the results of the first round of contracts awarded under the discipline of the 1988 LGA. The most interesting finding for our present purposes is that the way compulsory competitive tendering has been applied by the different councils has depended on their political complexion. As the author points out, 'only a tiny minority of the services covered by the LGA were contracted out when the council was Labour controlled. This is in stark contrast to the position for Conservative controlled authorities where complete or partial privatization was introduced in over half the services.'. Hence, 'the wide variation in the impact of the first round . . . reflects the political attitudes of different authorities towards the implementation of the legislation . . . [W]hereas Conservative controlled councils are committed to competitive compulsory tendering as defined in the LGA, Labour controlled councils are clearly in favour of public sector or in-house provision of the service, and determined to enhance services and maintain employment levels, wages and conditions for the workforce . . . Thus, the way in which compulsory tendering legislation works out on the ground can vary very significantly depending on the political attitude of the authority'.[51]

Conclusions

It follows that the restriction of the margin of discretion of contracting authorities to merely commercial grounds when awarding public contracts reflects a well defined political and economic approach based on the achievement of economic efficiency. It is not, however, the only approach possible. A second conception of public purchasing, that which goes beyond merely commercial considerations, defends the instrumental use of public procurement.

These two different approaches respond to two different conceptions of how the public interest and social welfare can be achieved. Compulsory competitive tendering responds to a neo-liberal philosophy which sees undistorted competition as the source of economic wealth. The concept of national interest is equated with the achievement of economic efficiency which would result in an increase of public welfare. Redistributory objectives

---

[50] A summary of the survey is to be found in Painter (above, n 35).

[51] Painter (above, n 35) at 201 and 207. Two other different groups of councils were described by the author. The first one related to non-committed councils which did not generally have a well developed ideological commitment either to privatization or to retaining in-house services in the public sector. A second group was composed of those councils which, although committed to maintaining in-house services, were prepared to cut wages, working conditions or jobs if that was necessary for them to become competitive and win the tender. This latter group was composed of both moderate Labour and Conservative councils.

such as the maintenance of employment levels, standards on working conditions and so on, are given preference over economic efficiency in the instrumental approach. This use of public contracting as a means of furthering general policies is more characteristic of a corporate conception of the State, where negotiation with social actors regarding the conception and implementation of government policies is preferred to the enactment of compulsory legal rules.[52]

The British case is prominent in this respect. Its legal system is far more entrenched than that of the Community and the binding force of statutory provisions is not questioned. Notwithstanding this, implementation of competitive compulsory tendering in public procurement has encountered great opposition at local level and the practical success of the ultimate objectives of the legislation has depended on the political colour of the different councils. The debate which took place in Britain as regards competitive compulsory tendering provides an example of how conflicting approaches at central and local levels can influence the way in which legislation is implemented. Even though one must be very cautious in translating to a supranational level the results of a typically national experience, it is submitted that this test case may well illustrate the greater difficulties which the Community policy on public procurement may encounter. It is true that the British case is concerned with the reduction of the provision of local services on the basis of in-house structures in favour of contracting-out. This is an issue which is not addressed by the public procurement Directives. This being said, the treatment of the relevant award criteria, as interpreted by the Commission, is similar at both levels. The Commission's approach is closer to that implemented by the British Conservative Government as regards local authorities than to that which defends free choice for contracting authorities. This begs the question whether the Commission enjoys the required legitimacy to impose such a policy choice on Member States without their explicit consent.

THE BALANCING APPROACH IN THE DIRECTIVES

At Community level, the tension between both conceptions was eased, however, as a result of the Community decision-making process. Certain provisions counterbalancing the strict 'economic rationale' approach were introduced at the initiative of the Member States. Contracting authorities were explicitly authorized to depart from the aforementioned award criteria

---

[52] Winkler, 'Law, State and Economy: The Industry Act 1975 in Context' (1975) 2 *British Journal of Law and Society*, 103, especially at 119 *ff.* Ganz (above, n 46) 347. In the Spanish context see Monedero Gil, 'Criterios de adjudicación del contrato administrativo en el derecho comunitario' (1986) No. 21 *Noticias CEE* 35 at 36–37.

in certain circumstances. The exceptions concerned both the instrumental use of public procurement for regional purposes as well as the social instrumental use of public procurement.

Articles 25(4) and 29(4) of the original public supply and public works Directives, respectively, sanctioned the validity of existing national rules which allow the award of the contract on the basis of criteria other than the lowest price or the most economically advantageous offer, when the aim of those rules was to give preference to certain tenderers by way of aid, on condition that the rules invoked are compatible with the Treaty, in particular Arts. 92 to 94 EC. The social dimension of public procurement was included therefore in the first regulation, although a stand still obligation applied.

The subsequent modifications of the public procurement Directives did not alter this balance. On the contrary, the instrumental element was reinforced by the introduction of new provisions transitorily admitting regional schemes.[53] Identical exceptions were introduced in the amended public works Directive,[54] as well as the Utilities Directive.[55] Both the Commission and the Council agreed that this type of scheme was at least to be allowed for a transitional period, until definitive substitute measures were designed. This agreement, however, was, as we shall see, to become the subject of dispute. The new public works Directive also attributed to the Commission a supervisory role as regards both types of instrumental schemes by requiring Member States to inform the Commission of the existence and implementation of national provisions having as their objective regional or social considerations.

It is worth noting the important role which the European Parliament played in this debate. Its position has generally been to support the existence of preferential public procurement.[56] Thus, during the decision-making process leading to the amendment of the new Directives, the European Parliament proposed the introduction of further social provi-

---

[53] Article 26 of the public supply Directive, as modified by Article 16 of Directive 88/295, stated that: 'this Directive shall not prevent, until 31 December 1992, the application of existing national provisions on the award of public supply contracts which have as their objective the reduction of regional disparities and the promotion of job creation in the most disadvantaged regions and in declining industrial regions, on condition that the provisions concerned are compatible with the Treaty and with the Community's international obligations.' OJ 1988, L127/1.

[54] Article 29 of the public works Directive, as amended by Article 21 of Directive 89/440, OJ 1989, L210/1.   [55] Article 28(2) of Council Directive 90/531, OJ 1990, L297/1.

[56] The Parliament stated its position regarding the instrumental use of public procurement in its First Reading Opinion on the Commission's proposal to the Council for a Directive amending Directive 77/62, where it held that 'public purchases and contracts may constitute an important part of a government's policy of job creation and regional assistance; [it] emphasizes therefore that any system regulating the placing of public supply contracts must take into account the need to reduce regional disparities and to create jobs and industries in those areas which are either underdeveloped or experiencing acute industrial decline; [it]

sions intended to favour female labour, ethnic minorities, handicapped persons[57] and youth and long term unemployment when awarding public contracts. It also adopted a resolution in which it defended the need to give preference in awarding public contracts to companies operating in underdeveloped regions or regions experiencing economic decline. Furthermore, it asked for the adoption of a specific Directive providing for a system of 'price preferences' for these companies when tendering for public contracts.[58]

Thus, the regime retained in the original Directives acknowledged, within certain limits, the instrumental use of public procurement. Whereas a competitive regime, justified on grounds of economic efficiency, was to apply in the award of regular contracts, the use of public procurement as a positive interventionist tool was permitted, provided it aimed at favouring regional cohesion or job creation or disadvantaged segments of the population. Ancillary restraints of trade which this could cause were considered admissible on the grounds of the legitimate aims pursued. National and supranational interests were compensated and, as a result, the two main functions of public procurement were harmoniously combined. The Directives therefore struck a fair balance between the two conflicting approaches to public procurement.

This balance was altered, however, due to a change in the Commission's position and the decisions by the Court of Justice. These events were interrelated and influenced each other. A dialectical evolution in the Commission's approach is noticeable. In 1963, in answer to a Parliamentary question, the Commission itself qualified preferential public procurement for regional purposes as a form of State aid and therefore susceptible to a derogation from Article 92 EC pursuant to Articles 92(3)(a) and (c) EC.[59] Equally, its reaction to most of the Parliament's proposals regarding the suitability of social clauses when the text of the public procurement

recognizes that public purchases and contracts may constitute an important part of government's policy of promoting equal opportunities at the workplace; [it] emphasizes . . . that any system regulating the placing of public supply contracts must take into account the need to reduce discrimination against women, ethnic minorities and the disabled at work', OJ 1987, C246/84 at 85.

[57] Ibid. As regards the modification of the public works Directive, see, for instance, the European Parliament's Opinion on the Commission's proposal for a directive amending Directive 71/305 concerning the co-ordination of procedures for the award of public works contracts, OJ 1988, C167/64 and Second Reading by the Parliament, OJ 1989, C69/69. These proposals were repeated in the context of the Utilities Directive (Parliament's First Reading, OJ 1989, C158/271).

[58] See the European Parliament's Resolution on the need to give preference to undertakings located in the less-favoured regions and the regions in decline when public works contracts are awarded, *Doc. B3–955/90*, OJ 1990, C149/125. See 'Europe', May, 21/22 1990, at 12.

[59] See Question écrite No. 48 du M. Burgbacher à la Commission, du 27 juin 1963, JO 1963, C2235/63.

Directives was being amended also indicated a more flexible attitude on the matter.[60] This lenient disposition changed in the late eighties probably due to the development among the Commission services of the 'economic rationale' thesis. After 1985 a school of thought within the Commission began to assess the merits of the preferential schemes in terms of Community law. This triggered a debate amongst different Commission services. Whereas the Internal Market and Industrial Affairs Directorate argued that such measures were illegal and opposed the use of public procurement to achieve regional or social objectives, the Commission Directorates in charge of Regional Policy and Social Affairs were understandably more cautious.[61] The merits of the instrumental use of public procurement and the compatibility of the schemes with the general principles governing the four freedoms and, in particular, the question whether preferential public procurement could qualify as a State aid, became recurring themes in the debates. An important role in this context was played by the cases concerning these issues which came before the Court of Justice. The initiation of the cases forced the Commission to clarify its position, and their final outcome determined, as we shall see, the judicial sanctioning of a certain approach and the abandonment of the regulation of the instrumental use in the Directives.

The position finally adopted rejected the legality of the preferential schemes. The Commission started negotiations with the Member States in 1989 to bring an end to the use of public procurement for regional cohesion purposes, although it never took direct action against preferential public procurement before the Court of Justice. It officially stated, however, that preferential schemes 'constitute an infringement of the EC Treaty, notably its Articles 30 and 59. Article 92 EC, notably its paragraph 2(c) and 3(a), might appear to provide a framework within which schemes which operate as State aids could be accommodated. However, even if some schemes could be considered to be State aids within the meaning of the Treaty, which is itself an arguable matter, this does not resolve the overriding problem of the infringement of Articles 30 and 59 for which a solution remains to be found'.[62] This position was applied in the Commission's submissions in the *Du Pont de Nemours* case, where it argued not

---

[60] The Commission included in its revised proposals most of the Parliament's proposed 'social' amendments, which were, in the last instance, rejected by the Council. For instance, even though the Commission incorporated Parliament's proposed amendment to favour female labour, ethnic minorities and handicapped persons when awarding public contracts, the Council dropped it when adopting the new public supplies Directive 88/295. See the Decision concerning the common position of the Council on the proposal of the Commission concerning a Directive amending Directive 77/62, OJ 1988, C13/62 at 66.

[61] Some authors have underlined the state of confusion in which the Commission has assessed this issue. Cox (above, n 11) at 153.

[62] EC Commission, COM (89) 400 (above, n 12) at para. 41.

only that preferential regional schemes were against Article 30 EC, but, in addition, that they could not qualify as a State aid measure within the meaning of Article 92 EC.[63]

The social use of public procurement was a more sensitive area. However, prior to the *Beentjes* judgment, the Commission applied a strict monitoring policy of social clauses and initiated several Article 169 EC proceedings.[64] Later, in its submissions in the *Beentjes* case in 1988, it argued that the impugned labour clause was incompatible with the requirements of the public works Directive 71/305. It avoided, however, any statement of principle on the matter and restricted its observations to the circumstances of the case.[65] After 1990, although it had previously supported most of the European Parliament's proposals in this respect, the Commission held that no social considerations were to be taken into account in the award of public contracts.[66] Its view was that to pursue social objectives through public procurement rules 'would reduce their effectiveness in meeting their principal goal of ensuring the non-discriminatory award of public contracts' and, as a result, it rejected all Parliament's amendments in this sense.[67] The final outcome has been that in the latest consolidated versions of the Directives, the instrumental use of public procurement has been abandoned.[68]

[63] Case C-21/88, *Du Pont de Nemours* (above, n 18) at 899 *ff*.

[64] The Commission opened Article 169 EC proceedings to challenge local labour clauses applied by local authorities in the UK (infringement cdo 88/115), the Netherlands (infringements S 87/406 and A 87/242) and Germany (infringement A 88/109).

[65] In fact, the Commission based its arguments on a formal interpretation of the applicable provisions of the public works Directive. Case 31/87, *Gebroeders Beentjes BV* v. *Netherlands* [1988] ECR 4635 at 4640 *ff*.

[66] With respect to the social clause amendments proposed by the European Parliament in the services Directive, Mr Bangemann, at the time Vice-President of the Commission, declared before the European Parliament that 'Tenders cannot be appraised on the basis of the tenderer's social attitude. Provided he acts lawfully, his tender may be assessed only by its objective quality, and I cannot therefore accept [the amendments]'. Debates of the European Parliament, 14 May 1991, No. 3–405/107–8.

[67] Amended proposal for a Services Directive, explanatory memorandum, COM (91) 322 at para. 7. See also, in the context of the Utilities Directive, the rejection by the Commission of a social clause proposed by the Parliament. COM (89) 380.

[68] See, however, the consideration made in the conclusions to Chapter 3.

3

Public Procurement in Context: The Political, Economic and Social Dimensions of Public Procurement in the EC (II)

The compatibility of the instrumental use of public procurement for social and regional purposes with the basic principles of the EC Treaty and the public procurement Directives has been tackled by the Court of Justice in several judgments. The two principal cases in which this issue was dealt with are, to some extent, contradictory. Whereas social policies pursued by means of preferential public procurement, such as job creation or favouring disadvantaged segments of society, were initially flexibly treated by the Court, the same is not true of regional policies. This section is devoted to a critical analysis of the Court's case law on the instrumental use of public procurement.

The Social Instrumental Function. The *Beentjes* case

The Facts

The *Beentjes*[1] case dealt with a contract whose object was the realization of public works for a land consolidation operation. The contract was not awarded to the plaintiff Beentjes, although it had presented the lowest offer, but to the next lowest tender. The Local Committee based the rejection on the grounds that Beentjes lacked specific experience to complete the work in question, that its tender appeared to be less acceptable and that it was not in a position to comply with the condition of employing at least 70 per cent of the work-force from long-term unemployed persons recruited through the regional employment office. The latter condition, the social clause, was explictly mentioned in the published contract notice as an independent contract condition.

Beentjes brought an action against the decision before the Dutch courts alleging, *inter alia*, that none of the reasons given by the contracting au-

---

[1] Case 31/87, *Gebroeders Beentjes* v. *The Netherlands* [1988] ECR 4635. For a discussion of the case, see Arrowsmith, *A Guide to the Procurement Cases of the Court of Justice* (Winteringham, 1992) at 73; Van Gerven, 'General Report to the 14th FIDE Congress' in FIDE, *L'Application dans les États Membres des Directives sur les Marchés Publics* (Madrid, 1990) 333 at 378 *ff*.

thority were in conformity with the rules concerning the award criteria established in the public works Directive. The Dutch court initiated a preliminary reference procedure under Article 177 EC. It asked the Court of Justice to state its position as regards the social clause which referred to the employment of long-term unemployed through the regional employment office.

The Judgment

The discussion concentrated on two issues. First, whether the disputed condition could be brought within Articles 25 and 26 of the applicable public works Directive which lay down the means of proof to determine whether a candidate is technically and economically qualified to carry out the contract properly.[2] Secondly, whether such a condition was a legitimate contract award criterion under Article 29.[3]

Advocate General Darmon, together with the Commission, reached the conclusion that it was neither. Ability to perform the social clause could not 'by definition be a reference capable of proving economic and financial standing in accordance with Article 25, and does not appear to have any relation to one of the indents of Article 26, which are . . . exhaustive'.[4] It fell therefore outside the permissible criteria for assessing the qualitative capability of the candidate. As regards the award criteria, he stated that Article 29 referred exclusively to the nature of the work to be carried out and that it excluded any considerations relating to the contractor itself.[5] Accordingly, the capacity of employing long term unemployed through the regional recruitment office bore no relation to the intrinsic qualities of the work to be carried out. On those grounds, he concluded that a contractor could not be excluded on the basis of his or her capability to fulfil the social condition.[6]

The Court took a different line of reasoning, however, and accepted the validity of such clauses under certain circumstances. The legal reasoning of the judgment is somewhat confusing and deficient. The Court made it clear that the local labour condition was not concerned either with the checking of the economic, financial and technical capacity of the bidders regulated in Title IV of the Directive, nor with the criteria to award the contract provided in Article 29 thereof. It was, in the Court's own words, 'an additional specific condition' and, therefore, was compatible with the Directive's provisions as it was not covered or explicitly prohibited by any of them.[7]

---

[2] These provisions concerned the means of establishing the financial and economic standing of the candidates (Article 25) and their technical knowledge and ability (Article 26).
[3] On the award criteria see Chapter 2.   [4] Case 31/87, *Beentjes* (above, n 1) at 4648.
[5] Ibid. at 4649.   [6] Ibid. at 4650.   [7] Ibid. at para. 28.

As regards the award criteria of Article 29, the Court held that the most economically advantageous criterion had the objective of limiting the choice of contracting authorities to criteria aimed at identifying the offer which is economically the most advantageous.[8] In order to do so, the decision had to be taken on the basis of objective criteria such as those listed by way of example in Article 29(2). Curiously, however, the Court made explicit reference to the exception in Article 29(4), which contemplates preferential public procurement in favour of disadvantaged tenderers.[9] Since no specific question to this effect was put forward by the national referring judge, the Court avoided the controversial issue of whether the local labour clause could come within the exception in paragraph 4 of Article 29 and, consequently, whether it could be held to be compatible with Articles 92 to 94 EC.[10] Instead, the case was resolved with respect to a formal interpretation of the provisions of the Directive. It is striking nonetheless that the Court adopted this hands-off attitude since the said provision was *prima facie* specifically concerned with situations such as the one at stake.

Thus, after holding that the local labour clause was not incompatible with the Directive, or rather, that it was alien to the Directive's provisions, the Court assessed whether such a condition was in line with the obligations arising under the EC Treaty and held that 'the obligation to employ long-term unemployed persons could *inter alia* infringe the prohibition of discrimination laid down in the first paragraph of Article 7 EC [now Article 6EC] if it became apparent that such a condition could be satisfied only by tenderers from the State concerned or indeed that tenderers from other Member States would have difficulty in complying with it'.[11]

It concluded that such a clause was compatible with Community law, as long as it was not a disguised means to discriminate against foreign undertakings, that is, that foreign undertakings were not in a more difficult position than national ones to perform the clause. It also required that such clauses be mentioned in the contract notice so that interested undertakings could be aware of them. In the Court's words, 'the condition relating to the employment of long-term unemployed persons is compatible with the Directive if it has no direct or indirect discriminatory effect on tenderers from other Member States of the Community. An additional condition of this kind must be mentioned in the contract notice'.[12] Thus, even

---

[8] Ibid. at 4657.

[9] 'Indeed, it was only by way of exception that Article 29(4) provides that an award may be based on criteria of a different nature within the framework of rules whose aim is to give preference to certain tenderers by way of aid, on condition that the rules invoked are in conformity with the Treaty, in particular Articles 92 *et seq.*' Ibid.

[10] In Case C-21/88, *Du Pont de Nemours Italiana* v. *USL No 2 di Carrara* [1990] ECR 889, the referring national court explicitly asked the Court of Justice to consider the question of Articles 92 to 94 EC. See later in this chapter.

[11] Case 31/87, *Beentjes* (above, n 1) at 4659.   [12] Ibid. at 4661.

if the contract is awarded on the 'most economically advantageous' offer criterion, an additional contractual condition regarding local labour may be introduced by contracting authorities, as long as it does not discriminate directly or indirectly against foreign bidders. Since it was a preliminary ruling under Article 177 EC, the Court of Justice itself did not pronounce specifically on the validity of that criterion. The duty to determine, in the light of all the circumstances of the case, whether the imposition of such a condition is directly or indirectly discriminatory was left to the national court. It is regrettable that the Court did not go into a deeper analysis of the clause.

Although the judgment is technically poor, it follows from the foregoing that the Court accepted this type of social clause as a valid factor to be assessed in contract conditions and one which is not *per se* incompatible with the public procurement Directives as they stand. The two sole requirements which the Court of Justice imposes upon contracting authorities is that the criteria used must not be directly or indirectly discriminatory and that those used have to be mentioned in the contract clauses. The question remains, however, whether a foreign undertaking unfamiliar with other Member States' labour market practices is indirectly discriminated against by such a clause, since it is not clear what should be regarded as indirectly discriminatory. Are domestic firms favoured in the sense that they are in a better position to comply with that requirement? Although it seems that in this case the answer may be negative, there could be other situations in which the response is not so evident.

The judgment has, in fact, given rise to numerous interpretations. Some authors maintained that it meant that the Directives did not restrict an authority's freedom to pursue secondary policies through public procurement by means of additional contractual conditions such as the one at stake in *Beentjes*.[13] The Commission for its part understood the decision as meaning that contracting authorities could take into account the ability of the contractors to perform certain contractual conditions incorporated into the actual contract terms.[14] This interpretation is ambiguous as it does not make clear the extent to which contracting authorities may exclude a particular tender which is technically, economically and financially eligible on the basis of such contractual conditions. We agree with some other authors that the Commission's interpretation is unmeritorious.[15] In any case this interpretation has become precarious as *Beentjes* seems to have been overturned by subsequent case law. It is submitted that, in practice,

---

[13] Arrowsmith, 'The Legality of "Secondary" Procurement Policies under the Treaty of Rome and the Works Directive' (1992) 1 PPLR 408 at 410 *ff*. See also Arrowsmith, 'Public Procurement as an Instrument of Policy and the Impact of Market Liberalisation' (1995) 111 LQR 235 at 248 *ff*.

[14] EC Commission, *Public Procurement-Regional and Social Aspects*, COM (89) 400 at para. 47.

[15] Arrowsmith (1992) 1 PPLR (above, n 13) at 411.

such contractual terms effectively act as selection criteria. In the instant case, Beentjes offer was rejected, although it was the cheapest, on the grounds, *inter alia*, that it could not perform the social clause. If a firm with the lowest or most economically advantageous offer is denied the contract because it cannot comply with a 'specific condition', the practical result is the same as if the latter had formed part of the applicable qualitative selection or award criteria.

The Application of the Articles on the Free Provision of Services

It is noticeable that the EC Treaty provisions on the free provision of services were not mentioned in the Court's reasoning in *Beentjes*, even though they are *prima facie* relevant, if not crucial, to the resolution of the case. Only Article 7 EEC (now Article 6 EC) was referred to by the Court, although it did not exclude the possibility of the social clause infringing other Treaty provisions. Subsequent cases have been dealt with differently by the Court and have called into question the authority of the *Beentjes* decision.

In the *Rush Portuguesa* case, the national court referred a question to the Court of Justice which concerned, *inter alia*, the compatibility with Community law of French labour law rules which granted an exclusive right to the *Office national d'immigration* to recruit nationals of third States for work in France. Rush Portuguesa had been carrying out some public works as a subcontractor in France for which purposes it had employed its own work-force from Portugal. The Court rightly situated the problem within the context of the free provision of services principles and held that Articles 59 and 60 EC must be interpreted as meaning that an under-taking established in Portugal which provides services in the construction and public works sector in another Member State may bring its labour force from another Member State for the duration of the works in question. In such a case, the authorities of the Member State in whose territory the works are to be carried out may not impose on the supplier of services conditions relating to the recruitment of manpower *in situ* (which was the situation in *Beentjes*) or the obtaining of work permits for the 'imported' workforce. 'To impose such conditions on the person providing the services established in another Member State discriminates against that person in relation to his competitors established in the host country who are able to use their own staff without restrictions'.[16]

It appears that the principle applied in *Rush Portuguesa* differs from that applied in *Beentjes*. In the former case, discrimination was explicitly held to exist on the basis of Articles 59 and 60 EC, whereas in the latter, this question was left open. The challenged measures had a similar effect in both cases, although their underlying policies were different. Could it not

---

[16] Case C-113/89, *Rush Portuguesa* v. *Office national d'immigration* [1990] ECR 1485 at 1144.

be argued that on the basis of *Rush Portuguesa* the social clause at stake in *Beentjes* was clearly contrary to Articles 59 and 60 EC? Why did the Court avoid the question in *Beentjes*? It is submitted that the difference in treatment was determined by the legitimate social policy aim of the long-term unemployed clause. The Court showed sympathy for the social clause and, arguably, refused to declare straightforwardly its incompatibility with Community law. The coherence of the Court's legal reasoning suffered as a result. It is worth noting in this context that at the time the judgment was rendered, the fight against long-term unemployment and the incorporation of young persons in the labour market had become primary objectives of the Community's social and economic cohesion policy which was being implemented through the regulation of the structural funds.[17]

In *Commission* v. *Italy*, an Italian law which reserved a proportion of public works contracts to subcontractors whose registered offices were in the region where the works were to be carried out was declared by the Court to constitute discrimination against undertakings established in other Member States. The Court held that, whilst it was true that the provision did not discriminate on the basis of nationality, as other Italian undertakings established outside the region were equally excluded, the fact remained that the subcontractors favoured by the provision were Italian. Thus, the Italian legislation was a clear restriction of the freedom to provide services.[18]

With respect to another provision of the Italian law, which accorded preference in the choice of undertakings invited to tender to joint ventures and consortia in which local undertakings were involved, the Court equally held that, although the provision applied without distinction to all Italian and foreign companies, it essentially favoured undertakings established in Italy, since such undertakings were much more likely to carry out their main activity in the region of Italy where the works were to be executed than undertakings established in other Member States. The Court held, moreover, that the preference represented a criterion of selection which was not contemplated by Articles 23 to 26 of the public works Directive and, therefore, constituted a breach of the said Directive.[19] The *Beentjes* 'contractual condition' interpretation was thus avoided by the Court, which did not follow its previous reasoning. This questions the legal force of *Beentjes*.[20]

---

[17] See Council Regulation 2052/88 and Council Regulation 4255/88 defining the goals of the Structural funds and the Social Cohesion Fund.

[18] This conclusion was facilitated by the previous *Du Pont de Nemours* judgment, expressly cited by the Court, in which the fact that the challenged system also discriminated against other firms established in Italy did not prevent the Court from declaring it contrary to Article 30 EC. See later in this chapter.

[19] Case C-360/89, *Commission* v. *Italy* [1992] ECR I-3415, noted by Arrowsmith (1992) 1 PPLR (above, n 13).

[20] In view of the judgment in Case C-360/89 *Commission* v. *Italy*, some commentators concluded that *Beentjes* had been overturned, see Arrowsmith (1992) 1 PPLR (above, n 13) at

Here again, the Court applied Articles 59 and 60 EC without hesitation. It could be argued that the obligation to hire 70 per cent of the required work force from the long-term unemployed registered in the regional employment office constitutes as much of an obstacle to the free provision of services as the need to have a registered office in the relevant region. In *Commission* v. *Italy*, the Court adopted a more strict stance than it had in *Beentjes*. Arguably, the fact that this decision was the result of an Article 169 EC proceeding may have affected the outcome, as the judgment was delivered by a full Court. This, however, does not explain the difference between *Beentjes* and *Rush Portuguesa* which was also a preliminary ruling under Article 177 EC. The ruling on *Commission* v. *Italy* was given after the *Du Pont de Nemours* decision (see below) and it followed the same strict reasoning applied in the latter case to similar preferential schemes with respect to the free movement of goods. The latest case law appears to have departed from the *Beentjes* precedent, although the issue remains unsettled.

The Application of the Free Movement of Workers Provisions and the Social Policy Question

A further question which was not addressed by any of the participants in *Beentjes* was the discriminatory effect of the clause as regards long-term unemployed labour established in other Member States. The Court only assessed the possibility of discrimination between tenderers in the light of the Treaty. Could it not be argued that the social clause went against the free movement of workers provisions? The labour force was to be recruited through the regional employment office. Although not a direct discrimination on the basis of nationality (since, arguably, foreign unemployed could be registered in the relevant local employment office and other unemployed Dutch nationals non-resident in the area were equally excluded), the fact remains that it is likely that the unemployed labour force favoured would be Dutch.[21] This could amount to indirect discrimination hindering the free movement of workers in the Community.[22]

In commenting on the judgment in *Beentjes*, the Commission did point out that although the Court only referred to discrimination between tenderers, discrimination may also occur as regards foreign unemployed persons. It hinted that in order to render the social clauses compatible with

414. See also Nielsen, 'Public Procurement and International Labour Standards' (1995) 4 PPLR 94 at 98–99.

[21] In the same vein Gormley, 'Some Reflections on Public Procurement in the European Community' (1990) 1 *European Business Law Review* 63.

[22] In this respect, it is worthwhile mentioning that Article 48 EC has been interpreted as covering the free movement of job seekers and unemployed workers. Case C-292/89, *R* v. *Immigration Appeal Tribunal ex p. Antonissen* [1991] ECR I-745.

the EC Treaty and avoid this discriminatory effect, contracting authorities should extend their preferential treatment to equivalent categories of beneficiaries in other Member States.[23] Indeed, if Article 48 EC was found to be applicable, the only means of bringing the clause in line with Community requirements is to eliminate its potentially discriminatory effect by extending its benefits to other Member States' nationals. This seems to be the policy preferred by the Commission which now requires Member States to extend the preference operated through national 'social clauses' to firms established in the EC which fulfil the established criteria.[24] This policy is equally applied to contract awards whose value falls below the Directive's threshold.

Although from a legal point of view such an extension is correct, some doubts arise as regards its convenience from a policy point of view. The Community's competence in the field of social policy[25] is marginal and subsidiary in character. Despite the existence of specific provisions in the EC Treaty dealing with social policy issues, the fact remains that the latter are subordinated and complementary to the main Treaty objective: the realisation of an internal market.[26] Apart from certain Directives which touch on social policy areas, no alternative binding secondary measures are available at the supranational level, nor does it seem that agreement in this sense is likely to emerge in the near future becasue of the position adopted in the TEU.

Due to the recalcitrant British stance, TEU amendments to existing EC Treaty social provisions have not brought any substantial innovation as regards the Community's legal powers in the field.[27] However, a Social

---

[23] EC Commission, COM (89) 400 (above, n 14) at paras. 54 *ff.*

[24] After the Article 169 EC proceeding initiated against certain provisions of the Italian Law No. 381 of 8 November 1991 on social co-operatives, the Italian Government and the Commission reached a compromise whereby the preferences favouring firms employing disadvantaged workers were extended to any comparable firms established in other Member States of the Community.

[25] Social policy is understood here to cover policies whose objective is primarily redistributory (see Majone, 'The European Community between Social Policy and Social Regulation' (1993) 31 JCMS 153 at 156 *ff*). This is something totally distinct from social regulation which is aimed at correcting market failures and externalities and in relation to which the Community has been attributed competence, by the Single European Act and TEU. For a detailed discussion of all political, institutional and legal issues relating to the social aspects of the common market, see Vogel-Polsky and Vogel, *L'Europe Sociale de 1993: Illusion, Alibi ou Réalité?* (Bruxelles, 1991).

[26] On the marginal character of the original Community social policy, see Vogel-Polsky, 'L'Acte unique ouvre-t-il l'espace social européen?' (1989) 2 *Droit Social* 177 at 178; Majone (above, n 25) at 154 and 160 *ff.*

[27] They only suffered technical amendments. For a general overview of the situation before and after Maastricht, see *inter alia* Whiteford, 'Social Policy after Maastricht' (1993) 18 ELRev 202; Szyszczak, 'Social Policy: A Happy Ending or a Reworking of a Fairy Tale' and Shaw, 'Twin Track Social Europe. The Inside Track' in O'Keeffe, and Twomey (eds.), *Legal Issues of the Maastricht Treaty* (London, 1993) 313 and 295 respectively; Watson, 'Social Policy after Maastricht' (1993) 30 CMLR 481.

Protocol and its related Social Agreement have been annexed to the TEU which authorise their signatories to have recourse to the institutions, procedures and mechanisms of the Treaty in order to adopt measures in the social field which go beyond what is permitted under the scope of the EC Treaty. The objective is to allow those Member States willing to proceed further in the adoption of common social measures to do so without being impeded by the constraints of the EC Treaty social provisions and the opposition of just one Member State. Even though the Agreement may be regarded as a significant advance,[28] its legal status in Community law remains unsettled. The Social Protocol provides that the provisions of the Agreement are without prejudice to the provisions of the EC Treaty. More importantly, the UK is not part of the Agreement and, therefore, the measures adopted under it are not binding upon it. In view of this, it has been suggested that the Agreement does not constitute part of Community law, but a mere intergovernmental agreement only affecting the signatories.[29] But, as pointed out by Whiteford, even assuming that the Agreement has shifted the balance of policy from the signatory Member States to the Community, it remains to be seen whether the signatories will 'be able to reach consensus on a body of social regulation'.[30] Moreover, it must be noted that the Agreement still requires unanimity for the adoption of a wide range of measures, amongst which are financial contributions for job-creation, without prejudice to the provisions relating to the Social Fund.[31] It follows that progress in this area is likely to be slow, since positions will be difficult to reconcile in a common 'Community' measure, even where qualified majority is required. It therefore looks as though Member States are still keen on retaining the main legal and political responsibility in the field of social policy.

In the absence of a Community measure, and following the rationale of subsidiarity, the definition of the content, the means and the resources devoted to the implementation of social policies is a national matter which generally affects national citizens. National approaches to social policy vary greatly from one Member State to another, depending not only on their economic wealth but also on their cultural attitudes and

---

[28] The Agreement annexed to the Protocol represents an advance with respect to the substantive social issues that may be regulated under its scope. It also increases the legal powers of the signatories to adopt binding legal measures in the social field, even by qualified majority. See Article 2(2) of the Agreement in relation to Article 2(1).

[29] See Barnard, 'A Social Policy for Europe: Politicians 1; Lawyers 0' (1992) *International Journal of Comparative Labour Law and Industrial Relations* 15 at 18. See Whiteford (above, n 27) at 211 *ff*.

[30] Whiteford (above, n 27) at 211. In this respect see also Watson (above, n 27) at 511 *ff*. A clear indication of Member States' reluctance to allow social policy matters to be controlled by the Community is evident in the discussions held in relation to the adoption of the EC Social Charter, the Social Protocol and Agreement and by the unanimity requirement for secondary legislation of Article 100A(4) EC, which relates to the rights and interests of employed persons.   [31] See Article 2(3) of the Agreement.

social values. These choices are politically accountable through national democratic institutions. Since citizens from other Member States do not usually have any legal or political connection with the State granting the social benefit,[32] no political or economic responsibility should result for the contracting public authorities of one Member State as regards other Member States' labour or population. Job creation schemes for the long-term unemployed come within the concept of national social policy and, at the present stage of Community law, may be restricted to the benefit of national citizens.

The way forward may be the establishment of a positive supranational European social policy. This may only be realized through political agreement, however. This philosophy supported the revision of the EC Treaty provisions on social policy which led to the adoption of the Social Protocol in the TEU and its annexed Agreement. Commentators who have analysed the gestation of both instruments and their potential for channelling the creation of a real supranational Social Policy are sceptical, if not overtly critical.[33] This being so, and although a pan-European employment policy and an extension of more favourable national social polices to all disadvantaged sectors of the population, irrespective of their place of residence, is a desirable and much needed development, as things stand at present it appears premature. To oblige Member States to extend the scope of their social policies, implemented through public contracts or other means, to other Community citizens on the basis of Article 7 EEC (now Article 6 EC) or Article 48 EC is a legalistic interpretation which disregards the actual stage of political integration in the Community and confuses the competence of national and supranational levels. This, however, must not preclude a worker or unemployed person from another Member State who has a direct link, be it economic, political or geographical (the most obvious case is that of residence), with the Member State granting the social benefit from enjoying the benefits available on the basis of the principle of non-discrimination. Thus, in the absence of Community horizontal measures, local labour clauses and similar social clauses should be admitted, provided they apply within a specific local area and not exclusively to the whole of the national labour market, and provided that they do not discriminate, directly or indirectly, on the basis of the nationality of unemployed persons residing in those areas. This interpretation however has been encumbered by the decisions in *Commission* v. *Italy* and *Du Pont de Nemours*.

The Commission's favoured solution could result in Member States withdrawing their social benefit schemes, or reducing their social policy

---

[32] Apart from a very vague notion of European citizenship. See generally O'Leary, *The Evolving Concept of Community Citizenship—From the Free Movement of Persons to Union Citizenship*, forthcoming (London, 1996).   [33] See above, n 27.

advantages, in order to avoid infringements of Community law, or their social welfare systems becoming overloaded as a result of claims by other Member States' nationals. It is therefore submitted that the Court's *Beentjes* judgment should be interpreted in the sense that public procurement may be used to implement legitimate national social policy choices with respect to national or assimilated citizens. The reference to Article 7 EEC (now Article 6) must therefore be read as meaning that no artificial conditions may be introduced in the contract clauses which discriminate against foreign tenderers. Support for this interpretation may be derived from the fact that the Court of Justice did not refer to discrimination between unemployed labour from different Member States. Discrimination with respect to such similar categories of beneficiaries established in other Member States should be acceptable at a time when political integration has not reached a stage when national public authorities become responsible for the well being of non-resident citizens of other Member States.

Conclusions

The *Beentjes* judgment must be welcomed from a policy point of view, as it took into consideration the reality of public procurement as a tool to pursue economic and social policies. The social instrumental function was therefore partially sanctioned by the Court of Justice. The legitimacy of the aim pursued by the local labour clause and the fact that the fight against long-term unemployment was seen at the time—and still is—with sympathetic eyes at the supranational level may have had some influence on the Court's lenient approach in *Beentjes*. However, the Court's legal reasoning is unsatisfactory and difficult to reconcile with susbsequent cases. The question remains whether this position will be maintained in the future in view of the Court's more recent decisions.

Nonetheless, for our present purposes, if *Beentjes* is still good law, the Court of Justice may accept certain departures from the strict 'buy efficient' approach which inspires the public procurement Directives. According to the Commission's interpretation of the judgment, other 'social objectives' may be pursued by similar contract conditions. The enhancement of employment opportunities for young people, professional training, health and safety, labour relations and the suppression of racial, religious or sex discrimination may legitimately be the object of positive policies implemented through public contracting. The Commission concludes that contracting authorities are free under Community law to pursue such objectives, provided that the Directives' procedures and the constraints of the EC Treaty are complied with. Thus, the discriminatory effect of these conditions is to be assessed on its own merits,[34] although

---

[34] EC Commission, COM (89) 400 (above, n 14) at para. 46.

the extension of these schemes to firms which fulfil the required conditions but are established in other Member States seems a prerequisite. This interpretation is subject to the criticisms developed above.

Some final remarks about the real impact of the social clauses in public procurement must be made. Even though it is a highly sensitive issue from a social point of view, its real repercussions may have been exaggerated. It is submitted that the relevance of the social instrumental function of public procurement for the purposes of the internal market is minor. Local labour clauses applying in the framework of public works contracts are not likely to act as substantial obstacles to the process of integration. For cost reasons, the work-force for the realization of public works is usually hired in the local labour market. Moreover, possible labour-costs savings which firms established in other Member States may obtain from transferring their own labour force to the public works site have largely been foreclosed by the ruling in *Rush Portuguesa*, which allows Member States to extend their legislation or collective labour agreements on working conditions to any person who is employed, even temporarily, within their territory, no matter in which country the employer is established.[35] Therefore, from the perspective of the integration of these markets, local labour clauses constitute a marginal complication. The same applies as regards other social contract conditions. Since they are intended to give preference to disfavoured sectors of the population, they are unlikely to cause noticeable disruptions in the functioning of the internal market since their scope of application is bound to be limited. The banning of such clauses is likely to cause public outrage, however.[36] Since responsibility for these groups must be a matter of national competence until Community legislation is enacted to substitute national schemes, the simplest solution would have been to allow them to operate at national level, provided no discrimination on the basis of the nationality of the workers existed. It is submitted that this issue appears to have been unnecessarily muddled by a far too legalistic approach by the Court of Justice.

The *Du Pont de Nemours* Decision. The Case of Regional Schemes

The *Du Pont de Nemours* judgment is of twofold interest. First, from a theoretical point of view, it tackles the specific question of the degree of freedom left to Member States to choose how to conduct their regional policies within the framework of the EC Treaty. Secondly, on a more practical level, the decision resolves the debate about whether national practices

---

[35] See Case C-113/89, *Rush Portuguesa* (above, n 16) at 1445.
[36] See the reactions to the British Government decision to withdraw the Priority Suppliers scheme in August 1994 on the basis of its incompatibility with Community obligations. See below, n 109.

as regards public procurement are compatible with the main objectives of the EC Treaty. Thus, the general background in which the judgment is to be placed is that of the conflict between market integration and regional cohesion on the one hand, and economically efficient public procurement and 'instrumental' public procurement on the other.[37] In view of the *Beentjes* decision, the same lenient approach could be expected to apply in the case of regional development policies implemented through public procurement. This impression was dispelled by the Court with respect to the free movement of goods provisions in the *Du Pont de Nemours* judgment. Moreover, the Court has extended the position adopted in *Du Pont de Nemours* to similar preferential systems applying in the field of public works and, therefore, to the free provision of services, which may detract from the applicability of *Beentjes*.[38]

Preferential schemes similar to the one at stake in the *Du Pont de Nemours* judgment aimed at influencing the spatial distribution of economic activities applied in other Member States.[39] The considerations made as regards the Italian quota must be generalized and are applicable to other schemes.

The Facts

By Law No 64/86,[40] the Italian State imposed on all public authorities, all firms with State participation, health authorities and universities, the obligation to obtain at least 30 per cent of their purchases from undertakings permanently established in the *Mezzogiorno* (southern Italian region), where in addition the required goods had to be manufactured or transformed. In applying this Law, the *Unità Sanitaria Locale* (USL) No. 2 of Carrara reserved 30 per cent of its procurement needs for undertakings fulfilling the legal requirements. It thereby excluded the *Du Pont de Nemours Deutschland GmbH* from the adjudication procedure regarding this portion of procurement, since it was not permanently established in the said region. By way of a response, this undertaking brought proceedings before Italian courts. The German firm questioned the compatibility of the

---

[37] This part of the chapter is based on previous work done in collaboration with Stehmann, published as 'Product Market Integration versus Regional Cohesion in the Community' (1991) 16 ELRev 261, reprinted in Snyder (ed.) *European Community Law*, Vol. II (Aldershot, 1993) 239.   [38] Case C-360/89, *Commission* v. *Italy* (above, n 19).

[39] Apart from Italy, Germany, Greece and the UK applied similar regional preferential schemes. For a description of these schemes, see COM (89) 400 (above, n 14) at paras. 38 *ff*. The German case has, however, come to the forefront due to the reunification of Germany. The German Government argued that similar price preference systems would need to be developed in favour of firms established in the ex-DDR to enhance its economic development. See Wainwright, 'Legal Reforms in Public Procurement' (1990) 10 YEL 133 at 139.

[40] For a full and detailed description of the Law see Merusi, 'Riserve obbligatorie e sistema sanitario nazionale' (1988) *Il Diritto dell'Economia* 35.

Italian measure with Community law. In an Article 177 EC reference, the national court posed two questions to the Court of Justice which are relevant for our present purposes. The first concerned the compatibility of such a preferential regime with Article 30 EC. The second referred to the characterisation of the 30 per cent reservation as an aid within the meaning of Article 92 EC, insofar as it intends to facilitate the economic development of a region where 'the standard of living is abnormally low'. These points will be analysed separately.

The Judgment

Does the preferential scheme qualify as a measure having equivalent effects to quantitative restrictions?

In a brief judgment the Court of Justice unceremoniously interpreted Article 30 EC as prohibiting the Italian measure. First it recalled its *Dassonville* case law, where measures which have equivalent effects to quantitative restrictions (MEE) were broadly defined.[41] Then the Court went on to examine the possible effects on intra Community trade of such a preferential scheme in the light of this definition, in order to appreciate whether it qualified as an MEE.

The conclusion of this analysis was straightforward. The scheme in question not only had restrictive effects on trade but was also discriminatory in the sense that it statutorily prevented Italian public bodies and administrative authorities from fulfilling 30 per cent of their procurement needs with foreign manufactured products. The determinate element in the Court's reasoning was that only goods of Italian origin were favoured by the preferential scheme, regardless of the fact that its territorial field of application was limited to part of the national territory, and as a result, it also discriminated against firms established in the north of Italy. According to the Court, the fact that the restrictive effects of a State measure do not benefit all national products but only part of them, is not sufficient to justify the non application of Article 30 EC to the said measure. In this sense, Advocate General Lenz rightly pointed out that the discriminatory character of the measure was aggravated by the fact that it affected 40 per cent of the Italian territory and concerned markets of an economic value ranging from 16 to 17 billion Ecus.[42]

Once the discriminatory character of the scheme had been established and, consequently, Article 30 EC deemed to be applicable, the Court proceeded to examine whether any justification for the regime could be found on the grounds of Article 36 EC, or the mandatory requirements

---

[41] Case 8/74, *Procureur du Roi* v. *Dassonville* [1974] ECR 837 at 852.
[42] Opinion of Advocate General Lenz in Case 21/88, *Du Pont de Nemours* (above, n 10) at 907.

of the *Cassis de Dijon* jurisprudence.[43] According to well-established jurisprudence, Article 36 EC does not include any exception based on economic grounds,[44] such as the need for economic development of underdeveloped regions. As for the latter, the application of the 'mandatory requirements' was out of the question insofar as the Italian measure was not indistinctly applicable to national and imported products. Only goods produced or transformed in the *Mezzogiorno*, and therefore of Italian origin, could benefit from the said preferential treatment.

Delimitation of the respective scope of application of Articles 30 and 92 to 94 EC

The second question considered by the Court referred to the vexed issue concerning the delimitation of the scope of application of Articles 30 and 92 EC. In essence the question by the Italian judge, as the Court understood it, was whether the eventual qualification of the scheme as a State aid could prevent the application of Article 30 EC. If that were the case, the State aid provisions would apply, which would eventually give the Commission the possibility, pursuant to Article 93 EC, to declare the measure compatible with one of the exceptions contained in Article 92(3) EC.[45] Furthermore, since Articles 92 to 94 EC do not have direct effect, national courts would not be competent to judge the compatibility of these measures as regards Community law.[46]

The 'state of uncertainty' in which the law concerning this matter stands at present derives, to a large extent, from the Court of Justice's ambiguous and even contradictory jurisprudence.[47] In *Iannelli* the Court partly followed the Advocate General and the Commission, and applied the *lex specialis* principle according to which Article 30 EC should only be used when there is no other more specific Treaty provision.[48] It underlined the different

---

[43] Case 120/78, *Rewe-Zentral AG* v. *Bundesmonopolverwaltung für Branntwein* [1979] ECR 649.

[44] See, for instance, Case 7/61, *Commission* v. *Italy* [1961] ECR 317; Case 95/81, *Commission* v. *Italy* [1982] ECR 2187; Case 288/88, *Commission* v. *Ireland* [1989] ECR 1761.

[45] The measure had been duly notified to the Commission by the Italian authorities as required by Article 93 EC.

[46] Case 74/76, *Iannelli & Volpi SpA* v. *Meroni* [1977] ECR 557 at 574 and 575. See also later in this chapter.

[47] Oliver, 'A Review of the Case Law of the Court of Justice on Articles 30 to 36 in 1985' (1986) 23 CMLRev 325 at 334, although he has partially modified his position; see Oliver, *Free Movements of Goods in the EEC*, 2nd edn. (London, 1988) at 80.

[48] The Advocate General in the case unequivocally argued that a State measure which fell under the scope of application of the State aids provisions could not be caught at the same time by Article 30 EC. Opinion of Advocate General Warner, Case 74/76 *Iannelli* (above, n 46) at 588. The Court for its part stated that 'however wide the field of application of Article 30 may be, it nevertheless does not include obstacles to trade covered by other provisions of the Treaty'. Case 74/76 *Iannelli* at 574. In the same sense, see Dashwood, 'Preliminary Rulings on the EEC State Aid Provisions' (1977) 2 ELRev 367 at 372; Oliver (1988) (above, n 47) at 77; Schramme, 'Rapport entre les mesures d'effet équivalent à des restrictions quantitatives et les aides nationales' (1985) 21 RTDE 487 at 501; Scheuing, *Les Aides Financières Publiques aux Entreprises Privées en Droit Français et Européen* (Paris, 1974) at 288 *ff.*

scope of application and functions of Article 30 EC and Articles 92 to 94 EC in the framework of the EC Treaty. Nevertheless, the Court went on to qualify this statement by introducing the so-called 'severability test' according to which:

> those aspects of aid that contravene specific provisions of the Treaty other than Articles 92 and 93 may be so indissolubly linked to the object of the aid that it is impossible to evaluate them separately so that their effect on the compatibility or incompatibility of the aid viewed as a whole must therefore of necessity be determined in the light of the procedure prescribed in Article 93. Nevertheless the position is different if it is possible when a system of aid is being analysed to separate those conditions or factors which, even though they form part of this system, may be regarded as not being necessary for the attainment of its object or for its proper functioning. In the latter case there are no reasons based on the division of powers under Articles 92 and 93 which permit the conclusion to be drawn that, if other provisions of the Treaty which have direct effect are infringed, those provisions may not be invoked before national courts simply because the factor in question is an aspect of aid.[49]

The 'severability test' is far from being watertight, since it involves many different concepts which lack precise content. As some authors have contended, it is nothing more than a difficult compromise which can only be arduously applied.[50] It seems that the main concern of the Court was to ensure that individual rights deriving from directly effective Treaty provisions were not ignored with impunity by Member States (by sneaking forbidden measures in 'the jungle of State aids'), while at the same time respecting the different scopes of application and functions of the various Treaty provisions. As for the solution of the case, the Court left the national judge to determine whether elements existed which were severable from the aid itself and which were not necessary for the attainment of its objective or for its proper functioning and, consequently, subject to the directly effective prohibition contained in Article 30 EC. In brief, from the wording of the *Iannelli* judgment one could safely conclude that Article 30 EC was viewed as a *lex generalis* in relation to Articles 92 to 94 EC.[51]

The turning point in the case law came in *Commission* v. *France*,[52] later confirmed by *Commission* v. *Italy*[53] and by the *Du Pont de Nemours* decision.

---

[49] Case 74/76 *Iannelli* (above, n 46) at 576–577.

[50] See Oliver (1986) (above, n 47) at 332, Dashwood (above, n 48) at 367. 'Indeed', as Oliver points out, 'the Court appeared to have difficulty in applying it' in the *Iannelli* case. For a favourable attitude towards this severability test as an adequate solution see Schramme (above, n 48) at 487.

[51] A similar, albeit not identical reasoning was applied in the subsequent case discussing this matter, the *Buy Irish* case: Case 249/81, *Commission* v. *Ireland* [1982] ECR 4005. Although the Court did not make any reference to its *Iannelli* precedent, it arguably applied the severability test to the facts. See further Fernández Martín and Stehmann (above, n 37) at 245 *ff.*   [52] Case 18/84, *Commission* v. *France* [1985] ECR 1339.

[53] Case 103/84, *Commission* v. *Italy* [1986] ECR 1759.

The Court reasoned similarly in all three cases and stated that 'Articles 92 and 94 cannot . . . be used to frustrate the rules of the Treaty on the free movement of goods or the rules on the repeal of discriminatory tax provisions. . . . [P]rovisions relating to the free movement of goods, the repeal of discriminatory tax provisions and aid have a common objective, namely to ensure the free movement of goods between Member States under normal conditions of competition'. Since the Court in *Du Pont de Nemours* defined the measure as an MEE contrary to Article 30 EC, there was no longer any reason for examining the Italian quota in the light of the State aids provisions. According to its previous jurisprudence, which it repeated, the mere fact that a 'national measure may possibly be defined as an aid within the meaning of Article 92 is . . . not an adequate reason for exempting it from the prohibition contained in Article 30'.[54] In other words, the Court gave priority to the free movement of goods provisions, even if not explicitly denying that the preferential scheme had some State aid features. This is quite clearly a departure from *Iannelli*.

The state of the law concerning this matter seems to be that when the two sets of provisions, those on the free movement of goods and those on State aids, might apply to the same measure, the former should be given priority.[55] The rules on free movement of goods are no longer *lex generalis* as regards the State aids provisions and the *Iannelli* precedent seems to have been abandoned.

We have argued elsewhere[56] that the Court's approach is unsatisfactory insofar as it is excessively formalistic, confuses the scope and functions of different Treaty provisions and disregards economic reality. First of all, when justifying its position, the Court of Justice stresses that both sets of rules seek to ensure the free movement of goods under normal conditions of competition. This is only partially true. The Court of Justice seems to neglect that State aids within the meaning of Article 92(3) EC have a secondary but no less important function of acting as incentive measures to close regional and economic gaps, that is, an economic cohesion function. Secondly, the Court's position may have certain undesirable consequences. It is clear that State aids, by nature, always have a negative effect on inter State trade since they artificially improve the competitiveness of domestic firms. They therefore may always come under the *imperium* of Article 30 EC according to the *Dassonville* formula, as can almost anything. *Dassonville*

---

[54] Case C-21/88, *Du Pont de Nemours* (above, n 10) at 922. See also Case 18/84, *Commission v. France* (above, n 52) at 1347 and 1348. On the evolution of the Court's position see Pescatore, 'Public and Private Aspects of the Community Competition Law' in Hawk (ed.) *US and Common Market Antitrust Policies* (New York, 1986) 383 at 401.

[55] For a more detailed analysis of the possible interpretations reconciling this case-law see generally Fernández Martín and Stehmann (above, n 37) at 247 *ff*.

[56] Fernández Martín and Stehmann (above, n 37) at 251 *ff*.

is, moreover, not subject to a *de minimis* rule.[57] Leaving aside possible jus-
tificiations on the basis of the *nemo auditur* principle in those cases where
no prior notification of the aid has taken place,[58] applying Article 30 EC
as broadly interpreted in *Dassonville* without engaging in deeper analysis risks obliterating Articles 92 and 93 EC.[59] Thirdly, the Commission's
wide discretion, recognised in Article 93 EC and sanctioned by the Court[60]
to accept aids as compatible with the common market would remain
impaired, since it appears that any State aid with restrictive effects on
trade is prohibited by Article 30 EC. This cannot certainly be the intention
of the Court and further clarification in subsequent cases is required.

This attitude is also worrying from an economic and political reading of
subsidiarity. From an economic point of view the Court's position favours
rapid market integration to the detriment of regional cohesion. The transition from national economies to a European economy and eventually to
a Monetary Union should be achieved smoothly so as to avoid an increase
in regional economic divergences. The speed with which trade barriers
are dismantled in the EC and the achievement of the TEU convergence
criteria sharply increases the need for quick measures to balance the adverse
effects on disfavoured regions. It is commonly agreed that economic integration certainly reinforces the already more competitive areas.[61] In the
specific case of Italy, while Italy as a whole may very well be better off
due to integration of the European market, the *divergence between regions* in
Italy is likely to increase. This again explains the need for transitional
countervailing measures which ideally should be adopted, or at least co-
ordinated, within the framework of a supranational regional policy.

However, measures undertaken at the supranational level to balance
these effects have so far been lacking. At the time of the *Du Pont de Nemours*
judgment, the Community's subsidiary role for regional policy had not
been adapted to the new situation, despite the introduction of provisions
in the SEA calling for greater attention to aspects of regional and social
cohesion when designing supranational policies. The changes introduced
with respect to the Community's Structural funds for the period 1988–
1993 within the framework of the new Community's social and regional
cohesion policy did not alter the subsidiary character of the supranational

[57] Flynn, 'State Aids: Recent Case law of the Court of Justice' (1987) 18 CMLRev at 135–
136; Schramme (above, n 48) at 501; Scheuing (above, n 48) at 249; and the Court itself in
Iannelli: Case 74/76 (above, n 46) at 574.
[58] Fernández Martín and Stehmann (above, n 37) at 247 *ff*.
[59] In this connection, see the Opinion of Advocate General Warner, Case 74/76, *Iannelli*
(above, n 46) at 588. The Court itself seemed to share this view in the same case. See Case
74/76, *Iannelli* at 575.   [60] Case 74/76, *Iannelli* (above, n 46) at 575.
[61] In this respect see EC Commission, *Competitiveness and Cohesion: Regional Trends. Fifth
Periodical Report on the Socio-Economic Situation and Evolution of the Regions in the Community*
(Luxembourg, 1995) at 9, 12 *ff* and especially at 145 *ff*.

schemes. Even though, at first sight, the doubling of the stuctural funds for the said period, following the introduction of Article 130d by the SEA and the new regulation,[62] may be regarded as a substantial financial effort at the supranational level, the majority of commentators agree that they were still insufficient for substituting national spending in redistributory policies in general and regional policies in particular. Not only was their operation complementary to national policies,[63] but the final amount devoted by the EC Budget to the five redistributory objectives set out in Regulation 2052/88 remained undersized, both in terms of the percentage of the total EC budget and the national spending in the same areas, to offset the unequal impact which the integration of the market would have in peripheral regions.[64] The fact that even the bolstered ERDF is not able to fill the gap can be seen by the fact that the reservation of 30 per cent of procurement purchases in Italy accounts for aid of between 16 to 24 billion ECU annually,[65] while the total payments of the ERDF to Italy amount only to roughly one billion ECU.[66]

Similar reasoning applies to the post-Maastricht situation. Due to the failures of Community structural policies between 1958 and 1993, these concerns were given more serious attention and social, economic and regional cohesion became a fundamental issue in the negotiations that led to the Maastricht Treaty.[67] The final TEU introduced several modifications stressing the importance of the economic and social cohesion objectives and makes the promotion of the latter a task of the Community.[68] The Commission and the less developed Member States, increasingly aware of the difficulties which underdeveloped regions would face in the event of open competition with core regions and acknowledging the bad economic performance of the weaker national economies in the recession in the early 1990s, insisted on the need to revise the operation of the structural funds and their financing.[69] In the Edinburgh Summit, Member States

[62] Council Regulation 2052/88, OJ 1988, L185/9.

[63] See EC Commission (1995) (above, n 61) at 125 *ff* and 132.

[64] Despite the Community's financial efforts, which have been implemented through the Structural Funds, the Commission recognizes that the situation has not been substantially improved with respect to the most lagging regions of the Community in the 1989–1993 period. EC Commission (1995) (above, n 61) at 9 and 12 *ff*.

[65] EC Commission, COM (89) 400 (above, n 14) at 9.

[66] Croxford, Wise and Chalkley, 'The Reform of the European Regional Development Fund' (1987) 26 JCMS 25 at 32.

[67] Kenner, 'Economic and Social Cohesion—The Rocky Road Ahead' (1994) LIEI 1 at 2. For a detailed account of the political negotiations behind the financial agreements reached at the Edinburgh Summit of December 1992, see Jouret, 'Les conclusions d'Edimbourg sur le Paquet «Delors II»' (1993) RMC 391, in particular pp. 395–397 discussing the issue of the structural funds.

[68] See Article 2 EC as amended and Title XIV on Economic and Social Cohesion and in particular the amended Article 130(a). For an analysis of the new provisions introduced by the TEU strengthening the Economic and Social Cohesion aspects, see Kenner (above, n 67) at 20 *ff*.

[69] The Commission's proposals were included in two Communications: *From the Single Act*

finally agreed to increase the financial resources available under the new structural funds for the period 1993–99 and agreed to a new regulation of the existing structural funds,[70] as well as to the creation of the so-called Cohesion Fund intended to provide a financial contribution to projects in the fields of environment and trans-European networks in the area of transport infrastructure.[71] Without entering into a detailed discussion of the new developments in the area, for our present purposes it must be noted that the period 1993–99, the structural funds will be increased by almost 45 per cent.[72] Even though it is undeniable that this increase in funds is substantial and contributes to a resolution of structural deficiencies in lagging regions, they are still insufficient in terms of budget and objectives. The principles of additionality and complementarity to national investments which govern the operation of the structural funds and the establishment of maximum ceilings of assistance clearly point in this direction.[73] In quantitative terms, between 1981 and 1986 State aids to industry were roughly ten times the size of the Structural funds and were still five times larger after the 1988 reforms. If those trends continue, the increase in the size of Structural funds after 1993 will still be insufficient to substitute national efforts in the area. Moreover, one has to note that these reforms responded to the concern of less developed Member States, led by Spain, that the realization of the Economic and Monetary Union as provided in the TEU would increase the divergence between core and poor regions. TEU requirements on national budget deficits impose serious budgetary constraints on Member States restraining them from increasing public finance for regional aid programmes.[74] Considering that, apart from Ireland, those Member States with serious difficulties in meeting the TEU convergence conditions are those with more Objective 1 regions, the aid provided by means of the structural funds is likely to be partially neutralized by the required restructuring of national budgets. In any event, the Commission estimates that by the end of the 1990s, Community regional policies will finance around 5 per cent of the total investments in Objective 1 regions. In conclusion, whereas the new regulation and the increase of the Structural funds is welcome, they still fall short of

---

to Maastricht and Beyond: The Means to Match our Ambitions, COM (92) 2,000 and *The Community's Finances Between Now and 1997*, COM (92) 2001, and in the document *Community Structural Policies—Assessment and Outlook*, COM (92) 84, the latter two are better known as the 'Delors II' Packet.

[70] See generally Kenner (above, n 67) and Frazer, 'The New Structural Funds, State Aids and Interventions on the Single Market' (1995) 25 ELRev 3.

[71] Article 130d EC as amended.

[72] Jouret (above, n 67) at 396. According to the Commission estimates, the increase for that period will amount to 41% with respect to 1993 funds. EC Commission (1995), cit. at 125.

[73] Regulation 2081/93 (OJ 1993, L193/5) and Regulation 2082/93 (OJ 1993, L193/20). See further Kenner (above, n 67) at 26 *ff*.

[74] See EC Commission (1995) (above, n 61) Chapter 11.

providing a sufficient supranational aid system which could substitute national efforts in the area. The same reasoning applies with respect to public procurement. The Commission has itself acknowledged that the total opening of public markets to European competition would bring a need for transitional restructuring measures in the short term[75]. It therefore proposed some policies in order to facilitate this restructuring,[76] but these policies have not brought about any practical results.

From a political perspective, pressure on Member States, as the ultimate responsible political actors before their own citizens, is thereby increased, to alleviate unilaterally the effects of increasing regional divergence and job losses. As a result, transitional corrective measures become mainly the responsibility of Member States. The principle of subsidiarity leaves regional policy in the hands of national governments, which feel obliged to offset, in the short term, the centrifugal pressure that rapid market integration provokes. These national corrective measures, which the debate before and after the TEU has shown to be objectively necessary,[77] should be carefully evaluated in the light of Articles 92 and 93 EC and possibly co-ordinated at supranational level. It does not seem reasonable to pursue radical positions as regards State aids when no substitute mechanisms have been developed at Community level. This formalistic application of Article 30 EC may generate a sharp reaction by Member States at a political level.[78]

The 'severability test' of *Iannelli* may be interpreted as a 'proportionality test'[79] which would allow the Commission on a case by case basis to weigh carefully the restrictive effects on trade of the aid scheme against its final objective, as well as considering alternative solutions. This is precisely the function of State aids provisions in the Treaty. It is up to the Commission, pursuant to Article 93 EC, to tune national and Community interests and eventually to declare the aid compatible with the common market, in accordance with the wording of Article 92(3) EC or propose less restrictive substitute measures which ensure the same degree of efficiency with respect to the achievement of the objective pursued.[80] The Court seems to

---

[75] EC Commission, COM (89) 400 (above, n 14) at para. 17.

[76] See ibid., sections III and IV.

[77] See EC Commission (1995) (above, n 61) at 13–14 where it is recognized that the Community policies will probably not be sufficient to improve the present situation and that national policies will play a fundamental role in this sense.

[78] By 'formalistic' we mean the straightforward application of Article 30 EC when a restrictive effect on trade is detected, without going into any deeper analysis and excluding the possible application of other EC provisions that could be better adapted to the case.

[79] See Case 74/76, *Iannelli* (above, n 46) at 576. In this sense see also Schramme (above, n 48) at 498; Flynn (above, n 57) at 133.

[80] For the Commission's responsibility when assessing notified aids schemes, see in general Winter, 'Supervision of State aid: Article 93 in the Court of Justice' (1993) 30 CMLRev 311; Gyselen, 'La transparence en matière d'aides d'État: les droits des tiers' (1993) 29 CDE 417 and Struys, 'Questions choisies de procédure en matière d'aides d'État' (1993) 30 RTDE 17.

have neglected these considerations in the latest decisions concerning this issue.

This is even more so since, as has been rightly suggested, after the TEU the Court of Justice is bound by the new provisions on social and economic cohesion to give preference to the latter objective over that of free competition and market integration. This would mean that the *Du Pont de Nemours* line of reasoning favouring market integration should be abandoned and a 'pro-State aid' interpretation preferred. So far, however, this interpretation has not filtered into the most recent case law of the Court on State aids.[81]

The Specific Case of the Italian Quota

Bearing in mind the observations made regarding the instrumental function of public procurement, this section focuses on an analysis of the Italian preferential scheme, from a legal and economic perspective. After examining the economic rationale behind the Court's ruling, it will be argued that the decision is far too concerned with economic principles and that, as a result, it neglects reality. Given the need for support for the *Mezzogiorno*, the increasing divergence of regions due to the '1992' and the Economic and Monetary Union processes, as well as the Italian socio-economic environment in which the quota was implemented, the challenged legislation was a necessary means of aid for a transitional period. In the light of this reasoning, a different legal solution which the Court might have adopted in order to take into account properly all social, economic and political circumstances surrounding the case is proposed. Although arising from the study of a specific test case, the conclusions reached are meant to be generally applicable to the instrumental use of public procurement for regional purposes.

The economic rationale behind the Court's rejection of the Italian quota

From a general economic perspective the quota can be rejected on two different grounds. First, there is *efficiency loss* which is caused by discriminatory procurement policy. Secondly, the quota can be held to be counterproductive as far as the aim of economic support to an underdeveloped region is concerned.

The quota works as an artificial increase in demand for firms operating in the *Mezzogiorno*. To have any aid effect the quota has to enable these firms to sell more than they would have done under full competition. Moreover, since these undertakings are isolated from international competitive pressure, they will be able to raise prices. The joint price and quantity effect is supposed to increase the firms' profits. As a consequence, these

---

[81] Frazer (above, n 70) at 16.

high profits will normally attract new entrants to the southern region, thereby increasing total output and employment. It is precisely this redistribution effect which was intended by the Italian government. However, the higher profitability of these firms will allow them to attract further scarce resources of production from other industries in order to increase their output. These resources (like qualified labour and capital) will be withdrawn from other undertakings which operate on a more efficient scale, and will, in turn, lead to an overall efficiency loss for society. The Court endorses the view that such a public procurement policy endures inefficient undertakings to the disadvantage of more competitive ones, hindering market efficiency and market integration. This economic rationale is comparable to that relied on by the Commission to justify its general policy on public procurement, as explained above.

The quota could alternatively be justified by claiming that the formerly inefficient and protected firms will 'grow up' and become competitive after a transitional period. This 'infant industry argument', although it is very popular, is disputable. It leads us to the second and even stronger argument in *favour* of the Court's ruling. It is questionable whether the protection implemented through a quota mechanism does bring about a more competitive industry in southern Italy. In fact, like all permanent artificial State protective mechanisms, the quota may very well hamper the south's development in the *long term. Collusion* among firms located in the *Mezzogiorno* becomes likely.[82] Since they are thus able to avoid competitive pressure, the need for technological innovation and lowering costs of production is reduced. Over time, while making high profits, these firms become less and less competitive compared with the outside world. There is no clear incentive to reinvest profits in cost reducing technology since higher costs are in any case borne by the State agencies which are obliged to fulfil the quota. Firms operating in the *Mezzogiorno* risk becoming structurally non-competitive if the quota is permanently maintained. On the other hand, if the quota is abolished while productivity is low, the whole industry is in difficulty. Given the structural problems of the region, politicians may very well refrain from this policy. Thus, they may be locked in by firms which find it more profitable to invest in lobbying for permanent (and rising) protection. The Italian system of *patronage* and their location in the underdeveloped south will offer these firms a good chance of success in achieving protection. Thus the quota is counterproductive

---

[82] Typically public procurement is concentrated on industries which have a relatively high degree of concentration (high tech industry, energy, military equipment, etc.) and where most firms are located in the industrialized parts of the country. Thus the number of suppliers in the *Mezzogiorno* is rather small. In this vein see Cox, 'Implementing 1992 Public Procurement Policy: Public and Private Obstacles to the Creation of the Single European Market' (1992) 1 PPLR 139 at 144–145.

from the *dynamic long term* perspective since it gives the wrong incentives to firms. A *permanent* fixed protection distracts firms from innovation towards other options of profit maximization. Thus, the *long term* effect of the quota is counterproductive for regional policy aims too.

The rationale for the quota: an Italian perspective. The quota as the 'second best strategy'

What then are the reasons explaining the Italian government's choice of the quota? Leaving aside the fact that instrumental public procurement is a legitimate policy choice of national governments and that reliance on it should therefore be acceptable as a matter of principle, the intention in this section is to concentrate on an economic analysis of the quota. The economic reasons leading the Italian authorities to prefer the quota to any other form of aid are explored. It is argued that, in certain circumstances, public procurement may be regarded as an efficient tool to apply regional policies.

If one assumes that cohesion in the Community necessarily implies convergence of living standards, then the need for support for the *Mezzogiorno* appears unquestionable. The Italian region fulfils the objective requirements to be eligible for regional aid performed through national measures within the meaning of Article 92(3)(a).[83] When choosing the means of transitional aid, one has to take into proper consideration the existing economic and political structure in which those means are to deploy their effects.

Direct financial aid to firms starting business in the *Mezzogiorno*, investment in its infrastructure and a higher level of education of unskilled workers are often regarded as policy instruments which are more likely to foster regional development than protectionist measures.[84] The former could increase productivity and thereby attract foreign investment while still leaving firms operating in the *Mezzogiorno* under competitive pressure from the outside. However, the disadvantages of these measures, if undertaken alone, are often neglected. For instance, investment in educational schemes may very well increase the labour cost of southern firms and lead to a drain of skilled workers to the northern part where salaries are higher. Moreover, the proposed infrastructural measures, if carried out by the

---

[83] The Commission points out that the areas comprised in the *Mezzogiorno* are amongst the less performing ones in the Community, maintaining high levels of unemployment. See EC Commission (1995) (above, n 61) at 119 *ff*. In all the Commission's assessments, the *Mezzogiorno* has always come within the Objective 1 regions, that is, those whose GDP is less than 75% of the Community average. The same status is maintained for the *Mezzogiorno* within the new regulation of the structural funds. See Frazer (above, n 70) at n 18.

[84] The Commission mainly favours the spread of information about procurement contracts to firms operating in the *Mezzogiorno*. It thereby neglects structural impediments which prevent southern firms from bidding competitively, even if they are fully informed. See in detail: COM (89) 400 sections IV and V.

State, have to be financed by raising taxes and must rely on the efficiency of the political bureaucracy. When the superiority of these measures is claimed, the underlying assumption is very often that the tax system is efficient, so that raising taxes itself will not lead to distortions. In addition it is assumed that tax collection works perfectly and that the spread of State aid follows economic and political criteria strictly. Instead, the inefficiency of industrial ventures (often related to infrastructural tasks) carried out by the Italian State is well known. Due to corruption and mismanagement, the costs of these undertakings regularly exceed all forecasts while public work projects remain unfinished.[85] Lastly, the tremendous public sector deficit[86] prohibits an increase in spending even if it were carried out in an adequate manner.

Thus, from the Italian Government's perspective, the quota may be regarded as a *'second best strategy'*[87] as it has two attractive features. First, it circumvents State bureaucracy and, second, it does not raise public spending directly. The support reaches the enterprises operating in the *Mezzogiorno* and, therefore, is less likely to be channelled into the purse of organized crime. Thus, in the short run, the quota becomes more efficient than tax-financed State aid which barely reaches recipients. Political support for such indirect aid is also easier to sustain. As local elections showed, voters in the northern regions are more reluctant to support interregional redistribution. An indirect support scheme operating via the large sector of public enterprises and, thus, to some extent disguising the redistributional effects, reduces the political pressure of regional separatism. Preferential public procurement is therefore not only a general policy choice in itself but, as has been submitted, an 'efficient' regional policy device in certain circumstances.

In fact, if this analysis is correct, the quota could be accepted as a 'second best device' for a *transitional* period.[88] It is not only necessary, since no sufficient supranational substitute measures are available, but given the drawbacks of alternative actions it is also more efficient from a national perspective. The alternative to national aid would therefore probably be even higher unemployment in the *Mezzogiorno* and an increase of State transfer payments which increases economic dependence and creates a mentality which is at least as detrimental as efficiency losses stemming

---

[85] For more detail see *The Economist* Survey Italy, 26 May 1990 at 21.

[86] See *The Economist* (above, n 85) at 11.

[87] If a constraint exists which prevents the optimum from being achieved, then the 'theory of the second best' claims that other conditions as well have to deviate from the optimum. Thus, from the point of view of total welfare, it can be suboptimal to maximize efficiency in public procurement policy if, as a consequence, the subsequent changes in regional policy lead to even further distortions.

[88] For other cases in which discriminatory public procurement can be welfare improving, see the studies cited by Hoekman and Mavroidis, 'The WTO's Agreement of Government Procurement: Expanding Disciplines, Declining Membership?' (1995) 4 PPLR 63 at 74 *ff.*

from the quota. Thus, the choice of the quota as an instrument of regional aid responds to economic and political arguments and not merely to a protectionist intention.

Coming back to a strict legal analysis and compared with its previous position in the *Beentjes* case, it seems somewhat bizarre that the Court maintains that social objectives may be pursued through 'selective' public procurement, while at the same time denying the same possibility for regional goals. These aims are objectively ascertained in the case of the *Mezzogiorno* and are far more important to the role of public procurement as an interventionist tool. It is believed that there is the same risk of discrimination in the *Beentjes* case as regards foreign unemployed labour as in the *Italian quota* case as regards undertakings not established in the *Mezzogiorno*, be they Italian or not.[89] Furthermore, as discussed above, the local labour clause at stake in the *Beentjes* decision benefited only those long-term unemployed registered in the local employment office, thereby discriminating against other Dutch nationals who did not comply with that condition. Unfortunately, as mentioned earlier, the reasoning of the *Du Pont de Nemours* decision has been extended to other instrumental uses of public procurement, which has questioned the validity of *Beentjes*.

In the *Italian quota* case, one should not ignore the fact that the measure had an explicit regional character and a well-defined object. It only deployed its effects with respect to the *Mezzogiorno*, affecting in a discriminatory manner not only foreign products, but also goods produced in northern Italy. It therefore was indistinctly applicable to a substantial portion of national industry, which is, it is submitted, an important factor overlooked by the Court. In addition, discrimination did not occur on the basis of nationality. Any undertaking, regardless of its nationality, could benefit from the scheme insofar as it was established in the *Mezzogiorno*. The case has certain particular features, therefore, which distinguished it from other Article 30 EC cases. These considerations are of relevance since any regional incentive, be it supranational or national, risks being discriminatory with respect to other European regions. These incentives should be implemented, however, since it is in the national, as well as in the Community interest to achieve a certain degree of regional cohesion. The Court could have considered these facts in more depth before deciding to apply Article 30 EC.[90] The question then turns out to be one of co-ordination between Community and national State aid policies, rather than an outright ban of national measures which have the same objective. At the very least, these reasons show that no formalistic approach should be implemented as regards State aids and that a close scrutiny should be required when

---

[89] See EC Commission, COM (89) 400 (above, n 14) paras. 54–56. See also the discussion above in this chapter.

[90] The same reasoning applies to the Court's judgment in Case C-360/89, *Commission* v. *Italy* (above, n 19) which concerned the free provision of services. See above in this chapter.

examining aid measures. Legal provisions are to be applied in context, carefully weighing all the factors involved.

From a more political perspective and considering that public procurement has traditionally been seen as a means to apply social and regional policies, the Court's approach leads to the withdrawal of a legitimate policy tool from Member States. By denying the relevance of regional development considerations in public procurement awards, the Court is partially imposing the 'efficient' public procurement approach of the Commission. If one considers that the social instrumental function of public procurement is of marginal relevance, in that it normally affects a minor number of persons, whereas regional preferential schemes play a more important role (bearing also in mind that the distinction between both functions is not clear-cut), the Court's position may increase the reluctance of national contracting authorities to abide by the rules. The balance between national and supranational interests has been struck down. It is suggested that a more positive solution from a Community law point of view could have been achieved, duly combining the latter interests, while at the same time remaining politically neutral. This alternative solution is developed in the following section.

The Italian quota as a State aid within the meaning of Articles 92 to 94 EC

The Court just avoided the question of the eventual qualification of the quota as a State aid, as it did in *Beentjes* with the social clause, although it did not deny that that could be the case. Could the preferential scheme have been treated as a State aid within the meaning of Articles 92 and 93 EC? Before entering into a formal legal analysis, it must be noted that, from an economic point of view, 'the purchase by the government or one of its agencies at a higher price than would otherwise be paid . . . is tantamount to paying a subsidy to the producer of that good'.[91]

The notion of State aid is not defined in the EC Treaty. On the contrary, Article 92 EC yields a very wide concept of what may be understood as State aid. The Court of Justice has interpreted the concept in equally broad terms.[92] From this it follows that any State measure, in so far as it has the effect of according aid in any form whatsoever, may be assessed on the basis of Article 92 EC for its compatibility with the common market. Commentators have deduced from both this jurisprudence and the broad

[91] Hindley in Lord Roll of Ipsden (ed.), *The Mixed Economy* (London, 1982). For a more complete economic analysis of the preferential schemes, see Hindley, 'The Economics of an Accord in Public Procurement Policies' (1978) *The World Economy* 279.

[92] See Article 92 EC. See Case 61/79, *Amministrazione delle Finanze dello Stato* v. *Denkavit Italiana* [1980] ECR 1205 at 1228 and the *Family allowances in the textile sector* case, Case 173/73, *Italy* v. *Commission* [1974] ECR 709 at 718. The notion of State aid has consequently been very extensively interpreted, both by the Commission and the Court of Justice. See Dony-Bartholmé, 'La notion d'aides d'État' (1993) 29 CDE 399 and Lasok, 'State Aids and Remedies under the EEC Treaty' (1986) 7 ECLR 53 at 54–60.

wording of Article 92 EC that one of the features an aid has to fulfil in order to qualify as such, is that it is awarded gratuitously, that is, that no return on the part of the recipient undertaking for the advantages received should take place. As a consequence, in the case of preferential treatment in public procurement and, since there is always a supply of goods or provision of services performed by the recipient undertaking, some authors have denied the qualification of State aids to those systems.[93]

However, whilst it is true that for preferential public procurement there is always a *contrepartie* performed by the aided undertaking, this does not mean that gratuitous economic advantages cannot be identified.[94] In the case under comment, three different advantages exist, all of which are measurable by an economic analysis. First, to make sense the quota has to be above the quantity which would be demanded by public enterprises if no preferential treatment were applied. Thus, together these firms are able to sell more. Secondly, they are able to charge a higher price. The advantage will then consist in the overprice paid by the State, which is intended to foster the attainment of economic and social objectives. The State will be gratuitously benefiting a specific undertaking by paying more than needed for certain goods or services. Lastly, the quota offers security. Whatever competitors outside the region do, the quota protects those firms eligible for the scheme from repercussions, therefore eliminating the normal entrepreneurial risks which otherwise exist under international competitive pressure. Here again the advantage is granted without there being any return on the part of the favoured undertaking. In short, the Italian scheme had certain elements which provided gratuitous advantages and, consequently, all things considered, the procurement preferential scheme could have been legally regarded as a State aid.

The Court could have returned to its earlier *Iannelli* jurisprudence and could have applied the *lex specialis* principle in order to analyse the measure in the light of the State aids provisions, or at least to check whether its restrictive effects were disproportionate to its objective. This would mean that the severability test would have to be applied to the Italian scheme. In this event, one could argue that the 30 per cent quota is precisely the aid and that, therefore, no severable elements can be detected. As a result, the quota could not be held to contravene Article 30 EC without affecting the aid's final objective, i.e., regional support to the *Mezzogiorno*, since not only is it not a severable factor from the aid scheme, but it constitutes the aid itself. In the event that the Commission deemed that the quota was disproportionate to its objective and that other less restrictive forms

[93] Schina, *State Aids under the EEC Treaty. Articles 92 to 94* (Oxford, 1987) at 15. Other authors deem that '[e]ven when full consideration has been given, aid may be considered as having been granted when a benefit has been received which would not have been received in the normal course', Quigley, 'The Notion of State Aids in the EEC' (1988) 13 ELRev 242 at 246.

[94] See Schramme (above, n 48) at 491–492.

of aid, such as direct financing, were preferable to render it compatible with Community law, the aforementioned arguments could provide solid grounds to uphold the choice of the preferential scheme. In this sense, less restrictive means of aiding the *Mezzogiorno* would not be as effective and appropriate as the quota.

The justification for this line of reasoning is that a more flexible legal approach could then follow. Once the system is defined as a State aid, paragraphs 2 and 3 of Article 92 EC, as well as Article 93 EC, could eventually apply, giving the Commission the possibility of evaluating in more depth all economic, social and even political aspects of such a system. This analysis might end with a declaration of its compatibility with Community law. Negotiations with national authorities throughout this process could also lead to the adoption of compromise solutions, by which transitional substitute measures could be devised.[95] Furthermore, the called-for co-ordination with existing supranational regional policies implemented through the structural funds could be put into practice and the needs of underdeveloped regions would be met. This would mean the assessment of the proportionality of such measures and their complementarity with the Community's regional policy measures. In brief, the declaration of such measures as State aids would set off the mechanisms provided for in the Treaty in order to balance Community and national interests. This is precisely their main function and represented the original compromise achieved in the decision-making process leading to the approval of the public procurement Directives and their subsequent amendments. In this way the institutional and political drawbacks mentioned earlier could be overcome and a more coherent policy could be followed.

Conclusions

The completion of the internal market and the eventual realization of the Economic and Monetary Union increase the pressure on national governments to raise regional aid in the short term in order to avoid further economic disparities. Both objectives will harm the Community's *cohesion* objective if no countervailing actions are undertaken. Further economic integration is likely to widen the divergence between regions while at the same time the Court with its strict jurisprudence withdraws national tools for regional policy from Member States. This situation is worsened by the fact that a supranational strategy which could help to overcome this divergence has not yet been sufficiently developed. Therefore the straight, formalistic and unconditional application of Article 30 EC pursued by the

---

[95] For a detailed discussion of the Commission's policy in the field of State aids see Evans and Martin, 'Socially Acceptable Distortion of Competition: Community Policy on State Aid' (1991) 16 ELRev 79.

Court is undesirable in the present Community context.[96] This could lead to tensions between opposing forces: national economic and social policies intended to encourage the development or restructuring of less favoured regions or sectors, against the product integration policy followed by the Commission and the Court.

In fact, the supranationalization of these national regional schemes, that is, their replacement by a Community scheme, must be regarded as the most sensible solution. This will allow the structuring of a general scheme of aid systems which will take account, at the Community level, of such regional disparities in a rational and co-ordinated way. In the meanwhile, until such measures are agreed upon and since Articles 92 to 94 EC leave room for a thorough analysis of all economic, social and political circumstances of each case, they seem a sound instrument to compensate for both Community and national interests in the light of the internal market and economic integration. This is the sense of recent suggestions calling for a more co-ordinated horizontal strategy between the Commission's Regional and Competition Directorates in order to harmonize the national state aid programmes and supranational regional initiatives.[97]

If the quota was to be analysed in the light of the State aids provisions, it is believed that it could have been declared a State aid and could probably have been examined in the light of Article 92(3)(a) or (c) EC, subject to the Commission's approval. This approach would allow for a more reasonable evaluation of the measure. Thereafter, it would be the Commission's duty to ensure that measures like the quota are *transitional* and regressive.

From a legal point of view, the reasoning finds support both in the SEA and the TEU. Article 7(c) EC, introduced by the Single European Act, already required the Commission to take into account 'the extent of the effort that certain economies showing differences in development will have to sustain' when drawing up its proposals for the establishment of the internal market. As regards the TEU, social and economic cohesion is given even more attention, to the point that it has been forcefully argued that it has become a primary objective which binds the Court of Justice in its interpretation of Community law. These provisions imposed an obligation on Community institutions to proceed in the direction defended above. The opening up of public contracts cannot be realized without

---

[96] The Court, after receiving criticisms (see for instance, White, 'In Search of the Limits to Article 30 of the EEC Treaty' (1989) 26 CMLRev 235) for its abusive interpretation of Article 30 EC, has limited the latter's scope in Joined Cases C-267 and 268/91, *Keck and Mithouard* [1993] ECR I-6097. See further Weatherill and Beaumont, EC Law, 2nd edn., (London, 1995) Chp. 17.

[97] The current Commission's approach on the co-ordination of its regional aid and competition policies has been subject to well deserved criticisms for its lack of overall coherence and even conflicting criteria. Wishlade, 'Competition Policy, Cohesion and the Co-ordination of Regional Aids in the Community' (1993) 14 ECLR 143. See also Frazer (above, n 70).

'compensatory' measures to smooth the economic and social costs which the less competitive areas and economic sectors in the Community will suffer.

All the discussion leads inevitably to the issue of subsidiarity. Assuming that regional policy competence is shared by national and supranational levels,[98] and that supranational measures are insufficient at present, subsidiarity could be read as implying that national institutions are entitled to carry out their own policies without undue interference from Community action. The above considerations relating to the necessity and legitimacy of regional policies, direct political responsibility for citizens' welfare and practical efficiency of the measures point to the direction that a wider discretion should be allowed to Member States in the field of State aids. Control of this discretion should of course be applied at Community level through the Commission's powers under Articles 92 to 94 EC and by the Court of Justice, but this should involve a more lenient approach to the requirements of economic and social cohesion when confronted with the competing value of free competition and economic integration. In the words of an MEP 'bearing in mind that public contracts are used as major instruments of sectoral policy in all our Member States, bearing in mind also that more than half of all public contracts, in terms of value, are carried out in the regions so that they are an important instrument of development policy for local and regional authorities, one cannot help wondering about a merely legal approach which is in danger of disintegrating as soon as it comes into contact with reality'.[99]

---

[98] It could be argued that regional policy has been transferred to Community institutions after the new provisions on social and regional cohesion introduced by the SEA and the TEU. According to this line of reasoning, all regional incentives have to be developed, or at least be approved, at Community level (see in this respect Van Gerven in FIDE (above, n 1) vol. I at 384). While this is basically true, first, Member States are also called upon to participate in the achievement of the objectives established in the new provisions. They are therefore not totally excluded. Secondly, and more importantly, these Articles do not constitute a derogation, neither explicit nor implicit, from Article 92(3) EC, which continues to be perfectly applicable.

[99] Mr Partrat, Debates of the European Parliament, 1988–89 session, Report of proceedings from 16 to 20 May 1988. Annex OJ 1988, 2 365/82.

General Conclusions to Chapters 2 and 3

The Commission's policy as regards public procurement may be subject to two types of criticism. First of all, from an integration policy perspective, the Commission has followed a straightforward economic efficiency approach to the regulation of public procurement, thereby neglecting other perspectives applied at national level. This attitude is likely to increase the opposition of Member States to comply with the rules and a parallel negative reaction by some national sectors. Competitive tendering conveys a certain political and economic approach as regards the function of public procurement which may not be shared by the political forces in power in the Member States.[100] As Mishan has argued, the efficient allocation of resources cannot itself be justified on purely economic grounds: an ethical consensus concerning allocative issues within which notions of efficiency can be introduced must exist.[101]

Secondly, if one concentrates on the economic merits of competitive tendering, it has been argued that it may be a positive choice in terms of economic efficiency, but that it has normally led to a degeneration in the quality of public services and working conditions as well as to job cuts.[102] Private contractors tend to pursue the maximization of profits to the detriment of the quality of the service and of working conditions. Moreover, strict competitive compulsory tendering has been challenged on the grounds that private contractors may deliberately underestimate their tenders in the hope of winning the contract and thereafter renegotiate its terms. Since private actors are not primarily concerned with satisfaction of the public interest, the latter is likely to be negatively affected unless close monitoring schemes are established. When commenting on the merits of competitive tendering, an MEP summarized the major criticisms with reference to a practical example: 'In my own constituency a cleaning

---

[100] See in this vein Turpin, *Government Procurement and Contracts* (Harlow, 1989) Chapter 9, at 258.

[101] Mishan, *Economic Efficiency and Social Welfare: Selected Essays on Fundamental Aspects of the Economic Theory of Social Welfare* (London, 1981).

[102] According to the Public Services Privatization Research Unit, the implementation of the Local Government Act competitive tendering has had a major influence on the 114,000 manual jobs lost in local government between 1988 and 1991. Equally, a survey carried out by the Low Pay Unit shows that enrolled nurses who had their jobs contracted out to private nursing homes received £1.70 and £2.40 an hour, while their counterparts in the National Health Service were getting £4.50 an hour. Reported in the Observer, 9 May 1993 at 3. See also Painter, 'CCT in Local Government: the First Round' (1991) 39 Public Administration 191 at 208. It is worth noting that where job cuts have been applied, they have mainly affected women workers.

contract for a hospital was put out to private tender. I shall tell you what the result was: 500 hours a month were cut from the cleaning contract. We found ants and cockroaches in the maternity ward. Women cleaners had their pay docked, their hours docked, they had their rights taken away, no more sick pay, no more maternity leave and we had an 18-month strike.'. He therefore insisted on the need for the Commission to accept the Socialist Group's amendments to the Commission's proposals for a services Directive which allowed authorities to give preference to contractors who would bring employment to less favoured regions.[103]

Going one step further, commercial criteria as the primary relevant grounds for economic decisions are particular to private actors in the market. In mixed economy systems, public authorities assume political and social responsibilities towards their citizens which enshrine prevailing values of the society. These in turn legitimize public action.[104] These responsibilities materialize in public authorities' activities in the social and economic spheres in different ways. Public contracting, like other activities of public authorities, is not alien to these concerns. Economic efficiency is not always the paramount motivation in allocating contracts. As one commentator has stressed, the 'overwhelming importance granted to the pursuit of efficiency is regarded as detrimental to wider administrative and political aims'.[105] What legitimate competence do the Commission and the Court of Justice have to impose such an unmitigated commercial approach?

In the Community system, where different economic and political approaches co-exist and where the integration process increases the tensions between economic cohesion and market integration, a balance between both forces has to be found.[106] The Commission has recognized that the application of strictly competitive criteria may provoke the need to restructure certain industrial sectors. However, in the context of the Cecchini

---

[103] Tongue MEP, Debates of the European Parliament, Report of Proceedings from 13 to 17 May 1991, Annex to the OJ 1991, No. 3–405 at 105.

[104] Habermas, *Legitimation crisis* (London, 1976).

[105] Parsons, 'Economic Principles in the Private and the Public sectors' (1988) 16 *Policy and Politics* 29. See, in the same vein, Painter ('*CCT in Local Government: the First Round*' 1991 39 Public Administration 191 at 194) who points out that in competitive compulsory tendering, financial criteria are accorded priority and questions of employment practice, democratic control over services, social desirability and effectiveness are subordinated to those of financial efficiency.

[106] For an exhaustive analysis of a case (the so-called sheep meat war) in which competing ideologies impeding the peaceful development of the integration process had to be resolved on the basis of a compromise settlement, see Snyder, 'Ideologies of Competition: Two Perspectives on the Completion of the Internal Market' in Snyder, *New Directions in European Community Law* (London, 1990) Chapter 3. See also Weiler 'The White Paper and the application of Community Law' in Bieber, Dehousse, Pinder and Weiler, *1992: One European Market?* (Baden-Baden, 1988) 337 at 347 under the heading 'Judicial activism: law without political consensus'.

report, the collateral implications of competitive compulsory tendering, especially the social costs of industrial restructuring and the decline of peripheral regions, have not been paid any particular attention.[107] It is regrettable that the Commission has not reflected on these draw-backs when designing its policy.

The outcome of *Du Pont de Nemours* and the subsequent case law on the free provision of services and the Commission's overall policy is that Member States are confronted with the withdrawal of an instrument of economic policy and with an obligation to follow strictly competitive criteria. The initial agreement, or 'ethical consensus', resulting from the decision-making process has been overruled. In fact, as a principal result of the *Du Pont de Nemours* decision, existing references to the instrumental use of public procurement have disappeared from the consolidated versions of the public supplies and services Directives. Only for 'historical reasons' and due to the impossibility of undertaking substantial amendments in the process of consolidation of a new codified text, certain references remain in the consolidated version of the public works and Utilities Directives, although they are considered irrelevant by the Commission.[108]

The political discretion of Member States as regards public contracting has been impaired. It is submitted that due to the lack of substitute measures, the Commission's policy will face opposition from contracting authorities when national regional policies implemented through public contracting are at stake. The primary political responsibility for the welfare of European citizens still resides in the hands of national governments and has not been transferred to the Community institutions. It should be up to them to decide the means and priorities of their national economic policies within the broad limits of the Community objectives and until Community measures are agreed. Public procurement is an activity of public authorities in which public interest considerations are always at stake. These factors should be carefully weighed by the Commission when defining its objectives and general policy. A formalistic interpretation of the Treaty leading to further reduction of Member States' margin of discretion in highly sensitive matters will certainly cause increasing conflicts in the future between the supranational and national levels and, as a result, an inadequate environment for the application of Community public procurement rules. It is unlikely that socially aware contracting authorities, politically responsible for the welfare of their voters, will regard in a positive light the restrictions imposed on their discretion by supranational institutions which are not answerable for their decisions and which do not provide alternative solutions to counteract imbalances

---

[107] See the consideration made in this respect in Chapter 2.
[108] Article 30(3) and (4) of consolidated public works Directive 93/37 and Article 35 of consolidated Uitilites Directive 93/38.

in the short term. A more cautious approach should have been followed at the supranational level. As things now stand, the conflictual setting in which Community legislation has to apply has been exacerbated.[109]

---

[109] Evidence that these reflections are not purely academic is provided by the controversy which arose in the UK when the British Conservative Government announced that, in view of its Community obligations, it had to abandon the so-called Priority Suppliers Scheme, which provided preferential public procurement to workshops employing disabled persons and prisoners. See further major British newspapers in August 1994. For a legal analysis see Arrowsmith (1995) (above, n 13) at 244 and Arrowsmith 'Abolition of the UK's Procurement Preference Scheme for Disabled Workers' (1994) 3 PPLR CS225.

4

The Ineffectiveness of the Rules (I): The Implementation Level

INTRODUCTION

Now that we have discussed, in the previous chapters, the political and economic context in which public procurement activities take place and the conflict which might exist at national and supranational levels, the aim of the following chapters is to go a step further in the analysis and examine, in more detail, the alleged reasons for the ineffectiveness of the Community rules both at the implementation and application levels. Before doing so, some preliminary remarks are made about the supranational nature of the Community and the legal and structural limits which derive from it. This provides an overview of the legal and structural framework in which Community rules have to operate.

The Main Features of the Supranational Structure and the Limits on State Action: the Principle of Effectiveness

The structure upon which the Community is built has certain distinctive traits which characterize the Community as a supranational system and which affect the manner in which Community rules apply in national legal orders.[1] These peculiar features also affect the operation of the public procurement rules. First, it is generally accepted that Community law is a higher rule of law with respect to national legal orders. This is the principle of the *supremacy of Community law*. The principle is founded on the conception of the Community as a unitary legal system. Community law forms an integral part of national legal orders in those areas subject to its jurisdiction and takes precedence over national rules.[2] Secondly, Community law, whether Treaty provisions or secondary legislation, may, under certain conditions, grant directly enforceable rights to private individuals which, as a result of the principle of supremacy of Community law, must prevail in domestic legal orders. These are *directly effective Community provisions*. Community rights originate at supranational rather than at national

---

[1] On the supranational features of the Community system and its overall impact on Community and Member State action, see generally Weiler, 'The Community System: the Dual Character of Supranationalism' (1981) 1 YEL 267; reprinted in Snyder (ed.), *European Community Law*, vol. I (Aldershot, 1993) 161.

[2] See generally Pescatore, *The Law of Integration* (Leiden, 1973) at 45.

level, while their enforcement is primarily left to national authorities.[3] Thirdly, a self-evident feature of the Community legal order is that it is subject to the imperatives of *the rule of law*, both at supranational level, as regards the relationships between its institutions, and at domestic level, as regards the respect of national authorities for Community rules.[4] As a consequence of this 'axiom', the respect and full enjoyment of individual Community rights, whether they are contained in directly effective provisions or not, must be guaranteed.

Lastly, the supranational entity to which Member States have freely adhered is not equipped with federal agencies for the implementation, application and enforcement of the norms which it enacts. With the exception of certain specific areas where the Commission has been attributed direct enforcement powers, whereas the legislative process takes place entirely through Community institutions and through autonomous decision-making processes, Community law is implemented, applied and enforced by national authorities in accordance with national constitutional systems. In legal terms, the system is defined as governed by the so-called principle of *institutional autonomy*.[5]

The principle of institutional autonomy is not absolute, however. Its unrestrained application would annul other basic Community law principles.[6] Irrespective of the fact that Community law relies on national procedures to be finally implemented and applied, the supremacy principle implies that the former, as a higher system of law, must prevail over national rules and legal approaches, in so far as these may impede the achievement of the objectives pursued by it.[7] The effectiveness of Community rules cannot be made dependent on national qualifications, concepts or procedural rules.[8]

The Court of Justice has sanctioned these limits to Member State discretion arising from the institutional autonomy principle through the

---

[3] The Court of Justice has developed far-reaching case law on the effective judicial protection of these rights which will be analysed when the enforcement level is dealt with. See further Chapter 7.

[4] See Case 294/83, *Parti écologiste 'Les Verts'* v. *Parlement Européen* [1986] ECR 1339 and Opinion 1/91, [1991] ECR I-6079 at 6102. For a general discussion see Hartley, *The Legal Foundations of European Community Law*, 3rd edn. (Oxford, 1994) at 339 *ff*.

[5] For a judicial application of the principle, see Joined Cases 205–215/82, *Deutsche MilchKontor GmbH* v. *Germany* [1983] ECR 2633 at 2665–67. For an academic definition of the principle, see Rideau, 'Le rôle des États membres dans l'application du Droit Communautaire' (1972) 18 *Annuaire Français de Droit International* 864 at 885.

[6] Bebr, 'Remedies for Breach of Community law' in (1980) FIDE Reports (London, 1980); Bridge, 'Procedural Aspects of the Enforcement of European Community Law through the Legal Systems of the Member States' (1984) 9 ELRev 28; Mertens de Wilmars, 'L'efficacité des différentes techniques nationales de protection juridique contre les violations du droit communautaire par les autorités nationales et les particuliers' (1981) 17 CDE 379.

[7] See for instance Case 20/72, *Commission* v. *Italy* [1973] ECR 161 at 172.

[8] In this vein, see Boulouis et Chevalier, *Grands arrêts de la Cour de Justice des Communautés Européennes*, T. 1, at 139 *ff*, esp. at 142–143.

introduction of the '*principle of effectiveness*' of Community law. According to this principle, in the absence of specific Community measures, national instances are under an obligation which flows from the general terms of Article 5 EC, to provide for effective mechanisms to give full effect to Community rules.[9] The consequence is that national legal orders are instruments which must evolve and adapt to the requirements of Community law whenever this becomes necessary to give full effect to supranational rules.[10] The Court of Justice has applied the 'effectiveness' constraint in various areas of Community law. Examples of this are its case law concerning the obligations of implementation and application of Community law by Member States,[11] the obligations of effective protection of individual Community rights,[12] and the controversial case law relating to the obligations arising for national authorities with respect to the effectiveness of competition rules.[13] The Court has, however, generally avoided giving a definitive definition of the principle and has preferred a flexible application to the circumstances of each case. However, in the *Simmenthal* decision, it held in general terms that:

every national court must, in a case within its jurisdiction, apply Community law in its entirety and protect rights which the latter confers on individuals . . . *[A]ny provision of a national legal system and any legislative, administrative or judicial practice which might impair the effectiveness of Community law* by withholding from the national court having jurisdiction to apply such law the power to do everything necessary at the moment of its application which might prevent Community rules having *full force and effect* are incompatible with those requirements which are the very essence of Community law.[14] (emphasis added)

It is submitted that this judgment enshrines the essence of the principle under examination. It is not in vain that it was cited as the relevant

---

[9] On Article 5 EC and the obligations it imposes on Member States, see Temple-Lang, 'Community Constitutional Law. Article 5 EEC Treaty' (1990) 27 CMLRev 645; Constantinesco, 'L'article 5 CEE: de la bonne foi à la loyauté communautaire' in Capotorti and others (eds.), *Du Droit International au Droit de l'Intégration: Liber Amicorum Pierre Pescatore* (Baden-Baden, 1987) 97.

[10] See, for instance, Case 54/81, *Fromme* v. *BALM* [1982] ECR 1449 at paras. 6–7. For a systematic analysis of the 'effectiveness' requirement see the opinion of Advocate General Verloren van Themaat in the same case, at 1470.

[11] Case 52/75, *Commission* v. *Italy* [1976] ECR 277. See also Temple-Lang (above, n 9) at 459 and the extensive case law cited therein.   [12] See Chapter 7.

[13] See Case 231/83, *Cullet* v. *Centre Leclerc Toulouse* [1985] ECR 305, at paras. 16–18. It is now generally accepted that the need to give full effect to the competition rules may, in certain circumstances, circumscribe the legislative freedom of Member States. On this matter see, *inter alia*, Gyselen, 'State Action and the Effectiveness of the EEC Treaty's Competition Provisions' (1989) 26 CMLRev 33; Hoffmann, 'Anti-competitive State Legislation Condemned under Articles 5, 85 and 86 of the EEC Treaty: How far should the Court go after *Van Eycke*?' (1990) 11 ECLR 11.

[14] Case 106/77, *Amministrazione delle Finanze dello Stato* v. *Simmenthal SpA* [1978] ECR 629 at 644. See also the Opinion of Advocate General Reischl in Joined Cases 66, 127 and 128/79, *Amministrazione delle Finanze* v. *Srl Meridionale Industria Salumi* [1980] ECR 1237 at 1271.

precedent in the most far-reaching applications of the principle in the *Factortame*[15] and *Francovich* cases.[16]

The principle of effectiveness obviously applies to all areas of Community law and governs all three levels of the integration of Community rules into national legal orders, that is, their implementation, application and enforcement.[17] In brief, the principle of institutional autonomy governing the delicate symbiotic relationship between national and supranational institutions at the political, legal and judicial levels[18] is subject to an effectiveness constraint or limit, which derives from the supremacy, direct applicability and direct effect features of Community law and has been developed by the Court of Justice on the basis of Article 5 EC. National systems must guarantee full force and effect to Community rules. Otherwise, any national provision or any legislative, administrative or judicial practice impairing their 'effectiveness' is incompatible with Community law. This effectiveness principle is equally applicable to the obligations arising from the public procurement rules. The implementation and application of public procurement rules must be examined bearing this legal context in mind.

THE IMPLEMENTATION LEVEL

As pointed out earlier, in its examination of the causes explaining the lack of impact of the public procurement rules, the Commission reckoned that the insufficiencies of Directives as harmonization measures, coupled with their inadequate implementation by Member States, was one of the causes which determined the marginal impact of the original public procurement Directives.[19] To combat these insufficiencies, changes in some domestic legal orders were required. In order to assess this reasoning and the pertinence of the corrective measures required, two different methods of implementation are compared both from a legal and practical perspective. In the light of this analysis, the influence which the chosen legal instrument and its implementation had on the meagre liberalization of public markets is discussed. Before starting it is important to note that the question of the means of implementation has been intimately linked with that of the requirements of effective protection of the individual rights contained in the Directives. The discussion of this aspect is, however, left to those pages devoted to the enforcement level.

---

[15] Case C-213/89, *R* v. *Secretary of State for Transport, ex p. Factortame-I* [1990] ECR I-2433, discussed at length in Chapter 7.

[16] Joined Cases C-6 and 9/90, *Francovich & others* v. *Italy* [1992] ECR I-5357, discussed at length in Chapter 7.

[17] The fact that it has achieved a more complete formulation and, in addition, a greater practical application in the context of the judicial protection of rights which individuals derive from Community provisions, should not prejudice its general character. For a full discussion of all these aspects see Chapter 7.　　　　[18] Bridge (above, n 6) at 29.

[19] EC Commission, *Public Supply Contracts. Conclusions and Perspectives*, COM (84) 717 at 7 *ff.*

Implementation of the Public Procurement Directives in National Law[20]

Directives have been used as the legal instruments which embody the Community's public procurement policy. On the legislative and executive levels, Directives are a paradigmatic example of the principle of institutional autonomy which inspires the political, institutional and legal dual-structure of the Communities. More recently they have been referred to as the normative embodiment of subsidiarity.[21]

According to Article 189 EC, Directives are binding as to the results to be achieved upon each Member State to whom they are addressed, but leave the choice of forms and methods to the national authorities. That is, the objectives sought by the regulation are adopted and drafted at the supranational level, whereas the means and methods to achieve them are left to the discretion of Member States in accordance with their national legal traditions. On this basis, each Member State implemented the original public procurement Directives as they thought suitable. The wide range of approaches prevailing throughout the Community in relation to public contracts inevitably meant that the means of implementing greatly varied from one Member State to the next. Thus, while in some Member States implementation was performed through the adoption of legally binding rules which created enforceable rights for individuals, in others it was done by means of mere administrative action. The United Kingdom and Germany belong to this latter group, whereas France and Spain are examples of the former. Through a comparative analysis of the two different approaches to implementation some conclusions can be drawn as regards the degree of influence which the choice of one means or the other had on the minimal impact of the provisions of the public procurement Directives.

Implementation through Administrative Action. The United Kingdom and Germany

United Kingdom[22]

Despite early claims by some commentators underlining the existence of certain peculiar features of public contracts which make them distinguishable

---

[20] For a survey of the implementation measures adopted in the different Member States, see D'Hooghe and others, 'Implementation of the Public Procurement Directives in the 12 States of the EC' Parts I and II in (1992) 1 PPLR 167 and 251; see also national reports submitted to the 14th FIDE Congress in FIDE, *L'Application dans les États Membres des Directives sur les Marchés Publics* (Madrid, 1990).

[21] Hilf, 'Die Richtline der EG-Ohne Richtung, ohne Linie' (1993) *Europarecht* 5.

[22] Reference to the United Kingdom is limited to the case of central government agencies and English law, save as otherwise stated. See generally Millet, 'Les Marchés Publics en Droit Comparé. Le Royaume Unie' in *Les Marchés Publics Européens. Droit Communautaire, Droit Comparé*, Travaux du Colloque organisé par l'Association pour le droit public de l'entreprise, 17–18 juin 1988, *Dossiers et Documents de la Revue Française de Droit Administratif*, 1989, at 37 and Turpin, *Government Procurement and Contracts* (Harlow, 1989) especially Chapter 4.

from those concluded between private parties and that, therefore, they were to be governed, to some extent, by different rules,[23] contracts of public authorities have been traditionally subject to the ordinary law of contract in the UK, and no public law principles apply.[24] Accordingly, no separate branch of the law existed in English law for the specific purpose of regulating the field of public contracts, to the exception of local authorities.[25] Public authorities enjoyed a wide margin of discretion as regards their freedom to contract.

Prior to the enactment of the Community Directives, a similar degree of discretion applied as regards the way in which contracting authorities decided to conclude a contract, as they were only subject to Parliamentary approval of the expenditure involved.[26] The general approach in the United Kingdom was to consider contracts entered into by public bodies as an activity subject to mere administrative guidelines.[27] In fact, legal rules never played a role in the regulation of contract award procedures. Statutory regulation of the award of public contracts has normally been restricted to the sphere of local government.[28] The source of such procedures and principles is to be found in the contracting experience of the departments themselves, which have been referred to as 'the principles of contracting' and these are normally followed in practice by the different government departments.[29] All these furnish a consistent set of administrative guidelines and principles which seem to be highly respected by contracting

[23] On the basis of the *Amphitrite* case (*Rederiaktiebolaget. Amphitrite* v. *R* [1921] 3 KB 500), which set down the principle that the Crown cannot fetter its future discretion by contract. See also *Birkdale District Electric Supply Co. Ltd* v. *Southport Corporation* [1926] AC 355; *R* v. *Inland Revenue Commissioners ex p. Preston* [1983] 2 All ER 300. Street, *Governmental Liability. A Comparative Study* (London, 1953) at 82. See also Mitchell, 'A General Theory of Public Contracts' (1951) 63 *Juridical Review* 60. His position is developed at length in his book *The Contracts of Public Authorities. A Comparative Study* (London, 1954). Turpin (1989) (above, n 22) at 85–90.

[24] Turpin (1989) (above, n 22) at 97 *ff*. For a critical assessment of this traditional view and a review of recent changes as regards the application of public law principles to the contractual powers of public authorities, see Arrowsmith, 'Judicial Review and the Contractual Powers of Public Authorities' (1990) 106 LQR 277; for a more detailed discussion, Arrowsmith, *Civil Liability and Public Authorities* (Winteringham, 1992) Chapter 2; Cane, *An Introduction to Administrative Law* 2nd edn. (Oxford, 1992) Chapter 13.

[25] With respect to local authorities, see the provisions of the Local Government Act 1988 discussed in Chapter 3.   [26] Turpin (1989) (above, n 22) at 91.

[27] Administrative principles and certain procedures have been developed by the Treasury and a number of Committees. For a description of these see Turpin (1989) (above, n 22) at 61 and Turpin, *Government Contracts* (Harmondsworth, 1972) at 77 *ff*.

[28] The Local Government Planning and Land Act 1980, the Local Government Act 1988 and the Local Government Act 1992 impose the compulsory competitive tendering requirement (CCT) on local authorities. The areas in which CCT applies have been increased since 1980. For an overview of the evolution see Bennet and Cirrell, 'The Local Government Act 1992: New Developments in Compulsory Competitive Tendering' (1992) 1 PPLR 242; Arrowsmith, 'Developments in Compulsory Competitive Tendering' (1994) 3 PPLR CS153.

[29] For an exhaustive analysis of the evolution of these principles and the agencies and processes by which these are established, see Turpin (1989) (above, n 22) at 73 *ff*.

authorities in practice. These did not, however, significantly reduce the margin of discretion of contracting authorities. The applicable principles were drafted in quite a loose manner and are intended to provide contracting authorities with an adequate margin of manoeuvre. Furthermore, such guidelines were not legally binding and contracting authorities could depart from them subject to mere administrative sanctions, rather than judicial control. Third parties could not, therefore, rely on the said internal administrative norms to initiate judicial actions.

In line with this general approach, Community public procurement rules were initially implemented by means of administrative circulars. The original public procurement Directives were incorporated into the United Kingdom by the Treasury through the adoption of Treasury guidelines[30] and by the Department of the Environment, as well as the Welsh Office, through the joint adoption of administrative circulars. These brought the Community provisions to the attention of the relevant public authorities and, in plain but brief language, explained the effects of the public procurement Directives.[31] No statutory provisions were adopted.

Germany[32]

In Germany, contracts entered into by public authorities were regarded as subject to private law in all their extremes. According to the traditional approach developed by Otto Mayer, only those acts in which a certain degree of public authority (*puissance publique*) is involved can be qualified as administrative acts. Since, by definition, contracts are concluded by parties legally regarded as equal, no degree of public authority in the acts of public authorities directed to enter into a contract with another party could exist. This approach was developed in the jurisprudence, confirming that public supplies and public works contracts belonged to the so-called *Fiskalische Verwaltung*, as opposed to the *Hoheitliche Verwaltung*. The former constitutes a fiction by which the courts characterize the administration as

---

[30] HM Treasury, *Guidance Notes on Public Sector Purchasing International Obligations: Supplies Contracts* and *Public Purchasing Policy: Consolidated Guidelines*. See Birkinshaw, 'British report to the 14th FIDE Congress' in FIDE (1990) (above, n 20) at 305.

[31] There were a number of different circulars of the Department of the Environment and of the Welsh Office. These circulars were very brief indeed and were limited to a mere reference to the Directives' provisions. See Millet (above, n 22) at 42; Birkinshaw in FIDE (1990) (above, n 20) at 305.

[32] See generally, Lupp, *Objektivität, Transparenz und Nachprüfbarkeit der Angebotswertung bei der Vergabe öffentlicher Bauaufträge* (München, 1992); Rittner, *Rechtsgrundlage und Rechtsgrundsätze des öffentlichen Auftragswesens. Eine systematische Analyse* (Freiburg, 1988); Niedzela and Engshuber, 'Enforcing the Public Procurement Rules in Germany' in Arrowsmith (ed.), *Remedies for Enforcing the Public Procurement Directives* (Winteringham, 1993); Remien, 'Public Procurement in an International Perspective' (1991) unpublished paper; Cleesattel, 'Government procurement in the Federal Republic of Germany' (1987) 21 *George Washington Journal of International Law and Economics* 59; Seidel, 'German Report to the 14th FIDE Congress' in FIDE (1990) (above, n 20) at 69.

acting as any legal person subject to private law. The latter refers to the public administration when it acts invested with *puissance publique* and, therefore, subject to administrative law and eventually to administrative courts. As a consequence of this approach, well-developed German administrative law did not play any relevant role in the regulation of the contractual activities of public authorities. Like the United Kingdom, Germany belongs to the category of States which regulate public contracts by means of non-binding administrative guidelines.

Apart from an early attempt to codify and give legal status to the rules applicable to contract award procedures which took place before the First World War,[33] no other legislative initiative was pursued to bring public procurement rules under the discipline of legal measures.[34] The present regulation finds its origin in the Weimar Republic, when a Commission composed of representatives of public authorities, industry and trade-unions (*Reichsverdingungsausschuß*) got together to elaborate the guidelines governing construction contract awards (*Verdingungsordnung für Bauleistungen*, VOB)[35] and the guidelines for all other contract awards apart from construction (and the *Verdingungsordnung für Leistungen— ausgenommen Bauleistungen*, VOL).[36] These regulations, with all their subsequent amendments, are still the applicable regime nowadays, although are being challenged before the Court of Justice.[37] Their amendment and adaptation to current circumstances are within the competence of two Commissions: the *Deutscher Verdingungsausschuß für Bauleistungen* and the *Deutsche Verdingungsordnungen für Leistungen—ausgenommen Bauleistungen*, which are responsible for works and all other contracts respectively.[38]

These *Verdingungsordnungen* are merely administrative guidelines. They derive their compulsory nature for contracting authorities from the fact that they are enacted by a hierarchically superior administrative body. They are therefore mere internal regulations with no effects outside the administrative sphere. Their correct application is therefore mainly ensured through the operation of internal administrative controls and checks, as well as political controls. Third parties do not derive any directly enforceable right from these administrative provisions. German authorities, however, defend the view that these provisions are rendered binding on contracting bodies by virtue of the relevant provisions concerning government finance.[39]

---

[33] A draft for an 'Imperial Act on Public Procurement' (*Reichgesetz für das Verdingnungswesen*) was presented to the Reichstag but was not finally adopted.

[34] Remien (above, n 32) at 7–8. See also Cleesattel (above, n 32) at 61.

[35] Adopted in 1926.   [36] Adopted in 1932–33.

[37] Case C-433/93, *Commission v. Germany*, still pending at the time of writing. See postscript to Chapter 10.

[38] These rules are complemented by a number of Ministerial orders which lay down the guidelines as regards prices. See Lupp (above, n 32) at 59.

[39] See Seidel in FIDE (1990) (above, n 20) at 71.

The original public procurement Directives were integrated into German law through the modification of the VOB and VOL.[40] They were, therefore, regarded as mere administrative norms.

Is Implementation through Circulars Adequate?

In view of the means of implementation adopted, the first question which needs to be tackled is whether the British and German practice of implementation through administrative circulars was in line with Community law. There is, in principle, no explicit prohibition upon Member States from using administrative provisions as implementing measures.[41] They may even be the most effective means of implementation in certain circumstances. Implementation through administrative action is equally envisaged by the current public procurement Directives themselves.[42] These provisions imply that both the Commission and Council considered implementation of the Directive through administrative provisions as a sufficient means effectively to achieve the desired results.[43] The final consequence of such an explicit recognition has been a certain legitimation of the implementation practice under examination, which has not favoured the adoption of more stringent measures and, as a consequence, a more correct application. As a matter of principle, one has to agree that a more rigid obligation regarding the legal means required to implement the Directives is to be preferred.

Thus, although not prohibited *per se* by the EC Treaty or the public procurement Directives, it must be recalled that the case law of the Court of Justice gradually limited this discretion on the basis of the effectiveness principle. In 1976, it held that the discretion left to Member States in Article 189 EC as regards implementation was made conditional on the adoption of the most appropriate means and methods to ensure the effectiveness

[40] Seidel in FIDE (1990) (above, n 20) at 71 and Seidel, 'Implementation of the public procurement Directives in the 12 States of the EC' (Part II) (above, n 20) at 257–258; Seidel, 'Die Anwendung der EG-Richtlinien für die öffentlichen Aufträge in der Bundesrepublik Deutschland' (1990) *Europarecht* 158.

[41] The Treaty itself recognizes the possibility of regulating certain matters relevant to Community law through the use of administrative norms and practices. Articles 49(b), 56, 57 and especially 100 EC explicitly contemplate that case and empower the Commission and the Council to adopt Directives for approximation and co-ordination of the different provisions laid down by law, regulation or administrative action which directly affect the establishment or functioning of the common market.

[42] See Article 34 of the consolidated public supplies Directive and Article 44 of the public services Directive which impose an obligation on Member States to bring into force the laws, regulations or administrative provisions, necessary to comply with the Directives. These clauses, which reproduced the wording of Article 100 EC, were intended to give legal coverage to the diverse national regulations of public contracts.

[43] Hen and Guillermin, 'Les marchés publics de fournitures et l'adoption de la directive du 21 décembre 1976' (1989) RMC 637 at 647.

of the directives.[44] Its general position was summarised in *Von Colson*, where the Court stated that 'although the third paragraph of Article 189 EC leaves Member States free to choose the ways and means of ensuring that the directive is implemented, that freedom does not affect the obligation, imposed on all Member States to which the directive is addressed, to adopt, within the framework of their national legal systems, all the measures necessary to ensure that the directive is fully effective, in accordance with the objective which it pursues'.[45] Thus, administrative provisions may be regarded as adequate means of implementation provided they ensure the full effectiveness of Community rules (Directives in this case) in the national legal orders. This is the crucial test.

Adequacy of national implementation measures has accordingly to be assessed on a case by case basis,[46] depending upon the result which the Directive wishes to achieve.[47] The Court has tackled the specific issue of implementation of Directives through administrative action in several cases. It follows from its case law that, in principle, administrative action will not be accepted whenever the national rules regulating the same subject-matter as the Directive in question have superior binding force.[48] More importantly, when Directives are intended to confer rights on individuals, the Court has been more reluctant to accept administrative provisions as implementation measures. After an initial ambiguous approach,[49] the Court has recently adopted a stricter interpetation on this point. In *Commission v. Germany*, which may be regarded as an expression of its current position, it held that 'a general legal context may, depending on the context of the directive, be adequate for the purpose [effective implementation of a directive] provided that it does guarantee the full application of the directive in a sufficiently clear and precise manner so that, where the directive *is intended to create rights for individuals*, the persons concerned can ascertain the full extent of their rights and, where appropriate, rely on

---

[44] See *inter alia* Case 48/75, *Belgium* v. *Royer* [1976] ECR 497.

[45] Case 14/83, *Von Colson and Kamann* v. *Land Nordrhein-Westfalen* [1984] ECR 1891 at 1906.

[46] In some circumstances the Court of Justice has been quite flexible when judging implementation techniques. In *Commission* v. *Germany* it held that 'the transposition of Community legislation into national law does not necessarily require the provisions of that legislation to be enacted in precisely the same words in an express and specific enactment; a general legal context may be sufficient if it is sufficiently clear and precise in order to ensure effectively the full application of the directive'. Case 29/84, *Commission* v. *Germany* [1985] ECR 1661 at 1667. See also Case 236/85, *Commission* v. *Belgium* [1986] ECR 3989 at 4007. See also Case C-59/89, *Commission* v. *Germany* [1991] ECR I-2607.

[47] Case 38/77, *Enka BV* v. *Inspecteur Invoerrechten en Accinjnzen Arnhem* [1977] ECR 2203. See also Case 152/79, *Lee* v. *Minister for Agriculture* [1980] ECR 1495.

[48] In *Commission* v. *Belgium*, it was stated that 'it is apparent from the whole of [the directives'] provisions and from the nature of the measures which they prescribe that the Directives in question are meant to be turned into provisions of national law which have *the same legal force* as those which apply in the Member States...' (emphasis added). Case 102/79, *Commission* v. *Belgium* [1980] ECR 1473.

[49] See Case 102/79, *Commission* v. *Belgium* [1980] ECR 1473.

them before the national courts'.[50] This judgment is particularly relevant as most of the discussion in the case related to the adequacy of administrative circulars to comply with the requirements of the Directive in question. With respect to this point the Court made clear that '. . . in the particular case of the circular [at stake] the Federal republic of Germany has not pointed to any national judicial decision explicitly recognizing that that circular, apart from being binding on the administration, has direct effect vis-à-vis third parties. It cannot be claimed, therefore, that individuals are in a position to know with certainty the full extent of their rights in order to rely on them where appropriate, before national courts or that those [affected by the directive] are adequately informed of their obligations'.[51] On this basis the Court held that Germany had failed to fulfil its obligations under the Treaty.

For our present purposes and on the basis of the case law of the Court, two different situations may be distinguished. Firstly, whenever Directives impose obligations with respect only to the internal administrative sphere, with no effects on third parties, the subject matter has been traditionally regulated through administrative action in the addressee Member States, and this administrative action is sufficient to ensure the accomplishment of the results sought by the Directives, implementation through administrative provisions is compatible with Community law. A second situation arises, however, when Directives provide third parties with benefits or rights. In these circumstances, implementation measures must be given sufficient publicity in order to make their content known to all possible beneficiaries and to ensure legal certainty. According to the Court, these conditions are not fulfilled by the mere adoption of administrative guidelines. Moreover, the Court has connected this issue with the 'effective judicial protection' principle which it has developed itself and according to which Member States are under an obligation to provide effective means of judicial redress to enforce rights arising from Community legislation at national level.[52] Since implementation through administrative guidelines renders the judicial enforcement of individual rights difficult, if not impossible, the conditions established by the Court's case law are not satisfied. Thus, implementation through administrative action is not permitted in this second category of cases.

---

[50] Case C-59/89, *Commission* v. *Germany* (above, n 46) at 2631. The same approach was adopted by the Court in its judgment on Case C-131/88 *Commission* v. *Germany* [1991] ECR I-825 and, in the specific context of the public procurement rules, in Case C-71/92 *Commission* v. *Spain* [1993] ECR 1–5923, where the Court added that '[the] requirements for clarity and precision are all the more stringent where . . . the transposition into national law is of exceptions and derogations from the rules laid down in the Directives'. Noted by Fernández Martín (1994) 3 PPLR CS73.

[51] Case C-59/89, *Commission* v. *Germany* (above, n 46) at 2632.

[52] See further Chapter 7.

Public procurement Directives belong to this latter category. Their provisions impose a compulsory award procedure whose object is to increase
transparency and ensure undistorted competition for the benefit of tenderers and, more precisely, foreign tenderers. Their effect goes well beyond
the administrative sphere and provides for individual rights.[53] In Germany,
administrative circulars do not produce legal effects outside the administrative sphere and, as a consequence, judicial enforcement of potential
individual rights arising from the Directives was seriously hindered.[54] A
similar situation occurred in the United Kingdom, where the fact that the
public procurement Directives were not transposed by means of statutory
norms had the effect of limiting the available judicial redress. As a
paradoxical consequence, individuals could only enforce their Community rights before their national courts through the direct effect doctrine
and only to a limited extent. Moreover, administrative circulars do not
usually have a binding character, since they act as mere recommendations
to lower government bodies.[55] The effectiveness of a Directive's provisions
in such cases depends, to a large extent, on the good will of the bodies
in charge of their application. Furthermore, publicity and legal certainty
were also limited by these means of implementation. Individuals had more
difficult access to information about their rights and obligations as the
Directives did not receive any publicity at national level.

In brief, pursuant to the Court's case law, the German and the British
implementation measures were not in line with Community law requirements.[56] The fact that in these Member States public contracts have been
traditionally regulated through administrative provisions could not justify
non-compliance with Community obligations. The absence of adequate
publicity and the absence of enforcement mechanisms at the disposal of
the tenderers hampered the effectiveness of the Directives. Whether these
legal insufficiencies had any impact on the non-liberalization of public
contracts will be discussed later on.

Despite the fact that case law supporting an eventual Article 169 EC
action had been available since the early seventies, the Commission never
challenged this obvious failure to comply with Community obligations
until 1985. The only Article 169 EC action for failure to implement the
original public procurement Directives which reached the Court of Justice

[53] EC Commission, COM (84) 717 at 8–9.
[54] This is precisely the problem in Germany where no subjective rights are provided and,
therefore, judicial review possibilities are highly reduced. See Chapter 10.
[55] See generally Wade and Forsyth, *Administrative Law*, 7th edn. (Oxford, 1994) at 871 *ff*,
although some ambiguity still exists.
[56] EC Commission, COM (84) 717 at 8–9; Remien (above, n 32) at 9. See in general,
Birkinshaw in FIDE (1990) (above, n 20) at 287 *ff*. See generally Curtin, 'Directives: the
Effectiveness of Judical Protection of Individual Rights' (1990) 27 CMLRev 709 at 714 *ff*,
especially at 717, reprinted in Snyder (ed.) (1993) (above, n 1), vol. I, at 395.

was the case of *Commission* v. *Italy*.[57] The reasons explaining this inertia must be linked to the general Eurosclerosis context in which the Communities had been developing during those years and the relatively dormant state of Community public procurement policy.[58] This lack of action did not favour a greater degree of compliance or the awareness of the relevant national authorities. The Commission bears part of the responsibility on this precise point, since it turned a blind eye on the matter.

This trend has radically changed in recent years. Nine Member States are currently facing the initial stages of Article 169 EC proceedings for failure to implement the public procurement Directives properly. Curiously, these enforcement actions do not refer exclusively to the new amendments but also to the original public procurement Directives. The current aggressive policy of the Commission in ensuring proper implementation in the public procurement area developed after 1985. The reorganization and strengthening of the Commission's own enforcement activities by the creation and staffing of a special enforcement service exclusively dealing with public procurement infractions has undoubtedly had an influence on this closer scrutiny of the implementation measures.[59] The political relevance attached to the public procurement area by the Commission in its internal market policy has also reinforced its diligence in monitoring public procurement.

This more aggressive policy is now bearing fruits. A substantial modification in national attitudes with respect to implementation through circulars has taken place. After talks with Commission officials, the United Kingdom has passed three Regulations in order to solve, properly and definitively, the inadequacy of previous implementation measures. These regulations are the Public Supply Contracts Regulations 1991 and 1995, the Public Works Regulation 1991 and the Public Services Regulation.[60] They substitute the applicable circulars and implement both the new amendments to the original public works and the public supplies Directives. They also incorporate the compliance Directive into British law. They provide a sort

---

[57] Case 10/76, *Commission* v. *Italy* [1976] ECR 1359, where the Court of Justice found that Italy had failed to adopt the measures necessary to comply with the Directive within the prescribed period. [58] See Chapter 1.

[59] Wainwright, 'Community Report to the 14th FIDE Congress' in FIDE (1990) (above, n 20) at 29.

[60] Supply Regulations; S.I. No. 2679/1991 and S.I. No. 201/1995 which contains all the rules on public supplies contracts in a consolidated form (on this latter Regulation see Arrowsmith, 'The Public Supplies Contracts Regulations 1995' (1995) 4 PPLR CS59); Works Regulation; S.I. No. 2690/1991; Services Regulation; S.I. No. 3228/1993. See O'Loan, 'Implementation of the Works, Supplies and Compliance Directives in the United Kingdom' (1992) 1 PPLR 88. O'Loan 'United Kingdom Implementation of the Services Directive 92/50' (1994) 3 PPLR CS 60. They were adopted under powers conferred by Parliament in section 2(2) of the European Communities Act 1972. Although this type of legislation does not need to go through Parliament, it has the same effect as an Act of Parliament.

of public procurement code, which was, until now, unknown in the United Kingdom. The structure reflects the general structure of the Directives themselves and the drafting is similar, if not identical, to the Directives.

The current Commission's position with respect to Germany is that the public procurement area needs to be regulated by means of measures of a legislative nature. There is currently a debate in Germany on this particular point. Some commentators share the view that such an important activity of public authorities may not be exempted from the application of the principles of administrative law. The need for a change in legal approach was already discussed by Fortshoff in the 1950s, who convincingly argued that public contracts constituted a particular category of contracts which greatly differed from private contracts and whose regulation was, accordingly, to be tackled on the basis of specific administrative principles.[61] Others emphasize that since the current system has proved efficient in Germany there is no need to guarantee subjective rights to tenderers nor to alter the administrative nature of the public procurement provisions.[62]

This latter view has so far prevailed.[63] Germany has finally implemented the Directives by upgrading the legal nature of both the VOL and VOB to administrative regulations, as opposed to mere administrative guidelines. This upgrading was meant to bring German law into line with Community requirements, including the Remedies Directive,[64] and was achieved through the revision of the Budgetary Principles Act (*Haushaltsgrundsätzegesetz*, HGrG). As regards public sector Directives, the Act introduces three new sections (57a to 57c) on the basis of which a so-called *Vergabeverordnung* (VgV) has been adopted.[65] This is a Federal Government Regulation and requires the application of the latest versions of the VOL-A (1993) and VOB-A (1992) by all contrating authorities mentioned in the HgrG. Even though the Regulation has now a binding character, it appears that it will only do so within the sphere of the Administration, but does not provide individuals with subjective rights enforceable before the ordinary administrative courts. For these reasons these measures do not seem to satisfy the requirements of Community law. In 1993, the Commission lodged an Article 169 EC action before the Court against Germany for failure to properly implement the public procurement Directives. This case is currently

---

[61] Fortshoff, *Traité de Droit Administratif Allemand*, 9e edn., translation by Fromont (Bruxelles, 1969), at 415 *ff.*

[62] See 'An explosive issue: 'Subjective rights' internal administrative controls?', briefly exposing the different positions in Germany (1993) 3 *EC Public Contracts* 10 and Wenzel, 'German solution not likely to last long. Four actions for Treaty violation', ibid. at 11. See further Chapter 10.

[63] For a defence of the traditional view, see Niedzela and Engshuber in Arrowsmith (ed.) (1993) (above, n 32) at 359.

[64] *Zweites Gesetz zur Änderung des Haushaltsgrundsätzegesetzes*, Bundesgesetzblatt, Jahrgang 1993, Teil I, p. 1928. See further Chapter 10.

[65] *Verordnung über die Vergabebestimmungen für öffentliche Aufträge—Vergabeverordnung*, Bundesgesetzblatt, Jahrgang 1994, Teil I, p. 321.

pending before the Court[66] and will be discussed at length later on. Whatever the final outcome of the dispute, Community law requirements have caused German authorities to rethink their traditional approach to public contracting. It is submitted that, in view of the ruling in *Commission* v. *Germany*[67] and considering that the public procurement Directives are intended to confer rights on individuals, the Commission's position now stands a better chance of being upheld.[68] As occurred in the United Kingdom, a judgment of the Court of Justice will lead to a substantial modification of the German legal treatment of public procurement.

Implementation through Statutory Instruments. France and Spain

Spain and France represent the other side of the coin of implementation in public procurement. Both Member States had well-developed legislation and jurisprudence in this area. The transposition of the Directives in both cases was done through the modification of statutory bodies of rules governing public contracts. This brought about the total 'nationalization' of the Directives' provisions. Even though adaptation of national legislation to Community law was necessary on specific minor points, the fact remains that no radical modification in existing legal approaches was needed in either country.

France[69]

The legal regime of contracts entered into by public authorities in France may be defined as being administratively oriented, since administrative law plays a crucial overall role in the preparation, award and enforcement stages. In general terms, French law distinguishes between two categories of contracts of public authorities: administrative contracts and private contracts of the administration.[70] The distinction is legally relevant for domestic law purposes, as it determines both the law applicable to

---

[66] Case C-433/93, still pending at the time of writing. See postscript to Chapter 10.

[67] Case C-59/89 (above, n 46).

[68] Advocate General Elmer has advised the Court to declare that Germany, by implementing the public procurement Directives through administrative action and thereby not conferring individual rights capable of being judicially enforced had failed to comply with its obligations under the EC Treaty. Opinion Case C-433/93 of 11 May 1995, not yet reported.

[69] On the French regime see generally, Laubadère, Moderne and Devolvé, *Traité de Contrats Administratifs* (Paris 1983); Bréchon-Moulènes (ed.), *Réglementation et Pratique des Marchés Publics* (Paris 1985); Goldman, 'An Introduction to the French Law of Government Procurement Contracts' (1987) 20 *George Washington Journal of International Law & Economics* 461.

[70] It must be noted that the said criteria have been developed by the jurisprudence of the *Conseil d'État*. Their lack of precise dogmatic boundaries has given rise to varying interpretations and theoretical discussions. For a complete discussion regarding the use and interpretation of such criteria, see Amselek, 'La qualification des contrats de l'administration par la jurisprudence' (1983) *Actualité Juridique-Droit Administratif* 3–7. There are voices in France, however, which defend the administrative nature of all contracts entered into by public authorities. Drago, 'Le champ d'application du Code' in Bréchon-Moulènes (ed.) (1985) (above, n 69) at 11 and 19.

the contract, namely, administrative or civil law, as well as the courts competent to interpret and enforce the contractual clauses. While the execution of administrative contracts falls under the exclusive competence of administrative courts, all other contracts are subject to common courts (*Judiciaire*).[71] This distinction has, however, little pertinence in relation to the EC public procurement Directives. These do not regulate the execution of contractual obligations and are only marginally concerned with the application of the accepted contract terms after their conclusion. On the contrary, their main target is to regulate the conduct of contracting authorities prior to the final award of a contract. That is, they regulate formation of the administration's will to enter a contract.

Whereas private parties generally benefit from the principle of freedom of contract as regulated in the *Code Civil*, all public authorities are obliged to follow a certain procedure in order to conclude a contract legally. Since public authorities are involved, this procedure is subject to administrative law. Due to the application of the principle of legality, French public authorities articulate their will to enter a contract by a 'sequence' of administrative acts, the corollary of which is the award decision.[72] All those measures and decisions are regular administrative acts whose legality, as a consequence, is subject to the control of administrative courts.[73]

With respect to public works, public services and public supplies contracts (generically known in France as 'marchés publics'), the applicable legal regime is contained *in extenso* in the *Code des Marchés Publics*.[74] The *Code* obliges only public authorities to abide by certain previously defined administrative procedures the disregard of which renders the conclusion of the contract illegal.[75] The administrative procedure consists of publicity acts, acts governing the selection of candidates and the final award of the contract, together with acts of approval. Respect for these measures guarantees equal opportunities for all interested tenderers, free competition and the protection of the financial interests of the administration, which is normally bound to contract either with the most economically advantageous offer or the lowest price. Since the very object of the Community rules on public procurement is to regulate the acts leading to the conclusion

---

[71] The origin of such a differentiation lies in the abandonment of the distinction made in the nineteenth century between *actes de gestion* and *actes d'autorité* of public authorities. The former were characterized by the absence of *puissance publique* on the part of the administration when performing them. Thus, contracts were considered as *actes de gestion* and were subject to private law and ordinary judges. After the Arrêt *Blanco*, (*Tribunal des Conflits*, 8 February 1873, *Aff. Blanco*) such a distinction was abandoned. For a complete exposition of the evolution see Laubadère and others (above, n 69) at 126 *ff*.

[72] Laubadère and others (above, n 69) at 472.   [73] See Chapter 9.

[74] Article 1 of the *Code* reads 'Les marchés publics sont des contrats passés, dans les conditions prévues au présent code, par les collectivités publiques en vue de la réalisation de travaux, fournitures et services'.

[75] On the *Code des Marchés Publics* see Bréchons-Moulènes (ed.) (1985) (above, n 69).

of the contract, the *Code* had to be duly modified in order to take Community requirements into account.

Thus, the original public supplies and public works Directives were implemented into national law through the modification of the existing *Code*, a modification which was carried out by means of Decrees.[76] Although subject to certain criticisms, the Decrees basically reproduced the Directive's provisions.[77] The same procedure was adopted for the public supplies Directive, which was implemented by Decree 79–98, and equally accompanied by an *arrêté ministeriel* with explanatory purposes.

As regards the amending Directives, the Decree transposing the new public supplies Directive modifies and adds new provisions to the *Code* itself.[78] Thus, Articles 378 to 388 were included, abrogating previous Decrees on any point contradicting the new rules. The situation was rather more complicated with respect to the new public works Directive.[79] The extension of its subjective scope of application to cover contracting authorities considered as private persons under French law and therefore subject to the ordinary law of contract, produced a significant change in the general domestic approach to the issue. Private parties, which until then benefited from freedom of contract, were now subject to binding rules governing the award procedures. The traditional division of competences between the civil and administrative jurisdictions as regards disputes relating to public and private contracts was thereby affected and different implementation measures were required.

The new public works Directive was implemented in various stages. First of all, a Decree of 18 September 1990, adapted the *Code's* procedures to the Directive's requirements once again. This Decree covered those public works contracts which were under the scope of application of the *Code des marchés publics*, that is, those awarded by public authorities subject to the *Code's* provisions. The Decree has modified *Livres II* and *III* and adds a

---

[76] The first public works Directive was the object of a Decree of 14 March 1973, and was complemented by an *arrêté ministeriel* of the same date, which explained and specified the scope of application of the new Community rules. See generally Hen 'Les incidences du droit européen sur le droit français des marchés publics' (1975) *Actualité Juridique-Droit Administratif* 496; Roquette and Lefort, 'Implementation of the public procurement Directives in the 12 States of the EC.' (Part II) (above, n 20) at 253. See Drago, 'Les incidences communautaires sur le droit des marchés publics et des marchés des entreprises publiques' in Rideau and others (eds.), *La France et les Communautés Européennes* (Paris, 1974) 859.

[77] See Drago in Rideau and others (eds.) (above, n 76) at 864.

[78] Decree No. 89.234 of 7 April 1989.

[79] On the implementation of the new public works Directive see further Cherot, 'La transposition de la Directive 89/440 CEE du 18 juillet 1989 portant coordination des procédures de passation des marchés publics de travaux' (1991) 16 *Revue de la Recherche Juridique* 981. As for the services Directive 92/50, a Draft Law and Decree are being discussed at the time of writing. The same applies to the implementation of the consolidated versions of the public supplies and Utilities Directives. At the time of writing, the Commission had initiated Article 169 EC procedures against France for failing to adopt the implementation measures in time.

new *Livre V* to the *Code*. With respect to the whole set of new 'private' contracting authorities which were not previously covered by the *Code*, the enactment of a legislative text was necessary. Thus, Law No. 91.3 of 3 January 1991 was passed, whose Title II explicitly incorporates the new obligations applicable to the 'new private' contracting authorities into French law.[80] This law was further complemented by Decree No. 92.311 of 31 March 1992, which enforced and specified the general framework laid down in Law 91.3.[81]

For present purposes, French implementation of the Directives has taken place by means of legally binding rules, which provide enforceable rights for tenderers and which formally respond to Community law requirements. Since Community rules have been implemented into the French legal order by means of their inclusion in the Code, they have acquired a legislative nature.

Spain

The special pre-eminent position which public authorities enjoy in the Spanish legal system as representative of the general interest is reflected in the contractual relationships entered into by public authorities. The legal regulation of contracts entered into by administrative bodies in Spain has been greatly influenced by French doctrine, although peculiarities still exist. Spanish law, like French law, distinguishes between so-called administrative contracts and private contracts by the administration.[82] As happens in France, the private or public legal nature of the contract determines the legal regime applicable to the contract clauses. It regulates its effects, enforcement, extinction, etc., as well as the courts competent to adjudicate eventual disputes. Thus, 'administrative contracts' are subject to administrative law and courts, whereas the enforcement and legal life of 'private contracts' of the administration are regulated pursuant to the common law of the contract by the civil law courts.[83] Although in theoretical terms such a distinction may be of interest,[84] it is generally irrelevant, however,

---

[80] See further Chapter 9.   [81] Roquette and Lefort (above, n 76) at 253.

[82] This distinction has its origin in the 19th cent. when, emulating the French example, certain contracts entered into by public authorities fell under the exclusive jurisdiction of administrative courts in order to protect their general operation from eventual judicial interference. Until then, civil law courts had been competent to resolve any contractual dispute, since the administration was treated like any other private party. For an overview of the historical evolution of the legal approach to public contracts in Spain, see Parada Vazquez, *Derecho Administrativo. Parte General*, T I (Madrid, 1989) at 184 *ff.*

[83] Articles 5 and 9 of the new Spanish Public Procurement Law (*Ley 13/1995, de 18 de mayo de Contratos de las Administraciones Públicas*, BOE No. 119 of 19 May 1995 (LCE).

[84] Whereas in France the distinction is still subject to doctrinal debate and is mainly dealt with by the case law of the *Conseil d'État*, a more practical approach has been followed in Spain. In fact, Article 5 LCE explicitly provides for the criteria defining a contract as either private or administrative, as well as the rules binding the competent review bodies.

with respect to Community public procurement Directives for the reasons already discussed with respect to France. Indeed, public authorities in Spain are always subject to administrative law and, therefore, administrative law courts, when it comes to awading a contract, irrespective of the contract's legal nature.[85] Even when public authorities actually conclude a contract subject to private law as regards its execution, the formation of their administrative will and its formal expression is subject to compulsory administrative procedures. These procedural constraints are inspired by the fact that public authorities are guardians of the general interest and consequently, pursuant to the principle of legality enshrined in Article 103 of the Spanish Constitution, their activities have to be previously sanctioned and regulated by a legal norm.[86]

Public procurement in Spain was governed since 1957 by the rules laid down in the *Ley de Contratos del Estado* and its executive *Reglamento* (Regulation).[87] As in the case of France, these two pieces of legislation exhaustively regulated public authorities' powers and prerogatives when entering into a contractual relationship with a third person, including the way in which they carry out the award procedure. The implementation of the first public supplies and public works Directives in Spain took place through the modification of the existing Law and Regulation and their adaptation to the requirements of Community law.[88] This adaptation took place through Royal Legislative Decree No. 931/1986 of 2 May.[89] Community rules thus became an integral part of national legislation, enjoying a binding legal status and the redress available against any

---

[85] Some commentators propose the definitive abandonment of the distinction in question in the field of contracts entered into by public authorities, claiming that it would simplify things if all contracts were regarded as administrative. See, for example, Parada Vazquez (above, n 82) at 194–195 who defines private contracts of the administration as a schizophrenic and residual category. In the same vein García Trevijano, 'Contratos y actos ante el Tribunal Supremo. La explotación del Hotel Andalucía Palace de Sevilla' (1959) RAP 147; Martin Retortillo, 'Institución contractual en el Derecho Administrativo: en torno al problema de la igualdad de las partes' (1959) RAP 50, and 'Reciente evolución de la jurisprudencia administrativa: actos separables admitidos por el Tribunal Supremo' (1961) RAP 227.

[86] García de Enterría and Fernández, *Curso de Derecho Administrativo*, 3ª ed., T I (Madrid, 1981) at 591–592.

[87] *Ley de Contratos del Estado*, approved by Decree of 8 April 1965, reformed by law of 17 March 1973 and *Reglamento General de Contratación del Estado* (RGCE) of 1967, reformed and updated by Decree of 25 November 1975, respectively. These pieces of legislation have been modified on different occasions, although for our purposes the sole important modification is that which brought the Spanish regulation into line with Community requirements.

[88] Since public procurement Directives were not the subject of any special regime in the Treaty of Accession of June 1985 as complemented by the Act of Accession, they were to be implemented into domestic law by the time Spain acceded on 1 January 1986.

[89] The Royal Legislative Decree was adopted by the Government on the basis of Law 47/85 of 27 December 1985, temporarily authorizing the Government to adopt all necessary legislative measures to bring the Spanish legal system into line with Community requirements. On the specific implementation measures in the field of public procurement, see the contributions to the monographic issue on *Los Contratos Administrativos en el Derecho Europeo*

violation of these Community provisions is the same as that which exists for infringements of national rules.

Although from a formal point of view the means of implementation were considered adequate by the Commission, it nevertheless questioned certain material aspects of the Royal Legislative Decree which were brought before the Court of Justice. In *Commission* v. *Spain* the Court partially upheld the Commission's claims and condemned Spain for failing to implement properly the first Directives from a material point of view.[90] Spanish Government representatives had recognized that some of the Commission's claims were well-founded, but argued that the alleged infringements would be remedied after the adoption of the new Law on Public Procurement, which was being prepared at the time by the Government. The enactment of this Law was, however, unduly delayed and the Commission engaged a new Article 171(2) EC procedure requesting the Court of Justice to impose a fine on Spain for failure to adopt the necessary measures to comply with its previous judgment. The formal letter of notice was sent in December 1994. However, in view of the final adoption of the new Law in April 1995 it is doubtful whether the Commission will maintain its Article 171 EC action.

With respect to the new amending and consolidated Directives, Spain enjoyed privileged treatment as regards the implementation deadline for the new public works and public supplies Directives which was extended until March 1992.[91] The public services Directive was to be implemented by July 1993[92] and the deadline for the implementation of the consolidated public supplies Directive was June 1994.[93] Spain, however, did not comply with any of its implementation obligations in time[94] and the Commission initiated an Article 169 EC procedure against Spain for failing to

---

(1986) No. 21, *Noticias CEE*; Juristo, 'La adaptación de la regulación española del contrato de obra pública a las Directivas de la Comunidad Económica Europea' (1986) REDA. On the relationship between the Spanish regulation of public contracts and the European rules, see generally Ojeda Marín, 'Contratos públicos en la CEE: La ley de contratos del Estado y su adecuación al ordenamiento jurídico comunitario' (1987) RAP 131.

[90] Case C-71/92, *Commission* v. *Spain* (above, n 50). The case examined the compatibility with Community law of some provisions of the LCE, RGCE and other specific provisions contained in other special statutes which affected public procurement. For a deatiled discussion of the judgment, see Fernández Martín (1994), 3 PPLR CS73.

[91] See Article 20 of the new supplies Directive 88/295 and Article 3 of the new public works Directive 89/440. According to the Preambles of the Directives, the reason for this was that Spain had just finished incorporating the original Directives and, therefore, any further changes at that stage would have adversely affected the adaptation of the private sector in Spain.   [92] Article 44 of the public services Directive 90/50.

[93] Article 34 of the consolidated public supplies Directive 93/36.

[94] A draft of the new Spanish Public Procurement Law was presented to Parliament at the beginning of 1993. The law was never debated, however, since the Spanish Government called a general election, which was held in June, 1993. This caused the suspension of all legislative activities. The adoption and discussion of the aforementioned Law on Public Procurement was therefore postponed.

notify the implementation measures of the amended public works and public supplies Directives.[95] The new Public Procurement Law (*Ley 13/1995, de Contratos de las Administraciones Públicas* (LCE)) which derogates from the previous 1965 Law and its Regulation,[96] was finally adopted in May 1995, three years after it was due.[97] The Preamble of the new Law declares its intention to adapt and update the regulation of public procurement to the changes which have occurred in the public procurement area since the last major modification of the Law in 1973[98] and to comply with the obligations arising from the Community Directives in the area. All the new public supplies, public works and public services Directives, as consolidated, are incorporated into the new Spanish Law almost word for word. As the implementation measure is a Law of Parliament, Community rules enjoy the same legislative status as they did before.

Comparison and Conclusions

The Impact of the Legal Instrument Chosen: the Directive

The advantages and the shortcomings of EC Directives have been the object of many studies.[99] On the positive side, Directives are restricted to the attainment of the harmonization of legal norms arising from different legal systems and traditions in order to ensure the achievement of a common objective. This leaves a wide margin of manoeuvre to Member States, thereby favouring a legal response better suited to national legal traditions and structures and avoiding excessive supranational interference at the national level. It therefore respects the subsidiarity principle. The lack of uniformity deriving from the different national approaches and the incorrect implementation by national administrations when a conflict between Community and national interests becomes patent can be identified as the most relevant disadvantages. National measures often distort a Directive's final objectives and political problems can hinder the

---

[95] See case C-92/328 *Commission* v. *Spain*, which in view of the adoption of the new law will probably be withdrawn.   [96] (Note 83, above).

[97] (Note 83, above).

[98] The major political, economic and legal changes which have taken place since then called for the adoption of rules more adapted to the new realities.

[99] A complete discussion of this question is beyond the scope of these pages. The most comprehensive is probably Siedentopf and Ziller (eds.) *L'Europe des Administrations? La Mise en Oeuvre de la Législation Communautaire dans les États Membres*, vol. I (Maastricht, 1988), especially the contributions by Siedentopf and Hauschild, 'La directive dans la Communauté Européene', and Capotorti, 'La problématique des directives et règlements et de leur mise en oeuvre'; Gaja, Hay and Rotunda, 'Instruments for Legal Integration in the European Communities: A Review', in Cappelletti, Seccombe and Weiler (eds.) *Integration Through Law*, vol. 1, book 2 (Berlin, 1986) 133; Weiler, 'The White Paper and the application of Community law' in Bieber, Dehousse, Pinder and Weiler (eds.), *1992: One European Market?: A Critical Analysis of the Commission's Internal Market Strategy* (Baden-Baden, 1988) at 337.

adequate implementation of its provisions.[100] Incorrect implementation at national level could lead to deficient application and, therefore, to the non-attainment of the established objectives.[101]

However, over the years these shortcomings have, to a large extent, been precluded by a substantial transformation of their legal nature both at the legislative and judicial levels. This has led to the progressive reinforcement of their binding nature and effectiveness. On the legislative level, due to diverse factors, their wording has become increasingly detailed, thereby reducing considerably the margin of discretion of Member States in choosing the means and methods for their implementation. In some cases, national discretion has amounted to a mere formal obligation to enact an identical national act. This practice of making Directives more detailed has never been questioned by the Court of Justice which, on the contrary, has validated it.[102] At the judicial level, the Court has developed a series of doctrines which have strengthened the legally binding nature of Directives. These doctrines are all encompassed in the more general principles of direct effect and effective judicial protection.[103] As a net result, this has brought about a practical identification between regulations and directly effective provisions of Directives as regards their effects.[104] Thus, Directives have gained in binding force by means of their increasing detail and, as a consequence, by the direct effect of their provisions. Furthermore, under Article 191 TEU, publication of Directives became compulsory. It is true that previously all Directives were published, but no legal obligation to that effect existed. Legal certainty and publicity of Directives' rules has therefore been improved.

On a practical level, effectiveness of Directives has also been enhanced by a stricter Commission stance as regards the monitoring of national implementation measures in the last decade. Its task has been facilitated by the introduction in all Directives of an explicit obligation on Member States to notify the Commission of adopted measures. Article 169 EC proceedings are likely to follow when these are absent or deemed inadequate.[105]

---

[100] In this context see the *Annual Reports of the Commission to the European Parliament on the Monitoring of the Application of Community Law* which provide for statistics as regards failures by Member States to comply with their implementation obligations.

[101] See Anderson, 'Inadequate Implementation of EEC Directives. A Roadblock to 1992' (1988) 11 *Boston College of International and Comparative Law Review* 91.

[102] See on this point Fernández Martín and Pellicer Zamora, 'Las ofertas anormalmente bajas en la contratción pública' *Gaceta Jurídica de la CEE, serie B, núm. 78*, 3 at 9.

[103] And more precisely the direct effect, indirect effect and *Francovich* doctrines. See on these points Chapter 7.

[104] Fernández Martín and Pellicer Zamora (above, n 102) at 10–11; Gaja, Hay and Rotunda (above, n 99) at 133. See also Capotorti, Hilf, Jacobs and Jacqué in *Le Traité d'Union Européenne* (Brussels, 1985) at 131.

[105] Dashwood and White, 'Enforcement Actions under Articles 169 and 170 EEC' (1989) 14 ELRev 388 at 399 *ff*. For further discussion of this point in relation to the public

Lastly, it is important to stress that it has been forcefully shown that, with respect to the implementation and application of Directives by national authorities, 'the general picture seems to be that implementation of Community legislation follows the same patterns and meets the same obstacles as the implementation of the respective national legislation'.[106] It is therefore axiomatic that once implementation measures are adopted, national authorities comply with them 'in the same impartial way as [they do with] any other national rule in the same area'.[107] Once Community rules on public procurement have been implemented, they are administered with the same degree of diligence employed when applying national rules on the same matter. It follows that, from a practical point of view, the legal nature of the measure becomes irrelevant provided that public authorities respect their general obligations in the area in question.

Public procurement Directives have benefited, in particular, from these improvements. For the most part, they impose obligations regarding the procedure to be followed when awarding contracts above the established threshold. Delays, subjective scope and objective scope of application, awarding criteria, etc., are thoroughly regulated by the Directives and do not admit many variations in relation to their own drafting. This implies a high degree of detail and does not leave much margin of discretion to the Member States. In fact, every time the Court of Justice has been called upon to judge the directly effective character of Community public procurement provisions to date, it has replied in the affirmative.[108] Most other provisions can be held to fulfil the direct effect test, i.e., clear, precise and leaving no margin of discretion to national authorities.[109]

It follows from the foregoing that the fact that public procurement rules have been integrated in Directives should not have affected their effectiveness to a significant extent. Their highly detailed character, the application of the direct effect doctrine and the fact that they provide for

procurement rules see Chapter 6. In the public procurement area this more aggressive policy of the Commission is reflected in the increasing number of Article 169 EEC procedures opened against faulty national implementation measures.

[106] Siedentopf et Ziller (above, n 99) at 58. For some authors this is due more to the substantial increase of the load of Community legislation to be implemented into domestic legal orders rather than the bad faith of national authorities. See in this sense Krislow, Ehlermann and Weiler, 'The Political organs of the Decision-Making Process in the US and the EC' in Cappeletti, Seccombe and Weiler (above, n 99) at 64.

[107] Siedentopf et Ziller (eds.) (above, n 99) at 58.

[108] Articles 20, 26 and 29 of the public works Directive 71/305 have been declared directly effective by the Court of Justice, Case 31/87, *Beentjes* [1988] ECR 4,635. Since the provisions of the public supplies Directive 77/62 are drafted in very similar (if not identical) terms, the declaration by the Court means that they obviously have the same effect. Article 29(5) of the public works Directive (corresponding to Article 25(5) of the public supplies Directive) has equally been declared directly effective in Case 103/88, *Fratelli Constanzo* v. *Commune di Milano* [1989] ECR 1839. Advocate General Lenz also considered Article 9 of the public supplies Directive directly effective, see his Opinion in Case C-247/89, *Commission* v. *Portugal*, [1991] ECR I-3659 at para. 15.   [109] In this vein see also Turpin (1989) (above, n 22) at 217.

rights to tenderers around Europe should have largely compensated for their shortcomings as harmonization measures and have constrained Member States' freedom of action in the field in question. The awareness campaign run by the Commission after 1985 has also contributed to the spread of information about the rules and the acquaintance of legal operators with these rules. Of course, this is not to say that it has not had any effect at all. Obviously, in the case of Germany and the UK more stringent means of implementation would have guaranteed further publicity of the rules and, consequently, a larger awareness of the parties involved. Equally, the adoption of a Regulation instead of a Directive would certainly have enhanced the binding nature of the Directives and would have overcome the difficulties arising from the cumbersome implementation process. But it is submitted that the improvements which would have resulted would have been marginal.

In this context, the Commission's failure in the 1970s and early 1980s to challenge original implementation measures needs to be highlighted. Nonetheless, after 1984, Community public procurement rules received widespread publicity. It is submitted, therefore, that the supranational legal measures used to regulate public procurement have not been conclusive in the failure to achieve the objectives pursued in this field. This submission will become more apparent when comparing the national implementation measures adopted.

The Impact of the National Implementation Measures in the Effectiveness of the Rules

With respect to Germany and the UK, a distinction has to be made between a legal analysis and a practical assessment. From a legal perspective, it appears that implementation of the public procurement Directives through administrative measures was contrary to Community law. It is doubtful, however, whether this had serious effects on the lack of effectiveness of Community rules or whether it constituted one of their essential drawbacks. In both Member States, administrative guidelines enshrined in administrative circulars are generally respected by competent national public bodies and all interested parties. Practice shows that contractors in Germany rely heavily on the contents of the VOL and VOB. Furthermore, in Germany, applicable provisions have a consensus character and are collectively drafted. This undoubtedly constituted a major incentive for compliance by all actors involved. Lastly, the *Bundeskartellsamt* as well as German courts normally take the conditions enshrined therein as a reference point to assess the respect by contracting authorities of the restraints of the Federal Law of Competition. If the said provisions are not complied with, a *prima facie* case of abuse of dominant position is said to exist.[110] Similar reasoning applies in the UK, where it is common practice to consult industry representatives when drafting the principles governing the public procurement policy of the British government.[111] Moreover, the British Report issued in the context of the European Public Administration Institute's project found that, in general, even where British civil servants are sceptical about Community legislation, they apply the latter the same way as they apply national rules. So far, no flagrant conflict has arisen in the UK between public authorities and contractors with respect to procurement policy or regulation, since the practice of contracting authorities has been consistent with the applicable principles. It is submitted that the application of Community rules enjoyed the same treatment as national rules in both States and were respected to the same extent. Both systems have, in fact, been considered as being rather open to foreign competition.[112]

As regards France and Spain, there is a general agreement that implementation through legislative action is the best means to ensure the attainment of the Directives' objectives and to guarantee a fair chance for all interested contractors. Apart from infringements of a minor nature, committed when translating the provisions of the Directives into national legal measures, the latin-continental system of implementation was in line with Community obligations and the national implementation measures were legally binding. The main difference between both systems of implementation referred, therefore, to the binding force of the national measures, which in turn determined the possibility for third parties to challenge alleged violations of the provisions of the Directives. One could have expected that the degree of compliance would have been greater in France and Spain than in Germany or the United Kingdom for two interrelated reasons. Firstly, the legally binding force of the national provisions adopted in the two former States is of a legislative nature. Secondly, in Spain and France, through the theory of the *actes détachables*, third parties who illegally discriminated could more easily impugn illegal conducts on the part of the administration. In comparison, in Germany and in the

---

[110] See Chapter 10.

[111] As Turpin points out, 'the legitimacy of [private contractors] is recognized by the government, which frequently consults with associations of suppliers and other representatives of industry on matters connected with government contracts' (1989) (above, n 22) at 65. Finally see also ibid. at 107.

[112] In Germany, three ministerial Decrees dating from 1960 already imposed the obligation of equal treatment for national and foreign tenders on contracting authorities. For a positive view of the German system in this respect, see Cleesattel (above, n 32) at 89. The same conclusion is reached with respect to the United Kingdom system where it is argued that 'foreign firms that qualify technically and financially for government procurement contracts are able to compete for such contracts on the same terms as British firms', Blyth, 'Government Procurement in the United Kingdom' (1987) 21 *George Washington Journal of International Law and Economics* 127 at 148.

United Kingdom, on the contrary, the right to bring proceedings because of non-compliance with an administrative circular is highly improbable, in so far as the latter did not create effects outside the administration.[113]

Available data shows, however, that the fact that implementation was performed through legislative action and that, as a consequence, judicial remedies were available, did not result in better compliance records in Spain and France when compared with the UK and Germany. As regards the obligation to publish contract notices in the Official Journal, the Commission found that the obligation to publish is increasingly being respected by all national contracting authorities, independently of the legally binding force of the rule imposing such an obligation. Indeed, the number of notices published by the four Member States under scrutiny have followed the same pattern in recent years.[114] Equally, complaints concerning public procurement before national courts are the exception rather than the rule in all four Member States.[115]

As far as the achievement of the Directives' main objective is concerned, that is, the actual liberalization of national public contracts to foreign competition, the percentage of public contracts awarded to foreign undertakings is equally insignificant in all four Member States.[116] Our main conclusion is therefore that the fact that in some Member States implementation was done through administrative circulars, whereas in others implementation took place through legislative action, did not have a conclusive influence on the lack of effectiveness of the Directives, nor did it produce substantially different patterns of compliance. In fact, no outstanding differences exist between the way in which the German and British on the one side and the French and Spanish contracting authorities on the other, have complied with the rules.

On the legal level, however, a second major conclusion arises from the analysis of the implementation level. Community regulation of public procurement clearly follows a latin-continental approach.[117] This approach is being imposed by Community law in those Member States which tackled the issue of public contracts from a private law perspective. This appears to be done regardless of effectiveness considerations. In the same context, modifications of national approaches long awaited by national academicians and business men have been speeded up (or will be speeded up) by

---

[113] See Chapters 9 and 10. [114] See the Tables annexed to this chapter.
[115] See Chapter 8.
[116] In 1987, import penetration in public purchasing was 1.6% in France, 3.8% in Germany and 0.4% in the United Kingdom. Data on Spain was not available (source National Accounts, Eurostat 1985. Atkins 1987). See EC Commission, *Communication from the Commission on a Community Regime for Public Procurement in the Excluded Sectors: Water, Energy, Transport and Telecommunications*, COM 88 (376) at 12.
[117] The public works and public supplies Directives are mainly inspired by the French approach to public procurement.

Community requirements. The impulse for these substantial modifications comes from supranational rather than national level, thereby contributing to the uniformity of the applicable regime. Whereas the uniformity achieved could be welcome by some sectors, doubts may remain as regards the adequacy of the system in achieving the Community objectives in the field of public procurement.

If implementation procedures have not determined the minimal success of the public procurement rules, the next step is to examine the application level in search of the reasons for failure. It is submitted that the decisive cause is related more to the structure of the market than the inadequacy of the implementation measures. This submission will be developed in the next chapter.

FIGURE 4: Public authorities notices published 1988–1994

Works   *Supplies*

Deutschland

	88	89	90	91	92	93	94
Tenders	1008	1213	1383	2005	3353	4769	5749
Awards	0	3	11	430	2320	2547	2881

	88	89	90	91	92	93	94
Tenders	723	841	1052	1103	1354	1420	1618
Awards	1	142	228	316	935	834	1054

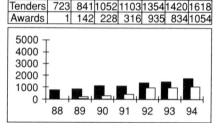

France

	88	89	90	91	92	93	94
Tenders	2462	2918	3233	1985	1700	1604	1376
Awards	0	617	946	699	613	683	742

	88	89	90	91	92	93	94
Tenders	1731	2290	2616	2665	3156	3141	3886
Awards	15	675	1050	1170	1413	1601	1903

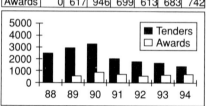
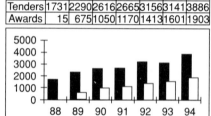

España

	88	89	90	91	92	93	94
Tenders	837	1430	1856	635	461	514	478
Awards	0	3	16	18	17	11	19

	88	89	90	91	92	93	94
Tenders	861	897	942	851	817	980	1202
Awards	1	6	1	8	9	10	14

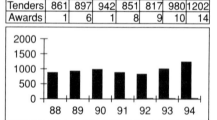

United Kingdom

	88	89	90	91	92	93	94
Tenders	1407	1861	1154	726	794	826	758
Awards	0	0	31	131	242	332	387

	88	89	90	91	92	93	94
Tenders	1141	1716	2493	3010	3715	4090	4573
Awards	268	701	1106	1649	2121	2540	2738

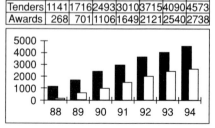

Source: TED database

5

The Ineffectiveness of the Rules (II): The Application Level

INTRODUCTION

It has been assumed by the Commission that one of the main obstacles to the achievement of an open competitive European market in the field of public procurement is that national contracting authorities apply discriminatory policies which favour national firms. The Economic and Social Committee and the European Parliament[1] and most commentators have accepted this explanation as valid without subjecting it to deeper critical analysis.[2] This position argues that public authorities consciously disobey their obligations under Community Directives thereby preventing the interpenetration of the market for public procurement. The negative effect of this attitude is that private firms neglect the possibilities of opening new markets as the investment needed to bid for foreign awards is not compensated by their chances of success. As pointed out earlier, available statistics show that intracommunity awards are the exception rather than the rule. These statistics support the main reason for the aggressive Community policy in this area.[3]

The purpose of this section is to test such an assumption against the reality of the public procurement market and to assess the merits of the Commission's policy. It would be naïve to deny the existence of a certain

---

[1] European Parliament, 'Report on the Communication by the Commission to the Council (COM (84) 717 final) on Public Supply Contracts—Conclusions and Perspectives' Doc. A2-38/85 (the 'Wogau Report').

[2] Most commentators seem to agree on this point. To this effect see *inter alia* Margue, 'L'ouverture des marchés publics dans la Communauté (1ère partie)' (1991) *Revue du Marché Unique Européen* 143 at 148; Bréchons-Moulènes, 'L'échec des directives travaux et fournitures de 1971 et 1976' (1988) *Revue Française de Droit Administrative* 753 at 759–760; Ojeda Marín, 'Hacia un sistema de contratación pública acorde con el mercado interior' (1988) *Revista de Instituciones Europeas* 821 at 832; Flamme, M. and Flamme, P. 'Vers l'Europe des marchés publics? (à propos de la directive fournitures du 22 mars 1988)' (1988) RMC 455 at 457; Flamme, M. and Flamme, P., 'La réglementation communautaire en matière des marchés publics. Le point sur le contentieux' (1993) *Revue du Marché Unique Européen* 13 at 19 *ff*; Weiss, *Public Procurement in European Community Law* (London, 1993) Chapter 2 especially at 10 *ff*. In this context see in particular Mclachlan, 'Discriminatory Public Procurement, Economic Integration and the Role of Bureaucracy' (1985) 23 JCMS 357, whose main argument corresponds to that followed by the Commission when analysing the causes for the lack of market integration in the public procurement area, and Mattera, 'Les marchés publics: dernier rempart du protectionnisme des États' (1993) *Revue du Marché Unique Européen* 5.

[3] See Chapter 1.

element of nationalism in the mind of contracting authorities. However, it is argued that this national attitude only constitutes a secondary cause for the lack of interpenetration of the public markets covered. In this section it is submitted that intrinsic features of public procurement and, especially, the economic structure of the 'ordinary' public supplies and public works contracts sectors play a far more relevant role in the lack of success of the legislation than the deliberate buy-national approach of contracting authorities.

THE COMMISSION'S ASSUMPTIONS. A CRITICAL VIEW

In its evaluation of the practical effectiveness of the original Directives, the Commission found that whereas procedural obligations, such as the publication of a notice, are increasingly being respected, no real interpenetration of public markets has followed. Since not enough cross-border awards are taking place and only a small number of foreign firms are successful in bidding for contracts in other Member States, the Commission concluded that there is a widespread disregard of the obligations under the Directives.[4]

The Commission's logic is open to scrutiny. It regards as axiomatic that public procurement markets at European level provide a high potential for intra-Community bidding and that European firms are eager to participate in foreign award procedures but that they are prevented from doing so by the attitude of national authorities. The merits of these assumptions may only be appraised by means of comprehensive, empirical research which examines, in detail, a representative number of award procedures, the reasons behind every individual award decision and the economic evaluation of the different offers presented. This ambitious research, which has not yet been undertaken, is beyond the scope of an individual study such as the present.[5]

An alternative methodological approach must therefore be devised. Some empirical research has been undertaken, which suggests that interest in intra-Community bidding[6] is not as high as the Commission presupposes, due to obstacles arising from the very structure of public procurement markets. If, as this author believes, these studies are correct, the conclusions reached and the assumptions on which the policy is based are weakened.

[4] See Chapter 1 and EC Commission *Public Supply Contracts—Conclusions and Perspectives,* COM (84) 717, at 15.

[5] In this connection, see the conclusions reached by Hartley and Uttley where they call for further statistical research in the direction suggested above in order to determine the practical implications of the EC public procurement policy. Hartley and Uttley, 'The Single European Market and Public Procurement Policy: The Case of the United Kingdom' (1994) 3 PPLR 114 at 122 and 125.

[6] The notion of intra-Community bidding refers to offers presented by firms based and established in a Member State other than the one in which the contract award is to take place.

By showing that this is the case, the difficulties in analysing whether substantial obligations are complied with will be overcome. But before entering into a more detailed development of the structural difficulties in ensuring European-wide bidding, the question why contracting authorities apply discriminatory procurement practices must be tackled.

The Alleged Reasons for Discrimination in Public Procurement

Do contracting authorities apply discriminatory practices systematically? If so, what are the reasons explaining this attitude? Two situations may be distinguished. First of all, discriminatory practices may be the result of complying with national regulations, rules or even political guidelines requiring such conduct from awarding authorities. The most obvious case of this occurs in the context of a preferential public procurement system. National contracting authorities are thereby placed under a legal obligation to favour national production or labour. This issue has been discussed at length in Chapters 2 and 3. For present purposes it is sufficient to recall that these schemes respond to legitimate concerns rather than pure protectionist impulses and have been preceded by political debate at the national level and are, therefore, subject to various degrees of public accountability. As already stated, this form of discrimination should be dealt with through political bargaining and compensatory measures agreed between national and Community authorities as a practical application of a political concept of subsidiarity.

A second scenario comprises biased decisions adopted outside the framework of binding obligations on the independent initiative of contracting authorities. These, on more or less equivocal grounds, would systematically favour national companies in open disregard of the applicable legal rules. This view seems to be supported by the undisputed fact that locally established firms are more likely to win a contract award procedure. From a public-choice perspective, this is explained as budget maximizing bureaucracies pursuing their own welfare by means of discriminatory awards which would ensure them votes or financial rewards.[7] This is more likely to be the case at local level, where the political class stands closer to the voters and their decisions directly affect local employment and industry. In most of these cases, however, local contracts rarely fall under the Directives' scope of application and are of marginal interest for Community purposes and of marginal interest to foreign firms.

In any event, for the purpose of Community rules, biased awards in favour of a particular firm seem the result of the latter's close links with the contracting authority, rather than its nationality. These links may be

---

[7] This is the main argument put forward by Mclachlan (above, n 2) and Mattera (above, n 2).

the result of many different causes, some legal, some illegal. On the legal side, when awarding supply contracts, public authorities may just be acting as sensitive consumers, who prefer to pass the contract to traditional suppliers whose reliability is already established. On the darker side, it is undeniable that in some Member States, mainly latin-continental ones, biased decisions are related to corrupt administrative practices. Although the examination of such practices is beyond the scope of this book, they must be mentioned since, unfortunately, they are anything but occasional. Several scandals at national level provide evidence that they are recurrent, especially at local and regional level. Notwithstanding this, it also emerges from press reports that interested firms are well aware of this course of action and that they assume it is just another variable when competing for public awards.[8] From a Community law point of view, although it may sound a bit cynical, the truth is that on these grounds discrimination affects national firms and foreign firms in the same manner and it is not restricted to the case of contracts subject to Community rules. Obviously, for foreign firms not established in those markets, the development of this type of proximity is necessary in order to increase their chances of success.

This being said, it is submitted that to blame the scarce percentage of contracts awarded to foreign-based undertakings on systematic discrimination is fallacious.[9] This position ignores the fact that applicable rules at national level already organized controls on contracting authorities and already required the use of competitive tendering.[10] Discrimination would flagrantly infringe the rules. Even assuming that the enforcement of a tenderer's rights may be a complicated affair and that existing judicial

---

[8] Continental political parties have obtained economic resources from the discriminatory award of public contracts. Successful undertakings receive the contract in exchange for a bribe which goes to the treasury of a political party holding public office or, in other cases, into the personal purses of those composing the awarding authority. Several scandals have come to light in different Member States. There are ongoing scandals in Italy (see the major Italian and European newspapers from April 1992 onwards) and in Spain (see the major Spanish newspapers for May 1993). Spain has in fact tackled this problem in its new Law on Public Procurement (Ley 13/1995 de Contratos de las Administraciones Públicas of 18 May) as the French Parliament had previously done when it passed a law exclusively aimed at bringing similar types of practices to an end in the aftermath of similar scandals. Law No. 91–3 of 3 January 1991 (whose Title II incidentally implemented the new public works Directive in French law) establishes a *Commission interministérielle d'enquête* to investigate the regularity of the award procedures. See also Mattera (above, n 2).

[9] With respect to the application of the supplies legislation in the United Kingdom see generally Hartley and Uttley (above, n 5).

[10] See generally Turpin, *Government Procurement and Contracts* (Harlow, 1989) Chapters 3 and 5 for the UK; Lupp, *Objektivität, Transparenz und Nachprüfbarkeit der Angebotswertung bei der Vergabe öffentlicher Bauaufträge* (München, 1992) at 54 *ff* for Germany; Monedero Gil, 'Criterios de adjudicación del contrato administrativo en el derecho comunitario' (1986) No. 21, *Noticias CEE*, 63, for Spain and Goldman, 'An Introduction to the French Law of Government Procurement Contracts' (1987) 20 *George Washington Journal of International Law & Economics* 461 at 468 for France.

review mechanisms may be considered ineffective,[11] internal administrative and political controls on contracting authorities are quite stringent. Budgetary controls of the expenses entered into by contracting authorities exist in all Member States. Hierarchical superiors also exert some monitoring powers on the correct use of public money. To assume systematic discrimination implies assuming systematic breach of applicable rules and the total ineffectiveness of financial and political controls on the activities of contracting authorities. Indeed, it must be remembered that public opinion also exerts considerable pressure.

The assumption that discrimination is systematically applied is also unfounded if we refer to other facts. It has been cogently established that once the provisions of Community Directives have become incorporated into national legal orders, no differentiation between nationally originated rules and supranationally originated rules is made by implementing bodies.[12] Thus, no *a priori* bad disposition on the part of national authorities should be assumed. On the contrary, certain commentators have described their national systems as relatively open to foreign bidders.[13] In the same vein, the fact that publication obligations are increasingly respected also questions the validity of the Commission's assumptions. If bad will exists on the part of contracting authorities, it appears unlikely that the notices published in the Official Journal would have increased so steadily.

From all this it follows that to assume bad will against foreign undertakings is to approach the question in too simplistic a manner and to question unnecessarily the good disposition of national authorities when awarding public contracts under Community rules. This is not to say that discrimination does not exist at all in public contract awards. It is submitted, however, that locally established firms are systematically given preferential treatment only when policy guidelines to that effect are imposed by hierarchically superior administrative orders, or by binding rules and that these are not as widespread as commonly believed. Furthermore, it was suggested earlier that these situations should be treated more flexibly by Community institutions when considerations other than economic efficiency apply, at least until substitute supranational measures are devised in order properly to take into account the needs of disfavoured regions or ailing sectors.

The reasons which may explain the ineffectiveness of the public procurement Directives in achieving intra-Community bidding and awards

---

[11] All these issues are exhaustively analysed in the part of the book devoted to the 'enforcement level' (i.e., Chapters 6 to 10).

[12] Siedentopf et Ziller (eds.), *L'Europe des Administrations? La Mise en Oeuvre de la Législation Communautaire dans les États Membres* (Maastricht, 1988) at 58. See the considerations made when discussing the implementation level in Chapter 4.

[13] See Cleesattel, 'Government procurement in the Federal Republic of Germany' and Blyth, 'Government Procurement in the United Kingdom' (1987) 21 *George Washington Journal of International Law and Economics* 59 at 89 and 127 at 148 respectively.

may therefore be structural. It is submitted that the structure of the markets targeted by the original public procurement Directives has had a more tangible influence on the non-achievement of the Directives' objectives. In the following pages the economic context in which public procurement activities develop and how this affects the application of Community legislation is discussed. On the basis of this analysis, it will be argued that a more selective policy in greater accordance with the legal and economic reality of public procurement and the principle of subsidiarity should have been and should be followed by the supranational institutions. Alternative areas where a more active policy should be implemented are proposed. Finally, some conclusions are put forward.

'ORDINARY' PUBLIC WORKS CONTRACTS AND PUBLIC SUPPLIES CONTRACTS. MARKET STRUCTURE AS AN OBSTACLE TO EUROPEAN WIDE COMPETITION

Ordinary Public Works Contracts

Public works contracts have very particular features since they concern markets which, in contrast with public supplies, do not have a repetitive nature. Construction, which includes building and civil engineering, is a service activity which requires the provider of the service, the contractor, to transfer itself to the site where the work is going to be carried out. Although referred to as one service, it concerns complex works comprising different heterogeneous activities, such as planning, execution and obtaining the supplies for carrying out the work.[14] These are normally ensured by the main contractor who may subcontract one or several of the constituent elements of the project.[15]

Due to these features, international construction markets are peculiar in many ways. Although at first sight it may appear a sector open to international competition, the fact is that within the framework of developed economies, the construction industry is normally locally based. Firms operating in this sector tend to hire their workforce and purchase the required materials as close to the site in which the public work is being carried out as possible. For economic reasons, it is cheaper to do so than to transfer their human and material resources from abroad.[16] Consequently, contractors willing to present an offer must be aware of

---

[14] For a lucid characterization of the public works contracts, see Clouet, 'Travaux publics et Marché Commun' (1969) RMC 83.

[15] See generally Nell, 'Analyse empirique de la portée matérielle d'une libéralisation des marchés publics suisses de travaux au niveau européen' (1993) 51 *Revue Économique et Sociale* 159.

[16] In this context, it is worth recalling the *Rush Portuguesa* case (Case C-113/89, [1990] ECR 1417), which has, as a net effect, reduced any competitive advantage which an undertaking using cheap labour may have in the EC context.

the local market structure in which the work is to be completed. This in turn leads firms taking part in international bids to operate in different national markets through local branches or agreements with local partners. Even firms which restrict their business operations to their own national market are likely to have a well developed network of local branches. These are, therefore, seen as a *sine qua non* for obtaining public works.[17] Apart from the necessary knowledge of the local market, familiarity with the requirements of public authorities seems to be an indispensable element of the commercial strategy of public works firms willing to obtain contracts abroad. Thus, 'what appears on the surface as one of the most international industries is in fact a set of local industries and operates world wide through subsidiaries which are local national companies'.[18] The latter are normally registered as national companies and are composed of experts familiar with the peculiarities of local markets.

In a European context, another important feature is that competitive advantages arising from technological breakthroughs are not common since technological know-how and innovations are relatively well spread amongst top European contractors. Thus, technological advantages play a minor role in the reduction of costs.[19] Thus, inter-state bidding between economically developed States is not common in public works contracts.[20] A different tale is told with respect to public works in developing and Far East countries. Competition for these is fierce because no local competitors exist. Major American, Japanese and European public works firms compete against each other for entry to these markets. The main potential for competition exists in this extra-European context.[21]

[17] Lozano, *International Construction Markets. EC, USA and Japan*, Advisory Committee for Public Procurement, CC/90/73, at 3.

[18] Lozano (above, n 17). The fact that 55% of the European construction market went to American contractors does not contradict this reality (Source: *Engineering News Record* of 17 July 1986). American construction companies are established in Europe through subsidiaries which are familiar with the European market. In the same vein, see Söffner, *Awarding Building and Public Works Contracts in the European Community*, IFO-Studien zur Bauwirtschaft 8/E, Institut für Wirstchaftforshung a. v. (München, 1984) at 149–150.

[19] Söffner (1984) (above, n 18) at 119 and 148.

[20] Barnes, Campbell, and Pepper, in 'Local authorities, Public Procurement and 1992' (1992) *Local Government Studies* 10 at 13. In 1979, the Federal German Statistical Office concluded that building firms carry out the bulk of their orders within a short distance of their head office (around 75% of their total works), *Der Regionale Wirkungsbereich der Beträge in Bauhauptgewerbe* (Wiesbaden, 1980). Another study has found that during the period between 1972 and 1982, German firms generated an average of 60% of their total turnover in their own urban or county district and that only 2% was obtained through building work abroad. This same study concluded that only large firms held an interest in foreign opportunities, and always to a negligible extent. Söffner, 'Kleiner Aktionsradius der Bauunternehmen' in *IFO Schnelldienst* Nr. 15/1979.

[21] Firms have argued that 'if they had an interest whatsoever in working abroad, they look to countries outside Europe, especially OPEC countries, where higher profits could be made, contracts covered lasted several years and relatively little competition was to be faced from local construction firms'. Söffner (1984) (above, n 18) at 147.

These assertions are supported by a comprehensive study on public works contracts carried out on behalf of the Commission, which examined both the demand and the supply side of the market.[22] When asked for the reasons for failing to participate in public invitations to tender in other EC countries, up to 58 per cent of the firms consulted replied that they faced cost disadvantages compared with local competitors. Of those firms which did present an offer, but which were not retained as successful bidders, 84 per cent explained their rejection on the grounds that their prices were too high. In fact, their greater distance from the site, which increases their overall costs, made their offers unacceptable.[23] As for the attitude of the consulted contracting authorities, 88 per cent also justified the rejection of foreign tenderers on the grounds that their proposed prices were too high. The study concludes by stating that 'one of the chief structural features of the construction industry is that it covers a small geographical area, and this is a major reason for the lack of interest in EC-wide tendering or in carrying projects in other EC countries'.[24]

More recent empirical studies point in the same direction. Surveys carried out at local government level in the UK lead to the conclusion that 'through whatever mechanism the Directives are applied, the evidence suggests that little additional interest in UK contracts has been generated from European-based contractors'[25] for public works contracts subject to the new Directive's discipline.[26] One of the possible explanations for this is that 'European contractors with an interest in competing in the UK local authority markets will do so through the acquisition in the British construction industry or joint ventures with domestic contractors rather than tendering for work from a base and in the name of a Continental contractor'.[27]

In this vein we should refer to Clouet who, as far back as 1969, argued that, whereas for public supplies contracts a certain degree of competition may exist between European manufacturers, in the case of public works the economic structure of the markets rendered similar competition unlikely. He also predicted that any attempt by Brussels to open up competition in public works at a European level would only be formally successful, but would hardly have any practical effect.[28] His arguments have largely gone unnoticed, however.

---

[22] Söffner (1984) (above, n 18).   [23] Ibid. at 141.   [24] Ibid. at 31.

[25] Paddon, 'EC Public Procurement Directives and the Competition from European Contractors for Local Authority Contracts in the UK' in Clarke and Pitelis (eds.) *The Political Economy of Privatisation* (London, 1993) 159 at 168.

[26] The local authority Association of Metropolitan Authorities (AMA) survey showed that no expression of interest was received from European contractors to public works contract notices published in the OJ in 1991. See AMA, 'Public Works and Europe, A Report to the AMA's Public Works Committee' 1991. Cited by Paddon (above, n 25).   [27] Ibid.

[28] Clouet (above, n 14) at 84.

Ordinary Public Supplies Contracts

In the case of public supplies contracts it is more difficult to draw general patterns since these involve a great variety of goods. These can range from the consumption of goods by public authorities to perform their daily duties, to highly sophisticated goods, such as telecommunications and computer equipment, aerospace, heavy electrical engineering and so on. The former will be identified as 'current' or 'ordinary' goods, whereas the latter category will be referred to as 'high-tech' goods. The examination of the case for 'high-tech' goods will be undertaken when discussing contracts of European interest.

As in the case of public works contracts, although for rather different reasons, the provision of 'ordinary goods' is likely to be done on a local basis and normally takes place in undistorted competitive conditions. Contrary to the construction sector, where public demand plays a significant role and larger contractors become specialized in public works,[29] the supply side of ordinary goods satisfies, in most sectors, both private and public demand.[30] As a result, the degree of market integration for these products is high, and imports of more competitive foreign goods have already taken place to satisfy the private demand. Multinationals operate through established local distribution networks which supply national private demand. These local distributors also fulfil the requirements of public authorities. Specific imports to meet public requirements are irrelevant or exceptional. Moreover, since the market price for 'current goods' is relatively homogeneous, transport costs are likely to foreclose any competitive advantage which foreign distributors or companies may have. In addition, profits arising from public contracts are normally limited by relevant national regulations to a 'reasonable margin'.[31] Apart from obvious language difficulties, the need to comply with the technical and financial requirements, as well as with the procedural rules involved in contract award procedures, adds further costs to engaging in tendering procedures in foreign countries.[32]

On the public demand side, public authorities behave on the market as

[29] In Switzerland, for instance, public demand in the construction sector was found to represent, depending on the period of time in question, between 35 to 44% of all demand. For civil engineering works above the Directive's 5 million ECU threshold, contractors depended almost exclusively on public authorities, whose contracts represented 88% of the total value. With respect to building, one fifth of all contracts above the threshold are of a public character, whose value represented 17.7% of the total value. See Nell (above, n 15) at 161–163.

[30] For a competent economic analysis of this point see Hindley, 'The Economics of an Accord on Public Procurement Policies' (1977) *The World Economy* 279.

[31] See Turpin (1989) (above, n 10) at Chapter 6; Lupp (above, n 10) at 139 *ff*.

[32] On the practical difficulties incurred in bidding abroad see Fischbein, 'Participation of SMUs in EC Government Contracts. Problems in Practice' (1992) 2 *EC Public Contract Law* 203.

normal consumers of goods, without enjoying any powerful market position. Thus, having a stable and reliable source of supply is regarded as a benefit, whatever short-term advantage there may be in contracting abroad.[33] 'Current goods' are purchased on a 'just in time off the shelf' basis due to limited storage availability, a factor which favours local suppliers. Delivery dates also become important. Thus, 'the most economical and practical method of purchasing supplies would be to buy through a large procuring body and from multinationals through local suppliers'.[34]

Since the market is already a highly integrated one on the private demand side, where subsidiaries and local distributors enjoy a naturally privileged position in competing for public contracts, intra-Community bidding for 'current goods' is therefore the exception rather than the rule. The level of imports in the national economies as a whole range from 19 per cent in the case of Italy to 43 per cent in the case of Belgium.[35] Intra-Community bidding is therefore marginal in overall terms, not because of discriminatory practices, but because direct imports to fulfil public demands are unnecessary. The public supplies contracts Directive would therefore cover only a small number of situations, which does not therefore amount to a real integration of public markets.

That bidding for 'ordinary' public supplies contracts is primarily a 'national boundaries' matter has recently been supported by some empirical studies. Hartley and Uttley have examined the extent to which foreign suppliers participated in UK public procurement markets in four specific sectors in 1992.[36] The authors reviewed a susbtantial number of contract awards advertised in the OJ after the amendment of the public supplies contracts Directive which came into effect in 1989 and was implemented in the UK in 1991. They found that 99.5 per cent of the contracts were awarded to UK based firms. However, an examination of the nationality of the ownership of the successful firm revealed that 64 per cent were UK-owned firms. The second largest group was, curiously enough, US-owned firms (16 per cent), with EC-owned firms obtaining 15 per cent of the contracts. The authors of the survey concluded that the 'cost of non-Europe research underestimated public import penetration by focusing only on contracts awarded to foreign based firms'.[37] Thus, whereas public import penetration measured in terms of the location of the successful tenderer amounts to 1 per cent, 'when ownership of firms is taken into

---

[33] This has, moreover, been recognized as a legitimate consideration to be taken into account with respect to award criteria by the Court of Justice in Case C-324/93, *R* v. *Secretary of State for the Home Department, ex. p. Evans Medical Ltd and Macfarlan Smith Ltd*, judgment of 28 March 1995, not yet reported, noted by Fernández Martín (1995) 4 PPLR CS80.

[34] Barnes and others (above, n 20) at 14.

[35] EC Commission, Communication from the Commission on a Community Regime for Public Procurement in the Excluded Sectors: Water, Energy, Transport and Telecommunications, COM (88) 376, at 12.

[36] These are medical products, shipbuilding, paper products and textiles.

[37] Hartley and Uttley (above, n 5) at 122.

account the analysis suggests import penetration rates are significantly higher'.[38] Equally, at local government level in the UK, a survey of the first two years of operation of the new supplies Directive, showed that out of 315 contracts awarded under the supplies Directives by thirty-one contracting authorities, only three were won by Continental based suppliers, that is, less than 1 per cent.[39]

It is submitted that the main bulk of the Community policy as materialized in the public sector Directives does not take proper account of these realities. The main thrust of the latter is to increase intra-Community bidding by making information available to foreign undertakings, restricting the contracting authorities' margin of discretion and requiring competitive tendering. This clearly implies the belief in a potential market for competition. The structural features which limit the interest of firms in presenting bids for public works contracts and public supplies contracts awarded in other Member States are overlooked by the Commission. It is submitted that the main reasons for the ineffectiveness of Community legislation in the public contracts area are likely to be structural. This is not to say that integration is not taking place in the public procurement area. But this is due more to the dynamics of the economic integration process rather than to the legislative efforts of the Community in the public procurement area. Firms which have established themselves in other Member States to gain access to the States' public markets have done so as part of their overall market expansion strategy and irrespective of the public procurement rules.[40]

THE ALTERNATIVE POLICY. PUBLIC WORKS AND PUBLIC SUPPLIES CONTRACTS OF 'COMMUNITY INTEREST'

The previous considerations should not be read as implying that there is no room for Community action in the field of public contracts. On the

---

[38] Ibid. at 124.

[39] The survey, which was carried out by the AMA, further established that out of 6,699 expressions of interest by candidates about the notices published, only 186 were from non-UK suppliers and that out of 3,844 bids presented, only 16 were from EC-based suppliers. AMA, 'Report by AMA Purchasing and Supply Group' 1991. Cited by Paddon (above, n 25) at 171. Further available statistics point in the same direction. Cox, 'Implementing 1992 Public Procurement Policy: Public and Private Obstacles to the Creation of the Single European Market' (1992) 1 PPLR 139 at 148. Equally, the data provided by Mr Wanstall before the House of Lords Select Committee on the European Communities, *Compliance with Public Procurement Directives*, session 1987–88, 12th Report at 4–5.

[40] This is also the conclusion arrived at by Paddon in his analysis of the local government works contracts (above, n 25) especially at 170 where he holds that 'The impetus for these strategies [acquisition of national companies in the area of public works or joint ventures with national companies] may come from an intention to establish European-wide contracting bases in preparation for the Single Market. But they are unrelated to the procedures of the Directives and point to the need for a more comprehensive and contemporary assessment of the actual patterns of concentration in these sectors so that the real likelihood of increasing competition for contracts can be evaluated'.

contrary, Community action may be useful and necessary as regards contracts which can be referred to as 'contracts of Community interest'. These contracts can be defined in general terms as those contracts which, due to peculiar features, are suited to European-wide competition and, as a result, are likely to give rise to a substantial interest amongst leading specialized European firms. Supranational action with respect to this type of contract is not only justified but necessary. Their more particular features depend, however, on whether their object concerns public works or public supplies.

Public Works Contracts of European Interest

In the case of public works, contracts of Community interest normally concern works of sizeable economic value inserted in large governmental infrastructure development projects. Even though they are of a sporadic nature, they ensure business to contractors for the considerable period of time in which the contract is to be completed. The expected profits are equally large. This type of contract certainly generates an interest in major specialized European firms which are ready to risk large investments in the hope of obtaining the contract. Competition for such contracts is reduced to large firms and, furthermore, the candidates are likely to combine their efforts and know-how to present a serious offer. These contracts are, by nature, bound to be few, although they will be of high value and considerable strategical importance. The number of eventual tenderers with sufficient capacity to present a bid is equally bound to be limited.[41] The IFO-study carried out by the *Institut für Wirtschaftsforschung*[42] showed that European contractors only have an interest in bidding for work contracts abroad when these consist of large special projects.[43]

It is with respect to this type of contract that the construction market acquires its real 'European' potential. The *Storebaelt* case clearly illustrates this statement.[44] The envisaged public works were part of a vast public works project aimed at linking the islands of Finen and Zealand to the Danish mainland. It consisted of the building of a bridge, which was to be complemented by the construction of another bridge and a tunnel. The Danish Government attached great economic and political significance

---

[41] In 1990, construction firms employing more than 400 employees amounted only to 10% of construction firms in Germany, 5% in Italy and 17% in France. Source: groupe de l'industrie suisse de la construction, *Rapport 1990* (Zurich, 1990) at 16.

[42] Söffner (1984) (above, n 18).   [43] Ibid. at 141.

[44] Case C-243/89, *Commission* v. *Denmark* [1993] ECR I-3353. For an exhaustive description of the facts and an accurate legal analysis of the subsequent case before the Court of Justice concerning interim measures, see Lamarca, 'Sospensione cautelare dell'appalto giá aggiudicato e conciliazione giuduziale. Il caso *Storebaelt*' (1991) *Rivista di Diritto Europeo* 803. On the strategic importance of the project as a public work, see Vickerman, 'Transport Infrastructure and Region Building in the European Community' (1994) 32 JCMS 1 at 8.

to the project, as it was one of the most important public works carried out in Denmark in modern times. The interest expressed by different European-based companies was high. The economic magnitude of the contract and the fact that it could lead to securing further contracts to be awarded in the framework of the same project, induced forty-nine firms, differently associated in consortiums in which they had pooled their efforts, to express their interest. The contracting authority, a company controlled by the Danish Government, short-listed five of these consortiums and invited them to present an offer. The number of firms involved was twenty-eight. Subsequent negotiations concluded in the award of the contract to the so-called European Storebaelt Group in June 1989. The consortium was composed of six firms, three Danish, one Dutch, one Swiss and one British.

The contract not only aroused pan-European interest, leading to intra-Community bidding but also to co-operation amongst firms. Supranational enforcement action, as we shall discuss later, is only effective and productive. as regards this type of contract. That contracting authorities respect the Directives' provisions as regards these projects should therefore be the major concern of the Commission's public procurement enforcement policy.[45] Its positive policy, aimed at establishing a European market for public works, should have concentrated on this type of project which, on account of its economic features, is subject to genuinely European competition. Further examples in which Community action could be especially beneficial include those projects concerning the development of European transport infrastructures, such as the network of High-speed railways,[46] or sizeable trans-national projects such as the Channel Tunnel.[47]

Not only is the Community better placed in practical terms to co-ordinate these initiatives, but after Maastricht it enjoys the legal basis to inititiate a policy in the field. The TEU introduced a new Title XII to the EC Treaty concerning 'Trans-European Networks'[48] which states that the Community is to contribute to the establishment and development of trans-European networks in the areas of transport, telecommunications and energy infrastructures. Even though the new provisions only enable the adoption of general guidelines covering the objectives, priorities and broad lines in the field, as well as the identification of projects of common interest, the Commission should take advantage of its powers of initiative and place Member States under increasing pressure to adopt a stance on the issue. This type of initiative is also of particular interest from the point of view of the Community, since it could be justified on regional

[45] See Chapter 6.
[46] See generally Ross, J., 'High-Speed Rail: Catalyst for European Integration?' (1994) 32 JCMS 91.
[47] For further examples of European infrastructure projects which may fulfil the conditions to qualify as of European interest, see Vickerman (above, n 44) at 8 *ff.*
[48] Articles 129(b) to (d) EC.

convergence grounds, it would foster greater economic integration,[49] the spread of technological innovation and, on a Keynesian reading, provide a stimulus for job creation. Through the elaboration of joint projects, it would also arguably favour the development of European systems of co-operation and would be a positive propaganda exercise.

So far, despite the existence of initial plans to give effect to the TEU provisions,[50] most infrastructure is planned and financed at national level.[51] Member States have also been reluctant to proceed with the TEU mandate and any decision on the subject has been delayed.[52] This should not prevent the Commission from claiming greater responsibility with respect to the financing of those projects.[53] In the field of public procurement, the Commission should exploit the new possibilities opened up by the TEU to the full and should call for further powers to co-ordinate, participate and closely supervise the development of these projects, including the award procedures and decisions.[54] In any event, the Commission could legitimately assume a larger role in controlling the respect of Community rules by national authorities in those projects financed through the Cohesion Fund, as it already does with respect to other national projects benefiting from funding from the Structural Funds.[55] This could be further supported by an 'effectiveness' related interpretation of the subsidiarity principle based on the considerations made above.[56]

It must be noted that this alternative policy for public works contracts,

---

[49] See generally Ross (above, n 46) and Vickerman (above, n 44).

[50] EC Commission, *Europe 2000: Outlook for the Development of the Community's Territory*, COM (91) 452; idem, *Proposal for a Council Regulation Introducing a Declaration of European Interest to Facilitate the Establishment of Trans-European Networks in the Transport Domain*, COM (92) 15; idem, *Communication on Transport Infrastructure.* COM (92) 231.

[51] Vickerman (above, n 44) at 13.

[52] See the outcome of the Cannes European Council Summit, June 1995.

[53] Article 29(c)1 provides for the possibility of Community financing of these projects, especially through the Cohesion Fund. So far, however, the only financing mechanisms agreed concern infrastructure projects financed through the Cohesion Fund. Vickerman suggests that in view of the insufficient European funding so far devoted to the development of these infrastructures, the creation of an Infrastructure Fund could provide a possible solution. Vickerman (above, n 44) at 15.

[54] See in this context Clouet (above, n 14) at 86 where he held that the most realistic way forward for Brussels would be '. . . en tout premier lieu—et l'on peut regretter qu'elle ne l'ait déjà fait—d'aborder la définition d'une politique européenne du Génie Civil, ou, plus justement, en considérant la fin et non les moyens d'une politique commune des infrastructures'. In this context see also the statements by the current EC Competition Commissioner Van Miert, 'A Community transport policy requires European networks' (1992) 2 *EC Public Contract Law* 201. For a similar claim for a supranational transport infrastructure policy, see Vickerman (above, n 44).

[55] The main principles guiding this initiative were laid down in a Commission notice to the Member States (Notice C(88) 2510 to the Member States on monitoring compliance with public procurement in the case of projects and programmes financed by the Structural Funds and financial instruments, OJ 1989, C22/3).

[56] See further below in Final Conclusions.

based more on co-ordination and joint programmes than on supranational uniform binding legislation, was initially contemplated by the Commission itself when designing its policy on public procurement.[57] However, the actual practice of the Commission post-1985 as described above shows that emphasis was placed, incorrectly it is submitted, on a more interventionist technique, regulating the area by means of a comprehensive set of detailed rules which have borne few practical fruits. The only scheme which partially responded to this alternative approach consisted in making the use of Structural Funds subject to strict compliance with Community public procurement rules by national contracting authorities.[58]

Public Supplies Contracts of European Interest

A similar selective policy should apply as regards public supplies contracts. Only those contracts which fulfil certain conditions should be the object of supranational policy. In general, this type of contract usually takes place in sectors where high-technology is involved (high-tech goods). The plea for supranational regulation is not only based on their economic significance but also on the great economic benefits which would result for the Community industry as a whole if they were subject to European-wide competition. Since a high potential for increased competition exists, with the economic benefits which would result from it, and the fact that public authorities do apply discriminatory procurement policies in these areas, more decisive action on the part of Community institutions is required.[59] To illustrate this point, the telecommunications sector is taken as the case-study, although any remarks made are *mutatis mutandis* applicable to other sectors dominated by public purchasing, such as transport, energy markets and so on.[60]

First of all, these are highly state-regulated sectors. Prior to 1984, the telecommunications service industry in most OECD countries had been structured on the basis of a monopoly: either state-owned or privately-owned and state-regulated. It was argued that since the industry was a natural monopoly, cost advantages in production were such that it was more efficient for one firm to serve the market rather than a competitive

---

[57] Emerson and others, *The Economics of 1992. The EC Commission's Assessment of the Economic Effects of Completing the Internal Market* (Oxford, 1988) at 67 *ff*.   [58] See above, n 55.

[59] These considerations are demonstrated by the Italian case. See Pontarollo, 'Procurement in the Utility Sector in Italy' (1994) 3 PPLR 1.

[60] Contracts awarded in these sectors normally include the provision of services such as installation, technical advice, after sale maintenance and so on. This is so for the telecommunications sector where 'the development of the regulatory, legal and operational framework has been such as to tie closely the service and equipment sides of the industry' (OECD, ICCP, *The Telecommunications Industry. The Challenges of Structural Change* (Paris, 1988) at 9). It is assumed for present purposes that the value of the goods supplied is higher than that of the services attached to them.

structure. As public welfare considerations viewed telecommunications as a public service based on the principle of universal service provision, it also required active State involvement.[61] Public authorities have traditionally maintained strong working relationships with the operating firms, which often materialized in a tight control of their activities, including purchasing.[62]

Secondly, in these key economic sectors, the public sector enjoys a dominant position in many cases, be it as a consumer or as a consumer and producer. In fact, the public sector is the main consumer (from 50 per cent to 80 per cent of total industry output).[63] In the telecommunications market[64] public purchasing claims up to 90 per cent of the industry's output.[65] Since this is the case, the purchasing power of public authorities has been regarded as the main barrier to entry. A further consequence of this is that, whereas public contracts in general can only act as a complementary tool to economic intervention, this function acquires special relevance in these sectors. The dominant position enjoyed by the public sector allows it to implement different economic policies through public contracts.[66]

Member States are most reluctant to let free competition take place in these particular areas. Most national policies applied in these sectors aim at the development of competitive national technology, an increase in national production levels and the maintenance of independence from foreign sources. Thus, telecommunication networks are supplied by national producers with, on average, more than 70 per cent of their needs. This figure can be as high as 90 per cent in certain cases, where the national enterprise is strong.[67] Thus, 'national champions' are consciously favoured and heavily protected from foreign competition through preferential public procurement. It is not a coincidence that the main sectors where the implementation of public procurement policies might have had a tangible economic effect were omitted from the first Directives.[68] Supranational

---

[61] ICCP, OCDE (above, n 60) at 10.
[62] EC Commission, COM (88) 376 (above, n 35) at 74.   [63] Ibid. Table 4 at 14.
[64] For a description of the telecommunications sector and its market structure see in general, EC Commission, COM (88) 376 (above, n 35) at 298 *ff*; OECD, ICCP (above, n 60); Roobeek, 'Telecommunications: an Industry in Transition', in de Jons (ed.), *The Structure of European Industry* (Doordrecht, 1988) 297; Scherer, 'Telecommunications and Public Procurement', paper presented at the *Europe-Japan Economic Research Center* seminar in Brussels, 25 May 1988.   [65] EC Commission, COM (88) 376 (above, n 35) at 14.
[66] For the use of public procurement in Japan and the USA to develop competitive national industries in high-tech sectors, see Richonnier, *Les Metamorphoses de l'Europe. De 1769 à 2001* (Paris, 1986) at 243. See also MacGowan and Thomas, 'Bureaucratic Rules versus Competition? An Alternative Approach to Utilities Procurement in the EC Electricity Sector'. Paper presented at the *Implementing and Enforcing the EC Procurement Directives* Conference, Birmingham, April 1993.
[67] EC Commission, COM (88) 376 (above, n 35) at 73 and 75.
[68] Although the original public works Directive 71/305 did not exclude telecommunications from its scope of application, the fact that many firms operating that sector enjoyed an

action is therefore justified *per se* to end traditional protectionism and systematic discrimination.

Moreover, the increasing need to develop a solid European telecommunications industry also reinforces the claims for stronger positive intervention by Community institutions. The market is becoming increasingly universal and competition with third countries, especially Japan and the USA, is fiercer and the European industry as a whole is currently in a disadvantaged position.[69] Economies of scale play an essential role in achieving economic efficiency and competitive structures. Domestic markets are not large enough to allow firms to capitalize on the necessary investments in research and development (R&D) which otherwise would give them an advantage in world markets. A total opening of public contracts to European-wide competition would bring better resource allocation, since contracting authorities would buy in the most advantageous economic conditions. Likewise, economies of scale, deriving from the restructuring of the different sectors along with market integration (in so far as national administrations would buy on a European-wide basis and not only on a national one) would be achieved. Finally, true competition in these areas will imply concentration of R&D efforts and dissemination of technological innovations which would increase the competitive position of European industry in world markets.[70]

In brief, the opening up of public contracts to European-wide competition in these key sectors is a necessary prior step to the development of a competitive European industry. Since the competition war occurs in a world context, protecting national markets is no longer a sensible policy. Industrial restructuring and a shift from a national to a European conception of industry is essential. Community intervention becomes especially suitable in these sectors. To use the words of an economist, 'international attention [to public procurement] should be focused on industries whose sole or dominant buyer . . . is the national government or its agencies'.[71]

These sectors have only recently been the object of Community action. A Directive on public procurement in the Utilities sectors was

---

autonomous legal status with respect to public authorities prevented the practical application of its rules.

[69] Richonnier (1986) (above, n 66) at 123 *ff*; Roobeek (above, n 64) at 301 *ff*. See generally, Pelkmans and Winters, *Europe's Domestic Market* (London, 1988), especially at 52.

[70] See the economic analysis regarding these sectors by Tovias, 'The Impact of Liberalizing Government Procurement Policies of Individual EC Countries on Trade with Non-members' (1990) *Weltwirtschaftliches Archiv* 722. In the light of his economic analysis he claims, at 733–4, that increased competition within the Community in the telecommunications sector, matched with temporary protection from third countries' competitive pressures, will result in the strengthening of European industry vis-à-vis third countries.

[71] Hindley (above, n 30) at 284.

adopted by the Council in 1990.[72] Its contents are excessively vague and non-compelling, however, and it is doubtful whether it will bring any substantial modification of present trends.[73] This Directive has been complemented by a Remedies Directive which is applicable to these sectors and which is equally flexible.[74] This is a small step in the right direction. However, even if a Directive is welcome as an initial measure, a more effective approach would have been the development of a more coherent and general policy favouring co-operation or partnerships between national firms in the elaboration of common projects in the excluded sectors.[75] The harmonization of technical norms, which constitute one of the hardest barriers to entry, should also be tackled. Supranational measures which minimize the negative economic results which an opening to European competition will inevitably bring in some Member States would also be required. Otherwise it is unlikely that substantial improvement would take place. In addition, tighter supranational control of public contracts conferring exclusive rights to national firms for the exploitation and management of networks in these sectors is also required. These aspects are missing from the Commission's approach and from the final Directive adopted.

Some authors have maintained that the liberalization of public procurement in these sectors should not be treated as the main priority. They argue that the key objective should be the creation of European-wide competition conditions for the provision of the sectors which have been protected. Once the obstacles to free competition are removed, Utilities would enter into direct competition which would inevitably result in the liberalization of public procurement policies. The need to cut down costs and buy from the most efficient sources in order to provide a better service at a better value for consumers, would dismantle inefficient procurement practices. The adoption of the Directives in their current form constitutes, according to this view, an unnecessary complication and a deviation of resources from other targets.[76] These considerations are obviously absent from the mind of the Commission, which seems to have placed high expectations on the practical impact of the Utilities Directive. In several decisions concerning the application of the Merger Control Regulation[77]

---

[72] Council Directive 90/531/EEC on the procurement procedures of entities operating in the water, energy, transport and telecommunications sectors, OJ 1990, L297. Substituted three years later by Council Directive 93/38 of 14 June 1993, in order to include the services contracts awarded by the covered entities (OJ 1993, L199/84). See Chapter 1 at n 127.

[73] After analysing the situation of three Utilities sectors in Italy and the possible impact of the Utilities Directive, Pontarollo reaches the conclusions that the 'desired opening of the public markets in the so-called excluded sectors does not . . . seem to be imminent'. The reasons for these conclusions are found in the lack of intention of interested parties, both supply and demand sides, in altering the status quo (above, n 59) at 14.

[74] Directive 92/13/EEC, OJ 1992, L76/14. See Chapter 1 at n 129.

[75] See below the conclusions to this section.   [76] McGowan and Thomas (above, n 66).

[77] Council Regulation 4064/89 of 21 December, OJ 1990, L257/14.

to the Utilities sectors, the Commission when assessing the impact of the mergers in question, seems to have overestimated the increase in competition which may result from the application of the Utilities Directive. From these decisions, it follows that the Commission, as Brown has rightly pointed out, is excessively 'over-optimistic in its expectations for the opening of markets as a result of the procurement directives . . . causing it to over-emphasise hypothetical sources of increased competitions which have yet to materialise'.[78]

The Public Services Contracts

Finally, mention must be made of the services market. For certain types of services where proximity to the customer is not a decisive factor, competition on a European basis is also likely to be feasible. Additional costs of providing services on a cross-border basis are a relatively small proportion of the total costs involved. A service provider may well develop the core of his or her activities from the home based office and travel around or communicate with contracting authorities. A financial adviser, a lawyer, an architect, a computer programmer, an insurance company and so on may clearly benefit from opening up the public markets, especially taking into account that services account for 25 per cent of total public procurement.[79]

A Directive covering this area has also been adopted by the Council.[80] Its main features correspond exactly to those studied for the main public works and public supplies Directives. Reference should therefore be made to the considerations made in relation to those measures. It is submitted that for those services where proximity is not a relevant factor, this Directive constitutes an important step in the overall procurement policy of the Community.

Defence Sector Contracts

Another sector where Community involvement is likely in the future is defence procurement. This issue initially lay outside the scope of the EC Treaty. The EC Treaty was not conceived as an instrument to co-ordinate and, potentially, integrate the Member States' defence policies.[81] However, military industry nowadays plays an important role in modern economies.

---

[78] Brown, 'High Hopes for Competitive Supply Markets: The Impact of Public Procurement on EC Merger Control' (1994) 3 PPLR 16 at 29. The author undertakes a complete critical analysis of the adopted decisions and the Commission's approach.

[79] De Graaf, 'Community Law: Latest Developments' (1992) 1 PPLR 317. See also Fischbein (above, n 32) at 203–204.   [80] EC Council Directive 92/50, OJ 1992, L209/1.

[81] See Cooper, 'Pre-conditions for the emergence of a European common market in armaments' (1983) *Centre for European Policy Studies*, No. 18, 7.

Public procurement in the field of defence amounts annually to a total of 40 to 50 billion ECU.[82] These amounts acquire further relevance if one considers the importance of military industry for the development of high-technology, which is afterwards used for civil purposes.[83] Furthermore, the costs of defence equipment are already high and there are indications of a trend towards rising costs.[84]

The situation of the military industry in the Community is highly inefficient. In their desire for independence and security, Member States have created compartmentalized national defence industries, with national champions heavily protected by the bias of 'buy national policies'.[85] As a result of this, there is no degree of market interpenetration whatsoever in this industry, which in turn leads to duplication of R&D costs, which small national markets can no longer bear, and to the impossibility of achieving economies of scale.[86] According to some authors, a *conditio sine qua non* to becoming competitive in world markets is to have an 'EC government procurement in the defence sector which could be used as a platform from which European firms can launch an attack on world markets'.[87]

It is in this context that Article 223(1)(b) EC operates.[88] Although not explicitly mentioned in the wording of this provision, public procurement is directly affected by it. In summary terms, Article 223 provides for a general exemption from the applicability of Community legislation for products intended *for specifically military purposes*. As a result, all secondary

---

[82] EC Commission, *Public Procurement in the Community*, COM (86) 375 at 1.

[83] As Richonnier points out, the micro-electronic revolution that placed the USA at the top of the world micro-electronic industry was greatly influenced by public purchasings linked to the military and aerospatial programmes. Richonnier (1986) (above, n 66) at 243 *ff*; Richonnier in 'Europe's Decline is not Irreversible' (1984) 22 JCMS 235. For the importance of defence procurement in today's commercial world, see further Strange, 'A Dissident View' in Bieber, Dehousse, Pinder, Weiler (eds.), *1992: One European Market? A Critical Analysis of the Commission's Internal Market Strategy* (Baden-Baden, 1988) at 73. For an analysis of the current situation of the armaments market in Europe, see the survey by *The Economist*, 3 September, 1994.

[84] For instance, each generation of new equipment might cost, in real terms, two to four times the cost of the equipment being replaced; Hartley, 'Public Procurement: a Community Market for Military Hardware and Technology' (1987) 25 JCMS at 237.

[85] The archetypal example in the European context being France. For an exhautive analysis of the French 'autarchic' policies in the field of defence see Kolodziej, *Making and Marketing Arms. The French Experience and its Implications for the International System* (Princeton, 1987) at Chapter 8.	[86] Hartley (above, n 84) at 238.

[87] Strange in Bieber, Dehousse, Pinder, Weiler (eds.) (above, n 83) at 76.

[88] Article 223(1)(b) EC: '(1) The provisions of this Treaty shall not preclude the application of the following rules:... (b) Any Member State may take such measures as it considers necessary for the protection of the essential interests of its security which are connected with the production of or trade in arms, munitions and war material; such measures shall not adversely affect the conditions of competition in the common market regarding products which are not intended for specifically military purposes.'. See further Wheaton, 'Defence Procurement and the European Community: the Legal Provisions' (1992) 1 PPLR 432.

legislation adopted with the aim of liberalizing national public procurement policies is not applicable to the aforementioned military goods.[89]

So far, the Commission's initiative has had a negative character in the sense that it is limited to clarifying the boundaries of the exception. Positive steps, however, have been announced. The Commission, in an answer given to a written question posed by Mr Scott-Hopkins in the European Parliament concerning a 'common defence procurement policy', declared that: 'The Commission has already stated . . . that it will now address as a matter of priority the question of defence procurement in the light of the provisions of the Treaty. The appropriate initiatives concerning the question of defence procurement will be considered with a view to adoption and implementation in accordance with the realisation of the internal market by 31 December 1992'.[90]

The political and economic connotations of military defence mean that the question of public procurement in the defence sector is highly delicate. The issue of military co-operation in procurement is a question which has only a political answer. There is no legal basis in the Treaty, except Article 235 EC which would allow Member States to follow a common defence strategy. Only a modification of the Treaties could provide for the basis of a common military industry. However, a first 'political' step taken in the framework of political co-operation was the adoption of Title III of the SEA, i.e., 'Treaty provisions on European co-operation in the sphere of foreign policy'. These provisions do not have a binding character, but have prompted the Commission to suggest that 'the question of defence procurement will also need to be addressed in the light of both the provisions of the EC Treaty and the European co-operation provisions on the SEA'.[91]

The situation has also been altered by the TEU and the introduction of the so-called second pillar, which is part of the Union but outside the EC Treaty framework. The issue of a security policy is explicitly tackled by Title V 'Provisions on a common foreign and security policy' which consists of Articles J, and J.1 to J.11 which lay down the legal framework in which the future common foreign and security policy is to be developed. Article J.4 provides for the institutional arrangements in the more specific field of a potential common defence policy. This will take place through

---

[89] A list of these products was adopted in a Council decision as long ago as 15 April 1958. Member States, however, have been broadly interpreting, or rather abusing, the exception. So, what was initially intended to be an objective and well-defined exception has, in practice, been extended to cover all purchasing made by defence agencies. The Commission, after an initial *laissez-faire* approach, has tightened up its policy towards procurement policies of defence agencies. A more inflexible interpretation of the wording of this provision is currently being applied. [90] 'Europe', 6 April 1989.

[91] EC Commission, *Report on the Progress made in Achieving the 1992 Internal Market*, COM (88) 650 at 17. See further Kirchner, 'Has the Single European Act Opened the Door for a Security Policy?' (1990) *Revue d'Intégration Européenne* 1.

a closer collaboration between the European Union and the operating Western defence organizations, NATO and the Western European Union (WEU). A so-called Western Armaments Group already exists within the WEU, in the context of which a policy on defence procurement is applied.[92] Article J.4 TEU could provide the legal basis for devising supranational initiatives in defence procurement. In fact, the issue of defence procurement is currently being subject to a thorough appraisal by the Commission's services and possible Community action in the field is being designed. The enhancement of the role of the WEU and its institutional relationship with the Community are being discussed at political level. It looks likely that any development in the area of defence procurement will come through the reinforcement of the WEU institutional structure and a more active participation of the Commission in it.[93] Within the specific context of the EC Treaty, a modification of Article 223 EC seems the only possible solution to bring defence procurement within the scope of the EC Treaty.

CONCLUSIONS

The public works and the public supplies Directives have been ineffective in achieving their established goal of enhancing intra-Community bidding and contract awards to foreign firms, since most of the public markets covered are supplied on a local basis. The Community policy is clearly inadequate and its legal implementation has not taken into account the structural features of the targeted markets. The first four public procurement Directives address what we have called 'ordinary public works and public supplies contracts', which are not often suited to European-wide competition. No relevant intra-Community bidding is likely to take place which renders the objectives of the Community rules irrelevant. Medium-sized and small undertakings lack the minimum structure required and are therefore unlikely to compete for public contracts abroad.[94] Any integration which has occurred is due to the effect of the market strategies of firms rather than the impact of the public procurement legislation.

Since 1985 the Commission has not only not changed its policy with respect to the main public works and public supplies contracts, but it has spent time and human and material resources in reinforcing its previous misguided approach. In fact, it has amended the original Directives by imposing more obligations on contracting authorities.[95] The likely result

---

[92] See further Arrowsmith, 'Public Procurement as an Instrument of Policy and the Impact of Market Liberalisation' (1995) 111 LQR 235 at 260 *ff*.

[93] See further Heibourg, 'A European Defence Industry: Dream or Reality?', *NATO's Sixteen Nations*, Dec 1988–Jan 1989.

[94] House of Lords (above, n 39) at 14; Cox (above, n 39) at 147.

[95] The only positive change seems to be the increasing of the threshold to 5 million ECU which is more in line with reality.

of this would be a substantial increase in bureaucratic costs involved in awarding a certain range of public works contracts which do not provoke any commercial interest in foreign firms. In this sense, Cox has pointed out with respect to the new Directives that tender costs are likely to be increased because 'firms will have to absorb more complicated and time consuming rules and adhere to an inflexible tendering time-table . . . The consequence of this is that firms will attempt to cover both the extra costs of a more sophisticated and complex contract process and the costs of their failure to secure the contract by increasing the prices for all their public contracts bids.'.[96]

Positive Community action in the sectors we have defined as of European interest seems a more effective target. This is also required by current trends in world market forces which call for the development of a supranational strategy. National markets have become insufficient on their own. The Commission's policy should aim at devising the means to allow for a smooth opening of these markets. This means putting a general process into operation which integrates the different national interests and gradually substitutes applicable domestic policies.

The main guidelines of this policy should be the favouring of co-operation between the main European firms through the launch of European projects. This would include major public works to be carried out in the framework of Trans-European networks which could be supervised by the Commission services and probably financed by it. This is a feasible task which would take into account the available Commission human and material resources as well as its competences under the EC Treaty. National reluctance could have been overcome by developing European projects similar to the Airbus, whose partial success has been guaranteed by the fact that most European governments have taken part in it.[97] More negotiations with the actors involved, imaginative alternatives and the selection of targets more relevant for the European economy should have been preferred, rather than the imposition of more bureaucratic obligations on contracting authorities and strict buy-efficient approaches.

In this sense, the SEA and the TEU furnish the legal basis on which this policy may be carried out. Article 24 SEA could provide for a partial legal basis on which supranational measures in the field of public procurement may be developed. This provision added a 'Research and Technological Development' policy to the existing policies of the Community which

---

[96] Cox (above, n 39) at 146. For another critical view based on similar arguments, see Boyle, 'Regulated Procurement—A Purchaser's Perspective' (1995) 4 PPLR 105.

[97] See Rallo, 'The European Community Industrial Policy Revisited. The case of Aerospace' (1984) 22 JCMS 245. Similar conclusions are reached by Hobday with respect to the European semiconductor industry. Its resurgence was favoured by State co-operation which took place within the framework of the Community EUREKA, BRITE, ESPRIT and RACE programmes, 'The European Semiconductor Industry: Resurgence and Rationalisation' (1989) 28 JCMS 155.

consists of Article 130(f) to 130(q) EC.[98] Within its framework, and pursuant to Article 130(f), the strengthening of the scientific and technological basis of the European industry becomes an aim of the Community.

Pursuant to that provision, the action of the Community in this field must be directed at favouring research and technological innovation through the encouraging of co-operation between industry and research centres so that undertakings are able to exploit the Community's internal market strategy to the full, 'in particular through the opening up of national public contracts'.[99] The simple mention of public contracts in Article 130(f) EC does not give a general legal competence to Community institutions to enact measures with the aim of opening up public contracts to European competition. However, once the link between public contracts and research and technological development is established, the Community institutions may 'exploit' this marginal reference to public contracts contained in Article 130(f) to adopt measures in the field of public procurement, provided these measures are connected with the pursuance of research and technological development in European industry.[100]

As for the TEU, the new Title XII on 'Trans-European Networks', together with the subsidiarity principle, afford new legal grounds on which the Commission may claim greater powers with respect to the control of contracts awarded in the framework of large infrastructure projects. It is up to the Commission to table imaginative proposals to enhance its role in these cases. In this context, it is worth noting the positive effects that have flowed from the Commission's decision to make the funding of projects and programmes by the Community's structural instruments conditional on compliance with the Community rules on public procurement. Thus, abiding by the public procurement rules is a prerequisite to benefit from the Community's Structural Funds.[101]

A cost-benefit analysis[102] suggests that supranational action should concentrate on those areas where most potential benefits for the European

---

[98] Previously, such measures could only have been based on Article 235 EEC. See generally Bosco, 'Commentaire de L'Acte Unique Européenne' (1987) 23 RTDE 377.

[99] See Article 130(f)(1) and (2). The Community follows the Japanese experience, whose predominant situation in the world market in most of the high-tech sectors is due to an active policy of co-operation between industry and research centres, led by the omnipresent Ministry for Industrial Affairs, the MITI. Richonnier (1984) (above, n 83).

[100] In this connection, see the decision of the European Parliament concerning the Council's common position on the Commission's proposal for a Directive amending Directive 77/62 in which it mentioned Articles 130 (a) to 130(f) as a suitable legal basis to adopt measures on public procurement (OJ 1988, C13/66).   [101] See above at n 55.

[102] A cost-benefit analysis is here understood as the process by which policy-makers 'determining the social goals to be achieved, identifying and assessing accurately and comprehensively the benefits and costs of proposed agency action, accounting for who will benefit by each option in a detailed manner and by whom the costs of each will be borne, and providing an exposition of alternatives detailing the foregoing information' choose 'among several possible actions (including non-action)', 'Project: the Impact of Cost-Benefit Analysis on Federal Administrative Law' (1990) 42 *Administrative Law Review* 545 at 552.

economy as a whole flow from the resources spent. Accordingly, Community action should have been aimed at securing undistorted competition in contracts defined as being of European interest. Not only is the Community framework the best one to bring together national interests, but from an organizational point of view, this would considerably reduce the Commission's workload and allow it to concentrate on a more selective and effective range of contracts, rather than on a vast number of little contracts irrelevant for the development of European industry. The Commission's efforts have been misdirected and its resources ineffectively spent in championing its previous policy. Although action has already been taken, the regulation of the excluded sectors and services has come late and the main policy does not seem to have been substantially altered.

The relevant question is, why has the Commission applied an inefficient policy in public procurement? The answer can only be speculative. It seems that the original Directives were not based on any thorough research.[103] The only evidence taken into consideration seems to have been the poor record of intra-Community awards and the fact that national authorities mainly fulfilled their public procurement requirements from local sources. Since no compromise could be reached to cover those sectors where public procurement policies really mattered in a transnational context, the legislation adopted was limited to the ordinary public works and supplies contracts.

Since 1985, administrative inertia and the political importance attached to the public procurement issue has led the Commission to persist in its original targets, despite the existence of at least some research questioning its assumptions. The only sensible modification of its policy was to increment the public works Directive threshold from 1 million to 5 million ECU which was, moreover, justified on the basis of the protection of local markets and small and medium-sized enterprises. It seems that the political momentum and the conception of public procurement as a politically important test case shadowed any other consideration. No overall cost-benefit analysis seems to have been applied and this must be criticized.

---

[103] The original public supplies Directive 77/72 was preceded in 1974 by a report in which two experts were charged by the Commission with the task of examining the reasons underlying the lack of market integration in the public procurement area. The authors concluded that the main reason was the lack of political will on the part of national administrations to open up their purchasing activities to European-wide competition. They stated that '. . . there is a deep-rooted feeling, common to politicians, officials and industry, and invariably supported by the organs of public opinion, that the taxpayers' money should be used to purchase domestic goods and not foreign goods', Charpentier and Clark, *Public Purchasing in the Common Market,* (Brussels, 1974), cited by Mclachlan (above, n 2) at 370.

6

The Enforcement Level (I): The Commission's Centralized Enforcement of Public Procurement Rules[1]

INTRODUCTION

An analysis of the available enforcement mechanisms to ensure proper application of Community public procurement rules must necessarily start with those provided at centralized level. The main questions addressed are whether the policy applied by the Commission and the use made of Article 169 EC proceedings to challenge infringements produce effective results in the public procurement area.

In the first section, Article 169 EC is analysed and its insufficiencies as a legal tool to ensure the proper enforcement of public procurement rules are discussed. Secondly, an examination of the current practice of the Commission is undertaken. In the light of this analysis, it is submitted that the Commission's early policy has been misconceived and that a more select-ive policy should have been followed. The main features of this possible alternative policy are then explored.

THE MEANS OF CENTRALIZED CONTROL: ARTICLE 169 EC

Preliminary Remarks

Centralized control in its pre-judicial stages is exercised by the Commis-sion of the European Communities in its role as guardian of the Treaties.[2] The main legal instrument by which the Commission implements this type of control is Article 169 EC, which lays down a cumbersome and time-consuming procedure aimed at bringing an end to alleged infringements of Treaty or secondary legislation by Member States. Article 169 EC con-tains two distinct phases, usually known as the administrative phase and the judicial phase. In the former, the Commission sends a formal letter of notice to the Member State concerned informing it of the existence of an alleged infringement of primary or secondary Community law on the part of a public authority, and inviting it to submit pertinent observations. If

---

[1] An earlier version of this chapter has been published in (1993) 2 PPLR 40.
[2] Article 155 EC.

the response is non-existent or unsatisfactory, the Commission then issues a reasoned opinion as a final step before the judicial stage of the procedure. The Commission must clearly establish its position as regards the alleged infringement therein, as well as the legal basis of the eventual reference to the Court of Justice. In cases where a Member State does not conform with the reasoned opinion, the matter is brought before the Court.[3]

Throughout this procedure there are regular contacts between Commission and national officials to discuss the matter and to attempt to reach eventually an amicable settlement. This is achieved in a high proportion of cases. In fact, normally the mere initiation of the procedure provokes settlement of the case before the judicial stage is reached.[4] This is possibly the main advantage of using Article 169 EC. Other advantages are that it leaves a wide margin of discretion to the Commission with respect to the infringements to be pursued and allows for a solution to the crisis through negotiation with the defaulting Member State.[5]

This general pattern also applies to the specific area of public procurement. In the period 1984–1990, (see Figure 6 at the end of this chapter) the Commission opened 99 infraction dossiers. These constitute the step prior to the formal decision to engage the Article 169 EC procedure. During this phase, informal contacts are initiated between the Commission services and the Member State in default. The opening of such a dossier implies that the Commission believes that there is a *prima facie* infringement, although, for different reasons, it may decide not to pursue it formally. In the case of infringements of public procurement rules, Article 169 EC proceedings usually follow the opening of an infraction dossier and a formal letter of notice is normally sent. In fact, all 99 infraction dossiers were transformed into Article 169 EC procedures. The 'reasoned opinion' stage was reached on 67 occasions, out of which only 18 cases (18 per cent) were brought before the Court of Justice. Thus, 32 cases (32 per cent) were settled after the sending of an Article 169 EC formal letter, while in another 33 cases (33 per cent) a settlement was agreed after the reasoned opinion was issued. The course to be followed in the remaining cases had not been decided by the Commission when this survey was

---

[3] See in general, Schermers and Waelbroeck, *Judicial Protection in the European Communities*, 4th edn. (Deventer, 1987), at 250–285; Dashwood and White, 'Enforcement Actions under Articles 169 and 170 EEC' (1989) 14 ELRev 388; Evans, 'The Enforcement Procedure of Article 169 EEC: the Commission Discretion' (1979) 4 ELRev 440.

[4] In this connection, see the studies by Krislov, Ehlermann and Weiler, 'The Political Organs and the Decision-Making Process in the US and the European Community' in Cappelletti, Seccombe and Weiler, (eds.), *Integration through Law*, vol. I, book 2, *Political Organs, Integration Techniques & Judicial Process* (Berlin, 1986) 66 *ff.* See also the annual reports of the Commission to the European Parliament on the application of Community law.

[5] Evans (above, n 3) at 449–450. See in particular Snyder, 'The Effectiveness of European Community Law: Institutions, Processes, Tools and Techniques' (1993) 56 MLR 19 at 27.

carried out (around 16 cases, or 16 per cent).[6] From this data it follows that most conflicts concerning public procurement, around 66 per cent, are settled between the Commission and Member States, without recourse to the Court of Justice.

The Scope of Article 169 EC. The Concept of State

The procedure under Article 169 EC may only be used by the Commission against Member States, that is, to challenge alleged infringements committed by the State. The notion of State for the purposes of Article 169 EC must be defined in the light of the Court of Justice's case law. National legal considerations become relevant, however, when the supranational criteria are applied to the facts of the specific case. The Court has given a very broad definition of what bodies and organs constitute the concept. The main decisions in this respect can be divided into two groups. The first category comprises cases in which the direct effect doctrine was at stake. A second group involves cases concerning the economic intervention powers of the State, especially in the field of State aids under the EC Treaty. An institutional definition has arisen from the former set of cases, whereas a definition based on the degree of control exercised by the State over the body in question has been applied in the context of the latter.[7]

The Institutional Definition

According to this definition, all bodies and organs belonging to the executive power of the State, that is, the public administration, including decentralized authorities, are embodied in the institutional definition of state for Community purposes. This notion obviously covers all central govern-

---

[6] The author tried to update this survey by requiring some information concerning the period 1991–1994 from DG XV officials. Unfortunately, and despite the general statements of the Commission concerning the need to increase transparency and accountability of Community action, some of the officials refused to provide any of the requested information. In view of this, the only data available are those in Figure 5 at the end of the chapter, although unofficially it was stated that the trend has not altered.

[7] The Court has described this second definition as a 'functional' one. This terminology is confusing. Indeed, a functional notion implies that the entity in question is defined with reference to its functions and not with reference to the degree of control that other entities exercise upon it. Moreover, a definition based on the functions rather than on the degree of control was applied by the Court in other cases such as *Johnston* and *Marshall I*. For these reasons and for the sake of greater precision, a different terminology is used in this chapter, even at the risk of departing from the Court's own terminology. For a discussion of the notion of State for Community purposes in the context of the direct effect doctrine, see Curtin, 'The Province of Government: Delimiting the Direct Effect of Directives in the Common Law Context' (1990) 15 ELRev 195; Hecquard-Theron, 'La notion d'Etat en droit communautaire' (1990) 26 RTDE 693.

ment agencies. Local and regional decentralized public administration and their agencies are equally included.[8] As regards other powers of the State, case law has extended the notion to cover infractions committed by 'whatever the agency of the State whose action or inaction is the cause of the failure to fulfil its obligations, even in the case of a constitutionally independent institution'.[9] Thus, the Court has held that national legislatures are accountable for the fulfilment of Community obligations.[10] As for national courts, they have been placed under the duty to observe Community obligations and to interpret their national laws to give full effect to applicable Community rules.[11] They may therefore also be held liable for non-fulfilment of their obligations under Community law.[12] Since *Marshall* it is also clear that this institutional notion of state for Community law purposes applies 'regardless of the capacity in which the [State] is acting, whether employer or public authority'.[13]

However, a grey zone existed as regards public bodies and other bodies not formally integrated in any of the three classic state powers, but which performed duties or functions closely related to those of public authorities. With respect to these increasingly numerous cases, the Court has developed a sort of functional definition, pursuant to which the notion of State for the purposes of the direct effect doctrine covers all so-called 'public authorities' or 'emanations of the State'.[14] Although the Court did not specify what conditions must be fulfilled for a body to fall within these concepts, it seems that it requires the performance of, or a close link with a traditional public function or duty.[15] Thus, professional organizations fall within the notion of State in so far as they are involved in the performance of a public duty.[16] In *Johnston*, the Court maintained that the respondent

---

[8] Case 197/84, *Steinhauser* v. *Ville de Biarritz* [1985] ECR 1819 and Case 103/88, *Fratelli Constanzo* [1989] ECR 1839. It is worth noting that both cases concerned the award of public contracts.

[9] Case 77/69, *Commission* v. *Belgium* [1970] ECR 243, at para. 15, Case 8/70, *Commission* v. *Italy* [1970] ECR 966.

[10] Joined Cases 314 to 316/81 and 83/82, *Procureur de la République* v. *Waterkeyn* [1982] ECR 4355 at para. 14.

[11] Case 14/85, *Sabinne von Colson et E. Kamman* v. *Land Nordrhein-Westfalen* [1984] ECR 1891; Case 79/85, *Harz* v. *Deutsche Tradax* GmbH [1984] ECR 1921; Case 222/84 *Johnston* v. *Chief Constable of the Royal Ulster Constabulary* [1986] ECR 1651; Case C-106/89, *Marleasing SA* v. *La Comercial Internacional de Alimentación SA* [1990] ECR 4135.

[12] See Dashwood and White (above, n 3) at 391 and the bibliography cited therein.

[13] Case 15/84, *Marshall* v. *Southampton and South West Hampshire Area Health Authority (Marshall I)* [1986] ECR 723 at 749.

[14] Case 15/84, *Marshall I* (above, n 13); Case 222/84, *Johnston* (above, n 11). The Court of Justice uses different terminology to refer to the same concept, which has caused certain confusion. For a more detailed analysis of these cases see Curtin (above, n 7) at 196 *ff*, especially at 199.   [15] See Hecquard-Theron (above, n 7) 696 *ff*; Curtin (above, n 7) 214 *ff*.

[16] Case 271/82, *Auer* v. *Ministère Public* [1983] ECR 2727. Hecquard-Theron (above, n 7) 697 *ff*.

body, the Chief Constable of the Royal Ulster Constabulary, by fulfilling the function of maintaining public order and safety, was to be regarded as an 'emanation of the State'. Finally, in *Foster*[17] the Court of Justice also gave a broad definition of what was to be understood by bodies coming within the concept of State. In answering a preliminary reference under Article 177 EC submitted by the House of Lords, it held that any directly effective provisions of a Directive can be relied upon against 'a body, whatever its legal form, which has been made responsible, pursuant to a measure adopted by the State and has for that purpose special powers beyond those which result from the normal rules applicable in relations between individuals'.[18]

The Court has left the duty to decide whether the conditions set down in its case law are fulfilled to the assessment of national courts. It has explicitly stated that 'the Court has jurisdiction in proceedings for a preliminary ruling to determine the categories of persons against whom the provisions of a directive may be relied on. It is for the national court to decide whether a party to proceedings before them falls within one of the categories defined'.[19] In other words, whilst the criteria are determined by Community law, the assessment of whether certain bodies fulfil those criteria will depend on their regulation by national law and whether the national court considers that a public function or duty is performed. Without entering into further debate on the concept of State, let us merely conclude that any alleged infringement of Community law, both primary and secondary, committed by all bodies coming within the concept of public authority as developed by the Court of Justice may be challenged by the Commission through the use of the Article 169 EC procedure. The evaluation of whether a particular body is part of the concept of State or not, for the purposes of Community estoppel, will depend on its main functions, purposes and characteristics. This may only be determined on a case by case basis and will certainly vary from one Member State to another.

---

[17] Case C-188/89, *A. Foster & others* v. *British Gas plc* [1990] ECR 3313.

[18] Case C-188/89, *A. Foster* (above, n 17) at 3348. Such a broad view conflicts with the narrower interpretation followed by English courts in similar cases. For a more detailed analysis of these cases see Howells, 'European Directives—The Emerging Dilemmas' (1991) 54 MLR 456. Curtin rightly argues that by failing to give a definitive Community concept of public authority, the Court has sown the seed for a non-uniform treatment of Community law in the twelve Member States. Curtin (above, n 17) at 199 *ff.* In the instant case, in view of the Court of Justice's decision, the House of Lords reversed the decision of the Court of Appeal and held that British Gas plc was an emanation of the State for the purposes of the direct effect doctrine (*Foster* v. *British Gas plc* [1991] 2 AC 306).

[19] Case C-188/89, *A. Foster* (above, n 17) at 3347. See also Case 152/84, *Marshall I* (above, n 13) at 749 where the Court avoided the question of whether the respondent authority was part of the State and left the responsibility to decide this matter to national courts in the light of the circumstances of each case.

The Definition based on the Degree of Control by the State of the Entity's Activities

This definition of State has been developed in the context of case law dealing with economic law controversies. It is therefore not surprising that this issue has also manifested itself in the area of public procurement. The main question is the extent to which the State may be held responsible for activities of bodies with which it has strong links, or which are under its supervision, although formally acting under the reign of private law. Which of these bodies' activities which infringe Community law may be imputable to the State as a breach of its obligations under the Treaty?

This broad definition of State was first applied by the Court in the *Buy Irish* case.[20] At issue was a campaign to promote the sale and purchase of Irish goods in Ireland which was run by the so-called Irish Goods Council which was an institution created under Irish company law. This campaign was challenged by the Commission on the basis of Article 30 EC. After establishing that the Council's activities were heavily financed, its members appointed and its broad guidelines defined by the Irish Government, the Court held that 'the Irish Government cannot rely on the fact that the campaign was conducted by a private company in order to escape the liability it may have under the provisions of the Treaty'.[21]

In the field of public procurement, the same approach was followed in the *Beentjes* judgment.[22] The case arose in the Netherlands in the context of a public invitation to tender issued by a so-called Land Consolidation Committee for Waterland. This body had been created by legislation, but was formally autonomous and did not form part of the State administration. One of the issues which arose was whether the Committee in question was subject to the public works Directive as a contracting authority. At that time, the Directive applied only to the State, regional or local authorities and to bodies specifically listed in the Annex, of which this body was not one.

The Court, after analysing the characteristics of the Committee, held that although it lacked any legal personality, public authorities had a large power of control over its activities and accordingly ruled that:

for the purposes of . . . the public works Directive the term the 'State' must be interpreted *in functional terms*.[23] The aim of the Directive . . . would be jeopardised if the provisions of the directives were to be held to be inapplicable solely because a public works contract is awarded by a body which, although it was set up to carry out tasks entrusted to it by legislation, is not formally a part of the State administration. Consequently, a body such as that in question here, whose composition and functions are laid down by legislation and which depends on the authorities for the appointment of its members, the observance of the obligations arising out

---

[20] Case 249/81, *Commission* v. *Ireland* [1982] ECR 4005.   [21] Ibid. at 4020.
[22] Case 31/87, *Gebroeders Beentjes* v. *The Netherlands* [1988] ECR 4635.
[23] See above, n 7.

of its measures and the financing of the public works contracts which is its task to award, must be regarded as falling within the notion of the State for the purpose of the above-mentioned provision, even though it is not part of the State administration in formal terms. (emphasis added)[24]

The decision of the Court in *Beentjes* is in line with its jurisprudence concerning the expanding notion of State developed in the field of State aids and Article 90 EC and corresponds, in general terms, with the definition adopted by the Commission in the 'Transparency Directive' whose subjective scope of application is defined in 'functional' terms.[25] The decisive criterion lies therefore in the degree of control of public authorities, whatever form this may take, financial or otherwise, over the contested activities of the organ or undertaking in question.[26] This approach requires a case by case analysis of the relevant facts. The result of this test determines whether the contested organ may be included within the notion of State for Community purposes and, consequently, whether it is subject to the Commission's control by means of Article 169 EC. In our case this will also determine whether the public procurement rules will apply to the body or not, irrespective of whether they are explicitly mentioned in the Directives, or of their national legal classification.

This case law was first codified in Article 1 of the new public works Directive and is now incorporated in all the consolidated Directives.[27] Needless to say, these provisions of the Directives are to be interpreted in the context of the general principles developed by the Court as regards the notion of State. Consequently, it is submitted that since the secondary rules on public procurement apply to the 'State',[28] any public authority which is either an integral part of national administration, understood in a broad sense, or is controlled by the State in any form whatsoever, although formally independent, should be considered as a contracting authority for the purposes of the application of the public procurement rules. It is further submitted that any breach committed by such a body is imputable to the State and consequently susceptible to challenge by the Commission under Article 169 EC, or by private individuals, before their national courts, provided the Directives' provisions are directly effective. No explicit inclusion in the public procurement Directives is required. Obviously, this

---

[24] Case 31/87, *Beentjes* (above, n 22) at 4655.

[25] Commission Directive 80/723 on the transparency of financial relations between Member States and public undertakings, adopted by the Commission under Article 90(3) EC Treaty, OJ 1980, L195. On this Directive see further Brothwood, 'The Commission Directive on transparency of financial relations between Member States and public undertakings' (1981) 18 CMLRev 207.   [26] See Hecquard-Theron (above, n 7) at 701–702.

[27] See Article 1 of Directive 71/305 on public works contracts as amended by Directive 89/440, OJ 1989, L210. See above, Chapter 2.

[28] See Article 1 of the different public procurement Directives defining their personal scope of application.

reasoning does not apply to bodies benefiting from a specific exemption provided for in the text of the Directives themselves. They must, however, respect applicable provisions of the EC Treaty.

The Effective Use of Article 169 EC Proceedings in Public Procurement Cases

The Different Types of Infringements

From a legal point of view, there are no obstacles to the Commission using its main control mechanism against breaches of Community public procurement rules. These infringements may, of course, refer both to original Treaty provisions or secondary Community provisions, in our case Directives. However, Article 169 EC is not always an appropriate tool to combat certain types of infringements from a supranational level.

One can differentiate between two types of infractions.

(1) **Major infringements**   These are all those infringements which are easily detectable by the Commission due either to the publicity involved and their economic importance or because they consist in the failure by Member States to fulfil an obligation which they specifically owe to the Commission, such as the need to communicate the implementation measures adopted at national level. The faulty implementation of the Directives at national level, legislative measures or administrative regulations subject to national publication procedures which overtly contravene the Community rules and infringements which occur in the course of the award of contracts which, due to their magnitude or economic importance, are widely reported in national press, fall within this category. Other examples are the preferential use of public procurement to aid underdeveloped regions sanctioned by a legal norm, general regulations obliging contracting authorities to discriminate in favour of their own nationals and so on. The main common feature of this group is that they are easily monitored from a supranational level.

(2) **Punctual or minor infringements**   This category refers to infringements which have an isolated character and do not result from legal obligations which bind contracting authorities. Procedural and punctual violations made during an average award procedure are included in this category. In contrast with the previous group, their detection from a supranational level, not to mention their correction, is rather complicated. They may only be spotted by means of a specific and direct scrutiny of a particular contract award procedure and are, therefore, more effectively monitored by participant firms. Only by means of direct complaints or the application of random monitoring procedures may they be pinpointed by the Commission. Lack of publication of the notice in the Official Journal, use of discriminatory technical specifications, refusal to accept correctly presented

offers from foreign firms and so on are typical examples of this group. They outweigh major infringements by far.

The Use of Article 169 EC for the Different Types of Infringement

Both types of infringements may be challenged by the Commission using the Article 169 EC enforcement mechanism. However, for legal and practical reasons, this only makes sense as regards the first type of infringement. Due to its limited manpower, the Commission is only capable of properly controlling the implementation of Community rules in domestic legal orders or major developments which take place as regards public procurement legislation in the various Member States.[29] The control of the implementation procedure is facilitated by the obligation imposed on national authorities, which is now contained in all Directives, to communicate national measures to give effect to the Directives. Once the Commission's experts have analysed the said measures, they are in a position to evaluate their conformity with the objectives and the wording of the original Directive. Supranational monitoring at this stage is straightforward.

It is possible that the use of Article 169 EC is most productive at this stage, since the monitoring of this step is usually crucial. The Commission should be especially vigilant with respect to the binding force of the transposition measures, since once the Directive has become an integral part of the national legal system, public officials charged with its application react to it in the same manner as they would do to any other similar national rules.[30] As already discussed, before 1985 the Commission failed to challenge national measures which were insufficient to implement the original public works and public supplies Directives.[31]

The same reasoning applies to those infringements which consist of an overt violation of Community legislation and also to those which take place in the course of contract awards related to large public works projects or highly expensive supplies, usually involving high-tech goods. The enactment of a national law or general regulation dealing with public procurement which expressly provides for discrimination as regards foreign products or undertakings is a paradigmatic example of the former type. The use of Article 169 EC is appropriate given the importance of the violation. The adoption of these measures is normally preceded by political

---

[29] This is not a problem exclusively restricted to the field of public procurement. The inability of the Commission to control all possible infringements of Community rules has been a recurrent theme since the early 1970s. See reply to Mr Vredeling (OJ 1973, C67/61). Evans (above, n 3) at 450. See also Weiler, 'The Transformation of Europe' (1991) *The Yale Law Journal* 2403 at 2419. The case of public procurement is specially acute.

[30] In general see the study by Siedentopf and Ziller, (eds.), *L'Europe des Administrations? La Mise en Oeuvre de la Législation Communautaire dans les États Membres,* Vol. I (Maastricht 1988). See the section headed THE THEORETICAL FRAMEWORK FOR ANALYSIS in Chapter 2, above.

[31] See further above, Chapter 1.

debate and subject to publication requirements in the Member States and is therefore easily detected by Commission officials. With respect to the latter type of contract, the great deal of publicity and press coverage which usually accompanies such 'extraordinary' contracts makes them rather conspicuous. Input by interested firms is equally likely in these cases, without prejudice to the actions which individuals might initiate before their national courts and tribunals.[32] The Commission may effectively monitor this type of conduct through the use of Article 169 EC.

With respect to minor infringements, Article 169 EC may be useful provided that the Commission has an interest in judicially establishing a legal principle or solid case law as regards a specific point relating to the public procurement rules. Article 169 EC leaves a discretion to the Commission as to the infringements which it may pursue.[33] Article 169 EC is a selective instrument. The Commission should select the test cases which may be useful to ascertain legal doctrine or solve unclear or debated legal points. In other words, the legal precedent importance of some cases may very well justify the launching of the heavy machinery of Article 169 EC.

As regards all other minor infringements which take place throughout the award procedure, Article 169 EC is not an efficient means to ensure their proper control and the subsequent correct enforcement of the Community rules on public procurement. This is due to the principal features of Article 169 EC[34] and to several reasons peculiar to the nature of public contracts. First of all, there are some obvious practical difficulties. In those Member States where the award process is of an administrative nature, the awarding act and all acts adopted in the course of the award procedure are considered to be administrative acts, which by their very nature have a singular character and are not of a general scope, or of legislative value. As a consequence, they are not susceptible to proper control on a centralized basis to the extent that they do not receive general publicity. Thousands of these acts are adopted every year, each constituting a potential breach of Community rules. The Commission is obviously not equipped to monitor them properly, even if it benefited from a consistent input by means of individual complaints. In those Member States in which public contracts are regulated under private law, apart from the publicity obligations contained in the directives, awarding authorities are under no duty to publish any information relating to the contract. Their monitoring, therefore, becomes an even more difficult task than in the case of administrative law countries, in which a certain degree of publicity always takes place.

---

[32] This is supported by the facts in the *Storeabaelt* case (Case C-243/89, *Commission* v. *Denmark* [1993] ECR I-3415). See later in this chapter.

[33] In general see Evans (above, n 3) and Dashwood and White (above, n 3) at 398 *ff*.

[34] See Weiler (above, n 29) at 2420.

A further practical disadvantage of centralized control as regards public procurement originates in the fact that a substantial number of the public contracts subject to Community rules are awarded by decentralized administrations, be they federal, regional or local. Under Article 169 EC the Commission is not entitled to challenge these bodies directly, as legal proceedings thereunder are restricted to State representatives and Community institutions. Only the central government is responsible before the Community institutions. The deterrent effect of an eventual intervention by the Commission is logically lower precisely because regional and local entities are not themselves involved in the infraction procedures. Furthermore, in some Member States, decentralized administrations publish contract notices in their own official journals.

Even if we assume that the Commission is in a position to monitor a relevant percentage of contract awards, Article 169 EC proceedings are notoriously insufficient to correct minor public procurement infringements. An action under Article 169 EC takes, on average, 30 months to resolve.[35] Since the introduction of an action before the Court of Justice does not have suspensory effect, unless the Court of Justice decides to grant interim measures under Articles 185 and 186 EC, national award procedures will proceed. By the time the judgment of the Court is delivered, the violation will have become irreparable in practice.[36] Under Article 169 EC the Court of Justice cannot impose any fine or sanction on the defaulting State, although the State is required under Article 171 EC to take all necessary measures to comply with the judgment.

Following the TEU, centralized enforcement has been enhanced by the introduction of Article 171(2) EC, which empowers the Commission to recommend the imposition of a fine on recalcitrant Member States which, in the Commission's view, have not adopted the necessary measures to comply with a previous judgment of the Court in Article 169 EC proceedings. This is intended to increase the pressure on national administrations to comply with the Court's decisions by the introduction of financial deterrents to non-compliance. The final decision depends on the Court of Justice's appreciation of whether the Member State has, or has not, taken the necessary measures. The Court's approach to the issue is still to be developed since no judgment under this new procedure has been adopted at the time of writing. As a result, the following considerations concerning this new procedure are only speculative. Its operation in public

---

[35] This period of time refers to the whole procedure, that is, from the first formal steps of the Commission until a decision of the Court of Justice is reached. Schermers and Waelbroeck (above, n 3) at 257. In the period from 1988 to 1992 it took the Court of Justice an average of 24.3 months to resolve direct actions. See also Editorial (1993) 18 ELRev at 177.

[36] See for example Case C-362/90, *Commission* v. *Italy* [1992] ECR 2353. See on this case Arrowsmith and Fernández Martín (1993) 2 PPLR CS2.

procurement cases, however, may not bring too many positive results. First of all, the economic sanction procedure will only take place after a final judgment condemning a Member State has been adopted as the outcome of a previous Article 169 EC procedure. This means that, unless interim measures have been decided by the Court, the impugned contract would have been executed by the time the first judgment is adopted. In such a case, Member States could claim that it is impossible to comply with the judgment, not because of their unwillingness to do so, but because it is just unfeasible to remedy the *fait accompli* situation. The only alternatives would be the granting of damages to injured undertakings, provided these overcome the procedural obstacles imposed by national rules on the subject, or the rescission of the contract, which, as we shall see, seems no longer to be favoured by the Court of Justice. A new Commission's action under Article 171(2) EC would not help to resolve this problem unless interim measures have been imposed by the Court but have been ignored by the contracting authority. It would not be fair to let the contract award procedure continue and then penalize the contracting authority by means of a fine for having done so. It is submitted that only evidence of bad faith or undue negligence on the part of the contracting authority may legitimize the imposition of a penalty under Article 171(2) EC. This could be the case where a Member State repeatedly refuses to adopt the required measures to comply with the Court's judgments.[37] In most public procurement cases, however, bad faith is unlikely to recur. Thus, if no interim measures are adopted, the infringement will become irreparable and the judgment will simply have a declaratory value with no practical effect. This will not be solved by the initiation of an Article 171(2) EC procedure. The Court, however, may adopt a different perspective, assume an activist role and adopt a 'punitive or exemplary damages' interpretation of Article 171(2) EC.

To illustrate the inadequacies of Article 169 EC in ensuring correct application of the public procurement rules, one case can be discussed. In *Commission* v. *Spain*,[38] the University Complutense of Madrid approved the execution of works of enlargement of one of its faculty buildings, the total cost of which was well above the threshold established in the public works Directive. No notice was sent, however, to the Official Journal of the Communities and the contract was awarded through a negotiated procedure.

The Commission formally engaged Article 169 EC proceedings against

---

[37] The Commission opened in December 1994 an Article 171(2) procedure agaisnt Spain for not complying with the Court's judgment in Case C-71/92, *Commission* v. *Spain* [1993] ECR I-5923. The action will be, however, withdrawn in view of the adoption by Spain of a new Law on Public Procurement. See above, Chapter 1 at n 90.

[38] Case C-24/91, *Commission* v. *Kingdom of Spain* [1992] ECR I-1989. For a more detailed analysis of the case see the note by Fernández Martín in (1992) 1 PPLR 320.

Spain. In December 1989 a formal letter of notice was issued. Dissatisfied with the Spanish representatives' claims, the Commission issued a reasoned opinion in October 1989 to which the Spanish Government did not oppose any new arguments. The matter was finally brought before the Court of Justice in January 1991. The Court gave its judgment in March 1992. In it, the Court held Spain liable for the University's failure to fulfil its obligations under the Treaty and the public procurement Directives. However, the final judgment of the Court of Justice merely had a declaratory value without any practical effect, as the challenged contract was executed and completed in October 1989, while the case was only decided in March 1992. The judgment is obviously not enforceable in practice. Could Spain be punished for not adopting measures to comply with the judgment? This case demonstrates the marginal effectiveness of the supranational enforcement mechanisms when it comes to correcting minor infringements of the public procurement rules. Such breaches must be challenged, but one wonders whether it is up to the Commission to do so.

The time and resources spent by Commission officials in monitoring this sort of minor infringement do not seem worthwhile.[39] Injured undertakings are certainly better placed than the Commission to redress these infringements by means of judicial complaints before competent national bodies.[40] Unless interim measures are obtained from the Court of Justice during Article 169 EC proceedings, the challenged award procedure is likely to proceed, irrespective of the fact that the Commission action has been initiated. Some positive aspects can also be identified, however. If a judgment is given, this provides legal support for a stricter Commission position in future negotiations with national representatives. National authorities can be required to make the obligations under the Directives more explicit for all the contracting authorities covered and competent national bodies should adopt a stricter control policy as regards the activities of the confracting authorities in the light of the Court's decisions. Equally, injured private parties may rely on these judgments to claim damages before national courts.[41]

Interim Relief in an Action under Article 169 EC

The above discussion underlines the importance of the availability of interim measures in order to avoid a *fait accompli*. This section concentrates

---

[39] See Weiler (above, n 29) at 2420.

[40] This is the underlying philosophy of the adopted Remedies Directive 89/665 (OJ 1989, L395/33). See Chapter 8.

[41] The success of this course of action is rendered difficult in most national orders, however, due to applicable procedural requirements. Difficulties refer mainly to the provision of evidence of a better right to win the contract. See Chapters 9 and 10.

on their role in ensuring effective application of the provisions of the Directives from a supranational perspective.[42] Article 185 EC provides that the introduction of an action before the Court of Justice does not have suspensory effect, although the Court may order that application of the act be suspended if it considers that the circumstances so require. The fact that actions before the Court have no suspensory effect corresponds, as it does in national legal orders, to 'the character of a public measure as the expression of public interest which is presumed legal until the opposite has been proven'.[43] Article 186 EC enlarges the powers of the Court of Justice by enabling it to prescribe any necessary interim measures. The latter are not restricted to the suspension of the impugned act.[44]

The Court has defined the objects and limits of an order on interim measures in the following terms:

> measures of this kind may be adopted by the judge hearing the application of such measures if it is established that their adoption is *prima facie* justified in fact and law, if they are urgent in the sense that it is necessary, in order to avoid serious and irreparable damage, that it should be laid down, and should take effect, before the decision of the Court on the substance of the action, and if they are provisional in the sense that they do not at this stage decide the disputed points to be given subsequently on the substance of the action.[45]

Interim proceedings in public procurement cases following Article 169 EC have reached the Court four times. There was a fifth case where the Commission asked for the suspension of the execution of a contract. The matter was withdrawn by the Commission after a settlement had been agreed before the Court could decide.

---

[42] For a complete discussion of the role of interim measures in practice of the Commission and the Court of Justice, see Borchardt, 'The Award of Interim Measures by the European Court of Justice' (1985) 22 CMLRev 203–206 and the bibliography cited therein; Oliver, 'Interim Measures: Recent Developments' (1992) 29 CMLRev 7. For an analysis of the role of interim measures in the context of Article 169 EC in the field of public procurement cases, see Lamarca, 'La sospensione cautelare degli appalti pubblici nel procedimento ex Article 169 del tratatto di Roma' (1989) *Rivista di Diritto Europeo* 383; Arrowsmith, 'Enforcing the Public Procurement Rules: Legal Remedies in the Court of Justice and the National Courts' in Arrowsmith (ed.), *Remedies for Enforcing the Public Procurement Rules* (Winteringham, 1993), Chapter 1 at 24 *ff*.   [43] Borchardt (above, n 42) at 206.
[44] The procedural requirements concerning interim measures are developed in Article 36 of the Statute of the Court and Arts. 83 to 89 of the Rules of Procedure. In brief, these provisions require that there must be a main procedure before the Court in the context of which an application for interim measures is made. Article 83(1), Rules of Procedure. In our case, this means that the Commission needs to have lodged a main Article 169 EC action before the Court in order to claim suspensory measures. The award of interim measures is also made conditional upon the existence of circumstances which give rise to urgency. Finally, a *prima facie* case on factual and legal grounds must be established for the interim measures applied for. Article 83(2) Rules of Procedure. They are temporary in nature, without prejudice to the decision of the Court on the substance of the main case and no appeal is possible.
[45] Case 20/81R, *Arbed* [1981] ECR 721. Borchardt (above, n 42) at 206–207.

The *Dundalk* case[46]

A Spanish-Irish company submitted the lowest tender in a contract award procedure the main object of which was the establishment of a water supply scheme intended to overcome chronic water shortage difficulties in the Dundalk region in Ireland. That tender was refused by the contracting authority on the grounds that it had not been certified by the Irish Institute for Industrial Research and Standards to comply with the standard specifications set out in the contract. Such a certificate was expressly required in the contract clauses. The rejected tenderer complained to the Commission, which took the view that the contested contract clause infringed Articles 30 to 36 EC and initiated Article 169 EC proceedings against Ireland. At the same time, the Commission asked the Court to adopt an interim order obliging Ireland to take such measures as may have been necessary to prevent the award of the contract in question, until such time as the Court had given final judgment or a settlement had been reached. This request was resolved by an Order of the President of the Court.[47]

The Court found that the Commission's submission concerning Article 30 EC raised a material argument which established a *prima facie* case in favour of the requested interim measure. The factual grounds presented were also held to be sufficient to admit the request. The Court was not satisfied, however, with the Commission's justification of the urgency of the measures requested. The latter contended that, if the contract in question was awarded in a manner contrary to Community law, irreparable damage would result, detrimental not only to the interests of the Community, but also to those contractors and their suppliers whose tenders were not considered as a result of the contested clause. The award of the contract would create a situation whereby the infringement would become progressively irreversible as the execution of the contract took place. The Court dismissed the Commission's application on the following grounds: 'although at first sight the problem seems to be a matter of some urgency, particularly since the damage to the Commission, as guardian of the interests of the Community, will arise as soon as the contract at issue is awarded, it may be necessary in proceedings for interim measures under Articles 185 and 186 of the EEC Treaty to weigh against each other all interests at stake'. In this case, 'the objective of the public works contract in question, namely to secure water supplies for the inhabitants of the Dundalk area . . . and the aggravation of the existing health and safety hazards for them if the award of the contract at issue is delayed tilt the balance of interests in favour of the defendant. It should be stressed that quite a different assessment might be arrived at in the case of other public works

---

[46] Case 45/87, *Commission v. Ireland* [1988] ECR 4929.

[47] Case 45/87R, *Commission v. Ireland*, Order of the President of the Court [1987] ECR 783.

contracts serving different purposes where a delay in the award of the contract would not expose a population to such health and safety hazards'.[48]

The *La Spezia* case[49]

A public body failed to publish a notice in the Official Journal concerning an award of a contract for works connected with the operation of a solid urban waste incinerator. The Commission applied for an interim order from the Court suspending the award. If the contract was awarded, the Commission requested, in the alternative, an order obliging Italy to adopt all the appropriate measures in order to cancel the award of the contract or, at the very least, to preserve the *status quo* until the final judgment was given in the main action. The Commission based its request on grounds similar to those alleged in the *Dundalk* case.

Italian representatives relied *inter alia* on Article 9(d) of the Directive, which exempts contracts from publication in case of extreme urgency brought about by events unforeseen by the awarding authorities. Given the public health interest involved in the prompt execution of the required works (since in the meantime solid refuse could no longer be satisfactorily disposed of), Italy opposed the concession of the interim measures demanded. The renovation of the incinerator was much more urgent and relevant to the public interest than compliance with the formal requirements of the Directive.

The Court rejected the Italian arguments concerning Article 9(d) of the Directive. The alleged urgency was not due to unforeseeable events, as required by the said Article, but to a lack of diligence on the part of the responsible authorities. As the chronology of the facts showed, the contracting authority had handled the matter slowly and ineffectively. More than five years had elapsed between the approval of the Decree requiring renovation of the incinerator and the issue of the invitation to tender. The Court concluded that there were sufficient factual and legal elements to allow it to assume that, *prima facie*, the Directive applied. A *prima facie* obligation to publish a notice therefore arose.[50]

With respect to the 'urgency' requirement, the Court recognized that any delay in the completion of the works could entail serious risks for public health and the environment. However, the contracting authority was responsible for the situation in which it found itself as it had not performed its duty efficaciously. On these grounds, the Court held that the balance of interests tilted in favour of the Commission and therefore ordered the Italian Government to adopt all measures necessary to suspend the challenged contract award until the date of delivery of the judgment determining the main action.

---

[48] Ibid. at 1378.
[49] Case 194/88R, *Commission* v. *Italy*, Order of the President of the Court [1988] ECR 5647.
[50] Case194/88R, *Commission* v. *Italy* (above, n 49) at 5653.

Once notified of the Court's decision on the issue of interim relief, the public consortium in charge of the operation of the waste incinerator decided to re-start the whole procedure *ex novo,* this time in accordance with Community law requirements. In view of this attitude, the Commission withdrew its main action before the Court.[51]

The *Storebaelt* case[52]

Although no decision was eventually taken by the Court, this case has some outstanding features which merit attention. In the case, the Commission requested for the first time the award of interim measures to suspend the execution of an already awarded contract. The Danish Government had awarded a public works contract to a Danish consortium despite the fact that the Commission had initiated an Article 169 EC procedure for breach of Article 30 EC. The Commission requested from the Court of Justice the suspension of the execution of the contract by the successful tenderers. Otherwise, the final judgment on the merits would be futile if the completion of the public work was not prevented, especially taking into account the magnitude and economic importance of the public works. Since the reinitiation of the whole award procedure and, as a result, of the public work, was out of the question, the only feasible means of enforcing the judgment would be the award of damages to the injured firms in accordance with domestic legislation (a possibility which appeared unsatisfactory). The Danish representatives opposed the grant of interim relief by referring to the crucial economic and social importance of the envisaged works which could not possibly be delayed without negatively affecting the general interest. Suspension of the works until final judgment was delivered would mean at least two years of inactivity. They argued, moreover, that the successful consortium had already furnished certain expensive services and that the award of the requested interim relief would imply the need to rescind the contract and, consequently, the grant of large amounts of compensatory damages for non-implementation of their contractual obligations. Indeed, from a legal point of view, the fact that the contract was already being executed had important consequences.

The economic and political importance of the work undoubtedly played a fundamental role in the development of the case. In fact, the application for interim relief never came before the Court. In an attempt to avoid the resolution of the request, the President of the Court after hearing the different allegations, prompted the two parties to reach a settlement on

---

[51] Lamarca, 'Sospensione cautelare dell'appalto già aggiudicatto e conciliazione giudiziale: Il caso *Storebaelt'* (1990) *Rivista di Diritto Europeo* 803 at 829.

[52] Case C-243/89, *Commission* v. *Denmark (Storebaelt)* (above, n 32). It must be noted that the published case refers to the judgment on the merits. For an exhaustive analysis of the case and its legal implications, see Lamarca (1990) (above, n 51).

the issue of the interim relief. According to him, the decision that the Court was to adopt would have been extremely important as regards both the interpretation, application and development of Community law and the economic interests involved.[53] On these grounds, the Commission and the Danish representatives reached an agreement *in extremis*, minutes before the oral hearings were due to start, and, as a result, the request for interim relief was withdrawn.[54] The Danish representatives, after accepting the Commission's claims as regards the illegality of the 'national origin clauses', made certain undertakings with regard to future conduct in contract award procedures as well as the establishment of an *ad hoc* arbitration procedure for the reimbursement of the costs of the unsuccessful tenderers.[55] The case is of great significance, especially in the assessment of the Commission's role in monitoring compliance with Community rules. This point is further discussed later on.

The *Lottery* case[56]

The most interesting aspect in this case is that the Court granted interim measures suspending the execution of an already awarded contract. The issues avoided in the *Storebaelt* case were tackled by the Court this time. An

---

[53] Cited by Lamarca (1990) (above, n 51) at 811.

[54] Order of the Court of 22 September 1989. The main action was decided in Case C-243/89, *Commission* v. *Denmark* (above, n 32) in favour of the Commission.

[55] One of the positive elements of this settlement was that according to this procedure, disappointed tenderers would not have to provide evidence that in the absence of the breach they would have won the contract. Other compensatory damages for further costs would be equally awarded in so far as the latter were directly caused by the inclusion of the illegal contract clause. Wainwright, 'Legal Reforms in Public Procurement' (1990) 10 YEL 133 at 137.

[56] Order of the President of the Court in Case C-272/91R, *Commission* v. *Italy* [1992] ECR I-4367. The Order of the President in the *Lottery* case meant that the works had to be suspended until a final decision on the substance was adopted. The case on the merits was resolved in favour of the Commission (Case C-272/91, *Commission* v. *Italy* [1994] ECR I-1409) noted by Fernández Martín (1994) 3 PPLR CS211). Arrowsmith forcefully argues that to give effect to the Court's judgment under Article 171 EC, the contract would need to be set aside. It does not make sense to order the suspension of the execution of an already concluded contract and thereafter, once judgment on the substance upholds the existence of the breach, allow the faulty Member State to proceed with the execution of the suspended contract (see Arrowsmith and Fernández Martín, 'Developments in Public Procurement in 1992' (1993) 19 ELRev 323 at 327). However, Article 171 EC leaves Member States discretion as regards the adoption of the 'necessary measures' to comply with a judgment of the Court of Justice. In its judgment on the merits the Court did not require the defaulting Member State to set aside the contract, but contented itself to hold that Italy had failed to fulfil its obligations. It is up to the Member State to adopt all necessary measures to comply with the judgment. If the Member State decides not to restart the contract award procedure on public interest grounds, compliance may well be attained through adequate compensation of the aggrieved tenderers, which will be determined in accordance with the relevant national legislation. However, applicable national rules may be unsatisfactory. Most firms would have to show a better right before competent national courts to be awarded any compensation at all. The situation is therefore intricate and some clarification on the part of the Court in this respect would have been useful. A further action by the Commission under Article 171(2) EC may help in this connection.

Article 169 EC action was brought before the Court against Italy, on the grounds that the Ministry for Finance had failed to comply with its obligations under Articles 30, 52 and 59 EC and Articles 9 and 17 to 25 of the public supply Directive with respect to the concession of the system for the computerization of the Lottery.

The Commission requested the Court to grant interim relief compelling the Italian Government to take all the necessary measures to suspend either the legal effects of the Decree of the Minister for Finance awarding the contract, or the legal effects of any contract which may have been concluded later. It must be noted that a previous judgment of the Court had already condemned Italy for restricting the conclusion of contracts for the development of the data-processing systems of public authorities to companies whose shares were mainly in public ownership. This practice was held to be contrary to Articles 52 and 59 EC.[57] Since the instant case did not materially differ, the Court of Justice found that there was a *prima facie* case in favour of the Commission. Once again the Court upheld the submission of the Commission according to which it could not await the outcome of the main proceedings without incurring grave and irreparable harm as the institution responsible for monitoring the application of the Treaty. If interim measures were not awarded, by the time the final judgment was delivered, the contract would have been executed and the Commission would not have any alternative but to accept the *fait accompli* which confronted it, even though a blatant infringement of Community law would have occurred.

The Court concluded by granting the requested measures since they would not cause any serious disruption to the public interest. In fact, since the successful tenderer did not become responsible for the various operations involved, the continued regular conduct of the lottery game was not prevented. The Court accorded the suspension of the legal effects of the Decree awarding the concession of the system for computerization of the lottery and the performance of the contract concluded for that purpose.

The *Transport* case[58]

This case is of particular interest for two reasons. First, because it was the first case in which the Utilities Directive was alleged as the main legal grounds before the Court of Justice. The defendant was a public entity in charge of running the public transportation of Wallonia, one of the Belgian autonomous regions. Secondly, and more importantly for our

---

[57] Case 3/88, *Commission v. Italy* [1989] ECR 4035. On the case see further Chapter 1 at *The free provision of services (Articles 59–66 EC) and right of establishment provisions (Articles 52–58)*.

[58] Order of the President of the Court of Justice in Case C-87/94R, *Commission v. Belgium* [1994] ECR I-1395.

present purposes, because the Court revised its previous case law and added some new elements to the subject of interim measures in public procurement cases.

The *Société régionale wallone du transport* (SRWT) issued a call for tenders for a public contract concerning the supply of buses for public transportation. Initially, part of the contract was awarded to the firm Van Hool, but after the unexpected intervention of the Wallon Ministry of Transport, this decision was reversed and SRWT awarded the contract to a different firm, EMI. Van Hool applied for the suspension of this decision before the Belgian *Conseil d'État* who finally rejected Van Hool's application for interim measures. Subsequently, the contract between SRWT and EMI was formally concluded in accordance with applicable national rules.

Van Hool had also introduced a complaint before the Commission. The Commission initiated Article 169 EC proceedings against Belgium and produced a reasoned opinion requiring Belgium to adopt measures suspending the legal effects of the contract. Since no satisfactory response was given, the Commission lodged the case before the Court of Justice alleging a breach of the obligations arising from the Utilities Directive 90/531. At the same time, it introduced an application for interim measures requesting the suspension of the legal effects of the award decision as well as the suspension of the contractual relationship between SRWT and EMI until a final decision had been adopted.

The Commission alleged that the urgency was manifest. The supply of the goods would lead to serious and irreparable damage in so far as the award of the contract and its partial execution would result in a *fait accompli* which the Commission, as guardian of the Treaty, would not be able to resolve. This would produce immediate and serious prejudice to the legality of the Community legal order. As long as the supplies continued to take effect, the final judgment on the merits would be ineffective if no interim measures were granted. Belgium referred to previous decisions of the Court of Justice[59] and claimed that a party was prevented from alleging urgency when the state of urgency had been provoked by the person alleging it, or was due to its own slowness in taking action. In the view of the Belgian representatives, this applied in the instant case, since it had taken the Commission five months to apply for the interim measures in the context of the judicial action. Belgium further argued that the Commission could not rely in abstract terms on its role as guardian of the Treaty to justify a serious and irreparable harm, but had to prove the existence of a more specific imperative substantiating the adoption of interim measures, such as the prevention of a breach of Community law before the award of the contract had taken place.

---

[59] E.g., Case C-194/88R, *Commission* v. *Italy* (above, n 49) at 5653.

The Court started by making it clear that the infringement of provisions of a Directive regulating the award of public contracts constitutes a serious prejudice to Community legality and that a later judgment by the Court declaring the existence of the infringement under Article 169 EC, usually after the contract has been executed, cannot eliminate the prejudices caused to the Community legal order and to the injured bidders. The Commission is entitled, as guardian of the Treaty, to apply for interim measures at the same time as it initiates an infringement procedure in the context of an award of a public contract.[60]

However, although the Commission could act in defence of Community legality whenever it wished, its intervention in public procurement cases was to be subject to certain conditions of effectiveness. The Court stated that the Commission had to intervene at the supranational level, as far as possible, before the conclusion of the contract or it must, at least, rapidly and unequivocally inform the defendant State of its views regarding an eventual infringement of the rules regulating the award procedure, or of its intention to apply for the suspension of the contract award procedure or the legal effects of the concluded contract itself. Once informed of the Commission's intentions, the defendant Member State could decide, at its own risk, to continue the contract award procedure or the execution of the concluded contract, but with the knowledge of the possible implications of its actions.[61]

The reasons justifying these new conditions on the Commission are to be found in the legal difficulties which arise when an already concluded contract is declared contrary to Community law. Every party involved is prejudiced.[62] The Court stressed this point by referring to the importance attached in most legal orders to the maintenance of contractual relationships and the need for speedy action before contracts are concluded. In this context, the Court of Justice mentioned the Remedies Directives[63] and underlined the fact that they allowed Member States to restrict the remedies available when a contract has already been concluded to an award of damages. It also pointed out in this connection that the Community legislator had left to national authorities the discretion to apply national rules regulating the effects of a judicial action on a concluded contract.[64]

From its previous decision in the *Lottery* case it appeared that the Court of Justice was ready to uphold the Commission's requests for interim measures and that this favourable attitude would not be influenced by the

---

[60] Order of the President in Case C-87/94R at para. 31.   [61] Ibid. at para. 34.

[62] See Chapter 8.

[63] Directive 89/665, applicable to remedies in the field of the public sector Directives, and Directive 92/13 applicable to remedies in the field of the Utilities Directive.

[64] Order of the President in Case C-87/94 R at para. 33.

fact that the contract had already been awarded. However, the *Transport* case represents a change in approach. Apart from the innovative stricter control imposed on the Commission, which seems now to be required by the Court of Justice to inform the defendant State of its intention to request the suspension of the contract in due time, the considerations of the Court of Justice are also significant because they indicate a preference for preventive action to avoid the conclusion of a tainted award procedure rather than sanctions once the contract is concluded. Despite the fact that in the *Lottery* case the Court of Justice had already granted interim measures suspending the execution of an already awarded contract, in this case it seems particularly conscious of the numerous difficulties in providing an effective remedy when an already concluded contract is found to be in breach of Community law. This may explain why the Court requires more efficient intervention by the Commission.

The Court of Justice then went on to analyse the specific circumstances of the case. It stated that the contract in question had been formally concluded in November 1993 and that the first supply of buses was scheduled for April 1994. It followed that when the application for interim measures was lodged, the contract was not only concluded but already being executed in so far as production of the buses had started. The Court was not satisfied with the Commission's attempt to justify the urgency of the measures requested. The Commission had not notified the Belgian Government of its intention to request the suspension of the legal effects of the award decision and of the contract until its reasoned opinion, that is, three months after Van Hool had lodged its complaint. Even though Van Hool had urged a prompt response from the Commission, the latter had not acted in a manner which enabled the contracting authority to realize fully the consequences of proceeding at its own risk with the execution of the contract. In other words, it had not made clear its intentions until the contract was being executed. The Court of Justice concluded from this fact that the Commission had not acted with due diligence when invoking the urgency necessary to justify an application for interim measures.

Subsequently, the Court of Justice turned to an analysis of the balance of the interests at stake. On this point it accepted, although reluctantly, the Belgian arguments to the effect that the concession of interim measures would put the security of public transport users and road users in general at risk. This argument was based on the precarious state of the buses currently running. Accidents had already occurred and any further delay in the acquisition of new buses caused by the suspension of the contract and the consequent need to commence a new award procedure would certainly aggravate the situation. The Court of Justice pointed out that most of the blame for the precarious state of the buses fell on the contracting authority itself for not acquiring new buses some years before and stated that, in normal circumstances, this would have meant that the balance of interests would have gone in favour of the Commission. However, in view of the serious risks which a suspension of the contract would entail for road users, public transport users and SRWT personnel, the Court, to avoid aggravating the situation, departed from its position in *La Spezia* and decided that the balance of interests tilted in favour of Belgium and therefore dismissed the Commission's application.

Conclusions as Regards Interim Measures at the Supranational Level

The Court, like national courts[65] when evaluating the need to award interim measures, balanced the different interests involved. Interim measures are dependent on the nature of these interests. A case before the Court of Justice usually lasts between five and thirteen months,[66] and if public interests are at stake they may well be harmed by such a long delay. Thus, in the *Dundalk* and *Transport* cases, the Court decided the imperatives of the general interest prevailed over any other consideration on the facts of the cases in question. Even though the Court ruled out the award of interim measures, it did so reluctantly and it seems that it will hold differently when the 'public interest' at stake is not as overriding as it was in both of those cases.

In fact, a stricter policy was applied in *La Spezia*. The Court recognized that the renovation of the waste incinerator was important to guarantee public health. However, the negligence of Italian authorities in performing their duties undermined the credibility of their arguments. The estoppel principle was applied and the balance of interests was tilted in favour of the Commission. A different approach was adopted in the *Transport* case where, despite recognizing negligence on the part of contracting authorities, the Court nevertheless denied the suspension in view of the tardy reaction of the Commission to the firm's complaint and the specific circumstances of the case.

In the *Lottery* case, the suspension of the effects of the already awarded contract was ordered since no overriding public interest would be harmed. The existence of a previous judgment condemning Italy for a similar breach probably played a role in favour of the award of the suspension. This favourable attitude to the Commission's requests for interim measures has, however, been qualified by the decision in the *Transport* case. The Court now seems aware of the disruption that the suspension of the execution of an already concluded contract may cause for both private and public

---

[65] For an analysis of the different national systems, see Arrowsmith (ed.) (1993) (above, n 42).   [66] Schermers and Waelbroeck (above, n 3) at 256.

interests involved.[67] It therefore adopted in the *Transport* case a cautious approach to the issue. It is in this context that the conditions imposed on the Commission with respect to making its intention known must be read. This decision may indicate a shift in the Court's readiness to award interim measures when the contract is being executed and a public interest is at stake.

But even if one assumes that the Court is favourably prepared to award interim measures, the practical effects of the requests of the Commission remain limited in the field of public procurement. Interim procedures before the Court of Justice are ancillary to the main action brought under Article 169 EC. The administrative phases of Article 169 EC have to be exhausted before judicial action can be initiated and interim measures demanded.[68] During this period, since the Commission has no power to suspend contract negotiations, the contract is likely to be awarded.

In any event, the Commission is not in a position to bring all possible unlawful acts before the Court. The adoption of interim measures at supranational level will only apply in the few cases where the Commission may detect the infringement in time. Moreover, the conditions required by the Rules of Procedure and the statute of the Court may not always be met. The fact that only five cases of interim measures in the public procurement area are reported (one of which was withdrawn) is clear evidence of the marginal relevance of this type of procedure as part of the Commission's policy. On the basis of these drawbacks, the Commission argued for extended suspension powers in the first Remedies Directive proposal, but these were not retained by the Council.[69]

Direct Complaints to the Commission

An important aspect of the supranational enforcement of public procurement rules relates to individual complaints of injured firms to the Commission. Arguably, the Commission could be aided in its enforcement task by the introduction of individual complaints concerning infringements of public procurement rules. The Commission's policy towards individual complaints has never been the subject of a specific regulation, but is pursued only informally on the basis of the Commission's internal rules

[67] The acquired rights of the successful tenderer and the effect of the final judgment on the suspended award procedure or the suspended execution of the contract pose delicate questions. One of these problems arises with respect to the right of the winning contractor to a fair hearing. Its rights have been affected by the Court's decision and by virtue of the principle of natural justice it should have been admitted to present its allegations before the Court. For an interesting discussion of these issues in the context of the *Storebaelt* case see Lamarca (1990) (above, n 51) at 837 *ff.*

[68] Due to the time-delays involved, this will usually mean twenty months of negotiations before a case is lodged before the Court. Audretsch, *Supervision in European Community Law*, 2nd edn. (Amsterdam, 1986) at 395.   [69] For a detailed discussion see Chapter 8.

of administration. Although the initiation of the Article 169 EC procedure is discretionary and not susceptible to challenge,[70] it is well known that the Commission's policy as regards infringements of public procurement rules has been to take action whenever the complaint is *prima facie* well founded.[71] Confidentiality as regards the complainant's identity is normally ensured and the costs of investigation and enforcement are normally borne by the Commission itself. Moreover, due to the privileged bargaining position of the Commission with respect to Member States, this route normally leads to a compromise settlement of most cases before they arrive at the judicial stage.[72] These various features should have acted as incentives for undertakings to resort to the Commission as a substitute for deficient national redress procedures. Is this the case?

Complaints concerning public procurement directly addressed to the Commission from January 1981 to 1994 amount to a total number of 269.[73]

TABLE 1:   Number of direct complaints by years

1981	1
1982	3
1983	4
1985	4
1986	3
1987	11
1988	26
1989	7
1990	21
1991	31
1992	35
1993	55
1994	68

As Table I clearly shows, complaints have considerably augmented after 1986 and 1993.[74] This is probably the result of the Commission's policy

---

[70] Case 48/66, *Lütticke* v. *Commission* [1966] ECR 19.

[71] This clearly stems not only from the Commission's practice but also from its statements and publications in the area. See Chapter 1.   [72] See Chapter 1.

[73] This data has been compiled by the author from the database of the Commission's General Secretariat for the period 1981–1986. The database is incomplete. However, it is the only source of information with respect to this matter. For the period 1991–4 the data was kindly supplied by DG XV/B/3.

[74] The poor record of 1989 is mainly due to the internal restructuring of the Commission's services during that year, when Directorate F of DG III, charged until then with all public procurement matters, was integrated with Directorate B. This created a great deal of confusion and most of the complaints received during that year were treated as if they

after 1985 which encourages firms to file a complaint whenever they became aware of an infringement in the area. After 1993, the increment in the number of complaints is due also to the entering into force of the Services Directive in 1993 and of the Utilities Directive in most of the Member States in 1994, which substantially increased the scope of application of the Community public procurement rules. Although at first sight the data seems to imply that undertakings are willing to take action as long as it does not affect their commercial position, it must be subject to a second reading. The number of complaints has certainly augmented, but it still remains negligible, especially when assessed in relation to the total number of contracts awarded pursuant to the Community rules.[75] A total of 269 complaints in fourteen years does not provide unquestionable evidence with which positive conclusions can be reached.

It is submitted that this 'passive' attitude of injured firms with respect to this safe method of complaint is explained by the fact that, in most cases, the complainant firm does not derive a direct benefit in the case in question. The Commission's actions are lengthy and encumbered by the need to proceed through the Article 169 EC proceedings. The Commission is not empowered to impose fines or claim damages on behalf of the successful complainant. The likely result of such a course of action is a compromise settlement between the Commission and the Member State, which normally involves the latter assuming a commitment to ensure that future contracts will be more closely monitored and addressing administrative instructions to contracting authorities concerning their obligations under the Directives.

The limited practical efficiency of the current complaint system could be overcome through the institutionalisation and regulation of a new supranational 'complaint mechanism' applicable to the public procurement area, similar to that applicable to the Competition area, albeit especially designed to take into account the special features of public procurement. The Commission could make the well-founded arguments of the complainants its own, while ensuring confidentiality regarding their identity. It would be empowered to suspend award procedures and fine

---

belonged to 1990. On the contrary, figures for 1988 are particularly high due to the fact that seven different complaints related to the same infraction. There was probably an agreement between the concerned parties to initiate action individually in order to increase the force of their complaint. Moreover, one company introduced four complaints against four different implementations of an allegedly incompatible national provision.

[75] Published notices concerning public supplies, public works and public services contracts in the last three years amounted to more than 75,000. In the same vein, Arrowsmith mentions that 90% of the alleged irregularities dealt with by the Commission between July 1990 and April 1991 (a total of 1,184) came to its attention through the application of monitoring programmes. Only 10% had their origin in individual complaints. In Arrowsmith (ed.) (1993) (above, n 42) at 9.

contracting authorities and would thereby exercise direct control over public authorities.

At present, however, several obstacles to the creation of this supranational enforcement mechanism exist. It would require, first of all, a huge increase of the Commission's staff which is unforeseeable in the medium term. Secondly, the EC Treaty does not provide a sufficient legal basis (with the exception, of course, of Article 235 EC) and political agreement between Member States regarding this issue is far from feasible. As already mentioned, a similar centralized enforcement mechanism, in which the power of the Commission to suspend an award procedure was contemplated in the first proposals for the Remedies Directive, was strongly opposed and ultimately rejected by the Council.

The Role of the Commission under Article 169 EC

The use of Article 169 EC in the field of public procurement may also be subject to more conceptual criticism. One may wonder whether the Commission is right in assuming the principal role in ensuring adequate enforcement of public procurement Directives. First of all, minor infringements in the public procurement area result from individual and specific acts by national officials. Recourse to Article 169 EC to combat this type of breach is not desirable. In fact, the previous practice of the Commission in other fields of Community law has been to ignore these particular infringements for the purposes of Article 169 EC, referring the matter to remedies at national level.[76] It is equally noteworthy that, in the past, the Commission has also decided not to challenge via Article 169 EC those infringements having slight effects with respect to Community law.[77] This is clearly the case concerning minor infringements committed in the course of average contract awards.

Secondly, assuming that the public procurement Directives provide for 'rights' for the benefit of contractors and suppliers, their legal enforcement is meant to be performed on a decentralized basis before national courts. The Commission should not substitute itself for interested firms in challenging breaches of public procurement rules. The purpose of Article 169 EC is not to uphold individual Community rights as the Court has explicitly held.[78]

---

[76] For a description of a case in which the Commission refused to open Article 169 EC proceedings albeit considering that a breach of Commuity law existed, see Evans (above, n 3) at 451. The Commission decided not to use Article 169 EC on the grounds that the breach was 'an individual one taken by the local authorities in the implementation of French rules and regulations and . . . the individuals concerned must seek redress in the appropriate courts if they feel the French authorities acted illegally'. Reply to a Written Parliamentary Question by Giraud and Schmidt, OJ 1976, C99/39.   [77] Evans (above, n 3) at 452.

[78] 'In fact proceedings by an individual are intended to protect individual rights in a specific case, whilst intervention by the Community authorities has as its object the general

It is submitted that most breaches of Community public procurement rules are not properly and efficiently corrected by means of the indiscriminate use of Article 169 EC. Not only is it not feasible for the Commission to detect a relevant number of infractions, but the legal nature of Article 169 EC equally acts as an obstacle. Even if the Commission counted on large enforcement resources, systematic challenges of breaches would result in an overloading of the Court of Justice, which would end up resolving minor administrative infringements. Moreover, injured undertakings, the ultimate beneficiaries of the public procurement rules, would not get proper redress. This does not mean, of course, that the Article 169 EC procedure is of no use at all. As regards public procurement, the Commission should proceed to a selection of those cases with special relevance which justify a 'constitutional' decision of the Court. In other words, it should use it as a means to make the Court pronounce on questions of principle regarding public procurement and not merely an action for general redress, or a system to attack specific infringements. Economically important contracts should also be the object of particular scrutiny by the Commission's services.

These considerations are not contradicted by the success achieved by the Commission in the *Storebaelt* case. Although the Danish case meant a victory for the Commission in the application of its present powers under the Treaty to control breaches of public procurement rules, its success must be assessed in the light of the circumstances of the case. This was an extraordinary case in many senses and is certainly not the standard type of infringement which comes before the Commission. The challenged public work, intended to link Denmark to the European mainland, was probably the biggest project undertaken in Denmark in modern times and it involved many economic as well as political interests. Evidence of the relevance of the case is provided by the fact that both the Commission and the Danish representatives were represented at the highest political level before the Court.[79]

The fact that the impugned clause was clearly contrary to Community law constituted a strong argument for a *prima facie* case in favour of the Commission and certainly put some pressure on the Danish side. The Danish Government could not face an order suspending execution of the contract, as this would have caused substantial economic hardship or would have meant entering into an open conflict with its Community obligations. The Commission, although intending to fight to the end with its request, feared a possible attitude of non-compliance by the Danish Government.

and uniform observance of Community law.' Case 28/67, *Firma Molkerei-Zentrale Westfalen/ Lippe GmbH* v. *Hauptzollamt Paderbon* [1968] ECR 143.

[79] The Vice-President of the Commission and the Danish Minister of Justice headed their respective representations.

This is particularly noteworthy if one considers that both the *La Spezia* and *Dundalk* precedents were arguments in favour of the Danish position. In fact, taking into consideration the economic and social importance of the envisaged work, as well as the sensitivity of Danish public opinion in the case, it seemed unlikely that the Court would have decided in favour of the Commission and suspended the execution of the contract. Nevertheless, both parties had a lot to lose, and the Court itself was faced with a delicate case. All these circumstances opened the way to negotiations. The case was also an exceptional opportunity for the Commission to show its commitment in the area of public procurement. The impugned breaches were quite flagrant and a large amount of publicity was to be gained.

Furthermore, the individual complainant at the origin of this Article 169 EC action was probably the biggest European firm specializing in public works and was determined to proceed to the end. Its determination certainly gave support to the radical stance of the Commission. The reasons for the firm's attitude related to the magnitude of the work which involved very high bidding costs and justified the action for their recovery. Equally, such projects only take place occasionally and the firm did not fear retaliation measures in future contracts, as it would probably not present offers for less significant contracts in Denmark. Its interest was limited to this particular contract. This is the type of contract which attracts foreign firms to present bids in other Member States.

In brief, the circumstances of the case were ripe and adequate for supranational action and the success obtained by the Commission in this case supports our claim for a more selective enforcement policy. These are the cases which justify the resources spent by the Commission in enforcing public procurement rules. Unfortunately, such cases do not always present themselves. Most of the time the Commission faces minor infringements in minor cases. As a result, one may not derive guidelines governing the Commission's role in preventing breaches of public procurement from this case. In more poetic terms, one swallow does not make a summer.

THE ACTUAL PRACTICE OF THE COMMISSION

All this being said, the actual practice of the Commission is a different matter. The Commission has often resorted to Article 169 EC to challenge all types of violations of public procurement rules. The policy seems to have been to attack any infringement which comes to the Commission's knowledge by any means. It may be argued that this is a mere consequence of the more vigorous general enforcement policy applied by the Commission since 1977.[80] This can only partially explain the Commission's activity

---

[80] See generally Dashwood and White (above, n 3) at 399–400; Weiler (above, n 29) at 2431 *ff.*

in the public procurement area. As discussed in Chapter 1, the political importance attached by the Commission to the opening up of public procurement to European-wide competition in the context of the 1992 internal market programme enhanced the Commission's enforcement efforts in the public procurement area.[81] Since 1985, the infraction proceedings initiated by the Commission have consistently increased, to the extent that they have been multiplied by a factor of eight in four years (see Figure 6 at the end of this chapter).[82] In the same vein, the Commission has consistently encouraged private parties to approach its services for advice and to lodge individual complaints indicating the existence of breaches in the field.[83] The practice of the Commission shows that Article 169 EC proceedings will normally ensue if the complaint is well-founded.[84]

Even though the mere initiation of the Article 169 EC procedure has, in many cases, brought existing infringements to an end and has contributed to the development of an increasing awareness by national authorities of the determination of the Commission, its systematic use constitutes a disproportionate response. A member of the European Parliament, when commenting on the general public procurement policy of the Commission, stated that 'we should resist the temptation offered by the Commission to use a blunderbuss to kill midges, and to miss them anyway'.[85] The same may be said about its supranational enforcement policy. These objections and possibly, practical experience, seem to have eroded the Commission's willingness to challenge minor infringements. A change of policy is currently taking place.[86] In fact, after the first impulsive years, the Commission is no longer challenging minor infringements on a systematic

---

[81] See EC Commission, COM (84) *Public Supply Contracts. Conclusions and Perspectives*, COM 84 (717) at 26 and EC Commission, *Public Procurement in the Community*, COM (86) 375 at 5.

[82] In 1986 only four Article 169 EC actions were initiated whereas in 1990 the total number was thirty seven.

[83] Thus, the Commission has stated that 'any supplier or contractor who considers that he has been harmed by an unlawful decision taken by a contracting authority is free to submit a complaint to the Commission. Complaints may be made at the same time as proceedings are instituted before a national court, but are in no way confidential on such legal action. Complaints can be handled confidentially, and there is no administration fee. To ensure that the Commission's action is effective, complaints should be lodged before the contract is signed'. EC Commission, *The Large Market of 1993 and the Opening up of Public Procurement* (Brussels, 1990) at 33. See also EC Commission,*Vademecum*, OJ 1987, L358 at 40; Wainwright (above, n 55) at 145.

[84] Magliano, 'Il contenzioso degli appalti pubblici nella prospettiva del mercato unico europeo' (1991) *Rivista di Diritto Europeo* 883 at 889. See the answer of the Commission to Parliamentary Question No. 2976/90 of Mr Simmonds, MEP.

[85] Von Wogau, Debates of the European Parliament. 1988–1989 session. Report of the proceedings from 16 to 20 May 1988, OJ Annex 1988, 2–365 at 78.

[86] Wainwright (above, n 55) at 145. See also the 'Commission's report to the 14th Fide Congress' in FIDE, *L'Application dans les États Membres des Directives sur les Marchés Publics* (Madrid, 1990) 13 at 29.

basis. Through an agreement with external consultants, national official journals are scanned on a random basis in order to individualize the existence of minor infringements such as disrespect of time limits or the non-publication of notices.[87] Instead of initiating Article 169 EC procedures against each of them, the Commission waits until a substantial number of such infringements is detected and thereafter notifies the competent national authorities. In this notification, the Commission merely requires the erring Member State to acknowledge the infringements and address general instructions to contracting authorities in order to remind them of their obligations under the EC Directives. If a major infringement is detected, however, proceedings under Article 169 EC may ensue. This shift in approach is only partial, however.

CONCLUSIONS

The nature of the legal tools at the disposal of the Commission, its limited manpower and the nature of the infringements in the public procurement area have rendered supranational monitoring inadequate. The early policy of the Commission has been ill-conceived. Too many resources have been wasted in running a system which is blatantly ineffective. Systematic challenge of infringements has provoked administrative inertia, preventing the development of a more selective enforcement policy and a better allocation of resources. At a supranational level, the emphasis should have been placed on challenging major infringements and monitoring large contracts with a European interest.

The supranational monitoring practice discussed is still being applied, however, and individuals are encouraged to resort to the Commission for assistance. Article 169 EC procedures are still frequently opened against alleged infringements. Nonetheless, the Commission is starting to acknowledge that the intrinsic features of public procurement enforcement render the use of Article 169 EC ineffective. In the Commission's own words, 'the penalties it has been able to impose . . . in response to complaints or on its own initiative had, in most cases, been imposed too late and have therefore proved counter-productive. Their ineffectiveness encourages infringements of the Community rules, and contracting authorities tend to regard the Commission's intervention under the procedure provided in Article 169 of the EEC Treaty as an arbitrary and unprovoked interference. Moreover, this ineffectiveness does not encourage contractors and suppliers to approach the Commission for assistance'.[88]

A shift in approach is being proposed. Emphasis is now being placed on

---

[87] Magliano (above, n 84) at 889.   [88] EC Commission, COM (87) 134 at 2.

the enhancement of decentralized control.[89] In its *Communication to the Council and European Parliament on the Principle of Subsidiarity*, the Commission stated that in the field of supervision and implementation 'it is important that more decentralised procedures be introduced for supervising the application of Community law in order to avoid 'apoplexy at the centre and paralysis at the extremities'. The best solution would be for the Member States to co-operate more closely in the examination of complaints for failure to comply with Community law. But first all national examining procedures would not have to show any marked differences in terms of guarantees and costs for plaintiffs . . .'.[90] The development of adequate means of redress at national level has therefore become one of the main elements of the Commission's public procurement enforcement strategy and rightly so. However, this strategy is still in the initial stages of its development and has not replaced the Commission's centralized efforts, at least with respect to individual complaints.

---

[89] The following chapters are devoted to the examination of the decentralized policy of the Commission and what its likely results will be.

[90] Reproduced in Europe Documents, Europe, No. 1804/05, 30 October 1992, at 14.

FIGURE 5:   Development of Article 169 EC procedures   1984–90

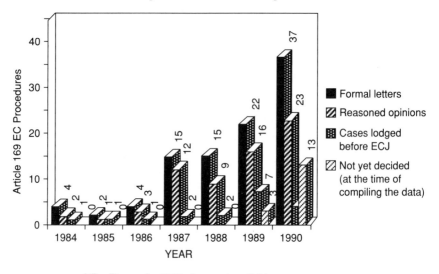

NB   Figures for 1991–4 are not available

FIGURE 6:   Article 169 EC Infraction procedures initiated in public procurement cases by year

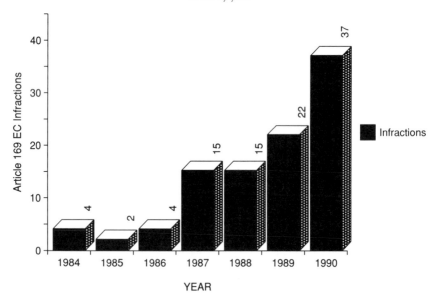

7

The Enforcement Level (II): The Community System and the Effective Judicial Protection of Individual Community Rights

INTRODUCTION

While individual Community rights originate at the supranational level, the main responsibility for ensuring their enforcement lies with national authorities and, more precisely, national courts, with the exception of possible direct individual actions before the Court of Justice.[1] As a corollary of the principles of supremacy, direct effect and the effectiveness of Community law, the applicable domestic proceedings must, moreover, ensure effective judicial protection of individual Community rights. When the national court is called upon to apply Community law, it is acting as a judicial organ of a unitary Community judicial power,[2] subordinate to the Court of Justice. It is up to national tribunals and courts, acting as Community judges, to ensure effective judicial protection of individual Community rights and, as a consequence, to control compliance by their national administrations with Community law obligations. It is not an exaggeration therefore to affirm that when performing their 'Community task', the attitude of national judges is of paramount importance and that they become the ultimate guarantors of the respect for Community law.[3] This is, in a nutshell, the basis of decentralized control in the Community, which is also referred to as the principle of dual vigilance.[4]

This duty on national judicial authorities is not only intended to satisfy the requirements of justice and the rule of law but also plays a crucial role in making the supranational structure workable. In a vast and heterogeneous legal, political and economic space such as the Community and given that the establishment of federal agencies of enforcement was not

---

[1] As the Court has established 'every time a rule of Community law confers rights on individuals, those rights, without prejudice to the methods of recourse made available by the Treaty, may be safeguarded by proceedings brought before the competent national courts'. Case 28/67, *Firma Molkerei-Zentrale Westfalen/Lippe GmbH* v. *Hauptzollamt Paderborn* [1968] ECR 143 at 153.   [2] Pescatore, *The Law of Integration* (Leiden, 1973) at 90.
[3] Rideau, 'Le rôle des États membres dans l'application du droit communautaire' (1972) *Annuaire Français de Droit International* 864 at 883.
[4] Weatherill, 'National Remedies and Equal Access to Public Procurement' (1990) 10 YEL 243 at 244.

envisaged,[5] effective control of compliance with Community law may only be achieved by involving national judicial systems in the task. The system is activated by judicial actions relating to Community legal issues brought by individuals before their national courts. In the words of the Court 'the vigilance of individuals concerned to protect their rights amounts to an effective supervision in addition to the supervision entrusted by Articles 169 and 170 EEC to the diligence of the Commission and the Member States'.[6] To round up the system and in order to guarantee a uniform interpretation of Community law in all Member States, Article 177 EC regulates the preliminary reference procedure. Needless to say, in order for the system to work correctly, individuals, in conjunction with their national courts, actively have to assume the role assigned to them.[7]

In the case of public procurement rules, decentralized control has acquired special importance for two main reasons. Firstly, the overwhelming quantity of public contracts subject to the Directives' provisions renders centralized monitoring and enforcement efforts ineffective. The pitfalls and insufficiencies of Article 169 EC proceedings may only be overcome by the establishment of efficient decentralized control, activated by injured undertakings and enforced by national judicial instances. Secondly, the very nature of the rights enshrined in the public procurement Directives is more effectively safeguarded by a decentralized rather than a centralized control mechanism. The Directives mainly provide for individual rights to be enforced against public authorities and, as the Court has pointed out, it is up to the repositories of such rights to assume the responsibility for their enforcement.[8]

THE PRINCIPLE OF PROCEDURAL AUTONOMY

Due to the interaction of the principle of institutional autonomy,[9] whereby Community law does not prescribe the remedies applicable in a particular

---

[5] With the exception of the Commission and Member States monitoring powers under Articles 169 and 170 EC. On these forms of action generally see Schermers and Waelbroeck, *Judicial Protection in the EEC*, 4th edn. (Deventer, 1987) 250–294.

[6] Case 26/62, *Van Gend and Loos* v. *Nederlandse Administratie der Belastingen* [1963] ECR 1 at 13.

[7] This explains why the Court's main concern in the initial stages of the Community was to make national courts and individuals aware and conscious of the importance of their role. See Stein and Vining, 'Citizen Access to Judicial Review of Administrative Action in a Transnational and Federal Context' in Jacobs (ed.), *European Law and the Individual* (Amsterdam, 1976) at 113 *ff*.

[8] 'In fact proceedings [brought before the competent national courts] by an individual are intended to protect individual rights in a specific case, whilst the intervention by the Community authorities has as its object the general and uniform observance of Commmunity law.'. Case 28/76, *Molkerei Zentrale* (above, n 1) at 153. See also Case 26/62, *Van Gend and Loos* (above, n 6). In this sense see also Coleman et Margue, 'L'action de la Communauté visant le respect des règles communautaires en matière de passation des marchés publics de fournitures et de travaux' (1989) RMC 546 at 548. [9] See Chapter 3.

situation, enforcement of the Community rights of individuals takes place via existing national judicial structures and, moreover, via the application of national rules of procedure. That is to say, the domestic body of rules governing the access to and conditions of judicial review by private individuals equally disciplines judicial actions concerning their Community rights.[10] This is the so-called 'principle of procedural autonomy',[11] enunciated by the Court in 1976.[12] Although merely a manifestation of the principle of institutional autonomy at the enforcement level, the principle of procedural autonomy has been discussed in detail by several commentators.[13]

Clearly, the assumption underlying the 'principle of procedural autonomy' is that national redress systems are self-sufficient in providing adequate mechanisms to ensure judicial protection of Community rights.[14] Although this assumption seems theoretically sound, its practical application demonstrates that it is not always correct for several reasons. Firstly, in a complicated and contingent legal system such as the Community's, where different legal traditions coexist, the declaration of the existence of individual rights at Community level is not always accompanied by a proper set of enforcement mechanisms at domestic level. Different legal approaches to individual rights often determine different redress mechanisms. Indeed, procedural rules are often designed as a parallel to existing individual rights. National approaches to judicial protection therefore vary from one Member State to another, depending on the substantial conception of the individual right or the context in which it is inserted.[15] If a

---

[10] Case 13/68, *SpA Salgoil* v. *Italian Ministry for Foreign Trade* [1986] ECR 453 at 462–463. This decision has however been the object of strong criticisms: see Kovar, 'Voies de droit ouvertes aux individus devant les instances nationales en cas de violation des normes et décisions du droit communautaire' in Larcier (ed.) *Les Recours des Individus devant les Instances nationales en cas de Violation du Droit Européen* (Brussels, 1978) 245 at 250. See also Case 6/71, *Rheinmühlen Düsseldorf* v. *Einfuhr- und Vorratsstelle für Getreide und Futtermittel* [1971] ECR 823.

[11] For a classic analysis of the principle, see Kovar in Larcier (ed.) (above, n 10) at 248 *ff*.

[12] Case 33/76, *Rewe Zentralfinanz* v. *Landwirtschaftskammer für das Saarland* [1976] ECR 1989 at 1997–8.

[13] See Bridge, 'Procedural aspects of the enforcement of European Community law through the legal systems of the Member States' (1984) 9 ELRev 28 at 30; Kovar in Larcier (ed.) (above, n 10); Mertens de Wilmars, 'L'efficacité des différentes techniques nationales de protection juridique contre les violations du droit communautaire par les autorités nationales et les particuliers' (1981) 17 CDE 379; Oliver, 'Enforcing Community rights in the English courts' (1987) 50 MLR 881; Steiner, 'How to Make the Action Suit the Case. Domestic Remedies for Breach of EEC Law' (1988) 13 ELRev 102.

[14] As Mertens de Wilmars plainly affirms, 'sans doute, à la base même de la solidarité qui rassemble les États et les peuples dans la Communauté, il y a l'adhésion aux institutions démocratiques qui implique, comme allant de soi, l'existence dans chaque État membre d'organes réalisant l'État de droit. Leur absence ou leur insuffisance notoire signifierait que ne sont pas ou ne sont plus réalisées les conditions de l'appartenance à la Communauté'. Mertens de Wilmars (above, n 13) at 381.

[15] For an analysis of how national approaches to public procurement determined the nature and extent of the legal remedies available in the area, see Chapters 9 and 10.

particular individual right is regarded as paramount in a given legal system, procedural safeguards of that right will be highly developed. On the contrary, where individual rights are subordinated to other social values considered of a higher importance, such as the public interest, procedural rules will benefit the latter to the detriment of the former. Moreover, a particular legal situation which in some States would confer an individual right, may only amount to a mere interest or legitimate expectation in others.[16]

In addition to this first level of difficulty, a further malfunction arises when Community law enters the picture. The objectives pursued by Community legislation may well be completely alien to national legal systems. Applicable procedural rules meant to serve as the enforcement vehicle of Community substantive rules become inadequate to respond to the requirements of Community law simply because they have not been designed to deal with them.[17] Either a positive attitude of national judges as regards the interpretation of those rights is needed in order to adapt them to national legal environments, or positive legislative action is required to overcome national procedural obstacles.

These considerations become more apparent when one analyses the case of the public procurement Directives. Until the adoption of the Remedies Directive,[18] no Community legislative initiative had tackled the harmonization of existing national redress procedures. As a result, the principle of procedural autonomy applied in absolute terms and any injured undertaking had to resort to national redress systems in order to have their public procurement Community rights judicially enforced. This situation was unsatisfactory. Although the correctness of domestic approaches as to the legal nature of contracts entered into by public authorities is not tackled by the Directives, nor should it be of Community concern, Community rules have a specific and well-defined objective: to open up public contracts to European-wide competition. The achievement of this objective requires the conduct of contracting authorities to be subject to a set of procedural obligations which increase the transparency and accountability of the award procedure. Both the Community objectives and the

---

[16] Which calls for a uniform notion of individual or subjective rights at Community level. On this point, see Fernández Martín, 'El efecto directo de las directivas y la protección de los derechos subjetivos comunitarios en la jurisprudencia del Tribunal de Justicia. Intento de sistematización' (1995) No. 126 *Noticias de la Unión Europea* 1.

[17] Rideau, 'Le contentieux de l'application du droit communautaire par les pouvoirs publics nationaux' (1974) *Dalloz-Sirey, chronique XIX,* 147 at 156. Once again in the words of Mertens de Wilmars, 'l'existence, dans chaque État membre, de systèmes de protection juridique assurés, fondés sur le droit et appropriés aux necessités et particularités nationales n'implique pas *ipso facto* une aptitude égale de ces systèmes à assurer une protection adéquate dans un ordre juridique commun, distinct par définition des ordres juridiques nationaux'. Mertens de Wilmars (above, n 10) at 381.

[18] Council Directive 89/665/EEC of 21 December 1989, OJ 1989, L395/33. Discussed at length in the following chapters.

procedural rules intended to achieve them were alien to some domestic legal systems.[19] Existing remedies at national level and even the understanding of national courts, could not foster an objective for which they have not been designed or are not conscious. In brief, different perceptions of the function and nature of public contracts in the Member States imply not only that existing remedies are substantially different, but that they may not be sufficient to guarantee a proper enjoyment and enforcement of individual rights deriving from the Community rules on public procurement. A new system of rights may thus require a new system of remedies to render the former effective.

The survival of national redress systems, where these prove insufficient to guarantee adequate enforcement of Community rights, is incompatible with the superior legal nature of Community provisions. The tension between the operation of the procedural autonomy principle and the requirements of the effectiveness of Community law has been the object of a far-reaching jurisprudence of the Court of Justice. The Court has gradually subordinated the application of the procedural autonomy principle to certain imperatives, which are analysed in the coming sections.

THE LIMITS TO THE PRINCIPLE OF PROCEDURAL AUTONOMY

Supremacy and Uniform Application of Community Law

The Court of Justice has consistently maintained that supremacy of Community law must prevail over the principle of institutional autonomy and, as a result, over the principle of procedural autonomy. Supremacy is the very essence of the Community legal order and means that Community law as a superior rule of law must be given full effect and force by national authorities over domestic legal approaches.[20] National legal considerations, of whatever nature, cannot serve as an excuse to escape the imperatives of Community law.[21] This position has been extended to cover national requirements of a constitutional nature.[22]

In the same vein, the principle of the uniform application of Community rights also calls for a limitation of the procedural autonomy principle. Since one of the pillars of the rule of law is that all citizens are equal (at

---

[19] Especially in those Member States approaching contracts of public authorities from a private law perspective such as Germany and the United Kingdom. See Chapters 4 and 10.

[20] Case 106/77, *Administrazione delle Finanze dello Stato* v. *Simmenthal SpA* [1978] ECR 629 at 644. See also Opinion 1/91 [1991] ECR I-6079 at 6102.

[21] Case 6/64, *Costa* v. *ENEL* [1964] ECR 1141. See also Case 52/75, *Commission* v. *Italy* [1976] ECR 277, See also Rideau (above, n 3) at 885–886.

[22] 'No provisions of municipal law, of whatever nature they may be, may prevail over Community law'. Case 11/70, *Internationale Handelsgesellschaft mbh* v. *Einfuhr- und Vorratsstelle für Getreide und Futtermittel* [1970] 1125 at 1127. See also Case 48/71, *Commission* v. *Italy* [1972] ECR 527 at 534.

least in formal terms), Community citizens, as the ultimate beneficiaries of Community rules, must be guaranteed a minimum degree of uniformity with respect to the application and enforcement of such rules throughout the Community.[23] This can only be achieved by means of positive harmonization measures. The Court of Justice has acknowledged this problem.[24] Despite the Court's pleas, Community legislative activity harmonizing procedures relating to actions based on Community law has been negligible to date.[25] This absence of positive action has led the Court to assume an active role and lay down minimum standards intended to provide a certain degree of uniformity. These standards, which have turned out to be far-reaching, have been developed in the context of the case law on the principle of effective judicial protection.

The Principle of Effective Judicial Protection[26]

The Early Definition of the Principle

The principle of effective judicial protection which developed on the basis of a wide teleological interpretation of Article 5 EC embodying the 'fidelity' principle,[27] places national authorities under a duty to ensure that individual rights arising from Community law enjoy effective judicial protection. In essence, it constitutes the application of the general principle of effectiveness to the enforcement level and is the most powerful constraint on national procedural autonomy.[28]

The first indication of the principle can be found in 1968, when the

---

[23] Case 94/71, *Schlüter & Maack v. Hauptzollamt Hamburg-Jonas* [1972] ECR 307 at 319. See also Joined Cases 205–215/82, *Deutsche Milchkontor Gmbh & others v. Germany* [1983] ECR 2633 at 2665 *ff.*

[24] Case 45/76, *Comet v. Produktschap voor Siergewassen* [1976] ECR 2043 and Case 33/76, *Rewe v. Landswirtschaftskammer* (above, n 12).

[25] See Curtin, 'Directives: the Effectiveness of Judicial Protection of Individual Rights' (1990) 27 CMLRev 709 at 726–727. The Court has even expressed its concern about the 'regrettable absence of Community provisions harmonising procedure and time limits' (Case 130/79, *Express Dairy Food v. IBAPI* [1980] ECR 1887).

[26] Dubois, 'A propos de deux principes généraux du droit communautaire' (1988) *Revue Française de Droit Administratif* 691; Curtin, (1990) (above, n 25); Curtin, 'The Decentralised Enforcement of Community Law Rights. Judicial Snakes and Ladders' in O'Keeffe and Curtin, *Constitutional Adjudication in European Community and National Law* (London, 1992) 33 *ff*; Oliver (1987) (above, n 13); Barav, 'Enforcement of Community rights in the National Courts: the Case for Jurisdiction to Grant Interim Relief' (1989) 26 CMLRev 369.

[27] See Temple Lang, 'Community Constitutional law: Article 5 EEC Treaty' (1990) 27 CMLRev 645; Constantinesco, 'L'article 5 CEE: de la bonne foi à la loyauté communautaire' in Capotorti and others (eds.), *Du Droit International au Droit de l'Intégration: Liber Amicorum Pierre Pescatore* (Baden-Baden, 1987) 97.

[28] It is submitted that the clearest and most decisive formulation of the effectiveness principle is contained in the *Simmenthal* judgment (Case 106/77, *Simmenthal* (above, n 20) at 644). See further Chapter 4. Most commentators, however, refer to the principle of effective judicial protection as an independent principle.

Court held that national courts are required 'to protect the interests of those persons subject to their jurisdiction who may be affected by any possible infringement [of the Treaty] by ensuring for them direct and immediate protection of their interests'.[29] In the *Rewe Zentrale* and *Comet* decisions the Court of Justice held that, 'in application of the principle of co-operation laid down in Article 5 EEC, national courts were entrusted with ensuring the legal protection conferred on individuals by the direct effect of the provisions of Community Law' and that consequently, national procedural remedies must not make it 'impossible in practice to exercise rights which the national courts have a duty to protect'.[30]

The Court of Justice has reiterated this principle on different occasions.[31] Some commentators, however, regard *Johnston*[32] as the definitive consecration of the principle.[33] According to the Court in that case 'the requirement of judicial control reflects a general principle of law which underlies the constitutional traditions common to the Member States' and is therefore also a Community law principle. Since Community obligations are legally binding and prevail over national law, 'effective judicial control as regards compliance with the applicable provisions of Community law and of national legislation intended to give effect to the rights for which the directive provides' is an imperious consequence of the principle in question.[34] In the same vein, the Court held one year later in *Heylens* that 'since free access to employment is a fundamental right which the Treaty confers individually on each worker in the Community the existence of a remedy of a judicial nature against any decision of a national authority refusing the benefit of that right is essential in order to secure for the individual effective protection'.[35] It is the responsibility of Member States,

[29] Case 13/68, *SpA Salgoil* v. *Italian Ministry for Foreign Trade* [1968] ECR 453 at 463. Barav (above, n 26) at 373.

[30] Case 45/76, *Comet* (above, n 24) and Case 33/76, *Rewe* (above, n 12). The Court went on to add a second limitation by ruling that national procedural rules 'designed to ensure the protection of the rights which individuals acquire through the direct effect of Community law' must not be 'less favourable than those governing the same right of action on an internal matter'. This second restriction is founded on the basis of the 'non-discrimination principle' of Article 7 EEC (now Article 6 EC) applied to access to judicial review. The principle of non-discrimination may not be construed in a manner which renders impossible in practice the actual enforcement of Community rights. In other words, the fact that national actions are not possible as regards similar claims cannot serve as a justification to deny actions intended to protect Community rights. 'Effectiveness' prevails over non-discrimination. Case 199/82, *Administrazione delle Finanze dello Stato* v. *San Giorgio* [1983] ECR 3595.

[31] See *inter alia* Barav, 'La répétition de l'indu dans la jurisprudence de la Cour de Justice des Communautés Européennes' (1981) 17 CDE 507; Hubeau, 'La répétition de l'indu en Droit Communautaire' (1981) 17 RTDE 442; Oliver (1987) (above, n 13).

[32] Case 222/84, *Johnston* v. *Chief Constable of the Royal Ulster Constabulary* [1986] ECR 1651.

[33] Dubois (above, n 26) at 693. See also Advocate General Van Gerven, Opinion in Case C-271/91 of 26 January 1993, not yet reported.

[34] Case 222/84, *Johnston* (above, n 32) at 1682.

[35] Case 222/86, *UNECTEF* v. *Heylens* [1987] ECR 4097 at 4117.

irrespective of their national legal traditions, to ensure that individual rights which derive from Community law 'are effectively protected in each case'.[36] The Court has also established that 'where Community legislation does not specifically provide any penalty for an infringement or refers for that purpose to national laws, regulations and administrative provisions, Article 5 of the Treaty requires the Member States to take all necessary measures to guarantee the application and effectiveness of Community law . . .'.[37] It is generally accepted, as a result of the Court's case law, that effectiveness of the judicial remedies available to protect the individual rights arising from Community law is an imperative obligation on Member States.[38]

The Court's reasoning could not have been otherwise. A fundamental right to effective judicial control applies in all democratic societies. More broadly stated, in any system subject to the rule of law, the existence of effective judicial remedies is an inescapable element of that concept. Indeed, anytime a legal right is conferred, the rule of law urges that such a right must be judicially enforced whenever it is transgressed.[39] The Community system has been held to be subject to the rule of law as an autonomous legal order.[40] Since Community rights form an integral part of the legal heritage of individuals,[41] individual Community rights are to be afforded judicial protection[42] at the appropriate levels, not only in the same manner as if they were rights of a domestic origin, but according to stricter standards due to their superior nature. Examples of stricter standards required by the Court in the context of the effective judicial protection principle are provided by the *Factortame* and *Francovich* cases. These judgments deserve particular and individual attention.

---

[36] Case 179/84, *Bozzetti* v. *Intermizzi SpA and Ministero del Tesoro* [1989] ECR 2301 at 2317–8

[37] Case 68/88, *Commission* v. *Greece* [1989] ECR 2977 at 2983. See also C-326/89 *Hansen* [1990] ECR I-2911, at para. 17; Case C-7/90, *Vandevenne* [1991] ECR I-4371 at para. 11.

[38] Barav (1989) (above, n 26) at 379; Curtin (1990) (above, n 25) at 729; Dubois (above, n 26) at 695.

[39] 'For a country to be under the rule of law, it is absolutely indispensable that it has a high court, with all the possible safeguards of independence, impartiality and competence, before whom can be brought an action to set aside any decision maintained to be contrary to law'. Duguit, *Leçons de Droit Public Général* (Paris, 1926) cited by Schwartz, *French Administrative Law and the Common World Law* (New York, 1954) at 112. Or in the words of Advocate General Darmon, 'the right to challenge a measure before the courts is inherent in the rule of law'. Opinion in Case 222/84, *Johnston* (above, n 32) at 1656. For a fuller examination of the meaning of the rule of law, see Schwartz, cit. at 108 *ff* and 307 *ff*.

[40] Case 294/83, *Parti écologiste Les Verts* v. *European Parliament* [1986] ECR 1339 and Opinion 1/91, [1991] ECR I-6079 at 6102. In the words of Advocate General Darmon, 'Formed of States based on the rule of law, the European Community is necessarily a Community of law. It was created and works on the understanding that all Member States will show equal respect for the Community legal order'. Opinion in Case 222/84, *Johnston* (above, n 32) at 1656.   [41] Case 26/62, *Van Gend and Loos* (above, n 6) at 12.

[42] In this vein see Dubois (above, n 26) at 700.

The *Factortame* decision[43]

The *Factortame* decision was a breakthrough in the Court of Justice's case law. It represents the first far-reaching application of the principle of effectiveness, or rather, the effective judicial protection principle, at the enforcement level. In that case the Court examined a fundamental principle of domestic constitutional law. This caused considerable legal turmoil in Britain.[44] There is no need to enter into an analysis of the material facts of the case since they are well-known and have been widely discussed.[45] It suffices to recall that the case arose before the Divisional Court of the Queen's Bench Division, went through the Court of Appeal and ended up in the House of Lords which posed a preliminary reference to the Court of Justice. The Court of Justice was asked whether Community law vested in national courts the jurisdiction to suspend the operation of a national legal provision alleged to contravene Community law, pending a conclusive determination of this issue, where such a power does not exist under national law.[46] The applicants, who alleged irreparable damages, requested the suspension of the application of an Act of Parliament which they claimed was contrary to Community law.[47]

What was really at stake was how far the Court of Justice would interpret the effectiveness requirement in view of the delicate domestic constitutional legal issues involved. On the one hand, if Community law was interpreted as requiring the suspension of the application of an Act of

[43] Case C-213/89, *R* v. *Secretary of State for Transport, ex p. Factortame* [1990] ECR I-2433. This case attracted well deserved academic attention: see *inter alia* Barav (1989) (above, n 26); Barav and Simon, 'Le droit communautaire et la suspension provisoire des mesures nationales. Les enjeux de l'affaire Factortame' (1990) RMC 591; García de Enterría, 'El problema de los poderes del juez nacional para suspender cautelarmente la ejecución de las leyes nacionales en consideración al Derecho Comunitario Europeo' (1989) REDA, núm. 63, 411; García de Enterría, 'Novedades sobre los procesos en el conflicto de pesca anglo-español' (1989) REDA, núm. 64, 593; García de Enterría, 'La sentencia *Factortame* del Tribunal de Justicia de las Comunidades Europeas' (1990) REDA, núm. 67, 401; Gravells, 'Effective Protection of Community Law Rights: Temporary Disapplication of an Act of Parliament' (1991) *Public Law* 180; Emiliou, Sharpston and Snyder, 'European Community Law' in Pettet (ed.) (1992) 45 *Current Legal Problems* (Annual review) 49; Oliver, 'Interim Measures: some Recent Developments' (1992) 29 CMLRev 7 at 10 *ff*; noted by Toth (1990) 27 CMLRev 573; Oliver, D., 'Fishing on Incoming Tide' (1991) 54 MLR 442 and especially Craig, 'Sovereignty of the United Kingdom after *Factortame*' (1991) 11 YEL 221 where the author revises the theoretical foundations of the concept of parliamentary sovereignty in the light of the *Factortame No. 1* decision.

[44] See the reactions of the British press to the judgment cited in Toth (above, n 43) at 583. Also Weatherill (above, n 4) 285 at n 234.

[45] See Barav (1989) (above, n 26) at 376; Oliver, D. (above, n 43) at 446.

[46] Barav (1989) (above, n 26) at 370.

[47] The alleged Community rights had only a putative character until the Court of Justice itself adopted a final decision and this was an important additional aspect of the case. All previous judgments urging national courts to ensure effective and immediate protection of individual rights arising from directly effective Community law provisions, had been made with reference to rights whose existence had already been established by the Court of Justice.

Parliament by national judges, traditional British constitutional principles denying such a power to courts would be overruled, and with it, according to some writers, the sovereignty of Parliament itself would be in question.[48] On the other hand, if the suspensory measures claimed were denied, the rights which the parties derived from Community law would be deprived of any effectiveness. The fact that irreparable damages would result unless the applicants were protected from the application of the challenged Act by way of interim measures was not disputed at any stage.[49]

In a very brief judgment, the Court of Justice began by redrafting the preliminary reference. It was simplified, maybe excessively, in the following terms: the question is whether a national Court which, in a case before it concerning Community law, considers that the sole obstacle which precludes it from granting interim relief is a rule of national law must disapply that rule. The Court, referring to its *Simmenthal* judgment, recalled the principle of supremacy of Community law which required that all directly applicable Community rules must be fully and uniformly applied in all Member States and the well-established obligation on national jurisdictions to ensure the legal protection of the rights which individuals derive from directly effective Community provisions. It stated that it would be incompatible with the inherent requirements of Community law to permit any provision of national law or any legal, administrative or judicial practice to impair the effectiveness of Community law by withholding from the competent national courts the power 'to do everything necessary at the moment of its application to set aside national legislative provisions, which might prevent, even temporarily, Community rules from having full force and effect'.[50]

In the light of these statements, the next step was obvious enough. The Court applied its reasoning to the case before it and concluded that '. . . the full effectiveness of Community law would be just as much impaired if a rule of national law could prevent a court seized of a dispute governed by Community law from granting interim relief in order to ensure the full effectiveness of the judgment to be given on the existence of the rights claimed under Community law. It follows that a court which in those circumstances would grant interim relief, if it were not for a rule of national law, is obliged to set aside that rule'.[51]

---

[48] Wade, 'What Happened to the Sovereignty of Parliament?' (1991) 107 LQR 1.

[49] In his Opinion, Advocate General Tesauro affirmed that 'the obligation imposed by Community law on the national courts to ensure the effective judicial protection' [*in other words, the principle of effectiveness operating at the enforcement level*] 'directly conferred on the individual by provisions of Community law includes the obligation, if the need arises and where the factual and legal preconditions are met, to afford interim and urgent protection to rights claimed on the basis of such provisions of Community law, pending a final determination and any interpretation by way of a preliminary ruling given by the Court of Justice'. Opinion in Case C-213/89, *Factortame* (above, n 43).

[50] Case C-213/89, *Factortame* (above, n 43) at para. 20.   [51] Ibid. at para. 21.

Thus, as a matter of principle, national courts are placed under the obligation to set aside any rule preventing them from granting interim relief where irreparable damages are foreseen. In *Johnston, Heylens* and *Bozzetti*, effective judicial control was seen as a prerequisite of Community law. In *Factortame*, the Court goes a step further by specifying that effective judicial protection may imply the award of interim measures, even if these are not available at national level. The practical consequence of the Court's decision, as pointed out in the British Government's submissions,[52] was to oblige national courts (and indirectly the national legislature) to create a parallel enforcement procedure at national level for alleged Community rights. This obligation derives from the general principle of effectiveness of Community law[53] and empowers national courts to award interim measures not provided for in the domestic legal order. It therefore goes beyond a mere statement of *de lege ferenda*, or what the law should be like.

This conclusion was debatable, however. First of all, it was in open conflict with the Court's previous statements in *Rewe*, where it held that national courts were 'under no duty to create new remedies for the application of Community law'.[54] Plaza Martín has explained the apparent contradiction by holding that the Court's affirmations in *Rewe* built upon the assumption that domestic remedies were adequate to protect individual Community rights in the instant case.[55] Equally, a more conservative interpretation argued that the Court limited itself in *Factortame* to obliging national courts to disregard norms preventing them from giving full effect to individual Community rights and that no positive action was in fact required. National courts were merely under a duty to search for an appropriate remedy amongst the whole panoply which the national legal system offers. Thus in the instant case, no real remedy was created, as the grant of interim measures is possible under English law, although not against the Crown.[56]

It is submitted that this position, although formally correct, ignores the practical consequences of the judgment. The reasoning used by the Court, duly supported by its previous case law concerning the protection of individual Community rights, seems to give a clear indication that the response

---

[52] See Report for the Hearing, Case C-213/89, *Factortame* (above, n 43).

[53] See Toth (1990), CMLRev 573; Barav and Simon (above, n 43) at 591; Curtin (1990) (above, n 26) at 709.

[54] Case 158/80, *Rewe Handelsgesellschaft Nord MbH & Rewe-mark Steffen* v. *Hauptzollamt Kiel* [1981] ECR 1805 at 1838.

[55] Plaza Martín 'Furthering the Effectiveness of EC Directives and the Judicial Protection of Individual Community Rights thereunder' (1994) 43 ICLQ 26 at 38.

[56] See s. 31 of the Supreme Court Act 1981 and *American Cyanamid Co.* v. *Ethicon Ltd* [1975] AC 396, which contains the common law conditions for the granting of interim relief. This position was maintained by Weatherill (above, n 4) at 285. In the same vein, commenting on Art. 6 of the equal treatment Directive and the *Marshall I* decision, see Prechal, 'Remedies after Marshall' (1990) 27 CMLR 451 at 468.

would have been the same, even if no interim relief was available at all in English law. In fact, one can argue that the impossibility of claiming interim relief against the Crown in the case under discussion meant that a remedy did not exist in the specific circumstances. The Court, however, smartly avoided tackling the specific issue of whether the creation of new remedies was required by re-drafting the national Court's preliminary reference. It thereby limited itself to considering whether, given the existence of relief, any obstacle to the grant of interim relief had to be dissapplied.[57] It is submitted that the 'principle of effectiveness', of which *Factortame* is merely an application, imposes an obligation on national courts to provide for remedies not contemplated by national law in a specific context.[58] This position is further supported by the *Francovich* decision which supplemented *Factortame*.[59]

The *Francovich* and *Bonifaci* case[60]

If *Factortame* caused great impact in Community law spheres, the *Francovich* and *Bonifaci* case was not far behind. In these joined preliminary references posed by two Italian courts, the Court was asked whether a private party who suffered a loss due to the failure of a Member State to transpose

[57] As Simon and Barav have pointed out, a result of the redrafting of the preliminary question was that many crucial points were left aside, especially the question whether Community law required national courts to create remedies *ex novo* in order to guarantee the effective protection of individual Community rights. This attitude of the Court attracted a strong criticism by both authors. Barav and Simon (above, n 43) at 549. In fact, it has been suggested that the Court deliberately simplified the reference to avoid entering into more turbulent waters. Arrowsmith, *Civil Liability of Public Authorities* (Winteringham, 1992) at 38. This strategy has merely enabled the Court to postpone the resolution of these questions until later. Joined Cases C-46 and 48/93 *Factortame III* and *Brasserie du Pêcheur* pending at the time of writing, require, *inter alia*, that the Court gives an anwer to this question.

[58] In this vein see also Curtin (1990) (above, n 25) at 755–756. In fact the Court of Justice's *Factortame No. 1* decision was interpreted by the House of Lords as requiring that interim relief must be available against the Crown when rights arising from Community law are at stake ([1990] 3 CMLR 375).

[59] *Factortame* was followed by the decision in *Zuckerfabrik*, in which the Court extended the duty of national courts to grant interim relief in those cases in which the legality of Community law was questioned by a private party (Joined Cases C-143/88 and C-92/89, *Zuckerfabrik Süderdithmarschen and Zuckerfabrik Soest* v. *Hauptzollamt Itzehoe* [1991] ECR I-415).

[60] Joined Cases C-6 and C-9/90, *A. Francovich and D. Bonifaci* v. *Italy* [1991] ECR I-5357. This decision, not surprisingly, has attracted even more attention than *Factortame*. See *inter alia* Barav, 'Damages against the State for Failure to Implement EC Directives' (1991) *New Law Journal* 1584; noted by Bebr, (1992) 29 CMLRev 557; Curtin, 'State Liability under Community Law: a New Remedy for Private Parties' (1992) 21 ILJ 74; Duffy, 'Damages against the State: a New Remedy for Failure to Implement Community Obligations' (1992) 17 ELRev 133; Gilliams, 'Effectiveness of European Community Public Procurement Law after *Francovich*' (1992) 1 PPLR 292; Lasok, K.P.E., 'State Liability for Breach of Community Law' (1992) 5 *International Company and Commercial Law Review* 186; Ross, 'Beyond *Francovich*' (1993) 56 MLR 55; Schockweiler, 'La responsabilité de l'autorité nationale en cas de violation du

a Directive into national law[61] was entitled to claim economic compensation against the State for the damages resulting from the State's breach of its obligations. The matter was further complicated by the fact that both Advocate General Mischo[62] and the Court found that the alleged provisions could not be considered as having direct effect. Even though the Court stated that the existence of different options in a Directive does not exclude the possibility of the Directive's provisions being directly effective, in the instant case the freedom left to Member States prevented this particular Directive's provisions from being unconditional.[63] This, however, according to the Court, and this is a crucial point, did not preclude the Directive from granting rights to individuals. These rights were just not sufficiently precise and unconditional to be invoked and applied as they stood, without further intervention by the addressee Member State.[64]

With respect to the question of damages, the Court of Justice, after citing its *Simmenthal* and *Factortame* case law,[65] recalled that national courts were obliged to give full effect to Community law rules and to protect the right which individuals may derive from them. The full effectiveness of Community norms would be questioned, and the protection of the rights they provide for weakened, if individuals could not obtain compensation when their rights had been harmed by a violation of Community law by a Member State.[66] Thus, the Court concluded that judicial protection of individual Community rights implies that the State is liable for all damages caused to individuals by breaches of Community law and that such liability is 'inherent in the scheme provided for by the Treaty'.[67] The Court based State liability on Article 5 EC, the provision on which the 'effectiveness principle' has been developed, since the obligation of effacing the illegal consequences of a breach of Community law, flows, amongst others, from

droit communautaire' (1992) 28 RTDE 27; Smith, 'The Francovich case: State liability and the Individual's Right to Damages' (1992) 13 ECLR 129; Snyder, 'The Effectiveness of European Community law: Institutions, Processes, Tools and Techniques' (1993) 56 MLR 19; Steiner, 'From Direct Effect to *Francovich*: Shifting Means of Enforcement of Community Law' (1993) 18 ELRev 3; Szyszczak, 'European Community law; New Remedies, New Directions?' (1992) 55 MLR 690; Temple Lang, 'New Legal Effects resulting from the Failure to Fulfil Obligations under European Community Law: the *Francovich* Judgment' (1992–1993) 16 *Fordham International Law Journal* 1.

[61] In a previous judgment the Court had condemned Italy for failing to transpose the Directive in question. Case 122/87, *Commission* v. *Italy* [1989] ECR 143.

[62] Opinion in Joined Cases C-6–9/90, *Francovich* (above, n 60) at para. 31.

[63] See Curtin (1992), ILJ (above, n 60) at 77–78. Steiner suggests that the Court's finding that the Directive lacked direct effect was deliberate beacause 'it wished to establish a remedy for Member States' infringements which did not depend on the need to prove direct effects. In this way, the problems associated with the directives arising from their lack of horizontal effect would be largely circumvented' (above, n 60) at 9.

[64] Opinion in Joined Cases C-6–9/90, *Francovich* (above, n 60) at para. 60.

[65] I.e., which developed the principle of effective judicial protection in more detail.

[66] Joined Cases C-6–9/90, *Francovich* (above, n 60) at paras. 32 and 33.

[67] Ibid. at para. 35.

that provision.[68] The Court then defined the conditions under which a State could be held liable and, consequently, when individuals derive a right to compensatory damages for losses resulting from the failure to implement a Directive into national law. First of all, the Directive must imply the attribution of individual rights. Secondly, the content of such rights must be capable of being ascertained on the basis of the Directive's provisions as they stand. Lastly, a causal link must exist between the breach of the obligation by the State and the prejudice suffered.[69] The Court finally held, in accordance with its previous case law, that it was up to national regulations of State liability to define the procedural details according to which compensation of the damage suffered is to be awarded, always bearing in mind the principles developed in *Comet* and subsequent case law.

As happens with any statement of principle, the ruling in *Francovich* remains ambiguous in many respects. Thus, most commentators discussing the judgment have concentrated on trying to define the parameters within which the *Francovich* principle may operate. Some have adopted a radical view,[70] whereas others have been more cautious.[71] A detailed discussion of these fascinating issues would take us away from our main subject-matter. Nonetheless, it is necessary to examine some of these questions, as they are relevant to the public procurement area.

The first issue is whether State liabilty under *Francovich* is limited to the case where the breach consists of the non-implementation or incorrect implementation of Directives enshrining individual rights. It is submitted that the principles established in *Francovich* cover any Member States' breach of Community obligations. It would make no sense to limit it to certain violations, since the decisive factor must be the existence of damages which are directly or indirectly caused by the State's failure to comply with its Community obligations. Furthermore, it seems illogical to recognize an obligation to compensate for failure to implement a Directive and not for failure to comply with original Treaty provisions. This conclusion is supported by the Court's statements in *Francovich* when it held that Article 5 EC obliges Member States to 'eliminate the unlawful consequences of a breach of Community law' and that this obligation is '*particularly* indispensable when . . . the full effectiveness of Community rules is subject to the condition of further action by the State . . .'.[72] In this case, the first two conditions established in *Francovich* will only be of relevance when non-directly effective provisions of Community law enshrining individual rights are at stake, independently of their nature.[73] On the other hand, the third

---

[68] Ibid. at para. 36.   [69] Ibid. at para. 40.
[70] Ross (above, n 60) at 71.   [71] Steiner (above, n 60).
[72] Joined Cases C-6 and C-9/90, *Francovich* (above, n 60) at para. 36.
[73] As we will discuss in the course of this chapter, the *Francovich* principle affects any Community provision which, although not fulfilling the criteria for direct effect, nevertheless

condition, relation of causality between the damage and the violation of Community law, seems of general application to any infraction.

Another interesting issue concerns the extent of State liability. This has given rise to varying interpretations. The Court has not explicitly required fault on the part of the State for it to be liable for damages. Moreover it did not follow Advocate General Mischo's suggestion that the relevant principles should be those developed by the Court itself in relation to the 'non-contractual' liability of Community institutions, which are quite restrictive. Does this imply that even *bona fide* breaches of Community law generate the liability of the State? Controversy also exists regarding definition of the boundaries delimiting the competences of national courts when awarding damages and the role to be played by national procedural rules governing the action. In line with its *Comet* decision, the Court of Justice has explicitly stated that procedural rules applicable to a claim for damages are those in force in the different domestic legal orders, always subject to the 'effectiveness principle'.[74] But how far may national courts go in applying national approaches to State liability? Must damages be granted automatically once a breach of Community law is held to exist, or are they empowered to balance the public and private interests involved in an action for damages, as is the normal practice in most Member States? What about the question of causation and remoteness? As Snyder rightly points out, the principle of State liability may prove a powerful political and legal symbol, which must therefore be cautiously judged.[75]

An answer to all these questions may be forthcoming when the Court delivers its judgment on Joined Cases C-46 and 48/93 *Factortame III* and *Brasseries du Pêcheur*. The *Bundesgerichtshof* and the Divisional Court (Queen's Bench Division) have submitted more than ten preliminary questions calling for clarification of the extent and limits of the State liability principle arising from *Francovich*.[76] These include whether *Francovich* may be extended to damages caused by breaches of Community law other than the incorrect, or lack of implementation of Directive, whether the degree

---

grants individual rights. This would include those provisions which do satisfy the direct effect test, but are being enforced by an individual against another individual, that is, on an horizontal relationship. This category not only includes Directives' provisions but also Treaty provisions from which the Court has only recognized vertical direct effect, such as Article 30 EC.

[74] Understood in its broadest sense as discussed above in this chapter and not only as developed in Case 45/76, *Comet* (above, n 24).

[75] Snyder (above, n 60) at 45. He quotes the following passage from Diver ('The Judge as Political Powerbroker: Superintending Structural Change in Public Institutions' (1979) 65 *Virginia Law Review* 43 at 80): '. . . a declaration of liability creates an abstraction, an absolute claim on public resources. Through its visibility and its authoritative source, it commands central attention on the crowded public agenda. A judicial declaration demands responsive action, and it stirs political actions to prepare such a response.'.

[76] The list of questions posed by both national courts may be consulted in OJ 1993, C94/13 and 92/4.

of fault on the public authorities may be considered, whether lost profit must also be granted and so on.

Pending the conclusions of those cases, a preliminary indication of the Court's future approach is provided by its decision in *Marshall II*.[77] The case, which was related to the previous *Marshall I* ruling,[78] dealt with Article 6 of the equal treatment Directive. Without entering into the details of the case (which also gives rise to a number of interesting questions with respect to horizontal direct effect),[79] one of the questions at stake was whether an upper limit on compensation established by applicable national rules is compatible with Article 6 of the equal treatment Directive and, more generally, with the principle of effective judicial protection as developed by *Francovich*.[80] The Court, elaborating on its previous approach to this subject,[81] quashed the statutory limitation of damages and held that whenever economic compensation is chosen by Member States as the means to ensure equal opportunities, it must, in order to comply with Community law requirements and 'in accordance with national rules on the matter', have a deterrent effect and, in any event, provide for full compensation of all damage caused.[82] The Court departed from the prudent position of Advocate General Van Gerven, who had suggested that 'at the actual state of Community law', the statutory limit of damages was to be sustained and, moreover, that an award of damages which does not fully compensate the actual loss suffered was to be admitted on public interest grounds.[83] The Court appears determined to apply an extensive interpretation of the conditions of State liability deriving from Community law.

However, this extensive interpretation is problematic. If fault is not required and damages may not be limited by public interest considerations,

---

[77] Case C-271/91, *M.H. Marshall v. Southampton and South West Hampshire Area Health Authority* [1993] ECR I-4367. Noted by Curtin (1994) 31 CMLRev 653.

[78] Case 152/84, *Marshall v. Southampton and South West Hampshire Area Health Authority* [1986] ECR 723.

[79] Advocate General Van Gerven suggested that the Court reverse its previous *Marshall I* decision and accept the possibility of horizontal direct effect which had been explicitly excluded in this judgment. Opinion Case C-271/91 (above, n 77) at paras. 11 and 12. The same attitude was adopted by Advocate General Lenz in his Opinion in Case C-91/92, *Paola Faccini Dori v. Recreb Srl* [1994] ECR I-3325.

[80] Section 65(1) of the Sex Discrimination Act 1975 (SDA) provides that an industrial tribunal can make an order requiring compensation to be paid where it finds that a complaint relating to sex discrimination in employment is well founded. Under section 65(2) of the SDA, however, the amount of such compensation may not exceed a specified limit.

[81] Case 14/83, *Von Colson and Kamann v. Land Nordrhein-Westfalen* [1984] ECR 1891. See also Case 79/83, *Harz v. Deutsche Tradax GmbH* [1984] ECR 1921 and Case 68/88, *Commission v. Greece* (above, n 37) 2983, which already provided for certain guidelines to determine the amount of economic compensation. In order to be effective, compensation had to be adequate in relation to the damages suffered, and have an effective, proportional and deterrent character. [82] C-271/91, *Marshall II* (above, n 77) para. 26.

[83] See Opinion of Advocate General Van Gerven in Case C-271/91 (above, n 77) at para. 17.

as the Advocate General had suggested they should be, individuals may claim unlimited damages, which would unfairly punish national treasuries. It would also clearly fetter the discretion of public authorities when adopting decisions in the public interest.[84] The Court is departing from national regulations of State liability which usually adopt a cautious approach to this subject. Furthermore, to require a stricter liability regime for breaches of Community law than that applicable to Community institutions themselves, or even national authorities in their domestic legal systems, would be going too far. Indeed, all national legal orders are built upon the rule of law and are the legal endorsement of democratic principles. Therefore, applicable domestic State liability regulations as applied and developed by national courts respond *prima facie* to democratic principles and therefore guarantee a fair balance between individual rights and the general interest.[85] It is submitted that the degree of liability should be made proportional to the degree of fault involved in the breach.[86] Inspiration may be drawn from current practices at the domestic level.[87] It is hoped that in its forthcoming decisions on the matter, the Court will weigh all aspects of State liability and that it will develop a reasonable approach to such an important issue.

The Case of Non-directly Effective Provisions

Francovich and *Factortame* have added to the Court's case law relating to the availability of remedies for individuals to make their Community rights effective. Some unresolved questions remain, however, with respect to the relationship between these cases and the direct effect doctrine. Both doctrines are inspired by the same objective: enhancing the effectiveness of Community law and the protection of Community rights at the national level. How do they interact with each other? Before both decisions were decided it was unclear whether the effective judicial protection principle was to be extended to non-directly effective provisions which were, nonetheless, intended to create individual rights.

Pursuant to the Court's initial case law, individuals could only claim the enforcement of 'precise and unconditional' provisions of Directives before national courts. However, if Member States have failed to transpose a Directive's provisions into national law, rights embodied in non-directly effective provisions were protected by means of so-called 'indirect effect'.

[84] For further discussion of current domestic approaches see Chapters 9 and 10.

[85] See Steiner (above, n 60) at 12 *ff.*

[86] In this connection, see the considerations of Judge Schockweiler (Case C-271/91) at 46. See also Steiner (above, n 60) at 17.

[87] On national State liability regulations generally, see Schockweiler, Wivenes and Godart, 'Le régime de la responsabilité extra-contractuelle du fait d'actes juridiques dans la Communauté européenne' (1990) 26 RTDE 27.

The furthest the Court had gone with respect to non-directly effective provisions was to state that national courts are under an obligation to interpret national legislation, either pre-dating or post-dating the Directive's implementation deadline, to the greatest extent possible in the light of the Directive.[88] If national legislation was openly in conflict with the non-implemented or faultily implemented Directive, commentators agree that under the 'indirect effect' doctrine, national courts are not required, although they may do so,[89] to set aside conflicting national law.[90] Since the literature dealing with this precise subject is vast, there is no need to discuss this issue in detail.[91] The same solution was also applied to provisions which, although fulfilling the direct effect test, do not enjoy horizontal direct effect according to the Court, but are being alleged against other individuals before national courts.

Following *Francovich* it is clear that the Court does not intend to limit the application of the effective judicial protection principle 'only to directly effective community provisions'.[92] This is what follows from *Wagner Miret*[93] and *Faccini Dori*,[94] which, until the decisions in *Factortame III* and *Brasseries du Pêcheur*[95] are delivered, constitute the latest judicial application of the effective judicial protection principle. *Wagner Miret* concerned the same type of Directive at stake in *Francovich*, that is, a non-directly effective Directive which nonetheless provided for individual rights. Spain

[88] 'In so far as it is given discretion to do so under national law', Case 14/83, *Von Colson* (above, n 81) at para. 28. See also Case C-106/89, *Marleasing* v. *La Comercial de Alimentación* [1990] ECR 4135.

[89] See the House of Lords decision in *Litster* v. *Forth Dry Dock and Engineering Co. Ltd* [1989] 2 CMLR 194.

[90] Galmot and Bonichot, 'La Cour de justice des Communautés européennes et la transposition des directives en droit national' (1988) *Revue Française de Droit Administratif* 1 at 20.

[91] As regards the evolution of the direct effect doctrine, see *inter alia*, Winter, 'Direct Applicability and Direct Effect. Two Distinct and Different Concepts in Community Law' (1972) 9 CMLRev 425; Easson, 'Can Directives Impose Obligations on Individuals?' (1979) 4 ELRev 67; Pescatore, 'The Doctrine of Direct Effect: an Infant Disease in Community Law' (1983) 8 ELRev 155; Arnull, 'The Direct Effect of Directives: Grasping the Nettle' (1986) 35 ICLQ 939; Mann, 'L'invocabilité des directives: quelques interrogations' (1980) 26 RTDE 669; Fernández Martín and Pellicer Zamora, 'Las ofertas anormalmente bajas en la contratación pública' (1990) 78 *Gaceta Jurídica de la CEE, Serie B*, 3 at 7 *ff*; Curtin (1990) (above, n 26); De Burca, 'Giving effect to Community Directives' (1992) 55 MLR 215; Dal Farra, 'L'invocabilité des directives communautaires devant le juge national de la légalité' (1992) 28 RTDE 634; Millán Moro, 'La eficacia directa de las directivas. Evolución reciente' (1991) *18 Revista de Instituciones Europeas* 845. For the difficulties of UK courts as to how far they may go in construing national law so as to conform with Community law, see Szyszczak in (1994) 19 ELR 214 at 215 *ff*. On Case C-106/89 *Marleasing* (above, n 88) see Stuyck and Wyttinck (1991) 28 CMLRev 205 and Mead (1991) 16 ELRev 490.

[92] *Contra* Oliver (1987) (above, n 13) at 884 and Oliver, 'Le droit communautaire et les voies de recours nationaux' (1992) 28 CDE 348.

[93] Case C-334/92, *Wagner Miret* [1993] ECR I-6911.

[94] Case C-91/92 *Faccini Dori* (above, n 79).

[95] Joined Cases C-46–48/93 *Factortame III* and *Brasseries du Pêcheur*, still pending at the time of writing.

had not adopted any implementation measure since, according to the Spanish Government, existing national rules already complied with the Directive's requirements. One of the questions posed referred to whether the applicant could claim compensation for the damages suffered due to the non-implementation of the Directive. Even though the Directive did not provide directly effective rights, the Court in *Wagner Miret* applied the effective judicial protection principle and held that, first of all, national judges had to apply an interpretation of national law which, to the greatest extent possible, conformed with the requirements of the Directive.[96] If that was not possible, which the Court (relying on the information provided by the referring court) assumed was the case with the applicable national rules, the national judge had to proceed with the application of *Francovich* and, provided all conditions were fulfilled, declare the State liable for the damages caused by the failure to implement the Directive properly. *Faccini Dori* confirms *Wagner Miret* and applies the same reasoning and reaches the same conclusion. The difference between them lies in the fact that the former case concerned a horizontal situation, that is, the case concerned an action between individuals. The plaintiff in the main action before the national court alleged her rights under a Directive in order to rescind a contract she had entered into with a private firm.

All these cases reveal that the direct effect test (clear, precise and unconditional) is no longer sufficient to determine Member States' obligations as regards effective judicial protection. The test for triggering the application of the principle is now whether the Community provision at stake is intended to provide individuals with ascertainable rights, irrespective of whether its terms are unconditional and precise or whether it is being enforced in a horizontal relationship. If this is the case, effective judicial protection must also be afforded to these 'imperfect' rights. Obviously, precise and unconditional provisions are *per se* enforceable against the State as the individual rights they provide are, by definition, clearly determined, otherwise they would not be considered directly effective. In the case of non-directly effective provisions, in contrast, individuals must convince national courts that the contents of the alleged rights can be ascertained from the terms of the provisions. Their judicial protection seems, therefore, to depend on the drafting of the provisions. The Court must draw up guidelines as to the degree of precision required for non-directly effective provisions to provide ascertainable rights. It is hoped that the Court will not adopt too demanding a stance, since this would reduce the practical impact of *Francovich*. Indeed, if the second condition of the *Francovich* test is interpreted too narrowly, there is a risk that only 'imperfect rights'

---

[96] According to the Court, that was especially the case whenever national authorities have understood that the pre-existing national rules already fully responded to the requirements of the relevant Community law rule. C-334/92, *Wagner Miret* (above, n 93) para. 21.

which do not qualify as directly effective on a minor point will benefit from effective judicial protection. In this way, the crucial innovation of *Francovich*, i.e., extending the case law to non-directly effective provisions, will be emptied of substance. Equally, when a Community law provision is denied horizontal direct effect but it is alleged against another individual, the same reasoning should apply, following *Faccini Dori*.

What sort of effective remedies are now required? The *Factortame*, *Francovich*, *Marshall II*, *Wagner Miret* and *Faccini Dori* decisions are to be read in conjunction rather than independently of each other, as concrete manifestations of the effectiveness principle.[97] Seen in the more general context of the Court's case law, they provide individuals with a right to effective judicial protection which may materialize in the application of the indirect effect doctrine, the award of interim relief, or damages when necessary. Thus, effective protection is not limited to damages but covers any other remedy which, in the opinion of the courts, may be effective (subject to the parameters to be developed by the Court).[98] Compensation through damages should in fact be seen as an alternative to the full restoration of the individual's right.[99] Only when individuals may not fully be restored to the legal position which they held before the breach was committed, should damages act as a substitutive compensation. If the ultimate objective of judicial enforcement is to allow individuals the full enjoyment of their rights, remedies other than an action for damages must be used. In fact, any other remedy which prevents the damages from arising is more desirable. The enforcement of the original right is always preferable, especially since there are cases where damages may only be calculated with difficulty, or where the computation of the economic equivalence of certain rights may be impossible. It seems much more reasonable to allow national courts a certain margin of discretion in ensuring effective protection of Community rights than to oblige them to condemn the State to pay damages.[100]

Conclusions

In view of the case law on effective judicial protection as a whole, national courts faced with an action relating to Community rights embodied in non-directly effective provisions must observe the following steps. First,

---

[97] Curtin (1992) (above, n 60) at 79.

[98] This position was already implied in the Court's general statement that, pursuant to Art. 5 of the EC Treaty, Member States are obliged to 'eliminate the unlawful consequences of a breach of Community law'. Joined Cases C-6 and C-9/90, *Francovich* (above, n 60) at para. 36.

[99] See in this vein Advocate General Mischo. Opinion, Joined Cases C-6 and C-9/90, *Francovich* (above, n 60) at para. 66.

[100] In this respect see Temple Lang (1992–1993) (above, n 60) at 26.

they must be satisfied that the provision is actually intended to provide the individual with rights and that the contents of those rights can be determined on the basis of the provisions. They must thereafter 'positively' interpret national legislation in the light of the Community provisions at stake, as required by the *Von Colson* 'indirect effect' doctrine. If the conflict between the applicable national law and the non-directly effective provision is unworkable, they must provide a remedy which effectively protects the disputed right. At this point, a difference in the remedy granted by the national courts arises from the nature of the defendant. If the State is the defendant, the national court is required to adopt an effective remedy, which may or may not be liability for damages. If the defendant is another individual who is benefiting from a failure by the State to fulfil its obligations under Community law, then damages against the State may be declared. Moreover, the *Francovich* decision empowers and requires national courts to create effective remedies when these do not exist.[101]

It is not excessive to compare this case law with other major landmark judgments, such as *Van Gend en Loos* or *Simmenthal* itself. These two cases belong to the first generation of decisions resolving substantial issues of legal integration (such as the hierarchy of norms, the direct applicability and direct effect of Treaty provisions). *Factortame* and *Francovich* on the other hand, deal with issues arising at a second level of the integration chain: the procedural norms governing the application and enforcement of the Community's higher rules of law. This second category settles the principles which guide the resolution of more practical problems relating to procedural requirements. Although the Court has gone far in the implementation of the principle of effective judicial protection, certain limits still exist to its full application. These limits derive mainly from external non-legal factors. In fact, the requirement of effectiveness in enforcing and protecting individual rights of Community origin cannot be interpreted to the extent of declaring any redress system which is inefficient as contrary to Community obligations. Those insufficiencies which derive from the structural pitfalls of national judicial systems are not covered.

The problem may lie not in the absence of well developed theoretical legal protection, but in the inefficiency of the implementation of such protection due to endogenous factors: overloading of the courts, delays due to under capacity, etc. It seems politically unreasonable to oblige Member States to proceed to a profound modification of their judicial systems just to give effectiveness to directly enforceable Community rights. The Court of Justice cannot go as far as imposing effectiveness requirements which cannot reasonably be performed by national administrations acting in good faith. Apart from being unrealistic, anything else would

---

[101] Schockweiler (1992) (above, n 60) at 47; Ross (above, n 60) at 68.

bring the political equilibrium between obligations deriving from the supranational level and their rational means of performance at national level to a dangerous impasse. What is correct, however, from a strict legal analysis, is the conclusion that the Court has obliged Member States to introduce, at least formally, indispensable modifications establishing a system which may, if operated correctly, ensure effectiveness.

The Incidence of the Effective Judicial Protection Principle in the Public Procurement Area

The application of the effective judicial protection principle to the public procurement area is of great relevance. The insufficiencies of the supranational monitoring system mean that the enforcement policy of the Commission has shifted towards the realm of domestic judicial enforcement mechanisms. Effective review procedures activated by interested undertakings are now seen as the only means by which contracting authorities can be controlled. In very simple terms, the case law studied means that effective judicial protection must be provided by national authorities in the public procurement area.

   However, the principle acquires special pertinence due to the characteristics of the Community rules on public procurement. Most provisions of the Directives are intended to confer rights on individuals.[102] The public works and public supplies Directives are intended to reduce the administration's margin of discretion when awarding contracts in order to increase the transparency of contract awards, prevent discriminatory practices and guarantee full information to interested undertakings so that they become fully aware of commercial opportunities which foreign public markets represent. This is achieved by the establishment of very detailed rules regulating the award procedures. The obligations imposed on contracting authorities transcend the administrative sphere of the original addressees and provide interested firms with rights to be effectively protected pursuant to the principle analysed. One may even go a step further and affirm that most of the provisions fulfil the 'direct-effect' test. Evidence of this is given by the fact that every time that the Court has been asked to decide whether a provision of a public procurement Directive was directly effective or not, it has answered in the affirmative.[103] The public procurement obligations therefore create individual rights capable of being enforced before national courts. Thus, the case law on effective judicial protection applies to most provisions of the Directives. The question of non-directly effective provisions is therefore of relative significance in this field since this type of provision is in fact rare. However, even if the

---

[102] See Temple Lang (1992–1993) (above, n 60) at 37–38; Gilliams (above, n 60) at 294 *ff*.   [103] See Chapter 4.

Court found some of the provisions non-directly effective, it is submitted that the content of the rights could easily be defined on the basis of the provisions of the Directives as they stand. For the reasons stated above, the same reasoning applies to the Utilities Directive, even in those cases where both parties are regarded as private. Thus, the doctrines of direct effect, indirect effect and State liability may be resorted to by individuals injured by breaches of Community public procurement rules.

On this basis, any infringement by a contracting authority of its obligations under the public procurement Directives may be brought before national courts by the individuals whose rights have been ignored or infringed. Rights conferred by Community rules, directly effective or not, have to be complemented by effective judicial protection guaranteeing their full enjoyment at the national level. If no remedy is available, under the *Francovich* and *Factortame* test, national courts must provide an adequate and effective remedy, which may include damages or interim relief.

IS THERE A NEED FOR A REMEDIES DIRECTIVE?

To answer this question, two positions may be confronted. If one takes the Court's case law on the obligation to provide for effective judicial remedies to its extreme, the adoption of a Remedies Directive can be considered a superfluous, redundant and unnecessary legislative act.[104] Such a non-interventionist, liberal position would argue that, once the need for 'effective judicial protection' has been elevated to the level of a Community law principle, national authorities would enjoy a broad margin of discretion to implement it in their domestic legal systems within the limits of the effectiveness requirement. Accordingly, the various national legal traditions would be better preserved and a better adaptation of Community rules to national perceptions and judicial uses would also be achieved. In brief, any legal provision imposing the effectiveness principle upon Member States is redundant to the extent that it would be a mere repetition of what the case law has already established, thereby withdrawing flexibility from the integration process by excessively centralizing and over-regulating the Community's legal environment. Moreover, effective enforcement mechanisms are clearly not restricted to the sphere of judicial actions

---

[104] In fact, a similar provision, Art. 6 of the equal treatment Directive, is viewed by most commentators as a mere 'juridification' of the case law requiring effective judicial protection of Community rights. Even if the Directive did not provide for such an Article, the obligation upon national administrations concerning effective judicial protection would still be binding. The same applies to the public procurement area. Oliver (1987) (above, n 13) at Prechal (above, n 56) at 467–468.

and Member States should be free to choose the system which better suits their peculiarities.[105]

There are also sound reasons, however, for supporting a positive harmonizing measure in this field. First of all, the case law establishing the effectiveness principle does nothing more than express the intrinsic aspiration of any legal rule, that it be effectively applied and enforced. The notion of 'effectiveness' is vague and is consequently open to many interpretations, which will in turn normally be influenced by national legal cultures and conceptions. In a 'supranational' system characterized by the co-existence of fifteen different legal orders which are immersed in an on-going integration process, the likely outcome of a unguided application of the Court's case law by Member States would be a whole range of domestic systems responding to their own perceptions of effectiveness. This in turn would lead to lengthy discussions about the adequacy of one chosen system over another and about whether a satisfactory degree of effectiveness is achieved. This conflict of views could only be settled in the last instance by the Court on a case by case basis, which would contradict the advantages which arise from a liberal approach. This is, moreover, a duty which corresponds to Community decision-making bodies rather than to a judicial organ.

However, even if one assumes that national systems of redress achieved an acceptable degree of effectiveness, another main objective of Community law, its uniform application, would still be jeopardised.[106] A harmonization measure assumes the responsibility of providing for minimum standards. As one commentator has put it, 'while it is true that the procedural rules and remedies of national law must, for the purposes of Community law, satisfy minimum standards, national law cannot satisfy such standards when Community law fails to specify them'.[107] Uniformity would therefore be established as regards these minimum conditions and flagrant disparities between Member States would disappear, thereby guaranteeing equal treatment between undertakings of different Member States.

There are other advantages which arise from the adoption of a legislative measure. Not only would a Directive be negotiated, taking into account

---

[105] For instance, in the Netherlands, the preferred system is arbitration which is, moreover, found to be very effective. Such a system remains discretionary for central government, however, is limited to the field of public works contracts and only covers those disputes which arise between the central government and contractors already involved in the award procedure. For an explanation of the system, see Glazener and others, 'Dutch Report to the 14th Fide Congress' in FIDE, 'Application dans les États Membres des Directives sur les Marchés Publics (Madrid, 1990), 219 at 237 *ff*. See also Van der Meent, 'Enforcing the Public Procurement Rules in the Netherlands' in Arrowsmith (ed.), *Remedies for Enforcing the Public Procurement Rules* (Winteringham, 1993) at 195 *ff*.

[106] The analysed case law does nothing else but stress the need for positive harmonizing measures. See further Snyder (above, n 60) at 42 *ff*; Steiner (above, n 60) at 12; Schockweiler (1992) (above, n 60) at 49.   [107] Bridge (above, n 13) at 40.

the various national peculiarities, as well as the diverse private interests concerned,[108] but they would also be specifically designed to cope with the particular features of public procurement. Accordingly, the most important element of positive legislative action would probably be to go a step further than the case law by specifying, through concrete procedural requirements, the means for achieving effective protection in public procurement, in accordance with the peculiarities of this field of law.

Last but not least, the adoption of a Directive is also important since it has a psychological component. Political and legal debate at national level precedes its adoption, especially if the Directive is innovative in many ways. Such debate favours the creation of a larger consciousness on the part of all the parties involved as regards the proposed legislation and its objectives. All bodies in charge of its implementation, enforcement and application directly participate in the elaboration process and, therefore, its chances of having a real impact are enhanced.

Summing up, the adoption of a Remedies Directive would have positive results provided it aids the establishment of adequate systems of redress specifically designed for public procurement cases. The removal of the blatant inadequacies of national systems, as well as the establishment of uniform judicial review for interested firms, would be ensured. It must be noted that all the Community institutions and parties involved share the feeling that there was a clear need to improve the redress situation available to secure compliance with public procurement rules. Existing domestic remedies do not favour a proper monitoring of contracting authorities' activities when awarding contracts under Community rules. The lack of transparency of the procedures in some cases, the Community system itself and the legal approach to public contracts generally have made this monitoring highly difficult.[109]

---

[108] As we know already the participation of the two Public Procurement Advisory Committees in the elaboration and design of the final text ensures that the views of private parties are taken into account.

[109] See Labayle, 'Le contrôle de la réglementation communautaire en matière de marchés publics' (1989) RMC 625 at 625.

8

The Enforcement Level (III): The Public Sector Remedies Directive

INTRODUCTION

In the last chapter it was submitted that despite the far-reaching case law concerning the principle of effective judicial protection, a harmonization measure laying down minimum conditions for effective remedies in the public procurement area was desirable. The Council adopted the Remedies Directive 89/665 on the co-ordination of the laws, regulations and administrative provisions relating to the application of review procedures to the award of public supply and public works contracts, on 21 December 1989.[1] The Directive was to be implemented in the different Member States by 21 December 1991.

The following chapters address whether the provisions of the Remedies Directive are suitable to guarantee a substantial degree of uniformity and effectiveness in the public procurement area and, therefore, act as a positive complement to the effective judicial protection principle. The assessment of the impact of the Remedies Directive cannot be completed without looking at the national implementation measures adopted. This is undertaken in the next two chapters. In the light of this analysis, some conclusions about the potential effect which the adopted measure may have in the national redress systems on public procurement are advanced. Even though the Directive was adopted some time before the *Factortame* and *Francovich* cases were decided, its relationship with the case law on effective judicial protection is considered. Naturally, for it to be worthwhile, the

---

[1] OJ 1989, L395/33. The Remedies Directive was later extended to cover the public services Directive 92/50. See generally Arrowsmith, 'Enforcing the Public Procurement Rules: Legal Remedies in the Court of Justice and the National Courts' in Arrowsmith (ed.) *Remedies for Enforcing the Public Procurement Rules* (Winteringham, 1993) at 50 *ff*; Coleman and Margue, 'L'action communautaire visant le respect des règles communautaires en matière de passation des marchés publics de fournitures et des travaux: problèmes et perspectives' (1989) RMC 546; Gormley, 'Remedies and Compliance' in Meredith (ed.) *European Initiatives in Public Procurement* (New York, 1990) 38; House of Lords, Select Committee on the European Communities, *Compliance with Public Procurement Directives*, Session, 1987–1988, 12th report; Labayle, 'Le contrôle de la réglementation communautaire en matière des marchés publics' (1989) RMC 625; Samaniego Bordiú, 'El control del derecho comunitario de los contratos públicos' (1990) RAP 401; Mestre Delgado, 'El control de la adjudicación de los contratos públicos a tenor del derecho comunitario europeo. Una nueva ordenación de las medidas cautelares' (1991) No. 74 *Noticias CEE* 35; Weiss, *Public Procurement in European Community Law* (London, 1993) Chapter 7.

legislative measure has to go further than the case law in that it should provide detailed procedural rules necessary to guarantee uniformity and effectiveness in the enforcement of the public procurement rules. A solution to this problem is proposed.

THE ANALYSIS OF THE REMEDIES DIRECTIVE

Its Origins

Baldwin has pointed out that 'in the case of those who are not well-disposed to comply, rules also tend to fail because the necessary enforcement strategy (or sanction) has not been applied'.[2] This statement was assumed by the Commission in the public procurement field. The Directives were not complied with due, *inter alia*, to a lack of proper domestic control mechanisms. After an examination of national situations which showed that complaints at domestic level were practically non-existent,[3] the Commission reached the conclusion that the insufficiencies of national enforcement systems were to be blamed.[4] In the 'White Paper', the Commission made clear its determination to entail 'more visible action in policing compliance with existing law' in order to increase the credibility of the Community's efforts to break down the psychological barriers to crossing frontiers'.[5]

Contrary to other Directives in other areas of Community law,[6] the public procurement Directives did not oblige Member States to introduce into their national legal systems such measures which are necessary to ensure adequate and effective means of redress in the form of claims by judicial process. National systems were to apply unchanged. Such a gap had to be overcome by the enactment of a specific piece of legislation. Furthermore, in the absence of a decentralized enforcement strategy, the entire responsibility fell upon the Commission's centralized enforcement efforts, whose shortcomings emphasized the need for enhancing decentralized control even more. These concerns finally materialized in the form of the Remedies Directive.[7]

The Directive relied on Article 100a EC as the appropriate legal basis. As a result, the co-operation procedure laid down in Article 149 EEC, which

---

[2] Baldwin, R., 'Why Rules don't Work' (1990) 53 MLR 321 at 329.

[3] EC Commission, Advisory Committee on the Opening-up of Public Procurement, *Extracts from the analysis of controls on compliance with the rules concerning public procurement in the Member States*, CCO/88/73 (Brussels, 1988).   [4] See the preamble to the Remedies Directive.

[5] EC Commission, *Completing the Internal Market* (the 'White Paper'), COM (85) 310 at para. 85. See also EC Commission, *Public Procurement in the Community*, COM (86) 375.

[6] See for instance Article 6 of the equal treatment Directive 76/207/EEC, OJ 1976, L39/40 and Article 4 of the misleading advertising Directive 84/450/EEC, OJ 1984, L250/17.

[7] Directive 89/665/EEC, OJ 1989, L395/33. See the preamble to the Directive.

has since been repealed by the TEU, was followed, and the three Community institutions were thus involved in the decision-making process. Due to the controversial character of the Commission's original proposals, this co-operation was quite intense. The adoption of the Directive took two years and the final text was the result of a compromise between the different institutions.[8] Even though the adoption of a regulation would have been more desirable as the detailed character of its provisions and its direct applicability would have enhanced the binding nature of the adopted rules, this option was probably unfeasible. A detailed regulation would have required a large degree of bargaining and elaboration and, arguably, would have faced stronger opposition from Member States.

The Remedies Directive is of a limited scope. It covers breaches of the obligations enshrined in the public works and public supplies Directives and the public services Directive, or in the national legislation implementing provisions of the Directives.[9] Its main purpose is therefore to support the effective application of the latter. It obliges Member States to take all measures necessary to ensure that, as regards contract award procedures falling within the scope of application of those Directives, decisions taken by contracting authorities may be reviewed 'effectively' and as rapidly as possible.[10] Accordingly, the Directive is not concerned with possible infringements of other rules in the same area which are not directly related to Community obligations. Disputes which may arise between parties to a contract as regards the enforcement of the contractual clauses are still, in the absence of Community rules, regulated by existing national provisions. The fact that the Community regime ignores substantial

---

[8] The Commission's first proposal (EC Commission, COM (87) 134) was amended in the light of some of Parliament's suggestions and was replaced by a modified proposal (EC Commission, COM (88) 733). The Council's common position emerged in July 1989 ('Position commune arretée par le Conseil le 24.7.1989 en vue de l'adoption de la directive portant coordination des dispositions legislatives, réglementaires et administratives relatives à l'application des procédures de recours en matière de passation des marchés publics de fournitures et de travaux', CCO/89/64). The Commission and the European Parliament did not oppose any substantial objections to the latter (European Parliament, 'Draft recommendation by the Committee on Economic and Monetary Affairs and Industrial Policy concerning the common position of the Council with a view to the adoption of a directive on the coordination of the laws, regulations and administrative provisions relating to the application of review procedures to the award of public supply and public works contracts', 14 September 1989, EP 134.123 (Report Beumer II) at 5).

[9] After the adoption of the public services Directive, the terms and conditions of the Remedies Directive were extended to cover the provisions in the services Directive (Article 41 of Directive 92/50/EEC). As already mentioned, a Remedies Directive specifically designed for the Utilities sectors was also adopted by the Council (Directive 92/13/EEC, OJ 1992, L76/14). As regards other breaches of directly effective EC Treaty provisions, on a literal interpretation of the Remedies Directive, they seem to be excluded from its scope. This seems to have been an overview by the drafters, as it does not make sense to require more effective remedies against certain types of breaches of Community law than against others.   [10] Article 1 of the Remedies Directive.

areas of public procurement where discrimination may occur has been criticized.[11]

The Directive's Regulation of Standing

Standing defines the conditions to be fulfilled by a particular plaintiff in order to be entitled to invoke the jurisdiction of the court.[12] In simple terms, the regulation of standing is intended to shelter the courts from frivolous actions and busybodies and to protect the public interest in the smooth operation of the activities of the public authorities. Even though national courts have adopted a very liberal interpretation of the standing of individuals against public authorities, the fact remains that they are required to show sufficient interest in the outcome of the action.

Taking into consideration that the Directive includes both the availability of interim suspensory measures and the award of damages, the Council decided that the public interest required standing to be limited to those cases where an interest on the part of the complainant could be shown. The requirement of affording a reasonable degree of legal certainty to other bidders also played a role in this sense. Although it has been suggested that individuals do not use relief mechanisms in a 'frivolous' manner,[13] it was thought that such a possibility was to be duly considered. The courts should be in a position to assess in the first stages of the review procedure whether a legitimate interest lies behind the action. Moreover this is the regime applicable in most Member States.[14]

Article 1(3) provides that any person having, or having had, an interest in obtaining a particular public supply or public works contract and who has been, or risks being, harmed by an alleged infringement must be granted standing to set off the review mechanisms. This combines both the need to ensure a broad access to judicial review for aggrieved undertakings, as well as concern to avoid abuses leading to the negative consequences mentioned above. As the English debate has shown,[15] the

---

[11] The European Parliament regretted that the Directive did not apply to infringements of other national rules on the subject. Report Beumer II (above, n 8) at 7. For a forceful argument in favour of overall regulation if the integration of the public works markets is to be realized, see Capper, 'Obstacles to Free Competition for Public Works Contracts. An English view', paper presented to the *Implementing and Enforcing the EC Procurement Directives Conference*, Birmingham, April 1993.

[12] Craig, *Administrative Law* 3rd edn. (London, 1994) at 479.

[13] As Scott has put it, 'The idle and whimsical plaintiff, a dilettante who litigates for a lark, is a spectre which haunts the legal literature not the courtroom'. 'Standing in the Supreme Court: A Functional Analysis' (1973) 83 *Harvard Law Review* 645.

[14] For a discussion of the national regulations of standing and their rationale, see Fernández Martín, 'A Critical Analysis of EC Public Procurement Legislation. Present Limitations and Future Prospects', PhD Thesis (Florence, 1993) at 295–300.

[15] Fernández Martín (above, n 14) at 297–298. See Craig (above, n 12) at 489 *ff*.

problem now is to give substance to the notions of 'interest' in participating in the contract award procedure and that of 'harmed or at risk of
being harmed'. It is up to national courts and, eventually, the Court of
Justice to develop the case law clarifying this matter, in the spirit of the
Directive. Since national courts have shown a readiness to facilitate access
to judicial review procedures it is submitted that conditions of standing
will be flexibly interpreted in the future. The Directive's broad definition
will include all those firms which, in one way or another, have explicitly
expressed an interest in taking part in an award procedure and whose
chances to participate or win the contract have been affected by the alleged
breach. The right to challenge infringements on a purely objective basis,
that is, in defence of legality, has been reserved to the Commission and
eventually Member States through the Article 169 EC procedure.

Lastly, Article 1(3) allows Member States to require the person seeking
review to first notify the contracting authority of the alleged infringement
and of his or her intention to seek review. This paragraph covers those
national situations where the introduction of an administrative complaint
is a prerequisite to the access to proper judicial review as, for example,
was the case in Spain.[16] Thus, contracting authorities may be given the
opportunity to correct alleged infringements which are caused by the
mere negligence or lack of attention of public officials. The Directive
does not specify further requirements as to the character, details, or consequences of such a notification. It seems, however, that this prior stage
should not act as an unnecessary delay to obtaining effective judicial protection. This has been a popular option amongst Member States as will
be seen later on.

The Conditions for Effectiveness of Remedies in the Public Procurement Area

The substantive aspects of the effectiveness of the public procurement
rules have been examined in Chapters 3 and 4. The following pages
concentrate on the procedural side of effectiveness.[17] For our purposes,
effectiveness at the enforcement level requires, first of all, the provision
of sufficient incentives for victims to seek compliance actively. Secondly,
it requires the existence of deterrents preventing the addressees of the
norms from escaping their legal obligations with impunity. Lastly, when a
breach is committed, injured parties must be guaranteed a full and satisfactory restoration of their transgressed rights. This, in turn, will ensure

---

[16] Coleman and Margue (above, n 1) at 550.
[17] For the defintion of procedural and substantive notion of effectiveness, see the General
Introduction to this book.

proper enforcement and, as a result, the achievement of the objectives pursued by the decision-making bodies.

How do these conditions materialize in the public procurement area? The following sections try to provide an answer to this question while taking into account the specific features of public procurement rules and the factors involved in their enforcement. Thereafter, the provisions of the Remedies Directive are analysed in order to assess whether they respond to these conditions.

Urgent and Rapid Review Mechanisms before the Contract is Awarded

A self-evident condition for effectiveness is that any applicable remedies should act as fast as possible once the irregularity is detected.[18] In public procurement cases, the determination of remedies must moreover always take place *before the contract is finalized*. The avoidance of definitive irreversible *de facto* situations which result from long and cumbersome review procedures is at the heart of this condition. Review procedures must allow for the resolution of the dispute before the award procedure comes to an end, so as to permit the re-establishment of legality and the progression of the award procedure under optimum competitive conditions. In addition, according to the Commission's findings, most of the alleged breaches take place before the final award of the contract is decided and consist in disrespect of the compulsory formal procedure, or the faulty implementation of one of its steps, with or without *mala fides*.[19] These are breaches which, provided they are immediately detected, could and should be corrected before the award procedure comes to an end.

Lastly, rapid remedies acting before the contract is concluded are required by the need to protect all public and private interests involved. The effects of already concluded contracts should be left untouched even if some irregularities have been detected, since to declare the contract null and void is not an effective solution. If a new award procedure has to be undergone, the satisfaction of public needs would be delayed and the

---

[18] Evidence of this assumption is given by the experience in the Netherlands, which demonstrates that the installation of an arbitration system providing for the quick resolution of disputes has brought a considerable increase in the number of complaints, to the extent that it has been held that this system has now become the victim of its own success. For a description of the system, see van de Meent, 'Enforcing the Public Procurement Rules in the Netherlands' in Arrowsmith (ed.) (1993) (above, n 1) Chapter 6 at 199 *ff*.

[19] EC Commission, COM 87 (134) at 6–7. See also EC Commission, COM (88) 733 at 6–7. Statistics provided by Arrowsmith point in the same direction in Arrowsmith (ed.) (above, n 1) at 9. As the Commission has put it: '. . . most such infringements differ from other types in that the irregularities committed are procedural. A procedural irregularity may be enough to exclude an enterprise from a given award procedure, and this encourages discriminatory practices'. COM (88) 733 at 7.

legitimate expectations of the successful tenderer would be frustrated. *Bona fides* tenderers would be unfairly punished.

This was the approach favoured in most domestic systems. In France, for example, the application of the theory of the *actes détachables*, means that a concluded contract is not affected by irregularities committed during the contract award procedure.[20] In Spain, although the law provides that illegalities in the award procedure imply that the contract itself must be rescinded and annulled, it nevertheless entitles the contracting authority to declare that the contract clauses must continue to be respected and performed if their annulment could involve a 'serious disturbance' of public services. Although the actual implementation of such a prerogative is subject to judicial control and, in any case, is considered only as a transitory solution by the law, in practice this leads to the permanence of a void contract.[21] In Germany, contracts entered into by public authorities are treated as subject to private law and, therefore, irregularities committed in the pre-contractual stages do not normally affect the validity of the contract, mainly on the basis of the protection of the successful contractor's rights.[22] In the United Kingdom the remedy requested in judicial review procedures may be refused at the full hearing if the order would cause serious disruption to the machinery of government,[23] or where the order would not be effective to restore the applicant to the situation he or she was in before the alleged breach was committed, or where the order would be futile in the circumstances.[24] Considerations of the same nature inform the Supreme Court Act (SCA) 1981, which explicitly protects both public authorities and the legitimate rights acquired by a *bona fides* contractor from delayed applications for judicial review.[25] These concerns were translated into the Remedies Directive's final text, whose Article 2(6) explicitly allows Member States to provide that 'after the conclusion of a contract following its award, the powers of the bodies responsible for the review procedures shall be limited to awarding damages to any person harmed by an infringement'. As will be seen, most Member States have made use of this discretion when implementing the Directive in their domestic legal orders. The Court of Justice also seems increasingly aware of these aspects of interim relief in public procurement cases.[26]

---

[20] See Chapter 9.

[21] Article 66(3) of the Spanish Public Procurement Law (*Ley 13/1995 de Contratos de las Administraciones Públicas* (LCE). In this context, see judgment of the Supreme Court (STS) of 20 May 1988, which held that whenever the illegally awarded work had already been executed, the Law provides other solutions for these situations, mentioning explicitly compensation through damages. Cited by Mestre Delgado (above, n 1) at 36.

[22] See Chapter 10.

[23] *R* v. *Paddington Valuation Officer ex p. Peachey Property Corporation Ltd* [1962] 1 WLR 1186.

[24] *R* v. *Bristol Corporation ex p. Hendy* [1974] 1 WLR 498.   [25] See SCA 1981, s. 31(6)(b).

[26] See Chapter 6.

The Need for Interim Relief[27]

The grounds supporting the need for rapid remedies in order to avoid the *fait accompli* are equally applicable to the debate concerning interim relief. In fact, both conditions are nothing less than two sides of the same coin. However, in public procurement cases, the grant of interim measures, although crucial, is to be approached cautiously since any unnecessary delay of the award of a contract due to the initiation of a review procedure would harm both private and public interests. As regards the former, remedies which would result in a long suspension of the award procedure, or the execution of an already awarded contract, could affect the economic interests of other bidders, when these bidders are in any way responsible for the breach. A suspension of the award procedure could force them to readapt their original bid to the new market context and this will normally bring additional costs. In the case of public works, contractors prefer to programme the contracted work in two summers and one winter rather than two winters and one summer, as costs are lower in the first case. Market prices for materials and components are also subject to fluctuations, normally positive increases due to inflation and original bids would thus have to be revised. The case is of special concern to contractors when the contract is awarded on a fixed price basis.

With respect to the public interest, increases in the price of the contracts would penalize public expenditure to the detriment of taxpayers. Equally, the fulfilment of a public demand would be delayed or encumbered, which would inevitably prejudice the basic needs of the population.[28] As a result, whereas the plea for easily accessible and flexible interim measures is a sensible one, such a power needs to be framed within very strict conditions. Resolution of interim relief procedures should be decided as rapidly as possible, preferably by means of special urgent procedures.

A comparative analysis of national systems shows that these concerns are well spread. National review procedures in public procurement cases do not have an automatic suspensory effect. The award procedure continues its course and the contract is awarded, despite the fact that an action may be pending before the competent review body. Moreover, interim relief is rarely granted at domestic level, since compensation through damages is seen as an adequate alternative remedy. Public interest imperatives override the need to ensure the correction of breaches.[29]

[27] On this point see in general Fromont, 'La protection provisoire des particuliers contre les décisions administratives dans les États membres de la Communauté' (1984) *Revue Internationale des Sciences Administratives* 309.

[28] This concern is also present in the case law of the Court of Justice. See Chapter 6.

[29] See Chapters 9 and 10.

The Need for Incentives and Deterrents at Decentralized Level

It is a well-known fact that in the area of public works and, to a lesser extent, public supplies, injured undertakings are not prepared to challenge breaches committed by their potential customers. In a study carried out on behalf of the Commission, the question whether judicial appeals by third parties against breaches of national legislation on public contracts were frequent, was answered in the negative in the vast majority of Member States.[30] At the supranational level, the ratio of public procurement cases resolved by the Court of Justice at the request of domestic courts largely departs from prevailing trends in other areas of Community law. The normal ratio of Article 177 EC preliminary references as regards Article 169 EC proceedings is 5 : 1 in favour of the former. Up to the end of 1994, in the public procurement area, the ratio is over 1 : 5 in favour of Article 169 EC proceedings.[31] The Commission has opened more than 300 infraction procedures during the 1986–94 period concerning alleged infringements of public procurement rules.[32] Such an intense monitoring at supranational level contrasts with the negligible level of activity at national level by disappointed contractors.[33]

The commonly accepted reason explaining this attitude by firms is that nobody bites the proverbial hand that feeds them. Firms have so far preferred to sacrifice short-term benefits which would have resulted from an ultimately successful judicial action for the possibility of winning future contracts. A judicial complaint entails the risk of being blacklisted by contracting authorities and subsequently losing future contract possibilities. In economic terms, it is not an efficient decision for an undertaking which acts according to commercial principles to bring an action unless the eventual remedies available compensate the risk of, first, not winning the contract and second, being blacklisted. With some exceptions, the mere

---

[30] EC Commission, Advisory Committee on the Opening-up of Public Procurement (above, n 3) CCO/88/73.

[31] In 10 cases out of 26 the decisions of the Court were given on the basis of preliminary references made under Art. 177 EC, whereas 16 were the result of Art. 169 EC proceedings.

[32] Infraction dossiers opened on the initiative of the Commission for the period 1991–94 amount to 76. Infractions dossiers opened on the basis of individual complaints for the same period amount to 199. See, however, the considerations made with respect to the insufficiencies of the indiviual complaints to the Commission in Chapter 6.

[33] This absence of complaints regarding Community rules may, however, be explained on grounds other than the mere reticence of firms to challenge contracting authorities. As the examination of the application level showed, there appears to be a lack of interest by foreign firms in most contract awards falling within the scope of the public works and public supplies Directives. Since Community rules are intended principally to benefit foreign contractors, if they do not avail of the opportunities provided by the Directives, then there will be few complaints regarding Community rules. This, however, does not detract from the fact that undertakings are not normally willing to proceed legally against public authorities as the studies carried out at national level demonstrate.

restoration of legality is not one of the criteria which move undertakings to lodge complaints or risk future relationships with their clients.

How may the stagnant situation concerning judicial actions at national level be remedied? Is it the case, as Labayle argues, that, '. . . l'insuffisance du contrôle national de la réglamentation communautaire . . . est propre à la matière, les marchés publics . . . et l'on ne voit guère comment la faillite du droit national pourrait se compenser au plan européen'?[34] An economic analysis of law would argue that the solution is one of incentives and deterrents. In simple terms, undertakings would initiate actions against illegal acts of contracting powers as long as the redress available under national law compensates the aforementioned risks.[35] On the other side of the equation, contracting authorities would be less likely to breach the rules if they faced suitable deterrent sanctions.

Damages as incentives

Since the maintenance of the contractual relationship once the contract has been concluded is seen as the most desirable solution in public procurement cases, injured undertakings may no longer enforce the rights vested in them by the Directives due to the final conclusion of the contract. The alternative remedy is the award of damages. The traditional approach followed at domestic level regards the main aim of the award of damages as '[providing] full compensation in the sense of placing the person in the same position as he or she would have been in had the injury not occurred, in so far as money can'.[36] The enforcement of the original right is always preferable, especially since there are cases when damages may only be calculated with difficulty, or where the computation of the economic equivalent of certain rights may be impossible. Thus, the grant of compensation has to be regarded as a 'second best choice' if the restoration of legality proves impossible. There is, however, a second aspect of the provision of damages which may be defined as an incentive aspect. From this perspective, an award of damages may combine a deterrent and incentive effect on law enforcement. As a deterrent, damages set at a high enough level will exercise pressure on contracting authorities which, fearing potential substantial claims, will be more cautious in complying with their legal obligations.[37] As incentives, the possibility of obtaining high damages

---

[34] Labayle (above, n 1) at 628.

[35] Becker and Stigler, 'Law Enforcement, Malfeasance and Compensation to Enforcers' (1974) *Journal of Legal Studies* 1 at 3.

[36] Veljanovski, *The Economics of Law. An Introductory Text* (London, 1990) at 53.

[37] See later in this chapter. See also the considerations of the Court of Justice requiring sanctions imposed at national level for breaches of Community rules to have deterrent and dissuasive effects on potential wrongdoers. Case 14/83, *Von Colson and Kamann* v. *Land Nordrhein-Westfalen* [1984] ECR 1891; Case 68/88, *Commission* v. *Greece* [1989] ECR 2977 at 2983; C-326/89 *Hansen* [1990] ECR I-2911, at para. 17; Case C-7/90, *Vandevenne* [1991] ECR I-4371 at para. 11.

will induce injured firms to take action against acts contravening Community rules. Assuming that injured firms are risk averse, the amount of damages would need to compensate for the actual loss plus the risk of being blacklisted. The archetypal example of the success of damages as incentives is provided by the 'treble damages' rule operating in US Antitrust law.[38] The same presumption could apply as regards Community public procurement cases.[39] Interested firms have acknowledged that the introduction of a provision on damages would constitute a desirable incentive encouraging them to monitor awards more actively.[40] It goes without saying that the more damages and the easier they can get them, the better. At national level, however, the 'incentive' element is non-existent against public authorities.[41]

The first aspect of damages is already covered by national regulations in the area, that is, the restoration of legality by means of economic compensation. In most Member States, however, evidence that the complainant would have won the contract, or at least had a serious chance of winning the contract which has been hampered by the alleged infringement, is normally required. In the absence of such evidence, national courts normally refuse damages.[42] It is unlikely that complainants can overcome the obstacle of proving a better right to the contract,[43] especially with regard to those contracts awarded pursuant to the most economically advantageous offer which, according to statistics, by far outweighs the lowest price criterion.

A supranational harmonization measure seeking to enhance decentralized monitoring should therefore concentrate on the development of incentive aspects. This would require the introduction of improvements not only regarding the amount of damages, but also regarding the procedural conditions under which they can be obtained, as high enforcement costs would deter victims from seeking compliance. These must be flexible and easy to fulfil. If undertakings are to be encouraged to initiate action, a major improvement compared with current domestic approaches seems necessary.

However, damages would be imposed on public authorities acting in

---

[38] Becker and Stigler (above, n 35) at 13. In the same vein, see the response of Prof. Schermers to the questions presented by the House of Lords Select Committee on the EC (above, n 1) at 13.

[39] However, the fact that in antitrust proceedings the actions are directed against competitors and not clients, as would be the case in public procurement cases, should not be overlooked.

[40] See the submissions concerning the desirability of damages by the representatives of the Confederation of British Industry to the House of Lords (above, n 1) at 59–63.

[41] See Chapters 9 and 10.   [42] See Chapters 9 and 10.

[43] See the submissions of the representatives of the Confederation of British Industry to the House of Lords Select Committee on the European Communities (above, n 1) at 14 and their reponse to questions 374–378.

the public interest.[44] If the Community legislation devised is to be realistic, this 'public aspect' cannot be overlooked. Damages are, after all, drawn from the public treasury. Imposing a disproportionate obligation to award damages on them would not constitute a fair solution, all things considered. Certain safeguards would need to be developed in order to prevent 'pirate firms' from unduly taking advantage of excessively liberal rules. This could be done through a careful design of *locus standi* conditions.[45] The public aspect also implies that the degree of fault involved and the direct incidence of the alleged infringement on the plaintiff's rights should be considered in order to determine the overall amount. Public authorities acting in good faith should not be unfairly punished by a large award of damages and minor irregularities caused by mere negligence should not be treated the same way as intentional discriminatory awards.[46] The effect of the infringement on the development of the procedure should equally be considered. A proportionality test would be advisable. In this sense, the practice of the French *Conseil d'État* could provide some inspiration.[47]

In a supranational context, the adoption of a system consisting of automatic damages to all those who fulfilled the *locus standi* conditions and calculated on the basis of the degree of culpability involved appears convenient if the objective of encouraging decentralized control is to be achieved. These should, in any event, cover bidding and enforcement costs, without prejudice to the right of injured contractors to obtain larger amounts if successful in establishing their better right. It is submitted that such a system would combine economic incentives to injured firms and the required minimum protection of public interest. As contended in previous chapters, firms in a European context will normally bid for public works and public supply contracts in another Member State on an irregular basis. They will generally bid for large contracts or contracts involving high technology.[48] This normally entails high bidding costs. A company in such a position is likely to be more attentive to the fact that the contracting authority abides

[44] See Chapter 7 when discussing the limitations of the *Francovich* decision.

[45] To require evidence from the plaintiff showing that he or she had a real interest in the challenged contract award and that a serious bid was presented would constitute a double safeguard against such a possibility. This would involve showing that the plaintiffs hold business interests in the area to which the contract relates, that they possess a reasonable technical, financial and economic capacity to present a serious bid and that their chances have been affected by the administration's misconduct.

[46] These concerns are present in the domestic regulation of State liability. See Chapters 9 and 10. For a comparative analysis of national public authorities' liability systems, see Schockweiler, Wivenes and Godart, 'Le régime de la responsabilité extra-contractuelle du fait d'actes juridiques dans la Communauté européenne' (1990) 26 RTDE 27.

[47] See Chapter 9.

[48] See the submissions of the Confederation of British Industry to the House of Lords Select Committee on the European Communities (above, n 1) at 14.

by the rules. Since its relationship with the contracting authority is only meant to be transitory, its predisposition to challenge an illegal act, which may in turn reduce its possibility of winning the contract, is greater. Of course this would only operate in those cases where the complainants are not willing to maintain a long term relationship with the contracting authority and where their financial solvency is not dependent upon future contracts with the same contracting body.

The need for deterrents

If one assumes that there is a certain degree of bad faith on the part of national bodies when it comes to the application of Community public procurement rules, this 'non compliance' attitude is reinforced by the absence of adequate deterrent provisions. Contracting authorities could be induced to abide by the rules through the imposition of economic fines for breaches committed. The deterrent effect of economic penalties does not need to be proved. It is in fact regarded as the most efficient means of ensuring compliance from an economic perspective.[49] The TEU has applied this rationale in its new Article 171(2) EC, which provides for the imposition of pecuniary sanctions on reluctant Member States.[50] Equally, under EC competition rules the power invested in the Commission to impose fines on private companies has contributed to the effective application of competition rules.

In the public procurement area, the first proposal for a Remedies Directive provided for a similar power invested in national review bodies which could impose fines on contracting authorities which committed a clear and manifest violation of Community law. The suitability of adopting a similar system in public procurement cases is, however, debatable. Drawing too close a parallel between competition and public procurement is not entirely appropriate when it comes to the imposition of fines for misbehaviour. Public procurement fines would be addressed to public authorities as distinct from private undertakings. This is a crucial point. Member States regard this type of interference with the conduct of their contracting authorities unfavourably and its introduction would require unanimity under Article 235 EC and would be very difficult to achieve. This possibility was therefore abandoned. Thus, in the final version of the Directive, the deterrent effect was limited to the obligation to allow

---

[49] It is well-established that increases in the severity of the punishment and the imposition of monetary fines constitutes the least costly law enforcement mechanism. See further Kadish, 'Some Observations on the Use of Minimal Sanctions in Enforcing Economic Regulations' (1963) 30 *The University of Chicago Law Review* 423. For an economic analysis of law perspective, see Becker, 'Crime and Punishment. An Economic Approach' (1968) 76 *The Journal of Political Economy* 169.

[50] For its potential effects on public procurement cases see Chapter 6.

review bodies to award damages, although the conditions in which the latter are to be confined are left to the discretion of Member States.[51]

The Regulation of the Remedies Directive. Effectiveness achieved?

The Regulation of the Rapidness Condition

An examination of the legal chronology of the Directive shows that concern for fast and rapid remedies was a leitmotif in the ears of all the institutions involved. The Commission,[52] the European Parliament,[53] and the Council itself,[54] shared this view. Such a generally shared feeling did not result, however, in the adoption of rigorous provisions. The final Directive refers to this aspiration in vague terms. The Preamble maintains that a prerequisite for the public procurement rules to have tangible effects is that rapid and effective remedies are available. Article 1 stresses that the decisions of contracting authorities shall be reviewed effectively and, 'in particular, as rapidly as possible'. The Directive contents itself with these requirements without giving guidance as to what the degree of satisfactory rapidness and effectiveness should be, nor the means to ensure it. Neither time limits, nor the establishment of urgent review procedures are imposed in the final text. This is particularly striking since legal proceedings are anything but rapid in most Member States. In this context, resort to the effective judicial protection principle would be of little use. As stated before, structural insufficiencies of national review systems cannot be tackled on the basis of this principle. The response of national authorities to this requirement shows that, whereas in some Member States means for ensuring rapidness have been put into place,[55] in others, the requirement has largely been disregarded.[56] This will not contribute to the attainment of the uniformity intended by the Directive. The Directive has been weakened by this failure to impose more concrete obligations as regards how to give practical validity to the requirements of rapidness.

---

[51] It must be noted, however, that in the Remedies Directive applicable to the excluded sectors, Member States are permitted to empower national review bodies to impose the payment of a dissuasive sum of money on defaulting contracting authorities. Article 2(1)(c). According to Article 2(5), the sum to be paid '... must be set at a level high enough to dissuade the contracting entity from committing or persisting in an infringement'.

[52] See the Commission's first proposal. COM (87) 134 at 2.

[53] See the 'Report drawn up on behalf of the Committee on Economic and Monetary Affairs and Industrial Policy on the proposal of the Commission to the Council of a directive co-ordinating the law, regulations and administrative practices relating to the application of Community rules and procedures for the award of public supply and public works contracts', EP Session Documents, 1987–88, 3 February 1988, EP 118.211 (Report Beumer I) at 11.

[54] Motivation Position Commune (above, n 8) CCO/89/64 at 3.

[55] See France, Chapter 9.   [56] See Spain, Chapter 9.

The Regulation of Interim Relief

Given the unsatisfactory situation at national level and the crucial importance of interim relief to achieve effectiveness in public procurement cases,
it is not surprising that this particular issue was a major preoccupation of
the Commission when drafting its proposals. The first proposal articulated
two sorts of intervention mechanisms in order to suspend contract award
procedures when a 'clear and manifest violation of Community law was
alleged'. One of them was to take place at a centralized level and was to
be directly initiated by the Commission itself. A second mechanism was
conceived to be performed at domestic level by nationally designed bodies
after an appeal was made. These schemes are examined separately.

The proposed powers of the Commission at centralized level

In addition to interim relief requests before the Court of Justice in the
context of an Article 169 EC procedure, the first proposal of the Commission contemplated an innovative 'supranational' interim relief procedure.
According to it, the 'Commission may, in case of urgency, suspend a contract award procedure for a period that may not exceed three months' on
its own initiative, or in response to a complaint.[57] The proposed suspension power could take place 'at any stage of the procedure where it has
been established that a clear and manifest violation of Community law
has been committed'. By way of example, a list of infringements in which
it was thought that a suspension of the procedure was justified was included. These corresponded to the most common breaches of Community rules.[58] The decision was to be notified both to the contracting
authority and to the Member State to which the latter is answerable and
could be published by the Commission in the Official Journal.[59] The suspension was to be unilaterally decided by the Commission, it would have
had an automatic effect and would have been legally binding on contracting authorities.

The Commission thought this power necessary 'in order to avoid any
irreparable harm that might result if the contract were awarded unlaw-
fully'.[60] Moreover, the unwillingness of undertakings to take action against
contracting authorities meant 'that the number of interim measures requested by way of a summary procedure by undertakings with a view to
the suspension of contract award procedures, even where these are manifestly irregular, was likely to remain small'.[61] Such a drawback was to be
resolved through more active Commission involvement. The insufficiencies
of Article 169 EC also called for the attribution of complementary powers

---

[57] Article 3 COM (87) 134.   [58] Article 4 COM (87) 134. See *supra* n 19.
[59] Article 4(2) COM (87) 134.   [60] EC Commission, COM (87) 134 at 2 and 4.
[61] EC Commission, COM (88) 733 at 22.

similar to those enjoyed in the competition area,[62] if effectiveness was to be attained.

The system would work as follows: 'the standstill imposed on the contracting authority would enable the Commission services to examine in detail whether or not the circumstances brought to its attention constituted an infringement of the Community rules in the field and to take the necessary corrective action'. The suspension was to be 'a temporary standstill and once it had expired, the contracting authority would regain the right to award the contract without prejudice to subsequent action which the Commission or contractor/supplier might take as to the legality of the award from the viewpoint of Community or national law'.[63]

Needless to say, the proposal provoked much controversy. First of all, doubts were raised about the compatibility with the Treaty system of division of powers it entailed. The Community legal and institutional system is governed by the 'institutional autonomy principle',[64] pursuant to which Member States are free to choose the way in which they comply with Community law within the limits of the effectiveness principle.[65] National discretion is subject to the control of the Commission and, in the last instance, the Court of Justice. However, with the exception of some specific fields,[66] as 'guardian of the Treaty' the Commission's monitoring powers are limited to the use of Article 169 EC when a 'clear and manifest violation of Community law' has been detected. This provision requires

---

[62] In Case 792/79, *R. Camera Care Ltd.* v. *Commission* [1980] ECR 133, the Court interpreted Article 3 of Council Regulation 17 implementing Articles 85 and 86 of the EC Treaty as empowering the Commission to adopt interim measures in Competition law proceedings, even though such a power was not explicitly mentioned in the Regulation. A similar regulation is lacking, however, in the field of public procurement rules. See generally Piroche, 'Les mesures provisoires de la Commission des Communautés européennes dans le domaine de la concurrence' (1989) 25 RTDE 439.

[63] EC Commission, COM (87) 134 at 4. In addition to the suspension powers, the Commission's proposal also required Member States to guarantee the possibility for the Commission to intervene in the administrative or judicial national procedures established pursuant to the Directive relating to infringements of Community rules on public procurement to 'ensure that the Community rules on public procurement were interpreted and applied uniformly and that contracting authorities were better informed of their obligations under those rules'. For a discussion of this specific issue, see Labayle (above, n 1) at 634; House of Lords Select Committee (above, n 1) at 12 and 20. This second power, although not as controversial as the power to suspend the award procedure, was also subject to various criticisms. See Coleman and Margue (above, n 1) at 552. The Council dropped the proposal during the adoption of its common position and although the Commission regretted this course of action, it did not regard the matter as sufficiently important, compared with the other objectives of the Directive, to jeopardize reaching a compromise agreement. See generally Beumer Report II (above, n 8) at 8.   [64] See Chapters 4 and 7.

[65] In this context the Court of Justice and the Commission have in the past been cautious when defining the duties and responsibilities of national courts with respect to Community obligations. See Evans, 'The Enforcement Procedure of Article 169 EEC: the Commission's Discretion' (1979) 4 ELRev 440 at 452. See also Chapter 6.

[66] Staff and competition cases, or when the Commission acts as a private individual.

Member States to account for any breaches of Community law committed by their administrative, judicial or even legislative organs. No direct action is envisaged against the defaulting organ itself.[67] In other words, the Commission's intervention powers are confined to the supranational level.

If the Member State does not comply with the Commission's requests, no direct sanction may be imposed on it and the matter must be brought before the Court of Justice for final adjudication. The 'institutional autonomy principle' operates even at this stage. Under Article 171 EC, competent national authorities are required to adopt the 'necessary measures' to comply with the judgments of the Court of Justice. The way in which they decide to comply is left to their discretion, provided the adopted measures are effective. The Commission in performing its monitoring role can only assess whether the adopted national measures are sufficient, but may not impose its view. After the TEU, if unsatisfied with the response of the Member State to the Court's judgment, it may bring an additional action under Article 171(2) EC and suggest the imposition of a pecuniary sanction on the defaulting Member State, but it cannot specify the measures to be implemented. Once again, it is up to the Court of Justice to decide, in the final instance, on the Commission's request. In brief, from this traditional perspective of the division of competences, vertical intervention by the Commission in national legal systems, including award procedures, has not been contemplated in the institutional structure established by the Treaties. On the contrary, the principle of institutional autonomy has operated in the opposite sense.

Further practical difficulties can be outlined. If the Commission found that a national act clearly and manifestly contravenes public procurement rules, that does not necessarily imply that its views are well-founded. Who would then be competent to monitor the correct use of this power? What would the rights of contracting authorities and injured tenderers be with respect to the review of the suspension decision? The determination of whether interim relief is needed to protect individual rights from irreparable damages is a competence reserved to judicial instances, both at the supranational and national levels. As the Commission would exercise this power through the adoption of decisions, complainants would have to proceed via a direct action under Article 173 EC and would have to claim eventual damages for non-contractual liability of Community institutions, which would seriously complicate access to effective judicial protection of firms suffering prejudices from the Commission's action.[68] Furthermore,

---

[67] Coleman and Margue (above, n 1) at 547.

[68] The Commission considered that 'the contracting authority and the injured firm or firms may, if the Commission abuses its power of suspension, invoke Article 173 of the Treaty in order to bring an action before the Court of Justice in respect of the decision to suspend the award procedure. Such an action may be brought with a view to seeking annulment by

the Court of Justice would function as an appeals court, which would exacerbate the current problem of overloading.

From a practical point of view, the effectiveness of such a power to enhance overall compliance is also doubtful. Although admittedly this power would have improved the enforcement scenario, its practical application would have been flawed by the same drawbacks discussed when analysing the centralized enforcement of the Commission.[69] It appears contradictory to justify the adoption of the Directive on the basis of the insufficiencies of centralized control and then (contrary to what its general enforcement policy indicated) return to inefficient centralized enforcement tactics.

The Council could, nonetheless, have adopted the proposal in the exercise of its decision-making competences on the basis of Article 235 EC. The fact that the opening up of public procurement represents an important aspect of the realization of the 1992 internal market would have justified such an 'extraordinary approach' to the issue. However, this possibility was only theoretical. The attainment of the unanimity required by Article 235 EC would have been rather unlikely, if not impossible, as the officials of certain Member States participating in the elaboration of the Remedies Directive indicated.[70]

Predictably, the proposal was unanimously rejected by the Council, after being watered down by the European Parliament.[71] It is worth noting that one of the reasons given by the Council for rejecting the proposed powers was the very serious economic consequences which such a power could bring.[72] The Commission, in view of the unanimous rejection, negotiated a less onerous intervention technique which, in essence, respected the Treaty division of competences. This compromise is enshrined in Article

the Court of the contested act and recovering damages from the Commission. Moreover, under Articles 185 and 186 of the Treaty, Member States, the contracting authority and the injured firm or firms may, when they bring their action, seek an order from the Court suspending the application of the Commission's decision.'. COM (88) 733 at 20.

[69] According to the Beumer Report II, 'the question is whether the Commission has the resources and staff it needs to ensure that the power of suspension (as originally proposed) is not applied arbitrarily to individual contract award procedures but is able to pursue a consistent policy in the field . . .' (above, n 8) at 9.

[70] While acting as a witness before the House of Lords Select Committee on the European Communities, Mr Jones, of Her Majesty's Treasury, stated in relation to this issue that 'I think in practical terms, in the discussions we have had so far on the works directive, there is hardly any possibility at all that the necessary unanimity could be obtained which is ultimately required under Article 235 EEC. I am sure it would not be possible.'. House of Lords Select Committee (above, n 1) question 88–89, at 14.   [71] Beumer Report II (above, n 8) at 9.

[72] The Council states in its common position '. . . une telle suspension est disproportionnée au but recherché, fait double emploi avec les mesures nationales applicables en la matière et peut avoir des conséquences économiques très graves', CCO/89/64 at 5. On the Council's reaction, see also Coleman and Margue (above, n 1) at 552. For the national reaction of public authorities, industry and academics to the proposed powers, see House of Lords Select Committee (above, n 1) at 11 and 18.

3 of the final Directive, which provides for a swift administrative procedure to be applied by the Commission in cases where a 'clear and manifest infringement of Community provisions' is detected. The Commission must notify the alleged infringement to the Member State and request its correction. The Member State, for its part, must communicate to the Commission the action undertaken with a view to correcting the infringement, in particular, whether the contract award procedure has been suspended or not, or when the Member State does not undertake any action, a reasoned submission as to why no correction has taken place. The Member State is equally obliged to inform the Commission of the developments in the case. That is, when and why the eventual suspension has been lifted and whether other award procedures on the same subject matter have been initiated. Although not explicitly stated in the Directive, it follows that if the Commission is not satisfied with the Member State's allegations or conduct, it may send a reasoned opinion under Article 169 EC, without the need to initiate an Article 169 EC infringement procedure from the beginning by sending a formal letter of notice.

This procedure had been used in Case C-359/93, *Commission* v. *The Netherlands*.[73] In it, the Commission formulated several complaints under the swift procedure of the Directive, which were communicated to the Netherlands six months after the notice of the contract in question had been published and just the day before the contract was entered into. The defendant rightly protested about the late use made by the Commission of this procedure. This delay obviously defeated the whole purpose for which the system was adopted.[74] The Advocate General explicitly criticised the Commission's delay in making use of the special procedure and endorsed the defendant's objections. The Court of Justice also hinted that the Commission had not acted in the spirit of the Directive.[75] Both concluded, however, that, although the behaviour of the Commission was criticisable from a policy point of view, legally its conduct could not exclude its right of action under Article 169 EC, as the Netherlands had contended.[76]

The Commission's course of action is certainly regrettable. The swift

[73] Case C-359/93, *Commission* v. *The Netherlands*, judgment of 24 January 1995, not yet reported. Noted by Fernández Martín (1995) 43 PPLR CS74.

[74] The Commission notified the Netherlands Government of the alleged 'clear and manifest' infringements on Friday 25 June 1992, more than six months after the tender notice had been published in the OJ. The notification only reached the relevant Ministry four days later, Monday 29 June 1992, the same day on which the contract was awarded. The Commission also communicated to the Netherlands Government that it should treat the notification as a formal letter of notice for the purposes of Article 169 EC and that the subsequent communication from the Netherlands Government would be treated as the observations provided for in that Article.

[75] C-359/93, *Commission* v. *The Netherlands* (above, n 73) para. 12.

[76] Opinion C-359/93, *Commission* v. *The Netherlands* (above, n 73) paras. 4–5.

procedure adopted was the result of a long and difficult decision-making process and its adoption was ultimately justified by the need to equip the Commission with sufficient means for monitoring the application of public procurement rules. The first time the Commission has used it, not only did it fail to prevent the award of the contract but it acted in a tardy and negligent manner. Even though, from a legal point of view, the conclusion of the Court of Justice and the Advocate General may be sound, the blatant misuse of the procedure by the Commission has done little good to the credibility of the Commission's monitoring policy and its constant claims for more powers for supranational enforcement of the public procurement rules. It would not be surprising if, from now on, Member States concede further enforcement powers even more reluctantly to the Commission services in an eventual revision of the Remedies Directive.

Interim relief before national courts at decentralized level

Article 2(1)(a) of the Remedies Directive provides that Member States must ensure that the measures taken concerning the review procedure specified in Article 1 include a provision for the authorities 'to take at the earliest opportunity and by way of interlocutory procedures, interim measures with the aim of correcting the alleged infringement or preventing further damage to the interests concerned, including measures to suspend or to ensure the suspension of the procedure for the award of a public contract to the implementation of any decision taken by the contracting authority'. This power is further qualified, however, in paragraph 3 of the same provision, which explicitly states that 'review procedures need not in themselves have an automatic suspensive effect on the contract award procedures to which they relate'. This paragraph was introduced by the Council while adopting its common position with the object of making clear that the award of interim measures was to be interpreted freely according to domestic legal approaches. In no case could the review mechanisms be understood as automatically interrupting the course of the procedure.

This restrictive approach of Member States is further revealed by the 'public interest' exemption enshrined in Article 2(4) which states that 'Member States may provide that when considering whether to order interim measures the body responsible may take into account the probable consequences of the measures *for all interests likely to be harmed, as well as the public interest,* and may decide *not to grant such measures where their negative consequences could exceed their benefits.* A decision not to grant interim measures shall not prejudice any other claim of the persons seeking these measures.' (emphasis added).

In all national legal orders public interest considerations are usually involved in the field of public procurement. It is not by chance that distinct principles alien to the ordinary law of contract apply to the area of public contracts. In Spain and France, the public interest is reflected not only at the enforcement level but also in the regulation of public contracts itself, through the attribution of numerous prerogatives which benefit public authorities.[77] Even in those Member States which approach contracts of public authorities from a private law perspective, principles protecting public interest have influenced the straight application of the ordinary law of contract, especially at the enforcement stages.[78] In fact, the application of the relevant rules has been eased when the general interest justified a discriminatory award.

This public interest aspect of the contracts of public authorities has largely been ignored by the main public procurement Directives. With the exception of the provisions admitting the preferential use of public procurement as a means of fostering regional development, (which is a manifestation of the general interest), and some Court of Justice decisions concerning interim relief requests by the Commission in which public interest has been taken into account, commercial considerations have prevailed in the Community legislation and in the Commission's policy in this area. Not surprisingly, the paragraph in the Remedies Directive was introduced on the initiative of the Member States and its objective is to correct this gap. However, the scope of such an exemption has been left undefined. What are the limits to the public interest exception? Is there a uniform approach to the notion of public interest throughout the Community? What should the interpretative guidelines be? The Directive's provisions fail to provide an answer to these questions and the responsibility of giving substance to this notion falls upon national courts and, in the last instance, the Court of Justice. It must be noted, however, that the Council and the Commission added a declaration concerning this provision in

[77] Spanish law provides for 'exorbitant' prerogatives in favour of contracting authorities, which are alien to the common law of contract, e.g., the power of unilateral interpretation, modification and annulment of the contract for reasons of public interest. See Article 60 LCE and STS of 10 February 1979 and STS of 22 February 1982. See in general Mestre Delgado, 'La posición singular de la Administración en la contratación administrativa y las garantías del contratista según la jurisprudencia contencioso-administrativa reciente' (1985) REDA at 425–448. The same types of prerogatives are awarded to French contracting authorities. See generally, Laubadère, Devolvé et Moderne, *Traité des Contrats Administratifs*, Tome I (Paris, 1983) paras. 840 *ff*; Goldman, 'An Introduction to the French Law of Government Procurement Contracts' (1987) 20 *George Washington Journal of International Law & Economics* 461 at 483 *ff*.

[78] In the United Kingdom, the principle of 'effectiveness in the government action' justifies certain departures from the application of the ordinary law to those contractual agreements entered into by the Crown. See generally Mitchell, *The Contracts of Public Authorities* (London, 1953), Chapter 4. Street, *Governmental Liability* (London, 1953) 82 *ff*; Turpin, *Government Procurement and Contracts* (Harlow, 1989), Chapter 4, 83 *ff*. In Germany, considerations relating to the public interest have been taken into account in the application of competition law rules to public authorities awarding contracts by the *Bundesgerichtshof*. See *Bundesgerichtshof* of 26 May 1987, *Wirtschaft und Wettbewerb* (WuW) 1987, 1009.

which they stated that they were of the opinion 'that the interests referred to in Article 2(4) must be substantive in nature and should conform with *the principles of national jurisprudence with regard to interim measures*' (emphasis added).[79]

The impact of the Court's case law on interim relief

The issue of interim relief has clearly been affected by the *Factortame* decision. The issue is whether the Directive's provisions add any substantial improvement to the specific case of public procurement. Oliver answers this question in the negative and states that the provision of the Remedies Directive on interim measures 'would appear to be declaratory in nature'.[80] In view of the restrictive provisions of the Directive, it is difficult to disagree with this judgement. Moreover, the provisions of the Directive, as supplemented by the above declaration of the Commission and Council relating to interpretative guidelines, amounts to nothing more than a mere codification of the practice of national courts. Much of its justification is lost because it falls short of imposing strict procedural conditions regarding this matter. It may even be regarded as consolidating a conservative approach.

Even though the Directive is disappointing, arguably national courts are bound by the Court of Justice's case law on interim relief in public procurement cases. This case law will furnish the relevant interpretative guidelines to be applied after the Remedies Directive has been passed. According to the Court, the test has been one of balancing private interests against public ones. It follows that a solution has to be found on a case by case basis. The nature of the contract, its object, the alleged urgency of the requested works or supplies and the effect of the measures on the public collectivity will have to be considered. As discussed in Chapter 6, despite its early case law, where the Court showed a readiness to suspend the contract award procedure and even the execution of an already concluded contract in the interests of legality,[81] its most recent position seems to have shifted to a more conventional position.[82] The current situation is ambiguous. If the first line of cases is accepted as establishing the Court's position, a presumption in favour of the suspension of the contract would need to be applied and the cautious treatment of national courts would need to be reconsidered.[83] Otherwise, things will remain unchanged.

As things stand, it is difficult to predict the way in which national courts

---

[79] Reproduced in Report Beumer II (above, n 8) at 12.
[80] Oliver, 'Interim Measures: Recent Developments' (1992) 29 CMLRev at 20.
[81] See Chapter 6. See also Arrowsmith in Arrowsmith (ed.) (1993) (above, n 1) at 63 *ff.*
[82] See Chapter 6.
[83] On the restrictive approach to interim relief by national courts see Chapters 9 and 10.

will react in the future and whether a change in their current approach is likely. Long standing traditions die slowly. Considering that delaying the execution of public contracts may well be considered a disturbance of the public interest, due regard to the long duration of legal proceedings as a consequence of endogenous factors and the fact that, in most cases, damages are seen as an adequate substitute ensuring effective judicial protection, it would not be surprising if interim relief is approached restrictively by national courts.[84]

The Regulation of Damages in the Remedies Directive

The provision on damages merely states that the Member States must ensure that the measures taken concerning the review procedures include provisions for the powers to award damages to persons harmed by an infringement.[85] Furthermore, a Member State may provide that after the conclusioñ of a contract following its award, the powers of the body responsible for the review procedure are to be limited to awarding damages to any person harmed by an infringement.[86] No other specifications are included.

The approach adopted therefore misses the whole issue of the incentive or deterrent aspects of damages.[87] It is regrettable that the Directive does not deal with the procedural conditions to be eligible for damages. It has completely avoided the hot potatoes which the Directive should have tackled. The scarce regulation of damages was due, according to the direct negotiators of the Directive, Coleman and Margue, 'au fait qu'en général la notion de dommages-intérêts et les montants à accorder relèvent de l'appréciation des juges. En outre, la jurisprudence en question est souvent d'application plus générale et n'est pas limitée au seul domaine des marchés publics. Il aurait donc été très difficile d'imposer des règles

---

[84] With respect to English courts, see Arrowsmith (1992), 'Enforcing the EC Public Procurement Rules: the Remedies System in England and Wales, 1 PPLR 92 at 112 *ff*; see also Weatherill 'Enforcing the Public Procurement Directives in the UK' in Arrowsmith (ed.) (1993) (above, n 1) at 285. The same conclusion is reached with regard to Spain, see Fernández Martín, 'Enforcing the Public Procurement Rules in Spain', ibid. at 259, 268 *ff*; Belgium, see D'Hooghe, 'Enforcing the Public Procurement Rules in Belgium', ibid. at 110.

[85] Article 2(1)(c).	[86] Article 2(6).

[87] In its first proposal, the Commission did partially tackle the question in the second paragraph of Article 1(3), which stated that 'the competent administrative body or court may take, among other things, the following decisions: . . . to award damages to the injured undertaking for the costs of *unnecessary studies, foregone profits or lost opportunities*' (emphasis added). Although these grounds for damages were optional, the proposal responded to the philosophy of ensuring compliance by attracting private actions through the possibility of obtaining high damages. COM (87) 134. The European Parliament acknowledged such a difficulty and recommended the deletion of the clause providing for foregone profits on the basis that they would be too difficult to assess in practice. Report Beumer I (above, n 53) at 12.

communes dans ce domaine, compte tenu notamment du principe de séparation des pouvoirs à la base des Constitutions de plusieurs États membres'.[88]

The impact of the Francovich *case law*

The provisions of the Remedies Directive on damages must be contrasted with the Court's statements in the *Francovich* decision. *A fortiori*, even if the Remedies Directive did not regulate damages such a right would result from the Court's case law on the effective judicial protection of Community rights by national courts. What, therefore, is the contribution of the Remedies Directive in this sense? Since it fails to adopt a more stringent provision on damages which would provide for an incentive element, or merely the procedural rules under which damages may be claimed, one may wonder what the final justification of the Directive is.

It is worthy of note that in its proposal for a Remedies Directive for the sectors previously excluded, the Commission attached special emphasis to the 'incentive' element of damages. Damages were to be awarded *automatically* to any complainant when an infringement was held to exist. The justification for this was given in the explanatory memorandum to the proposal:

... the injury inflicted on an interested party ... is to deprive the bidder of his right to a fair opportunity to compete for [a] contract. The bidder had a legitimate expectation that the bid would be fairly considered: this consideration contributed to his decision to incur the costs of bid preparation and submission. An infringement which materially affects the bid's chances of success therefore constitutes an injury to the bidder which should be repaired by the payment of damages, irrespective of whether it can be demonstrated that the bid would have been successful in the absence of the infringement.[89]

The Council accepted the inclusion of a provision in the final Remedies Directive applicable to the Utilities which reflected the general concern for the easier availability of damages, although subject to certain procedural limits.[90] Article 2(7) of Directive 92/13 provides that 'where a claim is made for damages representing the costs of preparing a bid or of participating in an award procedure, the person making the claim shall be required only to prove an infringement of Community law in the field of procurement or national rules implementing that law and that he would

---

[88] Coleman and Margue (above, n 1) at 551.

[89] Amended proposal for a Council Directive co-ordinating the laws, regulations and administrative provisions relating to the application of Community rules on the procurement procedures of entities operating in the water, energy, transport and telecommunications sectors, COM (91) 158 final at para. 24.

[90] For a discussion of this provision, see Gormley (1992) (above, n 1) at 261–263.

have had a real chance of winning the contract and that, as consequence of that infringement, that chance was adversely affected.'.

This provision constitutes a major improvement with respect to the position adopted in the general Remedies Directive. It balances the incentive element with the need to protect the public interest. Although it does not go as far as the Commission's proposal for automatic damages, the difficulties in providing evidence of having won the contract are overcome, since evidence of a real chance is deemed sufficient to be entitled to damages. Cow-boy complainants are therefore avoided. The amount is restricted to the bidding costs or preparation costs, although it is submitted that this should not prejudice the right to foregone profits and even loss of chance if a better right is shown.[91] One has to wait to see what the practical impact of this new provision will be, although it is suggested that it embodies the correct approach.

CONCLUSIONS

In order to accomplish a minimum degree of effective enforcement for Community purposes, remedies in the field of public procurement must fulfil three conditions. They have to allow for: (i) fast review procedures which allow for the resolution of the dispute before the contract is awarded; (ii) easily available interim measures which permit the resolution of the dispute before the contract is awarded; and if such a course of action is not possible due to the private or public interests involved, the most adequate solution would be to (iii) ensure injured bidders the award of compensatory damages under the conditions described above. Prevailing national approaches do not satisfactorily meet all three conditions, as national systems of redress tend to privilege the public interest behind public contracts, or, in more general terms, behind the activities of public authorities.

It was up to the Community harmonization measure to correct the insufficiencies of the national systems. The Remedies Directive is disappointing in many respects. Its provisions are vague and uncompelling and there is an absence of specific provisions tackling the core problems hindering the decentralized enforcement of the Community procurement rules by private undertakings. Moreover, it does not go beyond the case law of the European Court of Justice. It is nevertheless true that the *Francovich* and *Factortame* decisions were given after the Remedies Directive

[91] According to the explanatory memorandum of the first proposal, the amount of damages were deemed to be not less than 1% of the total contract value which, considering the type of contracts passed in the excluded sectors, is a rather important sum. COM (91) 158 at para. 22. This solution was not finally retained.

had been passed, but this does not justify the weakness of the measure adopted.

The analysis of the evolution of the Remedies Directive from the original proposals shows that the Commission's attempts to adopt effective mechanisms of redress were systematically defeated during the decision-making process. Why is this so? From a legal point of view, there was a need to strike a balance between the requirements of the effectiveness of redress mechanisms to achieve the aims of Community rules and the protection of the public and private interests involved. The Commission's proposals disregarded the public interest aspects and concentrated on effectiveness. An irreconcilable conflict between both aspects may exist. The supranational objectives, encouraging decentralized control through the establishment of incentives, may not be attainable as the 'public interest' aspects which prevail in national legal approaches impose limits on the extent and scope of possible mechanisms.

From an institutional point of view, the dual character of the supranational structure limits the possibilities of far-reaching integratory measures in the field of public procurement. Centralist tendencies, represented by the powers proposed for the Commission, have been systematically defeated by the Council. The political compromise between the Commission and the Council, which materialized in the adoption of the Remedies Directive, shows that national autonomy is still favoured by the Member States to the detriment of eventual effectiveness.

The establishment of a strictly autonomous supranational remedies policy, especially designed to render Community rules on public procurement effective and which differs substantially from the prevailing national approaches, implemented *ex novo* with respect to contracts of Community interest, does not seem to be feasible in the medium term. A Remedies Directive was enacted, despite these drawbacks. Has the Remedies Directive substantially altered previous national approaches regarding remedies in the field of public procurement? If so, to what extent? An answer to these questions will be sought in the following chapters once the implementation measures adopted have been analysed.

The Enforcement Level (IV): The Implementation of the Remedies Directive in France and Spain

INTRODUCTION

Article 5 of the Remedies Directive required Member States to adopt the necessary implementation measures by 21 December 1991. This chapter discusses the different means of implementation adopted to give effect to the requirements of the Remedies Directive and their potential effectiveness. The four countries analysed can be grouped into two different categories. The first group refers to those countries which can be defined as 'administrative law' oriented: Spain and France. The second category consists of Germany and the United Kingdom where public contracting has traditionally been regulated from a private law perspective. Where necessary, and in order to measure the impact of the Remedies Directive, reference is made to the main features of national systems as they stood before 1991.

FRANCE

Before the new public works Directive, the subsequent consolidated Directives and the Remedies Directive were implemented in France, only public authorities, as defined by the *Code des Marchés Publics*, were subject to the Community rules on public procurement. Third parties who were victims of a breach of Community rules by a public contracting authority had to resort, as a consequence of the theory of the *actes détachables*, to the administrative courts, in order to enforce their Community rights irrespective of the contract's private law or public law nature.[1] The situation became more complicated, however, after the modification of the scope of application of first the public works Directive and then the public supplies and services Directives.[2] Their new personal scope of application covers contracting authorities which were considered as private persons under French law and, therefore, were subject to the ordinary law of contract. This called for a significant change of the domestic regulation of remedies. Moreover, the applicable remedies had to be adapted in accordance with the requirements of effectiveness and rapidity which were imposed

[1] See Chapter 4.   [2] See Chapter 1.

by the Remedies Directive. In addition, recent case law suggests that the theory of the *actes détachables*, which governed available redress of public procurement cases for the most part of this century, seems to be losing relevance.

The Situation Prior to the Implementation of the Remedies Directive

Contracts of Public Authorities. The Theory of *Actes Détachables*

The position of third parties in France as regards the availability of judicial redress has been intimately linked to the theory of *actes détachables*.[3] Before its adoption by the *Conseil d'État* at the beginning of the twentieth century, the prevailing theory regarded the contracts of public authorities as *tout indivisible*. Accordingly, once the contract was concluded, all administrative acts adopted by the contracting authority in the course of the award procedure became indissolubly incorporated in the contract itself. Irregularities committed during the award procedure could not therefore be brought before the administrative courts without questioning the final contract at the same time. This theory caused a major problem. Once the contract started to produce legal effects, only those grievances presented by the parties to the contract, even though they referred to illegalities which occurred at the pre-contract stages, were admissible through a *recours en annulation en plein contentieux*.[4] Third parties, who are considered alien to the contractual relationship in force, were not allowed to judicially challenge alleged illegalities which had been committed during the pre-contract stages. This jurisprudence was based on the principle of respect for the acquired rights of successful tenderers. Thus, by way of example, if no publicity had taken place, or if the administration had not respected the requirements of fair competition but the contract had nevertheless been concluded, only the other party to the contract could challenge such a breach before the competent judge (*juge du contrat*) *en plein contentieux* with the object of declaring the contract null or invalid.

Commissaire Romieu introduced the theory of the *actes détachables*, substituting the idea of the *tout indivisible* in 1905. In his conclusions in the *Martin* judgment,[5] he held that all those administrative acts (that is, those

---

[3] Affaires *Commune de Gorre, Commune de Villers-sur-Mer, Commune de Messé*, concl. Martin, Petit, Camus et autres (Conseil d'Etat (CE) 11 December 1903, 22 April 1904, 29 April 1904, 4 August 1905, 19 December 1905 and 6 April 1906, S. 1906. III, 49.) For a detailed discussion of the evolution of the case law see Lefoulon, 'Contribution à l'étude de la distinction des contentieux. Le problème de la compétence du juge du contrat en matière administrative' (1976) *Actualité Juridique—Droit Administratif* 396 and Laubadère, Devolvé et Moderne, *Traité des Contrats Administratifs* (Paris, 1983) paras. 1823 *ff*.

[4] For a complete analysis see Auby et Drago, *Traité de Contentieux Administratif* (Paris, 1984) paras. 1367–1370.

[5] CE 4 August 1905, *Martin*, concl. Romieu; D. 1907. III 49; Lefoulon (above, n 3) at 397. Laubadère and others (above, n 3) at para. 1824.

acts unilaterally taken by the administration) which constituted the award procedure could be isolated from the contract itself, even when the contract had been definitively concluded. In a manner of speaking, their legal life was independent from that of the contract as long as they could be detached from it. This enabled third parties to question these acts before the administrative courts and seek to annul them through the correct legal proceedings. Furthermore, since the *actes détachables* were to be considered autonomous from the contract itself, the declaration of invalidity affecting one of those acts would not affect the validity of the contract. In this way, the principle of acquired rights was respected and the eventual rights of third parties were protected. The practical consequences of this theory are that any interested party may challenge an infringement which occurred throughout the contract award procedure, or even the award decision itself, before the administrative *juge pour excès de pouvoir*.[6] Where the contract has not been finally concluded and the action is declared well founded, the administration is banned from concluding it. On the contrary, if the contract has already been concluded, since the impugned act is presumed independent and autonomous of the contract itself, the eventual declaration of invalidity will be restricted to the impugned and separate act. This is without prejudice to the fact that the party to the contract, if it ever decided to do so, could allege such an infringement to quash the contract before the *juge du contrat*.[7]

Some commentators have contested the internal logic of this approach.[8] According to them, the declaration of nullity of one of the 'supporting' severable acts, as a result of an action *pour excès de pouvoir*, should automatically lead to the annulment of the contract itself. In this way, a variation of the theory of the *tout indivisible* would be reinstalled, since the nullity of an *acte détachable* would nullify the contract also. Partial authority sustaining this position is to be found in the judgment of the *Conseil d'État* of 7 July 1982,[9] where the lack of publication of the compulsory contract notice led to the nullity of the concluded contract itself. This decision, which seemed to be merely incidental in the case law of the *Conseil d'État*, has recently been complemented by a second decision in the same vein.

---

[6] Laubadère and others (above, n 3) at para. 1824. From 1964 the CE has extended the theory of *actes détachables* to cover acts of contracting authorities which relate to the execution of the contract clauses. Thus, any person with a sufficient interest may question contracting authorities' decisions regarding the execution of an already concluded contract. CE Sect., 24 April 1964, *Société Anonyme des Livraisons Ind. (SALIC)*.

[7] For a concise description of what the situation was with respect to those *actes détachables* and the position of third parties, see Lefoulon (above, n 3) at 399.

[8] Péquignot, 'Contribution à la Théorie Générale du Contrat Administratif', Thèse (Montpellier, 1945) at 559; Weil, *Les Conséquences de l'Annulation d'un Acte Administratif pour Excès de Pouvoir* (Paris, 1952) at 201 *ff*. In the same vein Laubadère and others (above, n 3) at para. 1834.

[9] *Commune de Guidel* c. *Mme Courtet*. For a full discussion of this case and its implications, see Laubadère and others (above, n 3).

Even though the case concerned a contract concluded under private law under which a local council decided to sell some property, it looks as though the principles underlying it may also be applied to public procurement contracts. The local council's decision authorizing the mayor to sell the property constituted an *acte détachable* which was challenged before the lower administrative court *pour excès du pouvoir*, where it was declared void. With reference to the prevailing doctrine, the court did not declare the contract itself void. The claimants appealed to the *Conseil d'État* which decided to impose a daily fine on the local council until they showed that they had brought the matter before the *juge du contrat* with a view to having the contract annulled. The judgment imposes an obligation on public authorities to undertake those steps necessary to have a concluded contract based on an irregular *acte détachable* declared null by the competent judge. As Martin points out, this decision establishes a direct link between the nullity of an *acte détachable* and the validity of the contract, thereby overcoming the *actes détachables* theory.[10] However, as the same author emphasizes, the procedure to obtain this is cumbersome as it requires, first, a judgment by the administrative judge declaring an *acte détachable* void; second, a referral to the *Conseil d'État* in order to obtain a decision requiring the public authority to bring the matter before the *juge du contrat* and, finally, a judgment of the latter declaring the contract void. These requirements may be overcome, however, with reference to the Law of 8 February 1955 concerning the organization of civil, criminal and administrative procedures. This provides that administrative judges are entitled to decide injunctions, which may be accompanied by daily fines, against public authorities in order for them to adopt all measures to comply with its decision. Thus, the administrative judge considering the validity of the *acte détachable* may order the contracting authority which is party to a concluded contract to bring it before the *juge du contrat* for a declaration of nullity.[11] It must be noted, however, that the use of this procedure is not common. This may change in the light of the latest decision of the *Conseil d'État*.

The Remedies Available before the Implementation of the Remedies Directive

Since the acts constituting the award procedure were autonomous administrative acts challengeable on their own accord, breaches of Community

---

[10] If the examined position is retained, one of the main objectives sought by the introduction of the *actes détachables* theory—that of protecting the acquired rights of *bona fide* contractors and successful tenderers—would be undermined. It must also be pointed out that third parties challenging a severable administrative act may not have any interest at all in obtaining the nullity of the concluded contract. See the statements by Romieu in this sense, CE 4 August 1905, concl. Romieu (above, n 5).

[11] See further Martin, 'Latest Developments in the Legal Procedures Applicable to Public Services Contracts' (1995) 4 PPLR CS . . .

rules on public procurement were impugnable through the same judicial means available against administrative acts. These were the *recours pour excès de pouvoir*, or eventually, a *recours en plein contentieux* for damages[12] before administrative courts.

The action for *excès de pouvoir* is the remedy through which any interested person may claim a declaratory judgment from administrative courts holding that an administrative decision is null and void.[13] It is of very limited scope, however, since the administrative judge cannot decide measures or remedies other than the mere declaration of nullity.[14] He or she may, however, address the pertinent Directives to the defaulting public authority in order for them to execute the judgment. This course of action is not usual however.[15] The practical effectiveness of this type of action was doubtful, as it did not provide the aggrieved tenderer with any practical benefit but only resulted in a mere declaratory judgment.[16] After the implementation of the Remedies Directive, doubts have been raised as to whether the *recours pour excès de pouvoir* is still available to injured third parties. This question is analysed later on.

A second option for aggrieved tenderers was to proceed through the action *en plein contentieux*. In this action the administrative judge is asked to decide not just on the validity or invalidity of an administrative act, but also upon the extent and effects of rights which individuals want to enforce against public authorities. This action is suitable if the plaintiff not only wants the annulment of a decision, but also compensation for all damages sustained. The *recours en plein contentieux* seemed to be the only judicial means by which damages may be obtained in the field of public procurement.[17] With respect to damages arising from breaches of Community rules committed by the State, it is clear since *Alivar*[18] that individuals have a right to compensation for any prejudice suffered as a direct result of the State breach, provided the conditions established by national law are

---

[12] For a detailed analysis of the peculiarities of each remedy and their interrelation, see Auby et Drago (above, n 4) at para. 1078 *ff.*
[13] See generally Auby et Drago (above, n 4) at para. 1078.
[14] A well-established jurisprudence going back to the 19th century. CE 25 June 1880, *Chebaud et Mille*, S. 1882. III, 2; CE 8 August 1896, *Cie. des bateaux à vapeur de la Guadalupe*, S. 1898, III, 110. [15] Auby et Drago (above, n 4) para. 1304.
[16] Even Commissaire Romieu acknowledged the insufficiencies of this action. See his conclusions in CE 4 August 1905, *Martin* (above, n 3). On the way in which this action applied to public procurement cases, see Bréchon-Moulènes, 'French Report to the 14th FIDE Congress' in FIDE *L'Application dans les États Membres des Directives sur les Marchés Publics* (Madrid, 1990) at 161.
[17] The principle of administrative liability in French law is governed by specific public law rules since the landmark judgment of the *Tribunal des Conflits* in *Blanco* (8 February 1973). See generally Laubadère, *Traité de Droit Administratif*, 9ème edn., Vol. I (Paris, 1984) paras. 1463 *ff.*
[18] CE 23 March 1984; see Barav and Green, 'Damages in the National Courts for Breach of Community Law' (1986) 6 YEL 55 at 76 *ff.*

fulfilled. French law requires that the plaintiff shows that the administration acted wrongfully (*faute de la part de l'administration*). This does not constitute a major obstacle since French jurisprudence considers that the existence of any illegal act constitutes a fault of the administration.[19] It has even regarded a mere error of appreciation committed in *bona fides* as indicating fault, and which thus engages the liability of public authorities.[20] The loss must be directly caused by the wrongful act.[21]

The amount of damages granted will cover the *damnum emergens*, that is, the actual costs incurred when preparing the offer.[22] The *Conseil d'État* seems to award *lucrum cessans* (lost profits) when there has been evidence of a 'serious chance' of winning the contract by the plaintiff, had the procedure been regularly developed. The difficulty lies in supplying evidence of a 'serious chance', especially when the contract had been awarded on the 'most advantageous offer' criterion. French courts will not normally involve themselves in the assessment of factual considerations. Nonetheless, it appears from more recent case law that the *Conseil d'État* is ready to grant damages for lost profit when the alleged wrongdoing of the contracting authority is flagrant and, in general terms, the plaintiff may be held to possess the same characteristics as the successful tenderer.[23] The determination of lost profit is left to an expert appointed by the court.[24] In general terms, it seems safe to conclude that the general approach of French courts to damages for breaches of Community obligations, including breaches of applicable public procurement rules, is satisfactory.[25]

It was possibly in its regulation of interim relief, however, that the French regime was most at odds with the requirements of Community law.[26] The introduction of a judicial action in France does not have suspensory effect on the challenged act, neither before the *Conseil d'État*, nor before the lower

---

[19] CE 26 January 1973, *Ville de Paris c. Driancourt*.
[20] CE 28 March 1980, *Centre hospitalier de Seclin*.
[21] CE 13 May 1980, *Monti c. Commune de Rans Pach*.   [22] CE 3 July 1967, *Sieur Lavigne*.
[23] CE 10 January 1986, *Société des travaux du Midi*, where the contracting authority had rejected the tender proposed to it by the assessment Commission without following the established procedure. The illegally rejected tenderer was awarded lost profits. See also *Tribunal Administratif de Pau*, 10 May 1979, *Sieur Bonneau*.
[24] *Tribunal Administratif de Pau*, 10 May 1979, *Sieur Bonneau*.
[25] In *Steinhauser c. Commune de Biarritz* (Case 197/84 [1985] ECR 1819) a German artist's application to participate in a tendering procedure for the allocation of rented lock-ups situated in a picturesque area of town was rejected by the Mayor of Biarritz on the grounds that the Conditions of Tender explicitly provided that only French nationals were eligible. In a preliminary reference under Article 177 EC, the Court of Justice ruled the nationality clause incompatible with Article 52 EC. The referring national court granted damages compensating for both the professional damage (including the loss of profits Mr Steinhauser suffered for not being able to work and present his paintings in this 'particularly favourable area') and the *préjudice moral* caused by the rejection. *Tribunal Administratif de Pau*, 15 November 1985. See Barav and Green (above, n 18) at 65–66.
[26] For a thorough analysis of interim relief before the administrative courts, see Auby et Drago (above, n 4) at paras. 942 *ff*.

administrative courts. Nonetheless, interim measures were accessible by means of interlocutory proceedings, either *le sursis à exécution* or *le référé*. The former alone is here examined, since the latter has hardly any incidence in the field of public procurement.[27] It must be stated, first of all, that the suspension of the effects of the act is the exception to the general rule. Therefore, the award of interim relief has been interpreted prudently and rather restrictively by the *Conseil d'État*. Lower courts, however, have been readier to suspend the act in question.[28]

The *sursis à exécution* is a request for interim relief which the complainant may lodge simultaneously with the main action. The main action must be based on serious grounds, or in other words, there must be a *prima facie* case in favour of the plaintiff and the prejudice which will result if the relief is not granted would be irreparable or very difficult to compensate.[29] Interim relief is discretionary, however, and the judge may refuse it even if the objective conditions are fulfilled. Such conditions are hardly ever met in public procurement cases, as national courts understand that compensation through damages is usually a sufficient means of redress. In any event, if the request for interim relief is introduced once the contract has been performed, the judge may only refuse it.[30]

The Situation after the Remedies Directive.[31] Law 92–10 and Decree 92–964

The adoption of the Remedies Directive meant that remedies available in French law were insufficient to respond properly to the requirements of Community law. On the one hand, with respect to contracts awarded under the *Code des marchés publics*, that is, by public authorities subject to the *Code*, certain improvements in existing redress mechanisms were required, in particular as regards the possibility of obtaining the suspension of the contract award procedure before the conclusion of the contract.[32] On the other hand, as mentioned earlier, the amending public works Directive adopted a broad definition of contracting authorities as well as of the contracts covered. This definition has been included in the consol-

---

[27] Bréchons-Moulènes in FIDE (1990) (above, n 16) at 163.

[28] Auby et Drago (above, n 4) at para. 957.

[29] See further ibid. at paras. 957 and 827 and the jurisprudence cited therein.

[30] Ibid. at para. 163.

[31] For a full account of the new situation and the problems it raises, see Valadou, 'Enforcing the Public Procurement Rules in France' in Arrowsmith (ed.), *Remedies for Enforcing the Public Procurement Rules* (Winteringham, 1993) Chapter 10. See also Arrowsmith, 'Actions to Enforce the Community Procurement Rules in France: Decree nº. 92–964 of September 7, 1992' (1993) 2 PPLR CS12.

[32] Roquette and Lefort, 'Implementation of the Public Procurement Directives in the 12 States of the EC' (1992) 1 PPLR 251 at 255.

idated versions of the public sector Directives.[33] These private law entities under French law are thus subject to the Directive's rules although previously their contracting activities were governed by the applicable civil law rules and, as a consequence, they enjoyed freedom of contract. Moreover, due to their private law nature, their contractual activities were only reviewable under applicable civil law provisions by civil courts. This situation was unsatisfactory, as the civil remedies available did not fully meet the provisions of the Remedies Directive. Article 34 of the French Constitution also reserves to the Parliament the power to regulate the civil and commercial obligations of private persons, that is, by means of an act of a legislative nature.

As a result, Law No. 92–10 of 4 January 1992[34] and Decree 92–964 of 7 September 1992[35] were enacted to implement the Remedies Directive into French law. They sought to establish a whole set of new remedies aimed at the resolution of any alleged infringement of the Community rules regulating the award procedure as incorporated into French law. The Law contains only two provisions which modify the existing situation as regards the powers enjoyed both by civil and administrative courts.[36] French authorities decided to maintain two separate jurisdictions for private law and public law contracts. If the contract is awarded by a contracting authority regarded as a private person under French law, the contract itself is considered to fall under private law. This in turn means that the civil courts (*judiciaire*) are competent and general civil law principles are applicable. On the other hand, if the contracting authority is a public authority, their contract awards are reviewable by administrative courts. The powers of each jurisdiction have been adapted to the requirements of the Remedies Directive.[37] In effect, the Law lays down a new hybrid system of pre-contractual remedies, granting courts specific powers to deal with breaches of public procurement rules before the contract is awarded.

Before entering into the detailed analysis of the innovations introduced, it is convenient to mention that its provisions do not alter the applicable rules governing the award of damages. France thought that domestic civil law and administrative law principles on liability were sufficient to guarantee proper redress. Any claim of damages will have to be based on the

[33] See Articles 1(1) and (2) of Directive 89/440 amending Article 1 of Directive 71/305. See further Chapter 1.   [34] Journal Officiel of 7 January 1992.

[35] Journal Officiel of 11 September 1992.

[36] The remedies refer only to those breaches of the rules enshrined in Book V of the *Code des Marchés Publics* (Articles 378 *et seq.* as introduced by Decree nº. 90–284 of 18 September 1990 as amended by Decree nº. 92–311 of 31 March 1992) and in Title II of Law 91–3 of 3 January 1991 implementing public works contracts Directive 89/440/EEC.

[37] Law 92–10 adds articles 11–1 and 11–2 to the Law regulating the powers of civil courts and a new section 4 headed 'Specific provisions relating to public contracts' to Book II, Title III, Chapter II of the *Code des tribunaux administratifs et des cours administratives d'appel.*

non-contractual liability principles provided in Articles 1382 *et seq.* of the Civil Code for contracts of a private nature,[38] and on the aforementioned provisions in the case of contracts awarded by a public authority.

The analysis of the future application of the principle of *responsabilité civile* to the public procurement area goes well beyond the scope of these pages. Let us simply mention here that, in principle, once a prejudice directly caused by the alleged infringement of Community rules has been proven by the applicant, he or she will be entitled to compensation covering *damnum emergens, lucrum cessans* and loss of chance, which will be assessed by the judge. As these private law contracts were not previously subject to any award procedure, the judicial treatment of damages for breach of the rules regulating award procedures and the evaluation of the plaintiff's chance of obtaining the contract is alien to civil courts. It seems likely that they will draw inspiration from the experience of their administrative law colleagues and apply, *mutatis mutandis*, a similar reasoning.[39]

Private Law Contracts

Civil law judges are competent to entertain any claims arising in the context of private law contracts.[40] The procedural rules to be followed are those governing the *procédure en référé*.[41] This provision is intended to comply with the rapidity requirement of the Remedies Directive and requires the action to be resolved by the judge in twenty days.[42] Needless to say, despite the fact that the procedural rules applicable are those for a request of interim measures, the judge actually decides on the merits of the case.

The applicant may ask the judge to adopt interim measures obliging the defendant to comply with its obligations regarding publicity and the use of the relevant competitive procedure; to suspend the award procedure or the execution of any decision relating to it, if necessary; or, lastly, to annul all decisions relating to the award procedure and to order the deletion of any contract clause or condition incompatible with the applicable Com-

---

[38] For a detailed examination of the *responsabilité civile* in general, see Weil and Terré, *Droit Civil. Les Obligations*, 4ème edn. (Paris, 1986).

[39] Valadou in Arrowsmith (ed.) (1993) (above, n 31) at 352.

[40] Article 1 of Law 92–10. Article R. 311–1 of the *Code de l'Organisation Judiciaire* (Code of Judicial Structure) and Articles 42–43 of the *Nouveau Code de Procédure Civile* (New Code of Civil Procedure (NCCP)). See further Valadou in Arrowsmith (ed.) (1993) (above, n 31) at 333.

[41] Article 1(3) of Law 92–10. This is the procedure which governs the requests for an interim ruling in civil cases which is regulated in Articles 484 to 492 of the NCCP. For a brief description of its main features, see Couchez, *Procédure Civile*, 6 ème edn. (Paris, 1990).

[42] Article 1 of Décret n⁰ 92–964 (JO 11 September 1992) adding Article 1441–2 to the NCCP.

munity obligations.[43] All these powers may be exercised separately or together. It must be emphasized that when the action is brought by a third party the law expressly requires that the action must be initiated before the conclusion of the contract.

This begs the question of what other remedies, apart from damages, remain available as regards private contracts when these have been concluded. Whereas in the case of administrative contracts, the theory of the *actes détachables* operated in favour of the permanence of the contractual relationship, in the civil law sphere one may wonder whether an injured third party may seek the annulment of the concluded contract on grounds of breach of the award procedure. The question is problematic. The power to set aside the contract is not mentioned in Law 92–10. By requiring the action to be brought before the conclusion of the contract, it seems that the intention of the legislator is clearly to limit the powers of the judge as regards private law contracts to the situation in which the contract has not yet been concluded. Notwithstanding this, if one assumes that once the contract is concluded the ordinary law of contract becomes applicable, then disrespect of the legislative provisions regulating the award procedure may be considered an infringement of a *loi imperative d'ordre public*, provided that one considers Community rules on public procurement as rules protecting the *ordre public économique*. These are rules which restrict the general freedom of contract of the parties by imposing certain obligations on them which are intended to protect the general economic interests of the State, or the interests of some social groups which are placed in a disadvantaged position when it comes to bargaining.[44] If this is the case, the contract may be declared as having an illicit cause according to Article 1133 of the French Civil Code,[45] which states that the cause of the contract is illicit when 'it is prohibited by *la loi*, or when it is contrary to the *bonnes moeurs* or to the *ordre public*'. Commentators and case law agree that any contract concluded in breach of rules of *ordre public* has an illicit cause which entails its absolute nullity with all the consequences attached to it. In other words, the contract is without effect *ab initio*, it must be rescinded and each party must restore what he or she has received. Moreover, any interested person[46] may seek its annulment before the civil courts and a

---

[43] Article 1 of Law 92–10 (above, n 37) adding Articles 11–1 and 11–2 to the Law nº 91–3 (above, n 36).

[44] Public procurement rules may well enter this category. For a complete discussion of these notions and the interpretative problems to which they give rise, see Weil and Terré (above, n 38) at paras. 240 *ff*, especially at para. 246. For a lucid and concise explanation of these same concepts in English, see Nicholas, *The French Law of Contract*, 2nd edn. (Oxford, 1992) at 33 *ff* and 128 *ff*, especially at 131–132.

[45] See also Article 6 of the French Civil Code.

[46] As defined by the case law, the interest must be directly connected with the nullity. It is submitted that any bidder having participated in the award procedure would fulfil the criteria.

judge would have to declare the nullity of the contract *ex officio,* even if the applicant in an action for damages has not raised this issue.[47] If this interpretation is correct, the annulment of the concluded private contract would follow automatically before the civil courts.

An alternative although more improbable solution, would be to adopt an *actes détachables* theory applicable to the civil jurisdiction. Once the contract is concluded, disrespect of the rules governing the award procedure would only entitle third parties to a claim for damages, provided their claims are well-founded. The contract would remain in force amongst the parties, unless one of them decided to challenge it before the *juge du contrat,* that is the civil judge competent to resolve the disputes arising from the execution of the contract clauses between the parties. The latest judicial developments discussed above suggest that, not only is the theory itself under revision, but it would also be rather innovative since it would introduce administrative law principles into the civil law sphere and would render inapplicable previously well-established civil law principles regarding the nullity of private law contracts. A final solution is to consider the new remedies as an exceptional autonomous category which is not subject to the general principles applicable to the civil jurisdiction. As Law 92–10 remains silent on this point, it will be up to the courts to clarify this situation.

Administrative Contracts

Law 92–10 adds Articles L.22 and L.23 to the *Code des tribunaux administratifs et cours administratives d'appel* (Code of Administrative Courts and Administrative Appeal Courts (CACAAC)). Contracts covered by these provisions are those which are of a public law nature, even though under certain circumstances they may be awarded by private persons.[48] The procedural rules governing the new action are those which regulate requests for interim measures in administrative law procedures.[49] As in the case of civil jurisdiction, this provision is intended to ensure the rapidity of the redress as the procedure *en référé* is one of urgency.[50] The ruling of the competent administrative judge is on the merits, even though it is issued according to the procedural rules regulating the request for interim measures.[51]

---

[47] Nicholas (above, n 44) at 133.

[48] For example, when the contract is awarded by a private person acting as an agent of a public authority. For a detailed description of the contracts covered by these provisions, see further Valadou in Arrowsmith (ed.) (1993) (above, n 31) at 331 *ff.*

[49] Article L.22 CACAAC *in fine* as introduced by Article 2 of Loi 92–10.

[50] The Decree n⁰ 92–964 of 7 September 1992 complementing Law 92–10, introduces a Chapter V to Book II, Title III of the CACAAC (*partie Réglementaire*), whose Article R. 241–21 imposes a time limit of 21 days on the judge to give a ruling.

[51] For an overview of the details of this procedure, see Chapus, *Droit du Contentieux Administratif,* 3 ème edn. (Paris, 1991) at 185 *ff.*

As for the powers conferred on the judge, these are similar to the ones analysed above for the civil judge. The main difference, however, is that in the case of public law contracts, the applicant is not explicitly required to introduce its action before the conclusion of the contract. Article 2 of Law 92–10 explicitly states that the judge '*may be* seized before the conclusion of the contract'. However, the range of remedies made available only makes sense if the action is introduced before the contract is awarded. Once the contract has been concluded, the law does not explicitly attribute to the judge the power to set it aside, nor does it explicitly exclude it, a matter which was left by the Remedies Directive to the discretion of national authorities.[52] It has been suggested that it follows from the silence of the law that the traditional approach arising from the theory of the *actes détachables*, which favours the permanence of contractual relationships between public authorities and other parties, has been preferred. Thus, remedies for third parties are limited to compensation in damages once the contract has been concluded.[53] However, under the most recent case law this should not prejudice the subsequent obligation of contracting authorities to seek the annulment of the contract before the *juge du contrat*, which, moreover, must be required by the judge entertaining the original action relating to the *acte détachable*.

The relationship between these precontractual remedies and the previously available *recours pour excès de pouvoir* is not clear, however. Would a third party still be entitled to bring an action for the annulment of an *acte détachable* under the *recours pour excès de pouvoir*? Valadou argues that, in the light of the principle of parallel judicial action which operates in French administrative law, the answer should be no. The *recours pour excès de pouvoir* is considered by French jurisprudence as a subsidiary action which may only be used when no alternative *recours en plein contentieux* is available and able to achieve the same outcome. A judicial action qualifies as a *recours en plein contentieux* when the powers enjoyed by the judge seized go beyond the mere annulment of the challenged act.[54] In view of the wide powers conferred by Law 92–10 it seems safe to classify the precontractual remedies as *en plein contentieux*. Therefore, injured undertakings will be prevented from introducing an action *pour excès de pouvoir* and will be limited to the more recent remedies. In practical terms it is suggested that

---

[52] Article 2(6) of Remedies Directive. French courts have so far ruled that actions under the new remedies must be brought before the contract is awarded. Otherwise the action should be dismissed. However, if the contract is awarded while the decision of the court is pending, the action must be accepted and resolved unless the request claims the grant of the suspension of the procedure. Martin, 'New Developments in Public Procurement in France' (1995) 4 PPLR CS53.   [53] Valadou in Arrowsmith (ed.) (1993) (above, n 31) at 351.

[54] On the principle of parallel action and the classification of actions between *contentieux en plein juridiction* and *le contentieux en annulation* or *en excès de pouvoir*, see Chapus (above, n 51) at 125. Also Laubadère and others (above, n 3) at paras. 1824 *ff.*

the distinction will not make much difference, as injured undertakings will certainly prefer to benefit from the new wider remedies, while the option to claim damages once the contract has been concluded will always remain open in the terms explained above.

Rules Common to both Jurisdictions

The French legislature has taken advantage of the possibility afforded by Article 1(3) of the Remedies Directive which allows national authorities to oblige any party intending to initiate a judicial action to request the relevant contracting authority in advance to comply with the obligations to which the alleged breach relates. Any person intending to initiate judicial action with respect to contracts of a private nature must first '*mettre en demeure*'[55] the private body acting as contracting authority by means of a registered letter. Only when the contracting authority rejects the complaint, or does not reply within 10 days, may the claimant commence judicial action within twenty days.[56] The same procedure applies when the challenged contract award is carried out by a public authority. A preliminary complaint (administrative complaint) must be forwarded to the contracting authority before the engagement of the judicial action. Procedure and time limits are the same as those for contracting authorities subject to private law.[57] In the administrative jurisdiction, the compulsory character of the preliminary administrative complaint has several effects: no judicial action can follow unless the preliminary complaint has been tried; if the contracting authority issues a response, the eventual judicial action must address this response rather than the original breach; finally, the complainant is constrained in his or her judicial action by the issues raised and the grounds set out in the complaint and is prevented from arguing new grounds which have not previously been mentioned.[58]

Conclusions

The French redress system was relatively ineffective prior to the implementation of the Remedies Directive. Due to the nature of the remedies available, aggrieved tenderers normally ended up, after proceedings which lasted two years on average, with a mere declaratory judgment which was impossible to enforce in practice, as the situation had become irreversible and the contract had been awarded. Difficulties in obtaining interim relief further aggravated the situation. There was no real possibility of intervening before the contract was awarded to prevent the contracting authority

[55] Send a letter of formal notice.
[56] See Article 1 of Decree 92–964 (above, n 42) adding a new Chapter V to the NCCP, Articles 1441–1 to 1441–3.
[57] See Article 2 of Decree 92–964 (above, n 56) adding a new Chapter V to Book II, Title III of the CACAAC, Articles 241–21 to 241–24.
[58] See Chapus (above, n 51) at 259–261.

from rendering a faulty award of a contract irreversible.[59] As a result, an infraction committed throughout the award procedure was usually satisfied by an award of damages following a second legal action *en plein contentieux*, provided that sufficient evidence was supplied. The approach to damages was, however, generous.

Against this background, the French measures adopted to implement the Directive have certainly improved the situation. Action before the contract is awarded is now available and competent judges enjoy a wide range of powers to avoid the *fait accompli*, amongst them, the power to suspend the contract award procedure.[60] The question remains whether injured parties will make use of these new possibilities and whether judges will be ready to suspend award procedures in order to uphold individual interests.

The situation has not changed as regards the possibilities of redress for third parties when the contract has already been concluded, as the implementation measures seem to limit redress to an award of damages. However, recent case law has raised the question whether contracting authorities are now bound to seek the rescission of a contract which is flawed by irregularities in one of its *actes détachables*. Some uncertainty remains, therefore, about the future position of the courts on this point. Equally, the judicial approach on damages as regards private contracts is still to be developed. It is hoped that the civil courts will follow the approach adopted with respect to administrative contracts which, overall, are satisfactory.

On the negative side, however, the maintenance of two different jurisdictions has not simplified matters. The dubious and complicated qualification of contracts as private or public will probably create confusion in the minds of potential applicants as regards which jurisdiction they should approach. Moreover, confusion will be heightened by the identical nature of the publicity and procedural obligations imposed on all contracting authorities. This will hamper the effectiveness of an otherwise satisfactory redress system. It is submitted that the creation of one specific body of a judicial nature which is exclusively competent in public procurement matters would have been a more suitable solution.[61] One is aware, however, of the difficulties surrounding the introduction of such an innovative system in a highly developed legal system such as the French.

With respect to the regulation of damages, due to the vague provisions of the Directive, the French situation may be held to comply with the Directive's requirements. No incentive element has been included, although

---

[59] For a brief description of the inadequacies of the system see Soulié, 'La Passation des Marchés Publics en France et la CEE', Thèse Paris I (Paris, 1987) at 130.

[60] For a case in which such a power was applied by a French court, see Martin, 'The Contractual "Référé" Procedures under Article L22 of the Administrative Tribunals and Administrative Courts of Appeal Code. Application in Practice' (1994) 3 PPLR CS112.

[61] This option was considered by national authorities as pointed out by Valadou in Arrowsmith (ed.) (1993) (above, n 31) at 328.

the practice of the *Conseil d'État* and lower courts in this respect is probably amongst the most satisfactory in the EU. Problems still remain with respect to the provision of evidence. Plaintiffs will normally have to prove their 'serious' chance of winning the contract to be awarded damages for lost profit. This normally entails evaluations of a subjective character which come within the margin of discretion of the contracting authorities. These problems will have to be resolved in cases which come before the French courts.

It is obvious nevertheless that the solution (adopted by the French) has willingly and honestly tackled the requirements of the Remedies Directive and this can only be welcomed. In addition, French law already counted on certain rules providing for criminal and administrative sanctions to ensure compliance with applicable rules on publicity and competitive award procedures, which add to the redress mechanisms established by the Law and Decree in question.[62] Finally, by subjecting private persons to the discipline of the public works Directive, Community law has required a partial modification of the existing French redress system.

SPAIN

The Implementation of the Remedies Directive

The Spanish Government notified the Commission that the current system of judicial remedies available against breaches of Community rules on public procurement responds adequately to the Directive's requirements.[63] Accordingly, no national measures have been adopted to implement the Remedies Directive into Spanish law. A brief analysis of the present system is necessary, therefore, in order to assess the validity of the Spanish Government's assumption.[64]

Available Remedies in Spanish Law

The Theory of Severable Acts

The legal regulation of contracts entered into by administrative bodies in Spain has been influenced by French doctrine. This is manifested in the adoption in Spain of the theory of severable acts. When awarding a contract, public authorities in Spain are always subject to the imperatives of administrative law and, therefore, to administrative law courts, through the theory of severable acts (*actos separables*), which is a replica of the French theory

---

[62] Valadou in Arrowsmith (ed.) (1993) (above, n 31) at 329.

[63] See the Preamble to the new Law on Public Procurement (*Ley 13/1995 of 18 May*) which explicitly states that no specific measures were required to implement the Remedies Directive since the current system of remedies already responds to Community requirements.

[64] See generally Samaniego Bordiú, 'El control del Derecho Comunitario de los contratos públicos' (1990) RAP 401 at 414.

of *actes détachables*. As in French law, these previous or supporting acts which make up the award procedure are typical administrative acts subject in their adoption, implementation and enforcement to specific procedures exhaustively regulated by administrative law, in this case, the recent *Ley de Contratos de las Administraciones Públicas* (LCE).[65] Moreover, they are exclusively reviewable by administrative courts in accordance with the general rules regulating their jurisdiction, irrespective of the contract's private or public legal nature.[66] The said theory was introduced into Spanish doctrine by the *Hotel Andalucia Palace* case.[67] However, as we shall discuss later on, important differences exist between the Spanish and French theories.[68]

This case law was later codified by the legislature and is now enshrined in the LCE, which explicitly recognizes the exclusive competence of administrative courts to entertain any dispute concerning those previous severable administrative acts, irrespective of the public or private nature of the final contract.[69] The legal regime applicable is therefore the general regime regulating judicial review of administrative acts, that is the *recurso contencioso-administrativo* regulated in the Law governing the access to and functioning of administrative courts (*Ley de la Jurisdicción Contencioso-Administrativa*).[70]

The Forum for Relief

Spanish law provides for two kinds of redress: administrative review of the act and judicial review before the administrative courts through the *recurso contencioso-administrativo*. Before the enactment in 1992 of the *Ley de Regimen Jurídico de las Administraciones Públicas y de Procedimiento Administrativo Común* (the LPA), both review mechanisms were intimately linked as the former was, and still is in most cases, a necessary prerequisite of the latter.

[65] *Ley* 13/1995 of 18 May.

[66] According to the Supreme Court, 'the intervention of a public authority as party to a contract, even if the latter is to be considered as a common law contract', provides the explanation for such an approach since this 'always implies the necessity of it abiding by certain formal steps and following a procedural path regulated by administrative law'. STS 19 October 1981. (Judgments of the Supreme Court are referred to as STS, followed by the date; those of the Constitutional Court are referred to as STCO; in case of Orders, they will be explicitly mentioned followed by TS or TCO respectively.)

[67] Order of the TS of 17 October 1961 and STS of 4 February 1965. According to this case, all acts adopted by contracting authorities during the contract award procedure, including the award decision, are to be regarded as 'severable' from the final contract and subject in all respects to the *imperium* of administrative law. See further, García Trevijano, 'Contratos y actos ante el Tribunal Supremo. La explotación del Hotel Andalucía Palace de Sevilla' (1959) RAP 147; Martín Retortillo, 'Reciente evolución de la jurisprudencia administrativa: actos separables admitidos por el Tribunal Supremo' (1961) RAP 227.

[68] See the section below entitled '*Relief other than Damages*'.

[69] See Article 9(2) LCE.

[70] *Ley de la Jurisdicción Contencioso-Administrativa* (LJCA), of 27 December 1956, as amended by the LPA.

Only if administrative recourse has been tried, and has proved unsuccessful, may the injured party bring the case before the administrative courts.

This requirement of lodging a previous administrative complaint is a peculiarity of the Spanish system compared with its Community counterparts. Its 'originality' lies in the fact that public authorities act both as judge and party in the resolution of the dispute. Although conceived as a guarantee for individuals, in practice, such a remedy has proved to be an ineffective formality, unnecessarily delaying access to judicial redress. In fact, public authorities have a tendency to neglect such recourses, letting delays expire without enacting a resolution. Such an attitude has been the object of well-deserved criticism by most commentators, some of whom have argued for the abolition of this requirement.[71]

In response to these criticisms, the new regulation introduced by the LPA is intended to ease access to judicial protection by reducing the cases in which a previous administrative complaint is required.[72] Although the new Law is well intentioned, it is far from clear in the LPA how, when and what is needed to gain access to the courts.[73] It provides that an administrative complaint is only required against acts which do not bring the administrative procedure to an end. On the contrary, those acts which are considered as closing the administrative procedure may be challenged directly before administrative courts, the only requirement being the need to inform the public authority of the initiation of judicial action.[74] In order to determine which acts are considered as bringing an administrative procedure to an end, reference needs to be made to the LPA, the LCE itself and other Laws.[75]

It is unclear in the field of public procurement which of the decisions of the contracting authority must be challenged at the administrative level before judicial action may be initiated. The situation is further complicated by the fact that previous provisions in the LCE concerning administrative complaints have been abrogated. The LCE now explicitly requires the introduction of administrative complaints in very few cases, such as the refusal by the competent body to grant a professional classification. In other cases direct recourse to judicial action seems possible, although

---

[71] García de Enterría and Fernández (1981), *Curso de Derecho Administrativo*, 3rd edn., T. II (Madrid, 1981) at 438–441 and Fernández Pastrana, 'Orientación antiformalista de la jurisprudencia en el agotamiento de la via administrativa previa' (1990) RAP 259 at 260. García de Enterría, 'Un punto de vista sobre la nueva Ley de Régimen Jurídico de las Administraciones Públicas y de Procedimiento Administrativo Común' (1993) RAP 205 at 208 *ff*.

[72] This has been substituted by a duty placed on the applicant who has to inform the public authority responsible for the challenged act of the initiation of the judicial action. Article 110(3) LPA.

[73] The new LPA has been the object of severe criticism by most authors. See, for instance, García de Enterría (1993) (above, n 71) at 208 *ff*.

[74] See Articles 107 and 110(3) LPA and Articles 37(1) and 57(2) LJCA.

[75] Article 109 LPA states that the resolution of administrative complaints in general, acts adopted by administrative bodies with no hierarchical superior and those acts explicitly declared so by a law or a regulation are acts which bring the administrative procedure to an end.

clarification by the courts is needed. As things stand, it appears that the award decision may be directly brought before the courts since the bodies empowered to adopt it pursuant to the LCE are regarded by other Laws as bodies whose decisions put an end to the administrative procedure. It must finally be noted that where a complaint is required, time limits for a resolution by the competent public authority are excessively long.[76]

The competent authorities at the *judicial stage* are administrative courts, as we have seen, whose jurisdiction is determined according to the general rules contained in the LJCA.

Damages

A broad right to damages is explicitly conferred by the Spanish Constitution, Article 106(2) of which asserts that individuals are entitled to be compensated in the terms established by the law for any injury they suffer to their rights or goods whenever such injury is the result of the functioning of public services. Damages for breach of public procurement rules are governed by the general regime regulating government liability, that is, for all damages which may be caused by government agencies or servants resulting from the normal or anomalous functioning of public services. The discussion is limited, however, to the examination of the regulation of State liability for damages deriving from the adoption of illegal administrative acts in the field of public procurement rules of a Community origin.[77] Thus, the considerations that follow should not be taken as a statement of general principles.

The applicable legal regime which develops the constitutional mandate is contained both in the revised LPA, which incorporates the substantial rules on damages, and the LJCA, which lays down procedural conditions to be fulfilled in order to lodge a judicial claim for damages when these result from the execution of illegal administrative acts. The courts have held that there is no link between the request for damages at the administrative and the judicial level. That is, they may be requested independently at either stage or at both.[78]

At the administrative level, Article 139(1) LPA acknowledges the individual's right to claim compensation from public authorities in similar terms to those of the Constitution. Paragraph 2 of Article 139 qualifies this broad and promising statement since it establishes the conditions to be fulfilled for damages to be accorded by public authorities. They have to be real, individualized and capable of economic evaluation. In addition,

---

[76] The new LPA grants up to three months to the competent authority to resolve the complaint (Article 117 LPA).

[77] For a comprehensive study of State liability in Spanish law, see Garrido Falla, 'La responsabilidad patrimonial del Estado' in *Estudios sobre la Constitución Española. Libro Homenaje al Prof. García de Enterría*' (Madrid, 1991) 2826.

[78] It must be noted that this has not always been the case. For a detailed discussion of this issue, see Blasco Esteve, 'La responsabilidad de la administración por daños causados por actos administrativos: doctrina jurisprudencial' (1980) RAP 206.

the existence of a direct causal link between the damage suffered and the public authority's act must be shown.[79] The LPA further states that the annulment of an act by the competent public authority or administrative court does not automatically entail a right to damages.[80] The LPA, however, does not contain the detailed procedural rules governing a claim for damages at the administrative stage, but leaves them to be developed by means of a government regulation, which must include an abbreviated administrative procedure to be resolved by the competent public authority in no more than thirty days.[81] Damages should be requested within a year from the moment the damage or administrative act took place. It must be noted that before the LPA was adopted, it appeared that damages were hardly ever granted at the administrative stage. It remains to be seen whether the new regulation will introduce any change in practice, although previous experience shows a reluctance on the part of public authorities to acknowledge damages.

Damages are to be specifically requested during the course of judicial action.[82] The procedural conditions to be fulfilled are regulated in Articles 42 and 28(2) LJCA. Despite the wording of these provisions, which seem to insist on the existence of a subjective right (a notion which may only be defined subject to controversy in the field of administrative law) which is illegally ignored by the contracting authority when adopting the act causing the damage, administrative courts have not applied a strict interpretation. Even when the plaintiff bases his or her action on a mere direct interest, the courts have admitted the claim for compensation for damages, on top of the mere declaration of nullity of the act.[83] Thus, damages may be claimed when all other conditions are fulfilled, even though no specific subjective right directly deriving from the legal order may be held to exist.

Damages are viewed at the judicial level as a final alternative. That is, they may only enter into play where there is no other means to restore the injured party to its 'individual legal situation' prior to the execution of the act. In addition, Article 139(2) LPA requires that evidence that the damages are real, individual, directly caused by the administration's act and capable of economic evaluation, must be supplied by the plaintiff. Under the present Spanish rules, lost profits require the undertaking to show that they would have won the contract had the procedure been legally followed. Only in the case of contracts awarded on an automatic 'lowest price' criterion, would undertakings stand a chance of successfully arguing their case. On contracts awarded on 'the most advantageous economic offer' criterion, a

---

[79] STS of 20 January 1984.   [80] Article 142(4) LPA.

[81] The Government Regulation was adopted by means of Royal Decree 429/1993 of 26 March. This Regulation also established the abbreviated procedure (Articles 14 to 17 of Royal Decree 429/1993) which, pursuant to the requirements of Article 143 LPA, will only operate in those cases where the causal relationship between the damage caused and the functioning of the public service, as well as its evaluation and calculation, are 'unequivocal'. Article 143 LPA.   [82] Article 43 LJCA.

[83] García de Enterría and Fernández (1981) (above, n 71) T. II, at 536.

certain degree of discretion on the part of the awarding authority always plays an important role. Not only would it be difficult to give evidence of the undertaking's superior right, but administrative courts will certainly be reluctant to substitute their appreciation for that of the administration.

Despite the fact that the right to be compensated for the effects of illegal administrative acts is widely and broadly recognized, the practice of Spanish administrative courts, backed by the fact that Article 142(4) LPA explicitly states that the annulment of an act does not entail a right to damages,[84] has been surprisingly restrictive and incoherent.[85] It is true that in the public procurement area there is quite an abundant case law according damages to private plaintiffs, but these cases concern compensation to the other party to the contract for the failure of contracting authorities to comply with the contract clauses. These have included not only the costs incurred but also loss of expected industrial profit which would have derived from the regular enforcement of the contractual agreement. To our knowledge, however decisions conceding damages to frustrated or excluded bidders are rare. An exception is STS 21 February 1983, which granted compensation for the costs incurred when preparing a tender when the administration illegally decided not to award a contract. More recently, the Regional Higher Court of the Canaries, after finding that objectively the applicant had a better right to the contract than the successful tenderer, granted not only bidding costs but also lost profit (judgment of 1 October 1993). These decisions are, however, exceptional since lost profit has generally been rejected by Spanish administrative courts.[86]

Interim Relief

It is a principle of Spanish administrative law that the acts of public authorities, including those adopted in the course of a contract award procedure, are self-executing. In other words, they enjoy a *iuris tantum* presumption of legality and they start to produce legal effects immediately after their adoption.[87] Only public authorities themselves or a definitive judgment establishing their invalidity, may interrupt their implementation.

---

[84] For a critical position on this provision, see Garrido Falla (1991) (above, n 77) at 2835.

[85] See generally Garrido Falla, *Tratado de Derecho Administrativo*, vol. II, 9ª edn. (Madrid, 1989) 224 *ff*. See the analysis of the case law by Blasco Esteve (above, n 78) especially at 204–215. See equally, García de Enterría and Fernández (1981) (above, n 71) T. II, at 195 *ff*. These comments are limited to the case of damages arising from illegal administrative acts. As regards other forms of State liability, Spanish courts have been rather generous with plaintiffs' claims. For an analysis of this latter case, see Garrido Falla (1991) (above, n 77) and Martín Rebollo, 'Nuevos planteamientos en materia de responsabilidad de las Administraciones públicas' in *Estudios sobre la Constitución Española* (above, n 77) 2781.

[86] STS 12 July 1954 and STS 21 November 1955.

[87] See Articles 57(1) and 94 LPA. The same principle applies in the public procurement context: see Article 60 LCE. For a judicial interpretation of such a principle, see Order of the TS of 15 April 1988. For a complete discussion, see García de Enterría and Fernández (1981) (above, n 71) T. I, at 424 *ff* and 487 *ff*; for a critical approach, see Parada Vazquez, *Derecho Administrativo, Parte General* (Madrid, 1989) at 161–162.

This is a principle which flows from the conception that the administration enjoys a privileged position as regards individuals as it pursues public ends and represents the general interest.[88] Its regular functioning may not be hindered by an individual judicial action which seeks to satisfy a private interest. A necessary consequence of such a principle is that the lodging of an administrative or a judicial action does not imply the automatic suspension of the effects of the disputed act.[89]

Notwithstanding this, the possibility of claiming interim relief is obviously available under Spanish law, both at the administrative and the judicial levels. Interim relief against administrative acts is restricted to the suspension of the effects of the impugned act. Although Spanish administrative law already envisaged interim relief as a guarantee against the executive character of administrative acts, after 1978 the case for effective interim relief was enhanced by Article 24(1) of the Spanish Constitution which recognized access to effective judicial protection as a fundamental individual right.[90]

Interim relief at the *administrative level* is regulated by Article 111 LPA, which states that while the introduction of an administrative complaint will not suspend the effects of the disputed act, the administrative public authority competent to resolve the action, after balancing the interests involved, may do so whenever the execution of the challenged act could entail damages which it would be impossible or difficult to compensate. It may also award interim relief when the recourse is based on grounds which, if well-founded, determine the nullity of the challenged act.[91]

As for the *judicial level*, interim relief is regulated by Article 122 of the LJCA, which is less explicit than its administrative counterpart which has just been analysed. In fact, it only establishes that the initiation of a judicial action does not prevent the administration from executing the challenged act. Nonetheless paragraph 2 of Article 122 states that the court entertaining the main action may grant interim relief at the instance of the plaintiff, when the execution of the act could lead to damages of 'impossible or difficult reparation'. The LJCA does not include the grounds for nullity as a basis for claiming interim relief at the judicial level. The Supreme Court's jurisprudence has, however, admitted such a possibility

---

[88] García de Enterría and Fernández (1981) (above, n 71) T. I, at 494. For a justification of this approach based on the general interest, see Boquera Oliver, 'Insusceptibilidad de la suspensión de la eficacia del acto administrativo' (1994) RAP 37.

[89] Articles 111 LPA for the administrative remedy and 122 LJCA for the judicial remedy.

[90] STCO, Case 66/1984, of 6 June, declaring that the right to an effective judicial protection is satisfied through the possibility that the executing character of administrative acts may be brought before a court, which, with the required urgency, decides about the grant of interim relief. See also STCO 32/1992 of 12 December. For an analysis of the evolution of the Constitutional Court's case law on this point, see Chinchilla Marín, 'El derecho a la tutela judicial cautelar como garantía de la efectividad de las resoluciones judiciales' (1993) RAP 167. [91] Article 111(2) LPA.

by expanding the scope of Article 122 by analogy with its administrative counterpart.[92] Thus, in the case of public procurement, interim relief has been granted by the Supreme Court in a case where the required open procedure was illegally substituted by direct negotiation.[93]

What is to be understood by irreparable damages? This notion has been equated with the feasibility of economically evaluating the prejudices caused by the challenged act. Whenever the courts found that economic compensation was easily calculated, applications for interim relief were dismissed. As a result, the grant of interim relief was exceptional and rare.[94] Naturally this approach was considered unsatisfactory by most commentators in so far as it placed the emphasis on the wrong problem. Indeed, interim relief procedures are intended to safeguard the requirements of 'justice' in a given case. Therefore, it is usually necessary to balance factors other than the mere feasibility of economic compensation.[95]

This alternative line of reasoning which is based on the balance of convenience is being favoured by the latest jurisprudence of the Supreme Court,[96] which is in turn inspired by the case law of the Constitutional Court. The 'balance of convenience' criterion, which is not mentioned in the wording of the applicable provisions and which is not without its critics,[97] finds its legal basis in the Preamble of the LJCA. This states that when deciding a request for interim relief, the court must weigh, 'first of all, the extent to which public interest requires the implementation' of the act. Thus, courts must proceed to balance the private interest in suspending the effects of the act and the eventual damages which such a suspension would cause to the public interest. From this operation they must determine whether or not interim relief is pertinent. The criterion of irreparable damages is, therefore, being rendered of secondary importance.

Nonetheless, and since the automatic implementation of the adopted act remains the general rule, the award of interim relief is still interpreted restrictively.[98] To date, public authorities have been favoured by the jurisprudence. Since both the administrative and the judicial instances enjoy

---

[92] Order of TS of 15 July 1988 and Order of TS of 21 March 1989. For formalistic reasons, however, interim relief claimed on these grounds will only be granted with difficulty. See further Fernández Martín, 'Remedies for Enforcing the Community Public Procurement Rules. The Situation in Spain' (1993) 2 PPLR 119 at 130.

[93] STS of 30 September 1964 and STS of 5 January 1968.

[94] García de Enterría and Fernández (1981) (above, n 71) T. II, at 547–549; Torno Mas, 'La suspensión judicial de la eficacia de la ley de la Jurisdicción Contencioso-Administrativa' (1986) *Revista Jurídica de Cataluña* 4 at 77.

[95] Torno Mas (1986) (above, n 94) at 77; Rodriguez-Arana, 'De nuevo sobre la suspension judicial del acto administrativo (1986–1987)' (1989) REDA 639; García de Enterría (1993) (above, n 71) at 209–210; Chinchilla Marín (above, n 90).

[96] Orders of TS of 3 June 1987 and 4 March 1987.   [97] Boquera Oliver (above, n 88).

[98] STS of 28 June 1972, Orders of TS of 5 November 1965, 27 September 1971 and 5 March 1970, although the general rule of automatic execution is recently being relaxed: Orders of 21 March 1988; 15 April 1988 and 15 July 1988.

a large margin of discretion when assessing whether the required conditions are fulfilled or not, the practical effectiveness of interim relief procedures in Spanish law as regards public procurement rules will depend, to a large extent, upon the attitude of the enforcement bodies when interpreting the law.[99]

Relief other than Damages

Although the theory of severable acts in Spain is a reflection of that developed by the *Conseil d'État*, its legal treatment under Spanish law differs substantially from the French approach, which is now being revised. In Spanish administrative law, contrary to the traditional position in France, irrespective of whether the contract has been finally concluded or not, the declared invalidity of any severable act entails the invalidity of the contractual relationship, which then enters a liquidation phase. Each party has to return what they have received and if this is not possible, its economic equivalent.[100] When the cause of invalidity is regarded as the administration's negligence, the successful tenderer is entitled to compensation, which includes the costs incurred and the loss of reasonably expected industrial benefits. These have been estimated by the Supreme Court in the case of public works contracts to be 6 per cent of the total value of the works.[101] If the contract has not been concluded, the declaration of invalidity of any of the 'severable acts' means that the contract may not be awarded until the infringement has been corrected. This clearly shows the importance of interim relief when judicial action is brought against a procedure.

Notwithstanding this, the recurring notion of public interest also becomes relevant at this stage. Thus, the continuation of a concluded contract may be decided by the contracting authority on grounds of public interest. The competent authority is entitled to declare that the contract clauses must continue to be respected and performed if their annulment could involve a 'grave disturbance' to public services until pertinent measures to prevent such disturbances are adopted.[102] Although the actual implementation of such a prerogative is subject to judicial control and, in any case, is considered only as a transitory solution by the law, it provides for an escape clause from the rigidity of the general 'nullity' rule of the contracts. In practice, the contracting authority may well continue to apply the contract clauses and finally decide to perpetuate the situation, until an eventual judgment applies. And even in this latter case, practice shows that de *facto* situations deriving from already executed contracts tend to remain untouched.

---

[99] The most recent case law seems to be in favour of relaxing the requirements to grant interim relief. See Rodríguez-Arana (above, n 95); García de Enterría (1993) (above, n 71) and Chinchilla Marín (above, n 90).   [100] Article 66 LCE.
[101] STS of 11 June 1985 and STS 13 December 1985.   [102] Article 66(3) LCE.

It is contended that the Spanish regulation on the effects of the invalidity of 'severable acts' is inadequate for several reasons. First of all, innocent bidders who may honestly have won the contract are penalized for wrongs beyond their responsibility. Secondly, it does not properly respond to the interests of complainants when they bring an action before the courts. It is difficult to see how the revocation of the contract may help their interests in any way. In practice, they would stand a weak chance of winning an eventual new award procedure. Thus, their interests may probably not be satisfied by the setting aside of an already concluded and executed contract. Compensation for the costs they have incurred is preferable. However, this solution may only be attained with difficulty in Spanish law. Finally, in relation to the defence of the public interest, such a radical solution may well result in interference with the satisfaction of public needs, as the contract will have to be awarded again, following the same cumbersome procedure.

Spanish regulation seems to have been exclusively designed to address the situation in which it is the party to the contract itself which challenges a severable act with the purpose of bringing his or her contractual relationship with the contracting authority to an end. From the perspective of Community rules on public procurement, such an approach is unsatisfactory, as it does not provide any incentive for undertakings who have been discriminated against to initiate judicial action.

Does the Spanish System Comply with the Requirements of Community Law?

An initial superficial assessment of the Spanish regime suggests that it is compatible with the Remedies Directive. Indeed, access to review procedures against those acts constituting the award procedure both at administrative and judicial level is reasonably broad. The same conclusions may be reached when one assesses the availability of interim relief and damages, for which Spanish law certainly provides. As the Directive does not impose more detailed obligations, but contents itself with requiring the mere existence of such possibilities, it may be concluded that Spanish law is already in line with Community obligations.

However, a more attentive analysis will uncover some of the inadequacies of the Spanish regime. If the Directive's ultimate objective is the deployment of effective remedies against breaches of public procurement rules, the essential question is how effective Spanish review procedures are in practice. Whether or not Spanish law complies with the Directive may not be quite as straightforward if one approaches it from this perspective. First of all, as a direct consequence of the general attitude of public authorities, the need to exhaust the administrative complaint procedure, where this is now required, hinders access to effective judicial protection. The automatic executive character of administrative acts, coupled with the fact that the mere introduction of a judicial or administrative remedy does not have automatic suspensory effect on the alleged illegal act, imply that the award procedure may follow its course and illegal situations tend to become irreversible. This is even more so since interim relief, although possible, has only rarely been granted and has always been interpreted restrictively. This contributes to a reduction in the efficiency of the system of redress, in so far as the effects of illegal acts are not normally prevented by the award of suspensory measures.

Although this does not exclusively affect infractions of the public procurement rules, one should not ignore the fact that delays in handing down judgments are extremely high in Spain. On average, a judicial action under administrative law takes more than two years to be resolved.[103] However, this is a problem requiring a political rather than a legal solution. In any case, such a lengthy judicial procedure may furnish an argument to the effect that the Spanish system does not comply with the requirement of 'rapidity' of the review mechanisms contained in Article 1 of the Remedies Directive. In this context, the need to exhaust the administrative complaints procedure can be seen as an unnecessary delay to effective judicial protection. Damages are also available in Spanish law. However, they are difficult to obtain and are probably insufficient to provide harmed undertakings with an incentive to initiate proceedings against a contracting authority.

Given these considerations, it may be concluded that the eventual success of the Spanish system of remedies in ensuring compliance with Community public procurement rules will depend, to a large extent, on the attitude which Spanish courts and the Spanish authorities adopt when applying the existing relief mechanisms. In so far as a large margin of discretion is left to them when deciding the award of interim relief or damages, only a change in their present attitudes will favour effective control of contracting authorities. A clear change in this direction will, in turn, transcend to market operators and encourage harmed undertakings to seek redress. However, this change in attitude takes time and since no special incentive (such as economic reward) exists in Spanish law, nor is this required by the Directive, it is submitted that the present situation, characterized by the resignation and indolence of interested firms when it comes to enforcing their rights, will not change in the short run.

---

[103] For an evaluation of the inadequacies of the Spanish administrative judicial review system, see Torno Mas, 'La situación actual del proceso contencioso-administrativo' (1990) RAP 103, especially at 114. Mestre Delgado, 'El control en la adjudicación de los contratos públicos a tenor del derecho comunitario europeo. Una nueva ordenación de las medidas cautelares' (1991) No. 74 *Noticias CEE* 35 at 37.

10

The Enforcement Level (V): The Implementation of the Remedies Directive in the United Kingdom and Germany

The Situation prior to the Implementation of the Remedies Directive[1]

Two separate families of remedies exist in English law: private law and public law remedies.[2] Private law remedies relate to the enforcement of private rights of action, whereas public law remedies are designed to ensure that public authorities carry out their public duties in a lawful and efficient manner. Since public authorities are the defendants, public law remedies provide a number of prerogatives and protective measures in their favour. The distinction between private law rights and public law rights becomes vital, since private law rights may not be enforced through judicial procedures particular to public law issues and vice versa.[3] In the face of the improvements introduced in the early eighties to the judicial review procedure in favour of individuals,[4] Lord Diplock held that the application for judicial review procedures was 'as a general rule' an adequate remedy to enforce 'public law rights'.[5]

---

[1] For a description of the available remedies in England and Wales for breaches of public procurement rules before the Remedies Directive was implemented, see Birkinshaw, 'British report to the 14th FIDE Conference' in FIDE, *L'Application dans les États Membres des Directives sur les Marchés Publics* (1990, Madrid) 287; Weatherill, 'National Remedies and Equal Access to Public Procurement' (1990) 10 YEL 243; House of Lords Select Committee on the EC, *Compliance with the Public Procurement Directives*, session 1987–88, 12th Report; Turpin, *Government Procurement and Contracts* (Harlow, 1989) Chapter 8.

[2] *O'Reilly* v. *Mackman* [1982] 3 All ER 1124. See also *Cocks* v. *Thanet Disctrict Council* [1982] 3 All ER 1135. Noted by Sunkin, 'Judicial Review: Rights and Discretion in Public Law' (1983) 43 MLR 645. This decision caused an open and interesting debate in English legal doctrine: Harlow, ' "Public Law" and "Private" Law: Definition without Distinction' (1980) 43 MLR 241; Samuel, 'Public and Private Law: a Private Lawyer's Response' (1983) 46 MLR 558; see generally, Arrowsmith, *Civil Liability and Public Authorities* (Winteringham, 1992) Chapter 1.

[3] This distinction was justified by the need to ensure that private plaintiffs did not evade the safeguards of Order 53 by resorting to private law remedies in order to enforce 'public rights'. Rules of the Supreme Court (RSC) Order 53, adopted under the authority of s. 31 of the Supreme Court Act 1981 (SCA), regulated the procedure for the application for judicial review. See Lord Diplock's considerations in *O'Reilly* v. *Mackman* (above, n 2) at 1134.

[4] After the 1977 and 1980 amendments to Order 53 and SCA 1981, the individual's position in judicial review proceedings was substantially improved.

[5] For a practical analysis of the judicial review procedures and related case law, see Gordon, *Judicial Review: Law and Procedure* (London, 1985); For an exhaustive analysis of the remedies available under judicial review, see Lewis, *Judicial Remedies in Public Law* (London, 1992) Chapter 3.

Although the most effective remedies for enforcement of Community obligations lie in private law actions,[6] it arguably followed from *Bourgoin* that breaches of public procurement rules were to be treated as falling within the public law category.[7] The principles applied in *Bourgoin* with respect to Article 30 EC were, *mutatis mutandis*, applicable to the public procurement Directives. Thus, in the absence of a specific remedy, breaches by contracting authorities of Community public procurement rules were to be challenged by means of an application for judicial review on the grounds of 'illegality, irrationality and procedural impropriety'. The remedies available under judicial review are (i) *certiorari*, to quash a decision already made; (ii) prohibition, to prevent the authority from implementing a decision which is unlawful; (iii) *mandamus*, to oblige a public authority to adopt a decision or perform other public duties; (iv) an injunction, to prevent unlawful action; (v) a declaration, by which the court declares the particular conduct of a public authority to be unlawful. All these remedies are discretionary.[8]

Unless a specific right to damages is conferred by the applicable rules,[9] damages are only available in judicial review procedures when a substantial right to damages arising under general liability law exists. This is the case when there has been a breach of statutory duty and in the case of misfeasance in public office. As regards damages for breach of statutory duty, since the public procurement Directives were implemented through circulars, no action for damages could be brought on this ground under national law. Such a right was also explicitly excluded in relation to breaches of Article 30 EC in *Bourgoin* and, arguably, in relation to directly effective provisions of similar characteristics, such as the public procurement Direct-

---

[6] Gordon (above, n 5) at 70–71 and the dissenting opinion of Oliver LJ in *Bourgoin SA and others* v. *Ministry of Agriculture, Fisheries and Food* [1985] All ER 585.

[7] The legal nature of Directives, the fact that they regulate the activities of public authorities, the function which public contracts perform in satisfying public needs and the fact that one may construe the final objective of the Directives as benefiting the Community as a whole and not just a particular class of person, argue in favour of the public procurement Directives imposing public duties on contracting authorities and giving rise to public law rights. See further Turpin (above, n 1) at 214 *ff*; Arrowsmith (1992) (above, n 2) at Chapter 3. However, substantial arguments supporting the conceptualization of public procurement rights as private law rights exist. In fact, in *Garden Cottage* v. *The Milk Marketing Board* [1983] All ER 770, the House of Lords admitted that an action in damages for breach of statutory duty existed against the breach of Article 86 EC, which is equally directly effective. To this effect, with regard to Article 30 EC, see the forceful dissenting opinion of Oliver LJ in *Bourgoin* (above, n 6) and the critical considerations by Barav and Green, 'Damages in the National Courts for Breach of Community Law' (1986) 6 YEL 55.

[8] Lord Diplock, *Council for Civil Service Unions* v. *Minister for Civil Service* [1984] 3 WLR 1174 at 1196. Craig, *Administrative Law*, 3rd edn. (London, 1994) at 596–597; Gordon (above, n 5) at 30 *ff*.

[9] Turpin (above, n 1) 213. In the field of public procurement, an explicit right to damages only existed in the case of contracts awarded by local authorities. See the Local Government Act 1988, s. 19.

ives. In his decision, Parker LJ considered that remedies provided through judicial review procedures afforded adequate protection against breaches of Article 30 EC when those breaches were committed *bona fides*. Conversely, an action for damages for misfeasance in public office would lie against breaches of directly effective Community law provisions committed by public authorities.[10] However, for this action to lie there must be a malicious, deliberate or injurious wrongdoing on the part of the defendant.[11] The practical relevance of this remedy is marginal both in general terms and as regards public procurement. Very few cases are reported. The reasons for such scarce case law relate not only to the excellence of British civil servants and public officers, but also to the fact that the disclosure of evidence revealing deliberate or malicious abuse of powers is practically impossible. Contract awards are equally affected by this difficulty. How may a contractor prove before a court that the decision he or she is challenging was flawed by malice and a deliberate abuse of powers? Due to these procedural obstacles, compensation for damages is not often awarded under judicial review procedures and would be unlikely for breaches of the public procurement Directives.[12] However, after the Court of Justice's decision in *Francovich*, according to which an explicit right to damages for loss suffered by breaches of Community law must be provided as a matter of Community law, English courts have to regard *Bourgoin* as bad law.[13]

In so far as interim relief is concerned, the situation was also inadequate since until the *Factortame* decision was enacted, interim protection was not available against the Crown nor against central government departments.[14]

---

[10] *Bourgoin* (above, n 6) at 631 g. For a critical assessment of the interpetation retained in *Bourgoin*, see Barav and Green (above, n 7) at 96.

[11] Malice will be held to exist whenever the decision has been taken with 'personal spite or a desire to injure for improper reasons'. *Ashby* v. *White* [1703] 2 LD Raym. 938 and subsequent case law. Misfeasance will equally exist whenever the authority is fully aware that it does not possess the power which it purports to exercise in adopting the decision. Supreme Court of Victoriain, *Farrington* v. *Thomson* [1959] VR 286.

[12] Millet, 'Les marchés publics en droit comparé. Le Royaume Uni' in *Les Marchés Publics Européens. Droit communautaire. Droit comparé (1989) Dossiers et Documents de la Revue Française de Droit Administratif* at 40–41; House of Lords (above, n 1) at 8. It is nevertheless true that the court may order the claim for damages to proceed as if they had been begun by private action when the application for judicial review is dismissed. Order 53 r. 9(5).

[13] See *Kirklees MBC* v. *Wickes Ltd* [1992] 3 All ER 717, where the House of Lords has indicated that *Bourgoin* may have been overruled by *Francovich*. See Chapter 7. See Ross, 'Beyond *Francovich*' (1993) 56 MLR 53 at 60. Weatherill, 'Enforcing the Public Procurement Directives in the United Kingdom' in Arrowsmith (ed.) *Remedies for Enforcing the Public Procurement Rules* (1993, Winteringham) Chapter 8 at 298.

[14] Weatherill (1990) (above, n 1) at 254–259. The situation has changed after the Court of Justice's *Factortame No. 1* decision (Case C-213/89, *Factortame* [1990] ECR-I 2433) which was interpreted by the House of Lords as requiring that interim relief must be available against the Crown when rights arising from Community law were at stake, although it was to be interpreted cautiously ([1990] 3 CMLR 375).

Moreover, the principles applied in the context of judicial review actions made the grant of injunctions in public procurement cases complicated.[15]

For the above reasons, prior to the implementation in the UK of the Remedies Directive doubts existed about the effectiveness of the remedies system available to third parties for breaches of public procurement rules.[16] The British case provided a clear example of the disparity between supranational rules and the existing rules at national level. In the UK, public procurement was an underdeveloped area of law, both at the legislative and judicial levels,[17] when compared with the position in most continental Member States. Since the main public procurement Directives draw inspiration from the French regulation of public procurement, existing British legal notions were ill-equipped to respond to the requirements of Community law. In the field of remedies, the approach to public contracts as an area governed by the ordinary law of contract and, therefore, not subject to specific rules, implies a certain disregard of judicial control by third parties of the conduct of contracting authorities in the pre-contractual stages.[18] The grounds which led contracting authorities to select one contractor or another came within the field of public law and did not create any subjective rights on behalf of contractors.[19] A general interest in public authorities acting in accordance with the principle of good administration is recognized, but no subjective right is derived from this. As in the German case, good administration and adequate expenditure of public money is guaranteed by means of political, financial and administrative controls.[20]

The rights which arise for European firms from the public procurement Directives were new to English law and, consequently, the national remedies system found itself at pains to deal with them. The award of contracts following the general administrative guidelines of the Treasury and Department of the Environment circulars[21] were subject to the general principles of good administration and to the review procedures provided to ensure the lawful implementation by public authorities of their public duties. As a consequence, the implementation of the public procurement

---

[15] Injunctions may be sought in an application for judicial review when an infringement of some private law right occurs. *Boyce* v. *Paddington BC* [1903] 1 Ch. 109; or when special damage particular to the applicant was suffered, *Benjamin* v. *Storr* [1874] LR 9 CP 400.

[16] House of Lords (above, n 1) at 8; Millet (above, n 12) at 41.

[17] Weatherill (1993) (above, n 13) at 299. See further Arrowsmith, 'Government Contracts and Public Law' (1990) *Legal Studies* 231; Arrowsmith, 'Judicial Review and the Contractual Powers of Public Authorities' (1990) 106 LQR 277.

[18] More recently, however, courts have indicated that administrative law doctrines can apply to the exercise of public authorities' contractual powers. See *R* v. *Lenfield LBC, ex p. Unwin* [1989] COD 466, and *R* v. *Lewisham BC, ex p. Shell UK Ltd* [1988] 1 ALL ER 938, discussed by Arrowsmith (1990), 106 LQR 227 at 289; Turpin (above, n 1) at 215.

[19] Turpin (above, n 1) at 213 *ff*.   [20] See generally ibid., Chapter 2.

[21] See Chapter 4.

Directives took place by means of circulars and, as a matter of national law, no individual statutory rights were provided against public authorities, which would entitle individuals to proceed through private law remedies.

The Situation after the Remedies Directive[22]

These insufficiencies placed the British Government under pressure to improve the situation with respect to Community law. After conversations with the Commission, all public procurement Directives were implemented by means of regulations which have a statutory character. Four comprehensive national Regulations in the area of public procurement were adopted. These not only bring into effect the requirements of the Remedies Directive, but equally incorporate the previous main public works and public supplies Directives (as amended into national law), giving them statutory force.[23] The situation in the United Kingdom has been substantially modified by the introduction of this 'statutory remedy', which is exclusively applicable to public procurement breaches.[24] In this way, the complexities discussed above have been largely overcome. Part VII of all Regulations is devoted to the question of enforcement of the obligations enshrined in the previous sections, which principally reproduce the provisions of the main Directives. As their texts are practically identical, the following references are of general application.

Locus Standi

The obligation on contracting authorities to comply with the substantive provisions of the regulations is a duty owed to contractors and suppliers. All Regulations define contractors and suppliers broadly as 'a person who sought, or who seeks, or would have wished, to be the person to whom a public works contract is awarded'. Thus, any breach of the duties owed to contractors and suppliers are to be actionable by any supplier or contractor who in consequence suffers or risks suffering, loss or damage.

The definition of standing is narrower than that which applies in judicial review procedures. A sufficient interest is the only requirement to

[22] The impact of the regulations adopted to implement the Compliance Directive have been analysed by Arrowsmith, 'Enforcing the EC Public Procurement Rules: The Remedies System in England and Wales' (1992) 1 PPLR 92; O'Loan, 'Remedies in the UK and Ireland', paper presented to the *Implementing and Enforcing the EC Procurement Directives Conference,* Birmingham, April 1993. Weatherill in Arrowsmith (ed.) (1993) (above, n 13) at Chapter 8.

[23] The Public Supply Contracts Regulations, SI 1991 No. 2679, which were followed by the Public Supply Contracts Regulations, SI 1995 No. 201 which implement the Consolidated Public Supplies Directive 93/36, the Public Works Contracts Regulations, SI 1991 No. 2680 and the Public Service Contracts Regulations, SI 1993 No. 3228. See further Chapter 4.

[24] For a general discussion of these types of remedies in English law and their relation with other existing remedies, see Wade and Forsyth, *Administrative Law* 7th edn., (Oxford, 1994) at Chapters 17–20.

enjoy standing under the SCA 1981, a notion which appears to be flexibly interpreted by the courts.[25] Although the wording of the Regulations is drafted in very generous terms ('. . . would have wished . . .') it is submitted that they restrict the category of persons entitled to bring an action to those able to show some sort of connection with the object of the contract, such as evidence of being involved in the relevant trade. Not every citizen with a general interest in public authorities abiding by the rules enjoys standing under the Regulations. In fact, the Regulations clearly state that the substantive provisions are duties only owed to suppliers and contractors. Lastly, standing is further restricted to nationals of, or individuals established in a Member State.

The action must be brought promptly and in any event before three months have elapsed from the date when the grounds for the bringing of the procedures first arose. This provision reflects the same concerns present in judicial review procedures to which the same general time limits apply and where the court may refuse relief where there has been 'undue delay' in bringing the application.[26] It follows that the principles developed as regards application for judicial review procedures could well be applied in the context of remedies under the public procurement Regulations. This implies that actions may be refused if they have not been initiated promptly, even if they are brought within the three months' time limit.[27] The court's discretion as regards this specific point is wide. It seems likely that it will tend to favour the smooth administration of public duties by public authorities.

The Available Remedies

Before a judicial action can be initiated, the complainant must inform the relevant contracting authority of his or her intention to bring proceedings. The Regulations remain silent on the consequences of such a requirement. It appears that this provision merely affords the contracting authority the possibility of considering the alleged breach and contacting the complainant in order to settle the question before a judicial action is initiated. In any case, it seems that the injured person may proceed immediately with the judicial action without waiting for a response.

The competent court[28] may adopt any of the following decisions: to suspend the award procedure or action taken by the contracting authority in the course of an award procedure by means of an interim order; it may also order a decision founded on a breach of the Regulations to be set

---

[25] Arrowsmith (1992), 1 PPLR (above, n 22) at 106.   [26] SCA 1981, s. 31(6).

[27] *R* v. *Stratford-upon-Avon DC, ex p. Jackson* [1985] 1 WLR 1319.

[28] The Session Court in Scotland and the High Court for the rest of Great Britain and Northern Ireland.

aside, or amended, and the award of damages to any tenderer who has suffered loss or damage, or both, as a consequence of the breach. Each remedy will be analysed separately.

The setting aside of decisions taken unlawfully or their amendment

As regards the power to set aside any unlawful decision, it appears that the effects of a decision of the court in this sense would be similar to those of a *certiorari*: the decision cannot be implemented by the public authority and a new lawful decision must be adopted.[29] The court is also empowered now to order contracting authorities to amend documents relating to the award procedure. This new power goes beyond the normal competences of the court under judicial review procedures, especially under the *mandamus* remedy. The object of a *mandamus* is to obtain an order obliging a public authority to perform one of its duties when it has wrongfully failed to do so. Under the new remedy, the involvement of the court is greater, as it seems that it would be entitled to lay down specific directions as to what the amendments should be. As pointed out by Arrowsmith, the importance of this remedy is that it may well prevent the setting aside of the whole call for tenders, if legality can be restored by simply amending the faulty award documents.[30]

Interim relief

Under the Regulations the courts are empowered to suspend the award procedure or the implementation of any decisions by interim order when a contractor is seeking the remedies described above. In theoretical legal terms, the situation of foreign tenderers has been substantially improved. National courts are now explicitly empowered by statute to adopt interim measures in claims concerning Community public procurement rules. This innovation is only relative, however. *Factortame* had already placed national courts under an obligation to provide for interim relief whenever this was needed to ensure the effective judicial protection of Community rights.[31]

The interesting question is whether the adoption of the Regulations under discussion has changed the situation in England and Wales with respect to the previous state of affairs. In other words, are English courts now obliged to approach the question of interim relief in public procurement cases brought under the Regulations differently? The wording of the Regulations is not forceful enough. They merely state that courts may grant interim relief without providing any further specification. It seems likely that British courts will draw inspiration from their previous practice as regards interim relief. Thus, the principles developed in *American*

---

[29] See further Arrowsmith (1992), 1 PPLR (above, n 22) at 100.   [30] Ibid.
[31] See Chapter 7.

Cyanamid and *Factortame No. 2* will provide the starting point.[32] Pursuant to these decisions, once satisfied that the plaintiff has a *prima facie* case, the court proceeds to balance the convenience of granting interim relief. In any case, where damages are seen as an adequate remedy, interim relief will be refused. Thus, in *Burroughs Machines Ltd* v. *Oxford Area Health Authority*, the plaintiff, a tenderer which had been rejected in an award procedure even though an advisory committee had judged its offer the most suitable one, challenged the award decision of the authority on the grounds that it was discriminatory. The judge refused interim relief on the basis that damages would be an adequate remedy. On appeal, this decision was upheld by the Court of Appeal, which took the view that the judge had exercised his discretion properly. Availability of interim relief will depend on the attitude of the courts as regards the availability of damages.[33]

Moreover, when the request for interim relief could mean the delay of public works or the provision of public services, courts must proceed to balance the interests involved and decide which should be given preference. Although the balance of convenience may only be established on a case by case basis and will depend on the nature of the alleged breach, the object of the contract, the effects of the suspension of the award procedure on the satisfaction of a public need and on the private interests involved, it is suggested that courts will have a tendency to refuse interim relief in public procurement cases. An indication of this is provided by the *Burroughs* decision. Interim relief was refused, *inter alia*, because the balance of convenience favoured the authority.[34] This is the case, moreover, since the Remedies Directive explicitly entitles them to proceed to a balance of interests when deciding interim relief requests. In conclusion, it must be noted that apart from the right to damages, all the described powers are discretionary and may be refused by the court. It is submitted that interim relief will be rarely awarded in public procurement cases.[35]

---

[32] The principles of *American Cyanamid* were explicitly applied with minor changes in the public law sphere by the House of Lords in *R* v. *Secretary of State for Transport, ex p. Factortame* [1990] 3 CMLR 375 which followed the Court of Justice's response to the preliminary reference, Case C-213/89, *Factortame* (above, n 14).

[33] *Burroughs Machines Ltd* v. *Oxford Area Health Authority*, 21 July 1983 (unreported) (1983) 133 *New Law Journal* 764. See however Arrowsmith (1992) 1 PPLR 92 (above, n 22) at 113 where she holds that this decision is to be regarded as exceptional since in most public procurement cases damages may not be regarded as an adequate remedy. On the relationship between the availability of interim relief and damages in procurement cases, see generally Weatherill in Arrowsmith (ed.) (1993) (above, n 13) at 284 *ff*.

[34] On appeal, Griffiths LJ explicitly stated that, on the facts, he would have reached the same conclusion.

[35] In the same vein, Weatherill in Arrowsmith (ed.) (1993) (above, n 13) at 285; House of Lords (above, n 1) at para. 65; Arrowsmith (1992) 1 PPLR (above, n 22) at 114. There is a recent case supporting this interpretation. In *R* v. *HM Treasury, ex p. British Telecom plc* both the Queen's Bench Divisional Court and the Court of Appeal refused to grant an order to disapply the contested provisions of the UK Regulations implementing the Utilities Dir-

Damages

The availability of remedies described above is limited, however, to actions initiated before the contract has been concluded. Whenever the contract in relation to which the breach occurred has been entered into, the competent court may only impose an award of damages. Thus, the contract may not be set aside or the implementation of the contract clauses suspended.

The British Government, like the French, has opted to limit the remedies available after the contract has been concluded to an award of damages. The competent court may award damages to a contractor or a supplier 'who has suffered loss or damage as a consequence of the breach'. Even though the Regulations only provide that the court *may* award damages, it is submitted that damages must be granted once the loss has been proven and no other remedy is available. In fact, it would be contrary to the spirit of the Directive to leave to the discretion of the court the decision to refuse to award damages once the contract has been concluded, provided the procedural requirements for the entitlement to damages are fulfilled.

The Regulations therefore make clear that a right to damages exists whenever loss has been sustained, thereby overcoming the confusion created by the *Bourgoin* judgment. The Regulations introduce a statutory right to damages. Once again, this improvement is only relative, however, as the same result has been achieved by the obligations imposed by the *Francovich* decision.[36]

As a consequence of the vague provisions of the Remedies Directive, the Regulations remain silent as regards the conditions to be fulfilled in order to be entitled to damages, the way in which the amount of damages should be calculated, or their nature. The task of fulfilling these gaps is left to national courts. As in the case of interim relief, the relevant principles likely to be applied are those developed in the context of claims for tort or breach of statutory duty. According to national case law, the plaintiff must be put in the same position he would have been in had the breach never occurred. Evidence of actual loss sustained is, obviously, a peremptory requirement for the success of the action. It must be proved that the loss is caused by the breach on a balance of probabilities.[37] That is, in the present context, the plaintiff will need to show a serious chance of having won the contract, a claim for which it may be rather difficult to provide

ective to BT pending the resolution of a preliminary ruling by the Court of Justice (Case C-392/93). For a detailed analysis of the background to the preliminary reference and a discussion of the grounds on which the interim order was refused, see Brown, 'Case C-392/93: Reference to the Court of Justice concerning United Kingdom Implementation of the Utilities Directive in the Field of Telecommunications' (1994) 3 PPLR CS30 at CS36 *ff.*

[36] See Chapter 7.   [37] *Hotson* v. *East Berkshire AHA* [1987] AC 750.

evidence. This is aggravated by the fact that English courts will try to avoid entering into speculative considerations relating to the margin of discretion left by the applicable rules.[38] If able to do so, the plaintiff may recover not only bidding costs but also lost profits. The latter, however, will be difficult to quantify.[39]

Damages could also be claimed on the basis of *Blackpool & Fylde Aeroclub v. Blackpool BC.*[40] The Court of Appeal adopted an approach similar to that applicable in German law in the context of the *culpa in contrahendo* theory.[41] The Court understood that, in certain circumstances, the invitation to present a tender made by a public authority may imply the establishment of a contractual relationship between the tenderer and the contracting authority. If this is so, it may be argued that the applicable rules governing the award procedure could be regarded as implied contractual conditions under which the tenderer submits his or her tender. Any breach of these conditions would give rise to a contractual breach enforceable under the general principles governing contract law, which are more generous than those applicable in tort. This would include a right to recover all costs incurred in reliance on the normal performance of the contract, unless the defendant could show that in the event that the contract had been duly performed, the plaintiff would not have recovered that expenditure.[42] The Court of Appeal did not find it necessary to examine the claim in tort, nor did it specify what other terms the implied contract contained. The extent to which *Blackpool* could be interpreted in such an extensive manner is doubtful. Commentators are sceptical about the possibilities left open by this decision and its practical effectiveness in the field of public procurement.[43]

Needless to say, English courts may, in practice, follow a more positive interpretation which brings together the Regulations and the principle of effectiveness as developed by the Court of Justice. According to Arrowsmith such an alternative interpretation may be developed on the basis of the

---

[38] Per Lord Brightman in *R* v. *Chief Constable of North Wales Police, ex p. Evans* [1982] 1 WLR 1155 at 1173. Turpin (above, n 1) at 214.

[39] On the problem of quantifying lost profits, see Weatherill in Arrowsmith (ed.) (1993) (above, n 13) at 289; Arrowsmith (1992), 1 PPLR (above, n 22) at 113 where she states that the difficulties in assessing lost profits 'will tend to the conclusion that damages are not an adequate remedy'.

[40] [1990] 3 ALL ER 237. Bingham LJ held that the invitation to tender was not a mere invitation but was a contractual offer which would be accepted by the submission of a tender, and that the resulting contract contained an implied term that all tenders which complied with the stipulations would be considered in *bona fides* alongside all other tenders. In the present case, he held that the parties must have intended that a contract would come into existence between them. See Davenport, 'Obligation to Consider Tenders' (1991) 107 LQR 201.   [41] See below in this chapter.

[42] *CCC Films* v. *Impact Quadrant Films* [1985] QB 16.

[43] Arrowsmith (1992) (above, n 22) at 111; Weatherill in Arrowsmith (ed.) (1993) (above, n 13) at 291.

rule in *Chaplin* v. *Hicks*,[44] a rule pursuant to which the plaintiff is awarded a proportion of what he or she would have gained if successful, including lost profits. The proportional amount would be determined in direct proportion to the plaintiff's chances of winning the contract. The drawback of this approach is that it may not be easy to evaluate the chances of success. Another alternative is to award damages to any bidder who had a reasonable opportunity of winning the contract, although in this case it seems sensible to reduce the amount of damages to the bidding costs, or a fixed proportion of the value of the contract, as several tenderers could claim a reasonable possibility of success. In any event, the impact of the new remedies is dependent, to a large extent, on the future attitude of English courts. If a conservative approach is adopted, the situation of injured bidders will certainly not be improved. Even though damages are now no longer discretionary, to provide evidence of a better right to the contract is an arduous task. In any event, the incentive element is absent in the Regulations.

Lastly, it is explicitly stated that the powers enshrined in the Regulations do not prejudice any other powers of the courts. It follows that pre-existing possible remedies, particularly judicial review remedies, are not excluded in the conditions described above. It follows that another means open to claim damages is through actions for damages for misfeasance of public office.

Impact of the Remedies Directive in English Law

Even if it is up to English courts to determine the ultimate impact of the Regulations, a fundamental legal change has taken place in the UK from a formal point of view. A big step has been taken from the previous situation in which no definite procedural avenue existed, to the current one, in which specific statutory remedies have been introduced to ensure compliance with public procurement rules. No one can dispute the fact that the impact of the Remedies Directive in the UK and, more generally, the impact of Community public procurement rules, has been material. It does not seem too exaggerated to affirm that well-established legal traditions have been altered and the autonomy of the UK with respect to the legal approach to public contracting has been substantially eroded by Community law.

In theory, these changes should improve the legal position of potential plaintiffs. Their new rights are no longer enforceable through, what would appear to a continental lawyer as the jungle of judicial review remedies. Statutory rights to damages and interim relief are now explicitly recognized. Whereas the legal position has been enhanced, one may wonder

[44] [1911] 2 KB 786.

what the practical effect of these legal changes will be. Will more actions be brought and if so, will they lead to satisfactory redress? It is suggested that, in view of the approach of English courts to interim relief and damages, the legal improvements will not be greeted with similar improvements in the enforcement of the rules. If this proves to be correct, this begs the question of whether the legal changes imposed and the erosion of national autonomy were justified.

GERMANY

Preliminary Remarks[45]

The situation in Germany at the time of writing is controversial. The Commission and German representatives could not reach an agreement as to the adequacy of the implementation measures adopted to give effect to the public sector Directives, including the Remedies Directive. One of the main arguments of the Commission refers to the fact that the German measures do not confer subjective rights to tenderers and contractors, thereby making it more difficult for them to enforce their rights effectively. Germany, for its part, considers that the whole of the German implementation measures, including those adopted to give effect to the Remedies Directive, although not providing for subjective rights, do guarantee an effective protection of the advantages conferred by the public sector Directives upon firms and are therefore in line with the requirements of the Remedies Directive. The controversy is currently pending before the Court of Justice. Prior to analysing the questions which arise from the case, some preliminary remarks with respect to the amended situation in Germany are made.

The situation in Germany was similar to the British one, yet less complex, due to a stricter dogmatic approach by German courts and writers with respect to the classification of contracts of public authorities as subject to private law. This conception finds its ultimate manifestation in the legal treatment of remedies for breaches of public procurement rules. The fiction by which the administration when entering a contract acts as *Fiskus* instead of *Hoheitliche Verwaltung* places contracting authorities in the same position with respect to their contractual agreement as any other private party, the applicable regime being that of civil law.[46]

It is somewhat striking that in Germany, with such a well-developed

---

[45] For a general overview of the situation as regards remedies for breaches of public procurement rules in Germany relating both to national and Community rules, see Lupp, *Objektivität, Transparenz und Nachprüfarbeit der Angebotswertung bei der Vergabe öffentlicher Bauaufträge* (München, 1992) Teil III. See also Niedzela and Engshuber, 'Enforcing the Public Procurement Rules in Germany' in Arrowsmith (ed.) (1993) (above, n 13) Chapter 11; Remien, 'Public Procurement Law in an International Perspective' (1991) unpublished paper.

[46] See Chapter 4.

administrative law tradition, the award of contracts of public authorities are excepted from this discipline. In fact, even though contracting authorities are seen as public authorities, the decisions adopted in the course of the award procedure are not 'administrative acts' from a domestic law point of view.[47] On the contrary, all these pre-contract acts performed by the contracting authority are regarded as belonging to a uniform private law transaction or act, which embraces the total award procedure and the award itself.[48]

In German law, the procedure to enter into a contract is regulated by the *Verdingungsordnung für Bauleistungen* (VOB) and the *Verdingungsordnung für Leistungen-ausgenommen Bauleistungen* (VOL),[49] which are mere internal administrative regulations with no effects outside the administrative sphere. As in the case of the United Kingdom, the VOL and VOB are intended to ensure that public authorities use public funds in an economic manner for the general public benefit. No 'subjective right' or individual right therefore arise for specialized firms and contractors, as they are not the direct beneficiaries of those provisions. Under administrative law, private parties may not rely on them to lodge a judicial complaint before the administrative courts since they have no subjective right to enforce against the administration.[50]

This does not mean that contracting authorities are totally free to disregard the obligations imposed on them by the *Verdingungsordnung*. A

---

[47] For a judicial decision see *Oberlandesgericht* (OLG) Köln of 29 April 1977, *Baurecht* (Baur.) 1977, 343. For a doctrinal assessment, see Rittner, 'Rechtsgrundlagen und Rechtgrundsätze des öffentlichen Auftragswesens. Eine systematische Analyse' in *Schriften zum öffentlichen Auftragswesen* (Freiburg, 1988); Badura, 'Wirtschaftverwaltungsrecht' in Von Münch (ed.), *Besonderes Verwaltungsrecht*, 8th edn. (1988) 344 *ff.*

[48] Some commentators have defended the application of the *Zweistufentheorie* or 'two step theory' which applies in other areas of German administrative law to these contracts. The theory distinguishes two different stages in certain activities of public authorities. The first stage occurs when the competent public body decides whether or not to carry out a certain course of action. This decision is subject to public law and is, therefore, categorized as an administrative act (*Verwaltungsakt*) impugnable before administrative courts pursuant to the rules governing this type of judicial proceeding. The way in which this decision is put into practice, usually by means of contractual arrangements, constitutes the second stage and is considered to be subject to private law. The enforcement and implementation of the contract clauses would, on the contrary, fall under the regime of private law. See Kopp, 'Die Entscheidung über die Vergabe öffentlicher Aufträge und über Abschluß öffentlichrechtlicher Verträge als Verwaltungsakte?', *Bayerische Verwaltungsblätter* 1980, 609–612. Lupp (above, n 45) at 195 *ff*; Niedzela and Engshuber in Arrowsmith (ed.) (1993) (above, n 13) at 359. Although the possibility of judicial redress for third parties would have been improved by the acceptance of this approach, German courts have explicitly refused it (*Bundesverwaltungsgericht* (BVerWG) of 6 June 1958, *Neue Juristiche Wochenschrift* (NJW) 1959, 115 and of 6 May 1970, *Deutsches Verwaltungsblatt* (DVB) 1971, 110 at 111 *ff* with annotations by Bettermann).

[49] See further Chapter 4 at the section entitled, **Germany**.

[50] In one case, however, a court admitted an action whereby an undertaking claimed to be accepted to participate in a contract award procedure. The basis of the judgment was not only the VOL and VOB, but more specifically Article 3 of the German Constitution which recognizes the right to equal treatment for all citizens. OLG Düsseldorf of 12 February 1980, *Die öffentliche Verwaltung*, 1981, 537 with a critical annotation by Pietzcker.

large set of internal administrative and political controls are provided by German law. However, these do not benefit injured bidders directly. The emphasis is therefore placed on the internal administrative controls as contracts follow private law principles and the will of the party escapes the control of judicial instances and third parties, unless 'pre-contractual obligations' may be held to exist, but then again a right to damages may only arise in private law. Thus, contract award procedures which disregard the provisions of the VOL and VOB only entitle aggrieved firms to resort to private law remedies. More precisely, the regulation of some areas of competition law and civil law provide for possible remedies.

Remedies Available in German Law

Remedies deriving from the Law on Restraints of Competition (*Gesetz gegen Wettbewerbsbeschränkungen* (GgW))

Certain provisions of the Law on Restraints of Competition have been held to be applicable to breaches by contracting authorities of the general provisions regulating contract awards. According to German case law and doctrine,[51] abuse of dominant position applies to those situations in which contracting authorities enjoy a privileged position on the demand side, that is, as consumers of goods and services, which allows them to impose on their suppliers measures which distort or threaten to distort competition.[52] Paragraph 22 GgW forbids the abuse of dominant position in the market either by the exploitation in an abusive manner of a favourable position in the market, or by the creation of obstacles, to fair competition. Paragraph 26(2) GgW states that any undertaking in a dominant position may not, directly or indirectly, unreasonably hinder another undertaking in business dealings regularly accessible to similar undertakings, nor may it discriminate against some undertakings unless such discriminatory treatment is objectively justified.

At the administrative level, the Federal Anti-Trust Enforcement Agency, the *Bundeskartellsamt* (BKA), takes the general provisions on contract awards (VOL and VOB) as a reference to determine the existence of abuse since, due to their consensual character, they are regarded as representing a fair balance between the different interests involved. As a consequence, on

---

[51] *Bundesgerichtshof* (BGH) of 26 October 1961 (Gummistrümpfe) *Wirtschaft und Wettbewerb/ Entscheidungen* (WuW/E) 422; BGH of 22 March 1976 (Autoanalyser) WuW/E 1469; for the Federal Administrative Court, see BVerWG of 13 March 1970, DVBL 1971, 111 *ff*; BVerWG of 10 November 1972, *Die öffentliche Verwaltung* (DöV) 1973, 244. As for the doctrine, see Stockmann, 'L'abus de puissance d'achat de la part de la puissance publique en RFA' in (1987) 9 *Journées de la Société de Législation Comparée* 535.

[52] Since the 1970s the *Bundeskartellsamt* has followed the policy of interpreting the notion of public enterprise as embracing public authorities when those authorities procure goods or services in the market like any other private person. Stockmann (above, n 51) 538; *Tätigkeitsbericht des Bundeskartellamtes* (TB) 1971, 23.

any occasion when public contracting authorities depart from these provisions without any objective reason, the BKA presumes that a *prima facie*
evidence of abuse of dominant position exists.[53] These would include those
cases when the award of the contract is made upon criteria or conditions
which have no direct connection with the object of the contract and which
prevent the attainment of the result which the correct application of the
general provisions on contract award would have produced.[54] Needless to
say, for these provisions to apply, a dominant position on the demand side
must exist. This reduces the relevance of these provisions considerably.

In so far as judicial application of the GgW to public procurement is
concerned, it appears that there are few cases. The remedies which a firm
which is the object of an abuse of dominant position is entitled to claim
before the courts are injunctions and damages.[55] Injunctions are to prevent the defendant from continuing to act in an allegedly illegal manner
and damages are to recover any loss sustained. In so far as injunctions are
concerned, lower courts have granted them in some public procurement
cases for disrespect of the obligations imposed by the VOB.[56] The authority of these rulings is questioned, however, by a subsequent decision of the
Bundesgerichtshof.[57] Finally, under para. 35 GgW, contracting authorities

[53] Memorandum of the 5th section of the BKA presented to the Conference 11/86 of
Authorities competent on the subject of Mergers, *Wirtschaft und Wettbewerb* (WuW) 1978, 444.
Cited by Stockmann (above, n 51) 543.

[54] For an overview of the practice of the BKA in applying the GgW to public procurement
cases, see Stockmann (above, n 51) 543–547.   [55] Para. 35(1), (3) GgW.

[56] The *Landgericht* (LG) of Berlin ruled that a public authority holding a dominant position
on the demand side of the market abuses such position by failing to provide precise specifications of the services requested, as required by VOB/A. This placed small and medium
sized enterprises in a situation of competitive disadvantage with respect to bigger firms, since
the bigger firms are better placed to face the expenses and difficulties of designing the
specifications on their own. It granted the injunction claimed, and therefore suspended the
award procedure. *Landgericht* (LG) Berlin of 1 November 1983, WuW 1985, 243. In another
case, the *Oberlandesgericht* (OLG) Düsseldorf granted an injunction and ordered a firm which
was systematically excluded from participating to be admitted to the award procedure. OLG
Düsseldorf of 12 February 1980 (above, n 50). This decision was based not only on paras.
26(2) and 35 GgW but also on Article 3 of the German Basic Federal Law which prohibits
unequal treatment of citizens unless objectively justified. The *Oberlandesgericht* held that since
the customer was a public authority, it was bound by Article 3 of the Constitution. This
judgment has been criticized for its confused legal reasoning: Pietzcker (above, n 50). See
also similar decisions by lower courts, LG München of 13 August 1986, WuW 1987, 938 and
LG Düsseldorf of 25 March 1987, WuW 1987, 942.

[57] BGH of 26 May 1987, WuW 1987, 1009. In this case, a public hospital decided to
appoint a public rescue team as the exclusive provider of transport for patients, to the
detriment of some private firms. Two lower courts had previously held, in similar circumstances, that the hospital was abusing its dominant position by excluding the private firms
without any objective reason for doing so. They granted injunctions and decided that the
decisions were to be set aside (LG München of 13 August 1986 and LG Düsseldorf of 25
March 1987 (above, n 56)). The Federal Supreme Court took a different position. It refused
to grant interim relief arguing that no contravention of the GgW existed. The hospital's
choice was justified on objective grounds, since the appointment of a public team guaranteed the promptness and availability of the service in all circumstances. The contracted
service, due to its public character, justified the exclusion of the private firms.

are under an obligation to compensate the injured firm for the damages caused by its abuse. However, to our knowledge, cases on the subject are rare.

Civil Law Remedies

Since contracts of public authorities are regarded as private law contracts and public authorities are seen as private parties, bidders injured by breaches of Community law rules have to resort to existing civil law remedies before the ordinary civil courts. German civil law remedies are generally quite restrictive with respect to interim relief. Interim injunctions are granted only when individual fundamental rights are at stake. These include an individual's life, health, property or personal integrity. Most other individual interests are protected by an *ex post facto* award of damages. As a result, injunctive relief in public procurement cases will only lie in exceptional cases.[58]

In civil law, therefore, the available remedies tend to be limited to the possibility of an award of damages. The concept of punitive damages is generally rejected in Germany. The *Bundesgerichtshof* has held, in relation to the liability of German public authorities for breaches of Community law, that authorities do not owe any obligation directly to the plaintiff whenever the plaintiff's losses were a result of foreseeable economic risk.[59] This principle may well apply to the public procurement sector. Even though the applicable situation as regards public procurement breaches is still not definite, since the German implementation measures are before the Court of Justice, it must be noted that these measures do not intend to modify the situation as regards damages. Thus, since Community provisions regulate the conduct of contracting authorities before the conclusion of the contract and since German law does not acknowledge the theory of severable acts, the applicable private law remedies with respect to damages are based on the civil law '*culpa in contrahendo*' theory.[60]

On the basis of this theory, aggrieved tenderers have a right to claim damages for the loss sustained which derives from infringements which occur during the contract negotiations or award procedure. Such breaches include cases in which the contracting authorities do not abide by the guidelines and the criteria enshrined in the VOB and VOL. Certain conditions must be fulfilled, however, in order for a tenderer to be entitled to this action. Firstly, a specific previous relationship must exist between the parties, which proved their intention to conclude a contract. This is the so-called *vertragsähnliches Vertrauensverhältnis*, which refers to a 'contractual-like'

---

[58] See Niedzela and Engshuber in Arrowsmith (ed.) (1993) (above, n 13) at 371.
[59] *Re Skimmed Milk Powder for Animal Feed*, Bundesgerichtshof, III ZR 146/85 [1988] 1 CMLR 265.
[60] See generally Höfler, "The Protection of the Interests of Bidders in the Precontractual Stage under German Procurement Law" (1995) 4 PPLR 159.

confidential agreement which emerges when two parties have contacted each other with the possible aim of subsequently concluding a contract. This situation exists in public procurement whenever the contractor or candidate submits a tender to a competitive award procedure, or is invited to present an offer by the contracting authority. There is, therefore, a serious intention on both sides to develop a procedure which may end in the conclusion of the contract. Secondly, for *culpa in contrahendo* to exist, one of the parties must have ignored his or her pre-contractual duties, either wilfully or negligently. Duties include exercising due care, keeping confidential information secret and, moreover, not abusing the reasonable reliance of the other party which was built up during contractual negotiations. German jurisprudence has held that contracting authorities passing a contract are under a duty to comply with the provisions of the VOL and VOB as the other party may reasonably rely on the contracting authority to respect these provisions.[61] Lastly, other conditions must equally be satisfied regarding the damages themselves. The liability of contracting authorities may be based on *culpa in contrahendo* when the damages sustained are directly caused by the alleged infringement of the 'pre-contractual' duties. If this is so, damages would only be granted if the plaintiff provides evidence that he or she would have been awarded the contract had the breach not been committed,[62] or would have refrained from presenting a bid at all had they known of the existence of the breach.[63] Thus, only those with a real chance of winning the award may be entitled to recover damages which compensate the costs incurred. German jurisprudence is therefore quite strict in assessing the chances of the plaintiff. They must show not only that they had a 'realistic' chance[64] or merely 'some' chance,[65] but that they had a 'very great chance' of winning the contract. All circumstances considered, plaintiffs will be in a position to argue their case only when the award is made on the lowest price criterion and, therefore, when no discretion is left to the contracting authorities.[66]

German courts have normally limited the amount of damages under

[61] OLG Hamm of 24 November 1971, *Betriebs-Berater* (BB) 1972, 243; OLG Köln of 29 April 1977 (above, n 47), OLG Düsseldorf of 3 June 1982, Baur. 1983, 377 and of 26 November 1985, Baur. 1986, 107–108.

[62] BGH of 26 March 1981 (Sporthalle), BB 1981, 1122 where a plaintiff was refused damages on the grounds that it was uncertain from the evidence provided whether he would have been awarded the contract had the procedure been correctly completed.

[63] OLG Düsseldorf of 27 January 1976 (Halleablad), NJW 1977, 1064 where the contracting authority had initiated a contract award procedure although the financing of the project was not yet secured.

[64] BGH of 12 April 1984 (Sport und Schwimmhalle) Baur. 1984, 631. In this case damages were awarded to first placed bidder, but were refused to the bidder placed fourth.

[65] BGH of 26 March 1981 (Sporthalle) (above, n 62).

[66] OLG Hamm of 24 November 1971 (Tiefbauarbeiten) (above, n 61) where the court accorded damages to the unsuccessful bidder since it would have had the 'very great chance' of winning the award had the procedure developed regularly.

this procedure to the so-called *Vertrauenschaden*. Its object is to bring successful litigants back to the position in which they would have been had the pre-contractual relationship never existed.[67] This means that they will normally be entitled to recover bidding costs.[68] Obviously, if a plaintiff is successful in proving a better right, he or she may be entitled to the *Erfüllungsinteresse*, or expectancy damages which may include the lost profit. These restore the plaintiff to the position he or she would have been in had the contract been concluded with them. This has been conceded in one case at least, where the plaintiff's offer was regarded by the court as the most acceptable one.[69]

Effectiveness of the German System

The German possibilities for remedies have been described as narrow.[70] The application of the GgW remedies is subject to the existence of a dominant position by public authorities in the market. However, this is the exception rather than the rule. Only in a few sectors, most of which have been excluded from the application of the Directives, may public authorities be found to enjoy a dominant position (this would be the case, for example, in the telecommunications, hospital equipment and energy sectors). The GgW will provide redress in only a handful of public procurement cases. Injunctions and damages under the provisions of the GgW will, moreover, be available only to firms operating in those specific sectors.

As regards civil law remedies, even though German courts have been open to claims based on *culpa in contrahendo*, their relevance is only partial. Difficulties relating to the fulfilment of the conditions determining *culpa in contrahendo* render the achievement of this redress complicated. Moreover, it does not provide for interim measures to prevent the award of the contract. The need to show a 'very great chance' of having won the award in order to be entitled to damages probably has a negative effect on potential plaintiffs.

Some commentators in Germany have advocated that the public procurement area needs to be the object of regulation through legislative measures. According to this line of thought, such an important activity of public authorities may not be exempted from the application of administrative law principles. Already in the 1950s, the need for a change in the legal approach was discussed by Forsthoff, who convincingly argued that

---

[67] OLG Frankfurt am Main of 26 July 1988 (Flugfeldbetankungsanlagen), Baur. 1990, 91 at 95; OLG Hamm of 24 November 1971 (Tiefbauarbeiten) (above, n 61).

[68] OLG Hamm of 24 November 1971 (above, n 61); OLG Düsseldorf of 27 January 1976, Schäffer/Finern, Z.2.11 Bl. 15; OLG Köln of 29 April 1977, *Schäffer/Finern*, Z 2 13 Bl. 53.

[69] OLG Düsseldorf of 15 December 1988 (Deckenarbeiten) Baur. 1989, 195.

[70] Rittner (above, n 47) at 146, n 34; Remien (above, n 45) at 31.

public contracts constituted a particular category of contracts which greatly differed from private contracts and that, therefore, their regulation was to be tackled on the basis of specific administrative principles.[71]

The Debate about the Implementation of the Remedies Directive

The question of remedies in Germany is directly linked to the question of the nature of the implementation measures adopted with respect to the public sector Directives, which, as mentioned earlier, were adopted by means of provisions which did not provide for individual rights. Germany implemented the Remedies Directive by establishing a peculiar system of redress which, in its view, fulfiled the requirements of the Remedies Directive.

The implementation of the Remedies Directive took place in Germany by means of a revision of the Budgetary Principles Act (*Haushaltsgrundsätzegesetz* (HGrG)).[72] The amendments consist of adding three new sections to the HGrG[73] which enable the government to enact regulations in the public procurement field. One of the Regulations adopted on the basis of these sections is the *Nachprüfungsveordnung*, which implements the Remedies Directive in German law. The review system envisaged consists of two different levels. The first level of review is *administrative* in nature and is the competence of the so-called *Vergabeprüfstellen* (Award Examining Bodies). Its duties are to initiate a review procedure *ex officio*, whenever it becomes aware of the existence of an alleged infringement of the rules contained in the VOB or VOL. It may be seized by any interested party. Its attributed powers are quite broad, including the possibility of ordering the suspension of the contract, setting aside unlawful decisions and ordering the contracting authority to adopt the required measures. Since this organ has an administrative nature, it is empowered to substitute its own decisions for those of the contracting authority, in so far as the latter is an administrative body itself. The suspension powers are subject to the public interest exception, and a balance of interests must be applied in order to grant the suspension. In addition, all these remedies may only be granted before the contract has been concluded.

With respect to damages, section 57(b) para. 4 of the Bill amending the HGrG states that the rules regulating damages before the civil courts are not affected by the amendments. It follows that the intention of the German Government is to leave the regulation of damages untouched and the principles regarding private law remedies will therefore remain applicable.

---

[71] Fortshoff, *Traité de Droit Administratif Allemand*, 9ᵉ edn., translation by Fromont (Brussels, 1969) at 415 *ff.*

[72] See Seidel, 'Implementation of the Public procurement Directives in the 12 States of the EC' (1992) 1 PPLR at 257. See Chapter 4. [73] Sections 57A, 57B and 57C HgH.

The second level of review is constituted by the possibility of appealing any decision of the *Vergabeprüfstelle* to the *Vergabeüberwachungsausschuß* (Commission for the Review of Contract Awards). This body is of a quasi-judicial nature and has been created pursuant to the requirements of Article 2(8) of the Remedies Directive.[74] Its powers are limited to act on appeal against any decision of the *Vergabeprüfstelle*, but only on matters of law. It is not entitled therefore to enter the assessment of questions of fact. It is entitled to submit preliminary references under Article 177 EC to the Court of Justice. Its final decision is to be implemented by the *Vergabeprüfstelle*, which must follow its instructions. The *Vergabeüberwachungsausschuß* may not, however, set aside the *Vergabeprüfstelle*'s decision nor substitute its own decisions for that of the latter.

It is suggested that a better solution would have been to provide individuals with subjective rights enforceable before the administrative courts according to the general principles which apply to the jurisdiction of those courts. This would give aggrieved contractors access to the well-developed system of administrative law remedies for breaches of public procurement law. This would mean that a sort of *Zweistufentheorie* would be adopted because pre-contract procedures would be subject to the jurisdiction of administrative law. This would also accommodate the demands for a change in the general approach towards public contracting.

The proposed legislation indicates that the German Government understands that this is not the case and seems determined to maintain the private law character of the public procurement activities of public authorities as regards their review. How otherwise may the creation of the specific administrative review body for breaches of public procurement rules be understood? In fact, the proposed measures do not provide contractors with subjective rights, despite the upgrading of the VOL and VOB. German authorities are reluctant to introduce such a radical modification.

In its submissions to the Court in Case C-433/93, the Commission claims that the German measures are not in line with the most recent case law of the Court of Justice concerning implementation of Directives by means of administrative provisions.[75] In the light of this case law, the Commission

---

[74] This provision requires that 'where bodies responsible for review procedures are not judicial in character [as is the case with the *Vergabeprüfungstellen*] . . . provision must be made to guarantee procedures whereby any allegedly illegal measure taken by the review body, or any alleged defect in the exercise of the powers conferred on it, can be the subject of judicial review or review by any other body which is a court or tribunal within the meaning of Article 177 of the EEC Treaty and independent of both the contracting authority and the review body . . .'. This provision was, in fact, included to take into account the German peculiarities.

[75] On the ongoing debate in Germany, see the report 'An Explosive Issue: 'Subjective Rights' or Internal Administrative Controls?', briefly exposing the government position in Germany (1993) 3 *EC Public Contracts* 10. See also Wenzel, 'German Solution not Likely to Last Long. Four Actions for Treaty violation', ibid. at 11. See Case C-59/89, *Commission* v. *Germany* [1991] ECR I-2607. discussed in Chapter 4.

argues that the public sector Directives are intended to confer individual rights and insists that implementation of the public sector Directives in national law must be done in a manner which ensures the conferral upon interested firms of subjective rights. In its view, the final outcome of the system adopted is insufficient, as it amounts to a mere administrative review of the alleged infringements without giving any substantial procedural guarantees to aggrieved tenderers. Germany, on the contrary, defends the view that the Court's case law leaves a certain margin of discretion to national authorities as to the form and means of implementation, provided the system effectively ensures the respect of the Community rules by contracting authorities and that an effective redress system is established. In this respect, for the German representatives, the question of whether individual rights are conferred at the national level is of secondary importance, as long as the requirements of legal certainty and transparency are complied with and, pursuant to the Remedies Directive, an efficient remedies system is established. In support of their position, which gives priority to the effectiveness of the redress system over the question of individual rights, German representatives relied on Article 2(8) of the Remedies Directive, which was precisely introduced in order to meet German demands and specifically allows for review systems of a non-judicial character. It must be conceded that the remedies situation would be substantially improved by the adoption of these rules, except as regards damages. But here again, the German approach would not differ from that prevailing in the other Member States examined.

This case certainly raises many interesting questions regarding the concept of individual rights at Community level and their treatment at national level, and the conflict between the Court's case law and the outcome of the decision-making process. A full discussion of these issues is beyond the scope of these pages, especially since the judgment has not yet been adopted.[76] Two different problems seem to be at stake, however. The first concerns the implementation of the public sector Directives and the question of individual rights which originate at Community level. It seems beyond doubt that the Directives provide for rights or advantages for tenderers and contractors. So far the Court has not ruled that the definition of individual Community rights is a matter for Community law and that national concepts or traditions are irrelevant. It has, however, declared, in a truly far-reaching case law, that Community rights are to be afforded effective judicial protection at national level. It is submitted that the Court should reserve the definition of the conditions necessary for an

---

[76] For an exhaustive discussion of these issues, see Fernández Martín, 'El efecto directo de las directivas y la protección de los derechos subjetivos comunitarios en la jurisprudencia del Tribunal de Justicia. Intento de Sistematización', (1995) No. 126 *Noticias de la Unión Europea* 1.

individual Community right to exist to Community law itself. In addition, these rights, in application of the procedural autonomy and effectiveness principles examined earlier, should benefit from the same status that individual or subjective rights enjoy at national level when this is more favourable or, in other cases, from effective judicial protection. It remains to be seen what features an individual legal situation requires in order to be classified as an individual Community rights (precision, unconditionality, feasibility amongst others, perhaps). The case pending before the Court provides a good opportunity to clarify this issue.

A second aspect involved is that the Court has gone quite far in developing the principle of effective judicial protection of individual Community rights. With regard to national implementation of Directives, the Court has been rather strict when the Directives were held to contain individual rights.[77] In this sense the German measures implementing the public sector Directives fall short of ensuring, on their own, effective judicial protection. However, once the Remedies Directive for public procurement matters was adopted, questions arose about whether compliance with the latter requirements is sufficient to fufil Community law requirements, or whether the conditions set down in the Court's case law must prevail. In other words, the case before the Court shows a conflict between the result of the decision-making process reflected in the Remedies Directive and the Court's case law requiring high standards of protection of Community rights. A solution to this conflict must be provided. Assuming that the Treaty is the basic constitutional charter of the EC[78] and that the Court of Justice is the constitutional Court, then an application of general principles of legal hierarchy suggests that its judgments must prevail and that the German implementation measures must be redefined. German Governments are right, however, to point out that their system guaranteees the requirements of the Remedies Directives in that it ensures review mechanisms which *prima facie* guarantee the effectiveness of the tenderers' and contractors' Community rights. This raíses the question of subsidiarity which the German representatives also put forward in their submissions. If their system is, *prima facie*, effective to ensure the objectives set out at the supranational level, why should they change it? Thus, a conflict between uniformity and 'centralization' of legal concepts and diversity and respect for national values and traditions also enters the picture. It is not easy to resolve this conflict. However, in the specific case of the definition of individual rights for Community purposes, it is submitted that, in order to guarantee equal treatment amongst individuals through the uniform application of Community rules and the development of a coherent Community legal

---

[77] See Chapter 4.

[78] See Case 294/83, *Parti écologiste 'Les Verts'* v. *Parlement Européen* [1986] ECR 1339 and Opinion 1/91, *Re a Draft Treaty on a European Economic Area* [1991] ECR I-6079.

system, the definition should be elaborated at supranational level and should prevail over national considerations.

The Impact of the Remedies Directive in Germany

To assess what the impact will be in Germany is a speculative exercise since the case has not been resolved by the Court at the time of writing. Nonetheless, on the basis of available information, the same conclusions reached with respect to the UK are applicable to Germany. Reference to them is made in order to avoid unnecessary repetition. What is also interesting about Germany, however, is that the long debated need for reform of the German regulation[79] of public contracting has been directly affected by the Community rules. Community law will induce changes which the German authorities have evaded for a long time. Once again, as was the case in the UK, the supranational legal approach will override and impose itself on long standing national legal traditions. Will the changes in practice compensate for the changes in law?

THE PROSPECTS FOR THE REMEDIES DIRECTIVE: SUCCESS OR FAILURE?

In view of the adoption (or absence) of national implementation measures, this section analyses what the impact of the Remedies Directive is likely to be on existing national systems.

Interim Relief

With the exception of Germany, where the opposite applies,[80] the grant of interim relief in public procurement cases followed the same principles which were generally applied to requests for interim relief against acts of public authorities. Their objective is to avoid irreparable damage and to guarantee effective judicial protection of individual rights. The award of such measures is, in most cases, left to the discretion of the competent authorities judging the claim. In assessing the convenience of interim relief, the standard approach by national courts is to 'proceed to consider the "balance of convenience",—that is, to weigh, on the one hand, the

---

[79] See Niedzela and Engshuber in Arrowsmith (ed.) (1993) (above, n 13) at 383.

[80] Only in Germany does the introduction of an action against an illegal administrative act have automatic suspensory effects on the execution of such an act. This principle does not, however, apply in the public contracts area, as the award of public contracts escapes the field of administrative law and consequently the control of the administrative courts. See in general, Fromont, 'La protection provisoire des particuliers contre les décisions administratives dans les États membres des Communautés européennes' (1984) *Revue Internationale des Sciences Administratives* 309.

detriment to the public interest which is likely to result from a delay to the procurement process against, on the other hand, the interests which may be prejudiced if no interim relief is given and the claim proves well founded'.[81] In public procurement cases, interim relief has rarely been granted by national review bodies. Injured rights are generally satisfied through an award of damages.

National legal orders either contemplated the possibility of interim measures in public procurement or have made the necessary modifications in order to comply with the Directive's requirements. In view of the implementation measures adopted, will this attitude change in the near future? In France and the UK, the implementation measures have explicitly empowered the courts to adopt interim measures in public procurement cases. They lack any detailed regulation of the conditions under which interim relief should be granted, however. In Spain, previously applicable rules have not been modified whereas the situation is still being debated in Germany. In view of the vague implementation measures, the solution remains in the hands of national judges and their willingness to interpret the applicable rules in favour of the award of interim relief.[82] Considering the prevailing national approaches to date, it is submitted that national courts will not change their attitude in the medium term. The final object, nature and effect of the contract in dispute on the public interest will determine whether suspension may be granted. Public interest considerations are likely to be favoured. In this context, it is noteworthy that a joint declaration of the Council and the Commission held that the interpretation of the balance of interests referred to in Article 2(4) of the Remedies Directive should 'conform with the principles of national jurisprudence with regard to interim measures'.[83] No 'particular' interpretation specific to public procurement Community rules is therefore required at national level and, consequently, current restrictive approaches may be tolerated by the Commission.

Of course, national courts may prove us wrong and adopt a more pro-European interpretation in accordance with the spirit of the requirement of effectiveness, the European Court's case law and the Directive's objectives. However, it seems that this will come about through individual judgments rather than general doctrines, at least in the coming years. This will give rise to a problem of lack of uniformity in the assessment of the convenience of interim relief, as decisions will vary considerably from one jurisdiction to another. The objective of uniform application sought by

---

[81] Arrowsmith (1992), 1 PPLR (above, n 22) at 113.

[82] See generally Lecourt, *L'Europe des Juges* (Brussels, 1976).

[83] Reproduced in European Parliament, 'Draft recommendation by the Committee on Economic and Monetary Affairs and Industrial Policy concerning the common position of the Council with a view to the adoption of a directive on the coordination of the laws, regulations and administrative provisions relating to the application of review procedures to the award of public supply and public works contracts', 14 September 1989, EP 134.123 at 12.

the Directive would then be frustrated. It is hoped that Article 177 EC procedures will be frequent in order to clarify the responsibilities of national courts. The Court of Justice must establish the parameters within which the award of interim measures is to be interpreted and which public interest circumstances justify the non-suspension of the award procedure. The scenario just described assumes that national judges will be fed with a substantial number of actions by injured undertakings allowing for the development of a substantial body of case law. On the basis of the information currently available, it remains to be seen whether this will take place.

Damages

Similar considerations apply as regards damages. As the Remedies Directive leaves the question of proof and the calculation of damages to national authorities, existing national approaches on damages are unlikely to change as regards breaches of public procurement rules. In fact, the implementation measures adopted (or not adopted as the case may be) have largely left the question of damages untouched. At the national level, damages in the field of public contracts are treated as a section of the more general issue of the liability of public authorities. Public interest considerations determine that the amount of damages and the procedural requirements to obtain them are confined within strict limits. No national system approaches damages as incentives to enhance active compliance with the rules. This aspect has not been altered by the Remedies Directive, despite its ultimate objective of enhancing decentralized enforcement. In the absence of incentives, the general apathy shown by firms in relation to initiating complaints will remain unchanged.

In public procurement cases, under relevant domestic case law, damages are granted if the plaintiff provides evidence that he or she would have been awarded the contract, or had a serious chance of winning it, had the breach not occurred. It is quite improbable that injured firms will be in a position to supply sufficient evidence demonstrating the most advantageous character of their offer as this criterion involves many considerations of a subjective character. Apart from the obvious difficulties in displaying evidence of a better right, it must be borne in mind that courts normally avoid entering the assessment of the material facts which lead the contracting authority to prefer one tenderer rather than another when the applicable rules allow for a certain margin of discretion. The traditional principle of the division of powers acts as an obstacle to this course of action.[84] As a result, damages for 'foregone profit or lost opportunities'

---

[84] As pointed out by the House of Lords (above, n 1) at 19, para. 71, 'litigation in which, in effect, the court or the administrative authority substitute their judgment for that of the procuring entity' is to be seen 'as inherently undesirable'. See also Monedero Gil, 'Criterios

will be 'extremely difficult to assess' as they involve an evaluation of the plaintiff's chances of winning the contract. Unfortunately, awards to the lowest bid, where no discretion is left to contracting authorities, are the exception rather than the rule. Nonetheless, if the plaintiff is successful in overcoming all these obstacles, he or she may also claim lost profits.

Apart from France where, in relative terms, damages may be regarded as adapted to the requirements of the Directives, quite a dramatic change in the way in which damages are awarded must take place at national level if the final objectives of the Remedies Directive are to be achieved. Taking into consideration both the nature of the implementation means (or the absence of them), such a radical change in attitude is unlikely however. An active role of the Court of Justice in this sense, specifying the procedural conditions left unresolved after *Francovich* is desirable.[85] However, the case law of the Court of Justice on the extra-contractual liability of the Community institutions does not provide a promising example for national courts. The Court has treated the extra-contractual liability of Community institutions for losses caused to individuals in quite restrictive terms. In its case law on Article 215 EC, which regulates this matter at the supranational level, the Court has maintained that the Community will not incur liability for damages caused by its unlawful economic legislation unless a particularly serious breach of a superior rule of law for the protection of the individual has occurred,[86] or unless the Community is found to have manifestly and gravely disregarded the limits of its competence and to have exercised its discretionary power in a manner verging on the arbitrary.[87] It seems inconsistent to require Member States to comply with more liberal principles at national level than those imposed by the Court on Community institutions as regards similar cases at the supranational level.[88]

Summing up, while a more stringent provision on damages could possibly have favoured compliance with the main Directives, it would have done so at the expense of present domestic approaches and considerations of fairness. Member States would not have accepted such an important step forward. To introduce the concept of 'incentive' or punitive damages as regards breaches of public procurement rules would mean a legal

de adjudicación del contrato administrativo en el derecho comunitario' (1986) No. 21 *Noticias CEE* 63 at 69.

[85] See Chapter 7.

[86] Joined Cases 83 and 94/76, 4, 15 and 40/77, *Bayerische HNL Vermetrungsvetrieb GmbH & Co KG* v. *Council* [1978] ECR 1209.

[87] Case 143/77, *Koniklijke Scholten Honig NV* v. *Council and Commission* [1979] ECR 3583.

[88] On the treatment by the Court of Justice of the issue of extra-contractual liability of the Community institutions, see in general Barav and Green (above, n 7) at 117. In *Bourgoin*, the Court of Appeal refused to grant damages for breaches of Article 30 *simpliciter* in view, *inter alia*, of the restrictive approach of the Court of Justice. Parker LJ held that the solution in *Bourgoin* was 'in harmony with European law as applied to the acts of its own institutions' (above, n 6) in fine.

revolution in most Member States and could certainly not be imposed by a sectoral Directive. State liability is a highly sensitive area, which goes beyond public procurement infringements.[89] It appears somewhat bizarre that a more progressive attitude towards State liability should be applied exclusively as regards public procurement infringements and not as regards other areas of state activity which may, moreover, be of far more importance to citizens.

Postscript to Chapter 10

The Court of Justice delivered its judgment in Case C-433/93 on 11 August 1995. It held that the pre-1993 implementation of the public procurement Directives by means of the VOB and VOL did not satisfy Community law requirements.[90] The Court repeated its previous case-law to the effect that whenever directives provide for individual rights, as the Court emphasised was the case with the public procurement Directives, national implementation measures must enable individuals to ascertain the full extent of their rights and, where appropriate, rely on them before national courts. The German implementation of public procurement Directives through administrative provisions fell short of these requirements. The Court also rejected the German argument that individuals could rely on the direct effect doctrine to enforce their rights under the public procurement Directives before German courts. It stated that the fact that direct effect could afford a certain degree of enforceability in German could not justify a Member State absolving itself from taking in due time measures sufficient to meet the purpose of the directive.

By strictly applying its previous case-law on the implementation of directives, the Court avoided entering into an examination of the degree of effectiveness achieved by the German system as regards guaranteeing respect for the public procurement rules by contracting authorities. It also did not analyse whether the objectives of the Remedies Directive were achieved by the German system.

The judgment only referred to the pre-1993 implementation situation in Germany, that is, the original VOL and VOB. However, in view of the requirement that individual rights arising from Community directives must be enforceable before national courts irrespective of the direct effect doctrine, the judgment of the Court begs the question whether the currently applicable German implementation measures will need to be modified in order to provide for enforceable individual rights under German law.[91]

---

[89] See the observations made by Snyder in, 'The Effectiveness of European Community Law: Institutions, Processes, Tools and Techniques' (1993) 56 MLR 19 at 45.

[90] For the background to the Case and the submissions to the Court, see Chapter 4, pp. 106–107 above.

[91] See further pp. 106–107 above.

General Conclusions to Chapters 7 to 10

The last chapters have analysed the Remedies Directive at two different levels. The question whether its final provisions fulfil the conditions to ensure effective enforcement at a decentralized level of public procurement rules was tackled first. Although the general approach of the Commission identifies the peculiarities of public procurement correctly and proposes adequate mechanisms to achieve an effective means of redress in that area, the final outcome of the decision-making process has not lived up to original expectations. On a second level, after examining the adopted implementation measures, some speculative forecasts as regards its eventual success have been put forward. It has been submitted that even though the Directive may always be used as a reference point for national enforcement authorities, it falls short of developing a competent and effective system of enforcement.

The adoption of a Remedies Directive was a good opportunity to establish a minimum common standard of protection of injured bidders and to go a step further in the specification of the 'effective judicial principle' case law in the field of public procurement. Advantage has not been taken of this opportunity. Given the far-reaching nature of the Court's case law, it is suggested that the Directive, due to the general, vague and compromised character of most of its provisions, which is further reflected in the national implementation measures adopted, will not have a substantial impact on enhancing the operation of decentralized control. No special incentives have been designed to encourage foreign bidders to perform their monitoring role. As data shows, this will not favour their active participation through the introduction of judicial complaints. Legal impact and practical impact will not necessarily go hand in hand.

Notwithstanding this, to hold that the Remedies Directive has no effect at the national level would be untrue. The Remedies Directive completes the supranational regulation of public procurement by adding procedural rules to the existing substantive provisions. Member States are now pre-empted from adopting conflicting legal rules in this area both in procedural and substantive terms. From a strict legal point of view, substantial changes in domestic redress systems have taken place at least in some Member States (Germany and the UK). Contractors and suppliers now enjoy (or will enjoy) subjective rights which may be enforced before national courts. In the UK and eventually in Germany, public contracting is no longer a purely internal administrative matter. The French general conception of public contracting and available remedies has been imposed (or will be imposed) on those Member States which previously approached public contracts from a private law perspective. One may wonder, however, whether these changes are merely formal and whether concrete, practical results will follow in the short term.

The Commission should have exploited the new paths opened by the case law of the Court of Justice in a more consistent manner and should have pressed national authorities to compromise and adopt a more far-reaching piece of legislation than the one finally adopted. Such an approach is not impossible in the future. The Commission may always go before the European Court and claim that the actual application by national enforcement agencies of the Directive's provisions fails to meet the intended 'effective' standard. Thus, an interpretation which combines both the case law and the spirit of the Directive may provide a basis for the Commission to specify and expand the realm of the Directive's provisions when it comes to their enforcement by national courts. The same road is open to the national courts. This possibility is rendered difficult, however, as the Directive provides for escape clauses, such as the public interest exemption, and fails to specify the conditions under which interim relief and damages should be awarded.

Article 4 of the Remedies Directive will also play an important role in this respect. No later than four years after the implementation of the Directive, the Commission, in consultation with the Advisory Committee for Public Contracts, must review the manner in which the provisions of the Directive have been implemented and, if necessary, make proposals for amendments. This will allow the Commission to assess the practical experience of national courts when applying the Directive's provisions and propose the pertinent modifications in order to correct and reinforce its practical effect. Stricter measures will probably be needed.

In brief, the opportunity to organize a more stringent enforcement system by means of a Community legislative act has been lost. As things stand, national judicial attitudes will determine the eventual success of the Directive. It is submitted that a change in attitude by national judges is not foreseeable in the near future, as national legal traditions and consistent jurisprudence are difficult to change.

From a strictly theoretical perspective, there is no such a thing as an enforcement problem. Complete enforcement can easily be ensured if sufficient resources, legal and material, are available for that purpose.[90] 'Complete enforcement is, [however] costly'.[91] Assuming resources are

---

[90] Resources are here taken to mean not only material resources, but also the costs involved in 'sacrificing' national sovereignty and domestic legal traditions for the purposes of improving the enforcement of supranational rules.

[91] Stigler, 'The Optimum Enforcement of Laws' (1970) 78 *Journal of Political Economics* 526 at 527.

scarce, the main question is, how much is society willing to spend for an enforcement mechanism directed towards the correction or prevention of particular types of infringements at a given moment? Society will normally give the enforcement agencies a budget which dictates a much lower level of enforcement than that which is required for complete enforcement.[92]

These theoretical considerations also apply to the enforcement of public procurement rules. If the Commission is attributed sufficient powers and staff, enforcement of public procurement would no longer be a problem. Equally, if high and automatic damages were available to victims for any infringements, even minor ones, complete enforcement would be close to being secured. However, is society ready to spend so many resources in guaranteeing complete enforcement of public procurement rules? In the Community system, society may be taken to mean Member States, as they ultimately decide how resources are allocated.[93] Any increase in the Commission's powers must flow from a general political consensus amongst the final decision-making organ, the Council. In the area of public procurement, Member States have proved quite reluctant to increase supranational enforcement mechanisms at the expense of national sovereignty and traditional legal approaches. The prior political consensus is lacking as Member States are not willing to attain effectiveness at no matter what cost.

The underlying dilemma is the conflict between the effectiveness of Community rules and the limitations arising from the supranational structure of the Community. The fragile equilibrium between national and Community interests is based on the existence of common objectives and on the mutual confidence between the centre and the constituent parts. The enlargement of the supervision powers intended by the Commission cannot solely be justified and brought into effect on the basis of the need for the effectiveness of public procurement rules, but only through shared political will.

On a more practical level, the potential success of decentralized control is dependent on the nature of the public procurement rules. As pointed out by some commentators, 'the amount of enforcement is ultimately determined by the rules to be enforced and the quality of enforcement'.[94] Apart from unavoidable difficulties relating to the supply of evidence, the position of national courts has not been improved by recent amendments. Even though the new information obligations imposed on contracting authorities with respect to both the Commission and participant firms will facilitate the provision of evidence by potential applicants, the fact

---

[92] Becker and Stigler, 'Law Enforcement, Malfeasance, and Compensation of Enforcers' (1974) 3 *The Journal of Legal Studies* 1 at 3.

[93] It is assumed that interested actors make their input in the Member States' decisions.

[94] Becker and Stigler (above, n 92) at 16.

remains that the award criteria are still loose. Judicial control may only be properly exerted in cases where flagrantly biased decisions are adopted or when clear and unconditional procedural rules are infringed. The ability of national courts to judge whether commercial reliance on the traditional contractor or supplier is an acceptable argument to exclude foreign firms from the award of the contract remains uncertain.

Further evidence of this is also provided by a detailed examination of the origin of individual complaints relating to breaches of public procurement rules received by the Commission.[95] Out of 83 complaints addressed to the Commission during the period 1985 to July 1991, 37 were made by nationals of the defaulting Member State, that is, more than 44 per cent. Only 29 complaints involved disappointed foreign tenderers (around 35 per cent). The origin of the rest was unreported. This data implies that direct complaints to the Commission have turned out to be a mechanism more often exploited by disappointed national tenderers than by foreign bidders, irrespective of the fact that Community legislation is intended to favour the latter.

The main breakthroughs have once again come from the Court of Justice through the 'active' performance of its role as the Constitutional Court of the Communities, when, in general, it acts unconstrained by the policy considerations of Member States. The compromise achieved in the Remedies Directive after two and a half years of negotiations, has been rendered largely redundant and outdated by the Court of Justice's case law on the effective judicial protection principle. Judicial activism of the Court of Justice is well noted in almost every field of Community law. One wonders, however, how much longer the Court may act irrespective of political consensus. The case of Germany is a good illustration of such a tension.

As we have attempted to demonstrate in the preceding pages, the type of infringements, their total number, the fact that they may occur all over the Community, the existing institutional structure of the Community and more particularly, the inherent economic, political and legal features of public procurement itself, greatly reduce the possibilities of achieving effective integration and judicial control as a result of supranational initiatives.

The Commission has, within the limits of its powers as developed in the Treaty, provided legal instruments (limited as they may be) and support to injured firms to improve their access to effective review and ensure restoration of their infringed rights. The European Court has also laid down the requirements for effective judicial protection. If the beneficiaries are

[95] Information on this point is only available in the Commission's database after 1985. More recent data was impossible to obtain from Commission services despite various efforts made by the author.

not willing to use the available means of redress at their disposition, this should no longer concern the Community institutions. If public procurement is to remain on the Commission's agenda in the coming years, other strategies more in accordance with the present limits of Community action and the peculiar features of public procurement need to be developed. However, this policy should be more selective than the one operating at present. Enforcement efforts originating at Community level should concentrate on ensuring that public contracts of European interest are open to competition.

Final Conclusions

THE FORMAL REVOLUTION, THE PRACTICAL IRRELEVANCE

From a legal point of view, the Directives adopted have brought about the establishment of an exhaustive supranational regulatory framework in the public procurement area. The declared intention of the Directives was not to establish a uniform and exhaustive set of rules, leaving Member States free to apply their own rules once they were adapted to the Directives. The truth is, however, that the detailed character of the rules, which has increased since 1985, and their binding legal nature, have resulted in a clear restriction of Member States' regulatory freedom in the area. Contracts subject to the Community rules have escaped national competence as regards the way in which they are awarded, the objectives sought by the award and, to a lesser extent, the remedies available against breaches of the rules. Moreover, since the applicable provisions must hereinafter be interpreted in the light of applicable Community law principles and the case law of the Court of Justice, it is likely that the 'autonomous character' of the supranational rules will be further consolidated in the future. It may, therefore, be safely concluded that the Community measures on public procurement have pre-empted national initiatives in the area and that future developments will come from the supranational rather than the national level.

At national level, the implementation of the Directives has caused a substantial modification in the legal situation of those Member States whose approach to public contracting differed most from the one followed by the supranational measures. Since the supranational measures have been greatly inspired by the French regulation, the consequence has been that previous divergent approaches have been harmonized on the basis of the Latin-continental treatment of public contracts. Member States which regulated public contracting from a private law perspective have been forced (or are being forced) to shift to a public or administrative law perspective in order to comply with their Community obligations. This has caused substantial hardship at the national level.

From a supranational perspective, the Community regulation of public contracts can be seen as an important step in the development of a Community system of administrative law.[1] National public authorities are

---

[1] Administrative law is here understood in its broadest sense, that is, those legal provisions which are specifically intended to regulate the behaviour of public authorities. Clearly, this European administrative law is not primary administrative law, that is, the rules governing the Community's own administrative system. This primary European administrative law is exhaustively analysed by Schwarze in his treatise on *European Administrative Law* (London, 1992).

bound, as regards a certain range of contracts, to respect the obligations and pursue the objectives enshrined in the Community rules. National rules are constrained to a secondary role. Although differences between the way in which the rules have been incorporated into national systems still exist, the fact remains that a certain degree of harmonization has been achieved. This will be further enhanced through the case law of the Court of Justice interpreting the provisions of the Directives.[2]

Although from a formal point of view the impact of the Community rules on public procurement has been substantial at domestic level, from a practical point of view a different story has to be told. The objectives sought by the Directives are far from being achieved. The reasons for this refer more to the misconceived policy adopted at the supranational level, than to the reluctance of Member States to abide by the rules. It is submitted that the Commission has failed to properly take into consideration the incidence of the market structure where the main public works and public supplies contracts covered operate and the economic characteristics of the latter. Since the Directives have been designed on the basis of assumptions which are partially wrong, the supranational legislative effort has been largely rendered irrelevant in practice. The modifications introduced after 1985 are not likely to resolve these insufficiencies. The new amending Directives are based on the strengthening of this previously misguided approach. If we put the legal and the practical conclusions together, one may wonder whether the effort in adopting the Community rules and the subsequent sacrifice of certain domestic approaches, together with the increment of formal cumbersome obligations on contracting authorities, are justified by the scarce impact which the Directives' provisions are likely to have in the future.

THE ALTERNATIVE APPROACHES. SUBSIDIARITY AND
SUPRANATIONAL REGULATION OF PUBLIC CONTRACTS

The subsidiarity principle enshrined in Article 3b of the EC Treaty is the object of great academic and political interest.[3] Article 3b states that:

---

[2] See in this context, Rivero 'Vers un droit commun européen: nouvelles perspectives en droit administratif' in Cappelletti (ed.) *New Perspectives for a Common Law of Europe* (London, 1978) 387 at 404.

[3] See EC Commission, *The Principle of Subsidiarity*, Communication to the Council and the European Parliament, reproduced in Europe, Documents, No. 1804/05, 30 October 1992. See also *inter alia* Constantinesco, 'Who's Afraid of Subsidiarity?' (1991) 11 YEL 33; Emiliou, 'Subsidiarity: an Effective Barrier against "the Enterprises of Ambition"?' (1992) 17 ELRev 383; Cass, 'The Word that Saves the Maastricht Treaty? The Principle of Subsidiarity and the Division of Powers within the European Community' (1992) 29 CMLRev 1107; Perissich, 'Le principe de subsidiarité, fil conducteur de la politique de la Communauté dans l'année à venir' (1992) *Revue du Marché Unique Européen* 5; Bribosia, 'Subsidiarité et répartition des compétences entre la Communauté et ses États membres' (1992) *Revue du Marché Unique*

In areas which do not fall within its exclusive competence, the Community shall take action, in accordance with the principle of subsidiarity, only if and in so far as the objectives of the proposed action cannot be sufficiently achieved by the Member States and can therefore, by reason of the scale or effects of the proposed action, be better achieved by the Community.

We shall not here enter the general debate on the general merits of the subsidiarity principle, its lack of specificity, its justiciability, or the difficulties surrounding its application in practice. In view of the conclusions reached as regards the ineffectiveness of the Community public procurement legislation, our aim is to explore, from a general point of view, how the principle of subsidiarity may apply to our topic.

Subsidiarity is meant to be the guiding principle governing the relationships between the supranational and the national levels and to provide the parameters according to which supranational action in the field of concurrent powers must be justified.[4] Taking into consideration the fact that the objectives of the principle of subsidiarity are to restrict Community action only to 'those policy powers which could clearly be done better or more effectively at the supranational level' and to avoid the over-interference of the Community at the domestic level,[5] subsidiarity can be interpreted as embodying the necessity of applying a cost-benefit analysis to any supranational action. This interpretation suggests that the subsidiarity principle should apply at two successive levels. Firstly, subsidiarity would justify Community action only where 'Member States are no longer capable of dealing with [certain matters] efficiently'.[6] This involves the application of the so-called comparative efficiency test.[7] Secondly, if the ultimate aim is to favour decentralized government action rather than unnecessary centralized intervention,[8] provided Community action is necessary, subsidiarity could

---

Européen 165; Mattera, Bangemann, Mertens de Wilmars, Mattina, Ehlermann, Gazzo and Constantinesco, 'Le principe de subsidiarité au service d'une Communauté à la dimension des problèmes de notre temps' (1992) *Revue du Marché Unique Européen* 189; Brittan, 'Subsidiarity in the Constitution of the European Communities', Robert Schuman Lecture, European University Institute, Florence, June 1992. See, in particular, the interesting view of Toth, 'The Principle of Subsidiarity in the Maastricht Treaty' (1992) 29 CMLRev 1079 and, for our present purposes, Wilke and Wallace, 'Subsidiarity Approaches to Power Sharing in the European Community' (1990) *RIIA Discussion Paper* No. 27.

[4] For a critical view of the way in which the question of concurrent powers is dealt with in Article 3b, see Toth (above, n 3).

[5] Dahrendorf, 'A Third Europe', Jean Monnet Lecture, EUI, Florence, 26 November 1979, as summarized by Wilke and Wallace (above, n 3) at 26.

[6] EC Commission, *Report on European Union* (1975) EC Bulletin, Supplement 5/75.

[7] In its Communication on the principle of subsidiarity the Commission stated that Article 3b 'implies that we have to examine if there are other methods available for Member States . . . in order to achieve the objectives in a sufficient manner. This is the test of comparative efficiency between Community action and that of Member States'. EC Commission, (1992) (above, n 3) at 2.

[8] For a discussion of the principle of subsidiarity as a limit to central government action justified on the presumption in favour of individual liberty, see Emiliou (above, n 3) 385–388.

be interpreted as limiting the scope of any supranational measure to that which is justified on a cost-benefit analysis.[9] A cost-benefit analysis is here understood as the process by which policy makers '.determining the social goals to be achieved, identifying and assessing accurately and comprehensively the benefits and costs of proposed agency action, accounting for who will benefit by each option in a detailed manner and by whom the costs of each will be borne, and providing an exposition of alternatives detailing the foregoing information' choose 'among several possible actions (including non-action)'.[10] The notion of costs not only refers to economic costs but also includes social and political costs, in particular, the loss of sovereignty involved and the lesser degree of democratic accountability of supranational action.[11]

In the public procurement area, it is submitted that subsidiarity may be interpreted as at the same time expanding and restricting the scope of measures that the Community may pursue. From a positive perspective, the 'comparative efficiency test' implies that the Community should legitimately assume the responsibility for the regulation of those sectors where national public procurement practices are hindering the development of competitive European industry. In Chapter 5 we have argued that as regards public supplies contracts, these sectors are those where public intervention is greater, the market in which competition takes place is a world market, European industry faces increasing competitive pressures from third countries and where national markets are in themselves insufficient to guarantee recovery of the investments needed to remain competitive. With respect to public works contracts, the Community is better positioned to co-ordinate the development of large national infrastructure projects in the context of an overall European policy. In brief, according to the principle of subsidiarity, Community action should concentrate

[9] In this sense see the Padoa-Schioppa Report, *Efficiency, Stability and Equity, a Strategy for the Evolution of the Economic System of the EC* (Oxford, 1987), cited by Wilke and Wallace (above, n 3) at 29. The Commission has stated that '. . . if it were concluded that a proposal passes the test of comparative efficiency, it would still be necessary to respond to the question, what should be the intensity and the nature of the Community action? This recalls the principle of proportionality . . . It is necessary to examine carefully if an intervention by legislative means is necessary or if other means which are sufficiently effective can be used. If it is necessary to legislate the Commission will as far as possible favour framework legislation, minimum norms and mutual recognition and more generally avoid a too detailed legislative prescription.'. EC Commission (1992) (above, n 3) at 2.

[10] 'Project: the Impact of Cost-Benefit Analysis on Federal Administrative Law' (1990) 42 *Administrative Law Review* 545 at 552.

[11] Greenwood defends the need to apply a serious cost-benefit analysis to European initiatives in the defence procurement sector. He argues that this analysis should not be limited only to economic efficiency criteria but must also take into account social policy and political considerations which apply at national level. According to him, this is the only way in which a realistic supranational policy with some prospects of success may be designed. Greenwood, 'Collaborative arms acquisitions in Western Europe, inhibitions and constraints' in Edmonds (ed.), *International Arms Procurement* (1981, New York) at Chapter 5.

on the liberalization of what we have defined as contracts of European interest. The supranational level is undoubtedly better equipped to define an overall policy in these sectors. The scope of these policies should subsequently be justified on a cost-benefit analysis and be therefore limited to what is strictly necessary to produce the maximum benefits at the minimum costs.

From a negative perspective, the current policy followed as regards the main public works and public supplies contracts may not comply with the requirements of the subsidiarity principle as interpreted above. We have suggested in Chapter 5 that a comprehensive cost-benefit analysis was lacking when the Commission designed its initial policy. This policy has not been altered by recent modifications of the Directives. After the examination of the economic structure of the markets where the Directives operated, this book has contended that the Commission's assumptions justifying its legal policy have been misled. Too many resources have been spent in seeking an objective which may not be attainable in practice. This has moreover caused substantial modifications of national regulations. If subsidiarity is interpreted from this second perspective, it is submitted that a more selective policy should be applied in the future. The main guidelines of this alternative policy are those explained above. On this basis, Member States could well argue that the modifications which their domestic regulations have suffered as a result of the Community public procurement rules will not bring the benefits expected. The 'intensity and the nature' of the Community's action is not justified by the overall gains. From the perspective of subsidiarity, the Community public procurement policy should be revisited. The 1996 Intergovernmental Conference is a good opportunity to address these issues and to identify those areas where Community involvement has so far been disproportionate and ineffective. Alternative policies should then be discussed.

With respect to the enforcement activities of the Commission, Chapter 6 has shown that the Commission's centralized enforcement efforts are ineffective. The application of the subsidiarity rationale demands a more selective centralized enforcement policy than the one applied by the Commission so far. The monitoring powers of the Commission should be directed to contracts of European interest, rather than focus on minor infringements. Nonetheless, we have also noted that although the main policy as regards centralized enforcement has not been modified, a more rational approach is now followed as the emphasis is placed on the enhancement of decentralized control. Due to the nature of the breaches committed, decentralized control is the most efficient way to monitor contracting authorities' activities. However, the Remedies Directive's provisions fall short of constituting a breakthrough in the search for better decentralized enforcement as it barely provides any incentives to injured undertakings. Following the analysis of the national implementation measures adopted, it has been concluded that, although the situation has formally changed in some Member States, no radical improvements may be expected in the medium term in the attitudes of national courts. Furthermore, it is submitted that since intra-Community bidding is not likely to increase in a substantial manner, complaints before national courts against breaches of Community rules will in any event remain exceptional.

Finally, on a political reading of the subsidiarity principle and after examining the political and economic connotations of public procurement, we have argued that the general policy of the Community may be excessively rigid and, arguably, illegitimate. Member States should be entitled to apply economic and social policies through the instrumental use of public contracting and any conflicts arising between the supranational and national levels should be resolved by means of political bargaining. This is particularly the case since the available supranational mechanisms which may substitute current national policies are insufficient. If the subsidiarity principle is applied in this context, Member States should be allowed to offset the negative regional, social and economic impact which the integration of the market will have on their economies until supranational measures have been agreed. In this vein, political responsibility for the immediate welfare of national citizens has not been transferred to the Community level but remains in the hands of national governments.[12] Member States should retain the means for the resolution of the economic, social and regional problems which affect their national populations until adequate substitute mechanisms are developed.

---

[12] On the concept of subsidiarity from a political theory perspective, see Wilke and Wallace (above, n 3) at 15 *ff*; Emiliou (above, n 3) at 385–388.

Bibliography

Amselek, 'La qualification des contrats de l'administration par la jurisprudence' (1983) *Actualité Juridique-Droit Administratif* 3.

Anderson, 'Inadequate Implementation of EEC Directives. A Roadblock to 1992' (1988) 11 *Boston College of International and Comparative Law Review* 91.

Ariño Ortiz, 'El concepto de contrato público en la CEE' (1986) No. 21 *Noticias CEE* 19.

Armin Trepte, 'Completion of the Internal Market for Procurement: The New Directives on Works, Supplies and Utilities' (1993) 2 PPLR CS118.

Armin Trepte, 'Extension of the European Community public procurement regime to public service contracts: an overview of the services Directive' (1993) 2 PPLR 1.

Armin Trepte, *Public Procurement in the EC* (London, 1993).

Armin Trepte, 'Remedies in the Utilities Sector. The European Dimension and Application in the UK', paper presented to the conference on *Implementing and Enforcing the EC Public Procurement Directives*, Birmingham, April 1993.

Armin Trepte, 'The GATT GPA and the Community Procurement Rules: Realignment and Modification' (1995) 4 PPLR CS 42.

Arnull, 'The Direct Effect of Directives: Grasping the Nettle' (1986) 35 ICLQ 939.

Arrowsmith and Fernández Martín, 'Developments in Public Procurement in 1992' (1993) 18 ELRev 323.

Arrowsmith and Fernández Martín, note on Case 362/90, *Commission* v. *Italy* (1993) 2 PPLR CS 2.

Arrowsmith, *A Guide to the Procurement Cases of the Court of Justice* (Winteringham, 1992).

Arrowsmith, 'Abolition of the UK's Procurement Preference Scheme for Disabled Workers' (1994) 3 PPLR CS 225.

Arrowsmith, 'Actions to Enforce the Community Procurement Rules in France: Decree no. 92–964 of 7 September 1992' (1993) 2 PPLR CS 12.

Arrowsmith, *Civil Liability and Public Authorities* (Winteringham, 1992).

Arrowsmith, 'Developments in Compulsory Competitive Tendering' (1994) 3 PPLR CS 153.

Arrowsmith, 'Enforcing the EC Public Procurement Rules: the Remedies System in England and Wales' (1992) 1 PPLR 92.

Arrowsmith, 'Enforcing the Public Procurement Rules: Legal Remedies in the Court of Justice and the National Courts' in Arrowsmith (ed.), *Remedies for Enforcing the Public Procurement Rules* (Winteringham, 1993).

Arrowsmith, 'Government Contracts and Public Law' (1990) *Legal Studies* 231.

Arrowsmith, 'Implementation of the Public Procurement Directives in the 12 States of the EC (part I)' (1992) 1 PPLR 174.

Arrowsmith, 'Judicial Review and the Contractual Powers of Public Authorities' (1990) 106 LQR 227.

Arrowsmith, 'Public Procurement as an Instrument of Policy and the Impact of Market Liberalisation' (1995) 111 LQR 235.

Arrowsmith, 'The Public Supplies Contracts Regulations 1995' (1995) 4 PPLR CS 59.

Auby and Bronner, 'L'Europe des marchés publics' (1990) *Actualité Juridique—Droit Administratif* 258.

Auby and Drago, *Traité du Contentieux Administratif* (Paris, 1984).

Audretsch, *Supervision in European Community Law*, 2nd edn. (Amsterdam, 1986).

Badura, 'Wirtschaftverwaltungsrecht' in Von Münch (ed.), *Besonderes Verwaltungsrecht*, 8th edn., 1988.

Baldwin, *Non-Tariff Distortions of International Trade* (Washington DC, 1970).

Baldwin, 'Preferential Government Purchasing Policies' in Jones and Kenen (eds.), *Handbook of International Economics* (Amsterdam, 1987) 602.

Baldwin, R., 'Why Rules Don't Work' (1990) 53 MLR 321.

Barav, 'Damages against the State for Failure to Implement European Community Directives' (1991) *New Law Journal* 1584.

Barav, 'Enforcement of Community Rights in the National Courts: the Case for Jurisdiction to Grant Interim Relief' (1989) 26 CMLRev 369.

Barav, 'La répétition de l'indu dans la jurisprudence de la Cour de Justice des Communautés européennes' (1981) 17 CDE 507.

Barav and Green, 'Damages in the National Courts for Breach of Community Law' (1986) 6 YEL 55.

Barav and Simon, 'Le droit communautaire et la suspension provisoire des mesures nationales. Les enjeux de l'affaire Factortame' (1990) RMC 591.

Barnard, 'A Social Policy for Europe: Politicians 1; Lawyers 0' (1992) *International Journal of Comparative Labour Law and Industrial Relations* 15.

Barnes, Campbell and Pepper, 'Local Authorities, Public Procurement and 1992' (1992) *Local Government Studies* 10.

Barton, 'Damages in Administrative Law' in Taggart (ed.), *Judicial Review of Administrative Action in the 1990s* (Oxford, 1986).

Batley, 'Allocation of Government Contracts in Peru and Venezuela' in Ghai, Luckham and Snyder (eds.), *The Political Economy of the Law. A Third World Reader* (Oxford, 1987).

Beaumont and Weatherill, *EC Law* 2nd edn. (London, 1995).

Bebr, note of Joined Cases C-6/90 and C-9/90, *Francovich* and *Bonifaci* v. *Italy* (1992) 29 CMLRev 557.

Bebr, 'Remedies for Breach of Community Law' in (1980) FIDE Reports (London, 1980).

Becker and Stigler, 'Law Enforcement, Malfeasance and Compensation to Enforcers' (1974) 3 *Journal of Legal Studies* 1.

Becker, 'Crime and Punishment: an Economic Approach' (1968) 76 *The Journal of Political Economy* 169.

Benazet, 'Marchés publics de travaux et Traité de Rome' (1963) *Revue Internationale des Sciences Administratives* 235.

Bennett and Cirrell, *Compulsory Competitive Tendering: Law and Practice* (London, 1990).

Bennett and Cirrell, 'The Interrelationship of European Community Public Procurement and Compulsory Competitive Tendering in the United Kingdom' (1992) 1 PPLR 280.

Bennett and Cirrell, 'The Local Government Act 1992: New Developments in Compulsory Competitive Tendering' (1992) 1 PPLR 242.

Bieber, Dehousse, Pinder and Weiler, (eds.), *1992: One European Market? A Critical Analysis of the Commission's Internal Market Strategy* (Baden-Baden, 1988).

Bieri, 'La politique des commandes publiques de l'État fédéral suisse' (1984) 72 *Annales de l'Économie Publique, Sociale et Coopérative* 183.

Birkinshaw, 'British Report to the 14th FIDE Conference' in FIDE *L'Application dans les États Membres des Directives sur les Marchés Publics* (Madrid, 1990).

Blasco Esteve, 'La responsibilidad de la administración por daños causados por actos administrativos: doctrina jurisprudencial' (1980) RAP 206.

Blyth, 'Government Procurement in the UK' (1987) 21 *George Washington Journal of International Law & Economics* 127.

Boquera Oliver, 'Insusceptibilidad de la suspensión de la eficacia del acto administrativo' (1994) RAP 37.

Borchardt, 'The Award of Interim Measures by the European Court of Justice' (1985) 22 CMLRev 203.

Bosco, 'Commentaire de l'Acte Unique Européen' (1987) 23 RTDE 377.

Boulois and Chevalier, *Grands Arrêts de la Cour de Justice des Communautés Européennes*, Tome I.

Bourcier de Carbon, 'Les marchés publics dans l'économie française' (1961) *Revue Administrative* 435.

Boyle, 'Regulated Procurement—A Purchaser's Perspective' (1995) 4 PPLR 105.

Bréchon-Moulènes (ed.), *Réglementation et Pratique des Marchés Publics* (Paris, 1985).

Bréchon-Moulènes, '1988, année "marchés publics"?' (1988) *Revue Française d'Administration Publique* 591.

Bréchon-Moulènes, 'French Report to the 14th FIDE Conference' in FIDE, *L'Application dans les États Membres des Directives sur les Marchés Publics* (Madrid, 1990).

Bréchon-Moulènes, 'L'échec des directives travaux et fournitures de 1971 et 1976' (1988) *Revue Française d'Administration Publique* 753.

Bribosia, 'Subsidiarité et répartition des compétences entre la Communauté et ses États membres' (1992) *Revue du Marché Unique Européen* 165.

Bridge, 'Procedural Aspects of the Enforcement of European Community Law through the Legal Systems of the Member States' (1984) 9 ELRev 28.

British Department of Trade and Industry, 'Public Procurement Review' (London, 1994).

Brittan, 'Subsidiarity in the Constitution of the European Communities', *Robert Schumann Lecture*, European University Institute, Florence, June 1992.

Bronckers, 'Private Enforcement of 1992: Do Trade and Industry Stand a Chance against Member States?' (1989) 26 CMLRev 513.

Brothwood, 'The Commission Directive on Transparency of Financial Relations between Member States and Public Undertakings' (1981) 18 CMLRev 207.

Brown, 'Case C-392/93: Reference to the Court of Justice concerning United Kingdom Implementation of the Utilities Directive in the Field of Telecommunications' (1994) 3 PPLR CS 30.

Brown, 'The Extension of Community Public Procurement Rules to Utilities' (1993) 30 CMLRev 721.

Bruetschy, 'L'ouverture des marchés publics à la concurrence communautaire' (1989) RMC 593.

Cane, *An Introduction to Administrative Law* 2nd edn. (Oxford, 1992).

Capotorti, 'La problématique des directives et règlements et de leur mise en œuvre' in Siedentopf & Ziller (eds.), *L'Europe des Administrations? La Mise en Œuvre de la Législation Communautaire dans les États Membres*, Vol. 1 (Maastricht, 1988).

Capotorti, Hilf, Jacqué and Jacobs, *Le Traité d'Union Européenne* (Bruxelles, 1985).

Cappelletti, Seccombe and Weiler (eds.), *Integration Through Law. Political Organs, Integration Techniques and Judicial Process*, Vol. 1 Book 2 (Berlin, 1986).

Capper, 'Obstacles to Free Competition for Public Works Contracts. An English View', paper presented to the Conference on *Implementing and Enforcing the European Community Procurement Directives*, Birmingham, April 1993.

Cartou, (1960) *Energies* no. 304, 2.

Cartou, 'Les marchés publics dans la Communauté Économique Européenne' in *Mélanges Dédiés à Gabriel Marty* (Toulouse, 1979).

Cass, 'The Word that Saves Maastricht? The Principle of Subsidiarity and the Division of Powers in the European Community' (1992) 29 CMLRev 1107.

Chapus, *Droit du Contentieux Administratif*, 3ème edn. (Paris, 1991).

Charpentier and Clark, 'Public Purchasing in the Common Market' (Brussels, 1974).

Cherot, 'La transposition en France de la Directive 89/440 C.E.E. du juillet 18 1989 portant coordination des procédures de passation des marchés publics de travaux' (1991) 16 *Revue de la Recherche Juridique* 981.

Chinchilla Marín, 'El derecho a la tutela judicial cautelar como garantía de la efectividad de las resoluciones judiciales' (1993) RAP 167.

Clarke and Pitelis (eds.) *The Political Economy of Privatisation* (London, 1993).

Cleesattel, 'Government Procurement in the Federal Republic of Germany' (1987) 21 *George Washington Journal of International Law and Economics* 59.

Clouet, 'Travaux publics et marché commun' (1969) RMC 83.

Coleman and Margue, 'L'action de la Communauté visant le respect des règles communautaires en matière de passation des marchés publics de fournitures et de travaux: problèmes et perspectives' (1989) RMC 546.

Constantinesco, 'L'article 5 CEE: de la bonne foi à la loyauté communautaire' in Capotorti and others (eds.), *Du Droit International au Droit de l'Intégration: Liber Amicorum Pierre Pescatore* (Baden-Baden, 1987).

Constantinesco, 'La coordination des procédures de passation des marchés publics de travaux. Directive du Conseil du 18 juillet 1989 modifiant la directive 71/305/CEE' (1989) RMC 597.

Constantinesco, 'Who's Afraid of Subsidiarity?' (1991) 11 YEL 33.

Cooper, 'Pre-Conditions for the Emergence of a European Common Market in Armaments' (1983) *Centre for European Policy Studies*, no. 18.

Couchez, *Procédure Civile*, 6ème edn. (Paris, 1990).

Cox, 'Implementing 1992 Public Procurement Policy: Public and Private Obstacles to the Creation of the Single European Market' (1992) 1 PPLR 139.

Craig, *Administrative Law* 3rd edn. (London, 1994).

Craig, 'Sovereignty of the United Kingdom after *Factortame*' (1991) 11 YEL 221.

Croxford, Wise and Chalkley, 'The Reform of the European Regional Development Fund' (1987) 26 JCMS 25.

Curtin, 'Directives: The Effectiveness of Judicial Protection of Individual Rights' (1990) 27 CMLRev 707. Reprinted in Snyder (ed.), *European Community Law*, Vol. I (Aldershot, 1993).

Curtin, note on Case C-271/91, *M.H. Marshall* v. *Southampton and South-West Hampshire Area Health Authority* (1994) 31 CMLRev 653.

Curtin, 'State Liability under Community Law: a New Remedy for Private Parties' (1992) 21 *Industrial Law Journal* 74.

Curtin, 'The Decentralised Enforcement of Community Law Rights. Judicial Snakes and Ladders' in O'Keefe and Curtin (eds.), *Constitutional Adjudication in European Community and National Law* (London, 1992).

Curtin, 'The Province of Government: Delimiting the Direct Effect of Directives in the Common Law Context' (1990) 15 ELRev 195.

D'Hooghe & others, 'Implementation of the Public Procurement Directives in the 12 States of the EC (Parts I and II)' (1992) 1 PPLR 167.

D'Hooghe, 'Enforcing the Public Procurement Rules in Belgium' in Arrowsmith (ed.), *Remedies for Enforcing the Public Procurement Rules* (Winteringham, 1993).

Dahrendorf, 'A Third Europe', *Jean Monnet Lecture*, EUI, Florence, 26 November 1979.

Daintith, 'Law as a Policy Instrument' in Daintith (ed.), *Law as an Instrument of Economic Policy: Comparative and Critical Approaches* (Berlin, 1988).

Daintith, 'Regulation by Contract: the New Prerogative' (1979) 32 *Current Legal Problems* 41.

Daintith, 'The Executive Power Today: Bargaining and Economic Control' in Jowell and Oliver (eds.), *The Changing Constitution* (Oxford, 1985).

Dal Farra, 'L'invocabilité des directives communautaires devant le juge national de la légalité' (1992) 28 RTDE 634.

Dashwood and White, 'Enforcement Actions under Articles 169 and 170 EEC' (1989) 14 ELRev 388.

Dashwood, 'Preliminary Rulings on the EEC State Aid Provisions' (1977) 2 ELRev 367.

Davenport, 'Obligation to Consider Tenders' (1991) 107 LQR 201.

De Burca, 'Giving Effect to European Community Directives' (1992) 55 MLR 215.

De Graaf, 'Community Law: Latest Developments' (1992) 1 PPLR 317.

De Smith, *Judicial Review of Administrative Action*, 4th edn. by Evans (London, 1980).

Dillemann, 'Les commandes publiques. Stratégies et politiques' (1977) *Notes et Études. La Documentation Française*.

Diver, 'The Judge as Political Powerbroker: Superintending Structural Change in Public Institutions' (1979) 65 *Virginia Law Review* 43.

Dony-Bartholmé, 'La notion d'aides d'État' (1993) 29 CDE 399.

Drago, 'Le champ d'application du Code' in Bréchon-Moulènes (ed.), *Réglementation et Pratique des Marchés Publiques* (Paris, 1985).

Drago, 'Les incidences communautaires sur le droit des marchés publics et des marchés des entreprises publics' in Rideau and others (eds.), *La France et les Communautés Européennes* (Paris, 1974).

Dubois, 'À propos de deux principes généraux du droit communautaire' (1988) *Revue Française de Droit Administratif* 691.

Duffy, 'Damages Against the State: a New Remedy for Failure to Implement Community Obligations' (1992) 17 ELRev 133.

Duguit, *Leçons de Droit Public Général* (Paris, 1926).

Easson, 'Can Directives Impose Obligations on Individuals?' (1979) 4 ELRev 67.

EC Commission, *From the Single Act to Maastricht and Beyond: The Means to Match our Ambitions*, COM (92) 2000.

EC Commission, Advisory Committee on the Opening up of Public Procurement, *Extracts from the Analysis of Controls on Compliance with the Rules Concerning Public Procurement in the Member States*, CCO/88/73.

EC Commission, *Communication from the Commission on a Community Regime for Public Procurement in the Excluded Sectors: Water, Energy, Transport and Telecommunications*, COM (88) 376.

EC Commission, *Communication on Transport Infrastructure*, COM (92) 231.

EC Commission, *Competitiveness and Cohesion: Regional Trends. Fifth Periodical Report on the Socio-Economic Situation and Evolution of the Regions in the Community* (Luxembourg, 1995).

EC Commission, *Completing the Internal Market*, COM (85) 310.

EC Commission, *Europe 2000: Outlook for the Development of the Community's Territory*, COM (91) 452.

EC Commission, *Guide to the Community Rules on Open Procurement*, OJ 1987, C358/19.

EC Commission, *Memorandum on Technological and Industrial Policy Programme* (Bruxelles, 1973).

EC Commission, *Public Procurement—Regional and Social Aspects, Communication from the Commission*, COM (89) 400.

EC Commission, *Public Procurement in the Community, Communication of the Commission to the Council*, COM (86) 375.

EC Commission, *Public Supply Contracts. Conclusions and Perspectives*, Communication by the Commission to the Council, COM (84) 717.

EC Commission, *Report on the European Union* (1975) EC Bull., Suppl. 5/75.

EC Commission, *Report on the Progress made in Achieving the 1992 Internal Market*, COM (88) 650.

EC Commission, 'Report to the 14th FIDE Conference' in FIDE *L'Application dans les États Membres des Directives sur les Marchés Publics* (Madrid, 1990).

EC Commission, *The Community's Finances Between Now and 1997*, COM (92) 2001, and in the document *Community Structural Policies—Assessment and Outlook*, COM (92) 84.

EC Commission, 'The Cost of Non-Europe in the Public Procurement Sector' in *Cost of Non-Europe*, Basic Findings Vols. 5/a and 5/b, Study carried out by WS Atkins Management Consultants (Luxembourg, 1988).

EC Commission, *The Large Market of 1993 and the Opening up of Public Procurement* (Bruxelles, 1990).

EC Commission, *The Principle of Subsidiarity*, Communication to the Council and the European Parliament, reproduced in Europe, Documents, No. 1804/05, 30 October 1992.

ECOSOC, *Opinion on the Communication by the Commission to the Council: Public Supply Contracts—Conclusions and Perspectives*, ESC (86) 399.

Ehlermann, 'The Internal Market Following the Single European Act' (1987) 23 CMLRev 361.

Emerson and others, *The Economics of 1992. The EC Commission's Assessment of the Economic Effects of Completing the Internal Market* (Oxford, 1988).

Emiliou, Sharpston and Snyder, 'European Community Law' in Pettett (ed.) (1992) 45 *Current Legal Problems* (Annual Review) 49.

Emiliou, 'Subsidiarity: an Effective Barrier against "the Enterprises of Ambition"?' (1992) 17 ELRev 383.

European Parliament, *Report on the Communication by the Commission to the Council (COM (84) 717 final) on Public Supply Contracts—Conclusions and Perspectives*, DOC. A2–38/85.

Evans and Martin, 'Socially Acceptable Distortion of Competition: Community Policy on State aid' (1991) 16 ELRev 79.

Evans, 'The Enforcement Procedure of Article 169 EEC: Commission Discretion' (1979) 4 ELRev 440.

Federal German Statistical Office, *Der regionale Wirkungsbereich der Beträge im Bauhauptgewerbe* (Wiesbaden, 1980).

Fernández Martín, 'A Critical Analysis of EC Public Procurement Legislation. Present Limitations and Future Prospects' PhD. Thesis (Florence, 1993).

Fernández Martín, note on Case 24/91, *Commission* v. *Kingdom of Spain* (1992) 1 PPLR 320.

Fernández Martín, 'El efecto directo de las directivas y la protección de los derechos subjetivos comunitarios en la jurisprudencia del Tribunal de Justicia. Intento de Sistematización' forthcoming (1995) No. 126 *Noticias de la Unión Europea* 1.

Fernández Martín, note on Case C-272/91 [1994] ECR I-1409 (1994) 3 PPLR CS 211.

Fernández Martín, note on Case C-359/93, *Commission* v. *The Netherlands* judgment of 24 January 1995, not yet reported (1995) 4 PPLR CS 74.

Fernández Martín, note on Case C-71/92, *Commission* v. *Spain* (1994) 3 PPLR CS 73.

Fernández Martín, 'Remedies for Enforcing the Community rules on Public Procurement: the Situation in Spain' (1992) 1 PPLR 119.

Fernández Martín, 'The European Commission's Centralised Enforcement of Public Procurement Rules: a Critical View' (1993) 2 PPLR 40.

Fernández Martín, 'Enforcing the Public Procurement Rules in Spain' in Arrowsmith (ed.), *Remedies for Enforcing the Public Procurement Rules* (Winteringham, 1993).

Fernández Martín and O'Leary, 'An Analysis of Judicial Exemptions to the Free Provision of Services' (1995) 1 *European Law Journal.*

Fernández Martín and Pellicer Zamora, 'Las ofertas anormalmente bajas en la contratación pública' (1990) *Gaceta Jurídica de la CEE, serie B,* num. 78, 3.

Fernández Martín and Stehmann, 'Product Market Integration versus Regional Cohesion in the Community' (1991) 16 ELRev 216. Reprinted in Snyder (ed.), *European Community Law,* Vol. II, The International Library of Essays in Law and Legal Theory (Aldershot, 1993).

Fernández Pastrana, 'Orientación antiformalista de la jurisprudencia en el agotamiento de la via administrativa previa' (1990) RAP 259.

FIDE, *Remedies for Breaches of Community Law* (London, 1980).

Finsinger, 'Non-Competitive and Protectionist Government Purchasing Behaviour' (1988) 32 *European Economic Review* 69.

Fiorio, 'Spesa pubblica investimenti nella CEE a apertura dei mercati indotti dalle pubbliche amministrazioni' in Lezione tenuta presso il *Centro Alti Studi Europei dell'Universita di Urbino*, 3 May 1989.

Fischbein, 'Participation of SMUs in EC Government Contracts. Problems in Practice' (1992) 2 *EC Public Contract Law* 203.

Flamme, M. and Flamme, P., 'La réglementation communautaire en matière des marchés publics. Le point sur le contentieux' (1993) *Revue du Marché Unique Européen* 13 at 19 *ff.*

Flamme, M. and Flamme, P., 'Enfin l'Europe des marchés publics. La nouvelle directive travaux' (1989) *Actualité Juridique—Droit Administratif* 651.

Flamme, M. and Flamme, P., 'La panoplie des directives 'marchés publics' se complète: les secteurs hiers exclus (eau, énergie, transport et télécommunications) ne le seront plus demain (analyse de la directive 90/531 du 17 septembre 1990)' (1990) RMC 346.

Flamme, M. and Flamme, P., 'Le droit européen des commandes publiques: après leur réglementation, voici les recours' (1990) *Journal des Tribunaux* 317.

Flamme, M. and Flamme, P., 'Vers l'Europe des marchés publics? (à propos de la directive 'fournitures' du 22 mars 1988)' (1988) RMC 455.

Flamme, M., 'La libéralisation de la concurrence dans les marchés publics au sein de la CEE' (1965) RMC 277.

Flamme, M., *Traité Théorique et Pratique des Marchés Publics* (Brussels, 1969).

Flory, 'Les marchés des fournitures et les accords du GATT' (1989) RMC 694.

Flynn, 'State Aids: Recent Case-Law of the Court of Justice' (1987) 18 CMLRev 124.

Fortshoff, *Traité de Droit Administratif Allemand*, 9ème edn., translation by Fromont, (Bruxelles, 1969).

Frazer, 'The New Structural Funds, State Aids and Interventions on the Single Market' (1995) 25 ELRev 3.

Fromont, 'La protection provisoire des particuliers contre les décisions administratives dans les États membres des Communautés européennes' (1984) *Revue Internationale des Sciences Administratives* 309.

Gaja, Hay and Rotunda, 'Instruments for Legal Integration in the European Communities: a Review' in Cappelletti, Seccombe and Weiler (eds.), *Integration Through Law*, Vol. 1 Book 2 (Berlin, 1986).

Galimot and Bonichot, 'La Cour de Justice des Communautés Européennes et la transposition des directives en droit national' (1988) *Revue Française de Droit Administratif* 1.

García de Enterría and Fernández, *Curso de Derecho Administrativo*, 3rd edn. (Madrid, 1981).

García de Enterría, 'El problema de los poderes del juez nacional para suspender cautelarmente la ejecución de las Leyes nacionales en consideración al Derecho Comunitario Europeo' (1989) REDA 411.

García de Enterría, 'La sentencia Factortame (19 de junio de 1990) del Tribunal de Justicia de las Comunidades Europeas. La obligación del juez nacional de tutelar cautelarmente la eficacia del Derecho Comunitario aun a costa de su proprio Derecho nacional. Trascendencia general de la Sentencia en el Derecho Comunitario y en el sistema español de medidas cautelares' (1990) REDA 401.

García de Enterría, 'Novedades sobre los procesos en el conflicto de pesca anglo-espanol' (1989) REDA 593.

García de Enterría, 'Un punto de vista sobre la nueva Ley de Régimen Jurídico de las Administraciones Públicas y de Procedimiento Administrativo Común' (1993) RAP 205.

García Trevijano, 'Contratos y actos ante el tribunal Supremo. La explotación del "Hotel Andalucia Palace" de Sevilla' (1959) RAP 147.

Garrido Falla, 'La responsibilidad patrimonial del estado' in *Estudios sobre la Constitución Española. Libro homenaje al Professor García de Enterría* (Madrid, 1991).

Garrido Falla, *Tratado de Derecho Administrativo*, vol. II, 9ª edn. (Madrid, 1989).

Geroski, 'Public Procurement as an Industrial Policy Tool' (1990) 2 *International Review of Applied Economies.*

Gilliams, 'Effectiveness of European Community Public Procurement Law after Francovich' (1992) 1 PPLR 292.

Glazener and others, 'Dutch report to the 14th FIDE Conference' in FIDE *L'Application dans les États Membres des Directives sur les Marchés Publics* (Madrid, 1990).

Goldman, 'An Introduction to the French Law of Government Procurement Contracts' (1987) 21 *George Washington Journal of International Law and Economics* 461.

Goodman and Saunders, 'US Federal Regulation of Foreign Involvement in Aviation. Government Procurement and National Security' (1985) *Journal of World Trade* 54.

Gordon, *Judicial Review: Law and Procedure* (London, 1985).

Gormley, 'Grandfather Clauses in Community Law' (1989) 14 ELRev 157.

Gormley, note on Case 76/81, *SA Transporoute et Travaux* v. *Minister of Public Works* [1982] ECR 417, (1983) *New Law Journal* 533.

Gormley, 'Remedies and Compliance' in Meredith (ed.), *European Initiatives in Public Procurement* (New York, 1990).

Gormley, 'Some Reflections on Public Procurement in the European Community' (1990) 1 *European Business Law Review* 63.

Gormley, 'The New System of Remedies in Procurement by the Utilities' (1992) 1 PPLR 259.

Gravells, 'Effective Protection of Community Law Rights: Temporary Disapplication of an Act of Parliament' (1991) *Public Law* 180.

Greenwood, 'Collaborative Arms Acquisitions in Western Europe, Inhibitions and Constraints' in Edmonds (ed.), *International Arms Procurement* (New York, 1981).

Grimes, 'Conflicts betweeen EC Law and International Treaty Obligations: A case Study of the German Telecommunications Dispute' (1994) 35 *Harvard Intenational Law Journal* 535.

Gyselen, 'La transparence en matière d'aides d'État: les droits des tiers' (1993) 29 CDE 417.

Gyselen, 'State Action and the Effectiveness of the EEC Treaty's Competition Provisions' (1989) 26 CMLRev 33.

Habermas, *Legitimation Crisis* (London, 1976).

Hainaut and Joliet, *Les Contrats de Travaux et de Fournitures de l'Administration* (Bruxelles, 1963).

Harlow, 'Public Law and Private Law: Definition without Distinction' (1980) 43 MLR 241.

Hartley and Uttley, 'The Single European Market and Public Procurement Policy: The Case of the United Kingdom' (1994) 3 PPLR 114.

Hartley, 'Public Procurement and Competitiveness: a Community Market for Military Hardware and Technology?' (1987) 25 JCMS 238.

Hartley, T., *The Legal Foundations of EC Law*, edn. (Oxford, 1988).

Hecquard-Theron, 'La notion d'État en droit communautaire' (1990) 26 RTDE 693.

Heibourg, 'A European Defence Industry: Dream or Reality?' *NATO's Sixteen Nations*, Dec. 1988–Jan. 1989.

Hen and Guillermin, 'Les marchés publics de fournitures et l'adaptation de la Directive du 21 decembre 1976' (1989) RMC 637.

Hen, 'Les incidences du droit européen sur le droit français des marchés publics' (1975) *Actualité Juridique—Droit Administratif* 496.

Hilf, 'Die Richtline der EG—Ohne Richtung, ohne Linie' (1993) *Europarecht* 5.

Hindley, 'The Economics of an Accord on Public Procurement Policies' (1978) *The World Economy* 279.

Hindley, 'The Mixed Economy in an International Context' in Roll (Lord of Ipsden) *The Mixed Economy* (London, 1982).

Hirsch, 'Objectif 1992: Le dossier-test marchés publics' (1988) RMC 1.

Hirtris, *European Community Economics* (London, 1988).

Hobday, 'The European Semi-Conductor Industry: Resurgence and Rationalization' (1989) 28 JCMS 155.

Hoekman and Mavroidis, 'The WTO's Agreement on Government Procurement: Expanding Disciplines, Declining Membership? (1995) 4 PPLR 63.

Hoffmann, 'Anti-competitive State Legislation Condemned under Articles 5, 85 and 86 of the EEC Treaty: How far Should the Court go after Van Eycke?' (1990) 11 ECLR 11.

House of Lords Select Committee on the European Communities, *Compliance with Public Procurement Directives*, session 1987–88 12th report.

Höfler, "The Protection of the Interests of Bidders in the Precontractual Stage under German Procurement Law" (1995) 4 PPLR 159.

Howells, 'European Directives—the Emerging Dilemmas' (1991) 54 MLR 456.

Hubeau, 'La répétition de l'indu en Droit Communautaire' (1981) 17 RTDE 442.

Jacqué, 'L'Acte Unique Européen' (1987) 23 RTDE 575.

Janot, 'Les accords internationaux sur les marchés publics: des résultats réels mais limités' (1985) *Revue Française d'Administration Publique* 26.

Jeanrenaud, 'Marchés publics et politique économique' (1984) 72 *Annales de l'Économie Publique, Sociale et Coopérative* 151.

Jeanrenaud (ed.), *Regional Impact of Public Procurement* (Saint-Saphorin, 1984).

Jeanrenaud and Meyer, 'L'incidence à moyen et long terme des commandes de material de télécommunication: deux études de cas (1984) 72 *Annales de l'Économie Publique, Sociale et Coopérative* 191.

Jouret, 'Les conclusions d'edimbourg sur le Paquet «Delors II»' (1993) RMC 391.

Juristo, 'La adaptación de la regulación española del contrato de obra pública a las Directivas de la Comunidad Económica Europea' (1986) REDA 85.

Kadish, 'Some Observations on the Use of Minimal Sanctions in Enforcing Economic Regulations' (1963) 30 *The University of Chicago Law Review* 423.

Kenner, 'Economic and Social Cohesion—The Rocky Road Ahead' (1994) LIEI 1.

Keohane and Hoffmann, 'Institutional Change in Europe in the 1980s' in Keohane and Hoffmann, *The New EC: Decision-Making and Institutional Change* (Boulder, 1991).

Keyzer, 'L'importance et la politique des achats publics' (1968) *Hommes et Techniques* 26.

Kirchner, 'Has the Single European Act Opened the Door for a Security Policy?' (1990) *Revue d'Intégration Européenne* 1.

Kolodziej, *Making and Marketing Arms. The French Experience and its Implication for the International System* (Princeton, 1987).

Kopp, 'Die Entscheidung über die Vergabe öffentlicher Aufträge und über Abschluß öffentlichrechtlicher Verträge als Verwaltungsakte?', *Bayerische Verwaltungsblätter* 1980, 609.

Kovar, 'Voies de droit ouvertes aux individus devant les instances nationales en cas de violation des normes et décisions du droit communautaire' in Larcier (ed.), *Les recours des individus devant des instances nationales en cas de violation du droit européen* (Bruxelles, 1978).

Krislow, Ehlermann and Weiler, 'The Political Organs and the Decision-Making Process in the U.S. and the European Community' in Cappelletti, Seccombe and Weiler (eds.), *Integration Through Law*, Vol. 1 Book 2, *Political Organs, Integration Techniques and Judicial Process* (Berlin, 1986).

Labayle, 'Le contrôle de la réglementation communautaire en matière de marchés publics' (1989) RMC 625.

Lamarca, 'La sospensione cautelare degli appalti pubblici nel procedimento ex art. 169 del trattato di Roma' (1989) *Rivista di Diritto Europeo* 383.

Lamarca, 'Sospensione cautelare dell'appalto gia aggiudicato e conciliazione giudiziale: il caso *Storebaelt*' (1990) *Rivista di Diritto Europeo* 803.

Larcier (ed.), *Les Recours des Individus Devant les Instances Nationales en Cas de Violation du Droit Européen* (Bruxelles, 1978).

Lasok, K.P.E., 'State Liability for Breach of Community law' (1992) 5 *International Company and Commercial Law Review* 186.

Lasok, 'State Aids and Remedies under the EEC Treaty' (1986) ECLR 53.

Laubadère, Moderne and Devolvé, *Traité des Contrats Administratifs* (Paris, 1983).

Laubadère, *Traité de Droit Administratif*, 9ème edn. (Paris, 1984).

Laviolette-Vanderpooten, 'Les directives européennes relatives aux marchés publics de travaux' (1972) RMC 474.

Lecourt, *L'Europe des Juges* (Bruxelles, 1976).

Lefoulon, 'Contribution à l'étude de la distinction des contentieux. Le problème de la compétence du juge du contrat en matière administrative' (1976) *Actualité Juridique—Droit Administratif* 396.

Lewis, *Judicial Remedies in Public Law* (London, 1992).

Lowinger, 'Discriminatory Procurement of Foreign Goods in the US and Western Europe' (1976) 42 *Southern Economic Journal* 451.

Lozano, 'International Construction Markets. EC, USA and Japan', Advisory Committee for Public Procurement EC Commission CC/90/73.

Lupp, *Objektivät, Transparenz and Nachprüfbarkeit der Angebotswertung bei der Vergabe öffentlicher Bauaufträge* (Munich, 1992).

Magliano, 'Il contenzioso degli appalti pubblici nella prospettiva del mercato unico europeo' (1991) *Rivista di Diritto Europeo* 883.

Majone, 'The European Community between Social Policy and Social Regulation' (1993) 31 JCMS 153.

Maldague, 'La politique des commandes publiques: instrument de politique économique? Le cas Belgique' in (1984) 72 *Annales de l'Économie Publique, Sociale et Cooperative* 173.

Mann, 'L'invocabilité des directives: quelques interrogations' (1990) 26 RTDE 669.

Margue, 'L'ouverture des marchés publics dans la Communauté (1ère partie)' (1991) *Revue du Marché Unique Européen* 143.

Margue, 'L'ouverture des marchés publics dans la Communauté (2ème partie)' (1991) *Revue du Marché Unique Européen* 177.

Marissing, van, *Liberalization of the European Market for Public Procurement: a Lengthy and Extensive Process* (Diemen, 1989).

Martín Rebollo, 'Nuevos plantamientos en materia de responsibilidad de las administraciones públicas' in *Estudios sobre la Constitucion Espanola. Libro homenaje al Professor García de Enterría* (Madrid, 1991).

Martín Retortillo, 'Institución contractual en el derecho administrativo: en trono al problema de la igualdad de las partes' (1959) RAP 50.

Martín Retortillo, 'Reciente evolución de la jurisprudencia administrativa: actos separables admitidos por el Tribunal Supremo' (1961) RAP 227.

Martin, 'New Developments in Public Procurement in France' (1995) 4 PPLR CS 53.

Martin, 'The Contractual 'Réferé' Procedures under Article L22 of the Administrative Tribunals and Administrative Courts of Appeal Code. Application in Practice' (1994) 3 PPLR CS 112.

Mattera, Bangemann, Mertens de Wilmars, Mattina, Ehlermann, Gazzo and Constantinesco, 'Le principe de subsidiarité au service d'une Communauté à la dimension des problèmes de notre temps' (1992) *Revue du Marché Unique Européen* 189.

Mattera, 'La libéralisation des marchés publics et semi-publics dans la Communauté' (1973) RMC 206.

Mattera, *Le Marché Unique Européen. Ses Règles. Son Fonctionnement* (Paris, 1990).

Mattera, 'Les marchés publics: dernier rempart du protectionisme des États' (1993) *Revue du Marché Unique Européen* 5.

McCrudden, 'Public Procurement and Equal Opportunities in the European Community. A study of "contract compliance" in the Member States of the European Community and under Community law' (Brussels, 1994).

McGowan and Thomas, 'Bureaucratic Rules versus Competition? An Alternative Approach to Utilities Procurement in the EC Electricity Sector', paper presented to the conference on *Implementing and Enforcing the European Community Procurement Directives*, Birmingham, April 1993.

McLachlan, 'Discriminatory Public Procurement, Economic Integration and the Role of Bureaucracy' (1985) 23 JCMS 357.

Mead, note on Case C-106/89, *Marleasing* (1991) 16 ELRev 490.

Meredith (ed.), *European Initiatives in Public Procurement* (New York, 1990).

Merten de Wilmars, 'L'efficacité des différentes techniques nationales de protection juridique contre les violations du droit communautaire par les autorités nationales et les particuliers' (1981) 17 CDE 379.

Merusi, 'Riserve obbligatorie e sistema sanitario nazionale' (1988) *Il Diritto dell'Economia* 35.

Mestre Delgado, 'El control de la adjudicación de los contratos públicos a tenor del derecho comuniatrio europeo. Una nueva ordenación de las medidas cautelares. (Comentario a la Directiva 89/665/Cee de 21 diciembre 1989)' (1991) No. 74 *Noticias CEE* 35.

Mestre Delgado, 'La posición singular de la administración en la contratación administrativa y las garantías del contratista según la jurisprudencia contencioso-administrativa reciente' (1985) REDA 425.

Michel, 'La jurisprudence de la Cour de Justice sur les marchés publics' (1994) *Revue du Marché Unique Européen* 135.

Millán Moro, 'La eficacia directa de las directivas. Evolución reciente' (1991) 18 *Revista de Instituciones Europeas* 845.

Millet, 'Les marchés publics en droit comparé. Le Royaume Uni' in *Les Marchés Publics Européens. Droit communautaire. Droit comparé* (1989) *Dossiers et Documents de la Revue Française de Droit Administratif.*

Ministerio de Economía y Hacienda, *Memoria de la Junta Consultiva de Contratación Administrativa* (Madrid, 1994).

Mishan, *Economic Efficiency and Social Welfare: Selected Essays on Fundamental Aspects of the Economic Theory of Social Welfare* (London, 1981).

Mitchell, 'A General Theory of Public Contracts' (1951) 63 *Juridical Review* 60.

Mitchell, *The Contracts of Public Authorities. A Comparative Study* (London, 1954).

Monedero Gil, 'Criterios de adjudicación del contrato administrativo en el derecho comunitario' (1986) No. 21 *Noticias CEE* 63.

Mougeot and Naegelen, *Les Marchés Hospitaliers. Analyse Théorique et Application aux Achats des Pharmacies Hospitalières* (Paris, 1984).

Nell, 'Analyse empirique de la portée matérielle d'une libéralisation des marchés publics suisses de travaux au niveau européen' (1993) 51 *Revue Économique et Sociale,* 159.

Nicholas, *The French Law of Contract,* 2nd edn. (Oxford, 1992).

Niedzela and Engshuber, 'Enforcing the Public Procurement Rules in Germany' in Arrowsmith (ed.), *Remedies for Enforcing the Public Procurement Directives,* (Winteringham, 1993).

Nielsen, 'Public Procurement and International Labour Standards' (1995) 4 PPLR 94.

O'Leary, *The Evolving Concept of Community Citizenship—From the Free Movement of Persons to Union Citizenship,* forthcoming (London, 1996).

O'Loan 'United Kingdom Implementation of the Services Directive 92/50' (1994) 3 PPLR CS 60.

O'Loan, 'An Analysis of the Utilities Directive of the European Communities' (1992) 1 PPLR 175.

O'Loan, 'An Analysis of the Works and Supplies Directives of the European Communities' (1992) 1 PPLR 40.

O'Loan, 'Implementation of the Works, Supplies and Compliance Directives in the UK' (1992) 1 PPLR 88.

O'Loan, 'Remedies in the UK and Ireland', paper presented to the conference on *Implementing and Enforcing the EC Procurement Directives,* Birmingham, April 1993.

OECD, *Government Purchasing in Europe. North America and Japan* (Paris, 1966).

OECD, ICCP, *The Telecommunications Industry. The Challenges of Structural Change* (Paris, 1988).

Ojeda Marin, 'Hacia un sistema de contratación pública acorde con el mercado interior' (1988) 15 *Revista de Instituciones Europeas* 821.

Ojeda Marin, 'La Comunidad Europea y el GATT en el moderno sistema de contratación pública' (1988) RAP 409.

Ojeda Marín, 'Contratos públicos en la CEE: La ley de contratos del Estado y su adecuación al ordenamiento jurídico comunitario' (1987) RAP 131.

Oliver, D., 'Fishing on the Incoming Tide' (1991) 54 MLR 442.

Oliver, 'A Review of the Case-Law of the Court of Justice on Articles 30 to 36 in 1985' (1986) 23 CMLRev 325.

Oliver, 'Enforcing Community Rights in the English Courts' (1987) 50 MLR 881.

Oliver, *Free Movement of Goods in the EEC,* 2nd edn. (London, 1988).

Oliver, 'Interim Measures: some Recent Developments' (1992) 29 CMLRev 7.

Oliver, 'Le droit communautaire et les voies de recours nationaux' (1992) 28 CDE 348.

Oliver, note on Case 76/81, *SA Transporoute et Travaux* (1982) 7 ELRev 233.

Paddon, 'EC Public Procurement Directives and the Competition from European Contractors for Local Authority Contracts in the UK' in Clarke and Pitelis (eds.), *The Political Economy of Privatisation* (London, 1993).

Painter, 'CCT in Local Government: the First Round' (1991) 39 *Public Administration* 191.

Parada Vazquez, *Derecho Administrativo. Parte General* (Madrid, 1989).

Parker, 'The 1988 Local Government Act and Compulsory Competitive Tendering' (1990) 5 *Urban Studies* 653.

Parsons, 'Economic Principles in the Private and Public sectors' (1988) 16 *Policy and Politics* 29.

Pelkmans and Winters, *Europe's Domestic Market* (London, 1988).

Pelkmans, 'A Grand Design by the Piece? An Appraisal of the Internal Market Strategy' in Bieber, Dehousse, Pinder and Weiler (eds.), *1992: One European Market?* (Baden-Baden, 1988).

Péquignot, 'Contribution à la Théorie Générale du Contrat Administratif', Thèse (Montpellier, 1965).

Perissich, 'Le principe de subsidiarité, fil conducteur de la politique de la Communauté dans les années à venir' (1992) *Revue du Marché Unique Européen* 7.

Pescatore, 'The Doctrine of Direct Effect: an Infant Disease in Community Law' (1983) 8 ELRev 155.

Pescatore, 'Public and Private Aspects of the Community Competition Law' in Hawk (ed.), *U.S. and Common Market Antitrust Policies* (New York, 1986).

Pescatore, 'Some Critical Remarks on the Single European Act' (1987) 24 CMLRev 7.

Pescatore, *The Law of Integration* (Leiden, 1973).

Piroche, 'Les mesures provisoires de la Commission des Communautés Européennes dans le domaine de la concurrence' (1989) 25 RTDE 439.

Plaza Martín 'Furthering the Effectiveness of EC Directives and the Judicial Protection of Individual Community Rights thereunder' (1994) 43 ICLQ 26.

Pomeranz, 'Towards a New International Order in Government Procurement' (1979) *11 Law and Policy in International Business* 1263.

Ponssard et De Pouvourville, *Marchés Publics et Politique Industrielle* (Paris, 1982).

Pontarollo, 'Procurement in the Utility Sector in Italy' (1994) 3 PPLR 1.

Prechal, 'Remedies after Marshall' (1990) 27 CMLRev 451.

'Project: the Impact of Cost-Benefit Analysis on Federal Administrative Law' (1990) 42 *Administrative Law Review* 545.

Quigley, 'The Notion of a State aid in the EEC' (1988) 13 ELRev 242.

Radford, 'Competition Rules: the Local Government Act 1988' (1988) 51 MLR 717.

Rainuad, 'Les marchés publics dans la CEE' (1972) RMC 365.

Rallo, 'The EC Industrial Policy Revisited. The Case of Aerospace' (1984) 22 JCMS 245.

Rapport du Groupe Stratégie Industrielle: Travaux Publics (1987) *La Documentation Française.*

Reboud (ed.), *L'Achèvement du Marché Intérieur Européen. Signification et Exigences* (Paris, 1987).

Remien, 'Public Procurement Law in an International Perspective' 1991 (unpublished paper).

Report, 'An Explosive Issue: 'Subjective Rights' or Internal Administrative Controls?' (1993) 3 *EC Public Contracts* 10.

Richonnier, 'Europe's Decline is not Irreversible' (1984) 22 JCMS 235.

Richonnier, *Les Métamorphoses de l'Europe. De 1769 à 2001* (Paris, 1986).

Rideau et al., *La France et les Communautés Européennes* (Paris, 1974).

Rideau, 'Le contentieux de l'application du droit communautaire par les pouvoirs publics nationaux' (1974) *Chronique XIX Dalloz-Sirey* 147.

Rideau, 'Le rôle des États membres dans l'application du droit communautaire' (1972) *Annuaire Français de Droit International* 864.

Riga, 'Recent Council Directives and Commission Proposals Affecting Public Procurement in the European Communities' (1989) 12 *Boston College International and Comparative Law Review* 387.

Rittner, 'Rechtsgrundlagen und Rechtgrundsätze des öffentlichen Auftragswesens. Eine systematische Analyse' in *Schriften zum öffentlichen Auftragswesen* (Freiburg, 1988).

Rivero 'Vers un droit commun européen: nouvelles perspectives en droit administratif' in Cappelletti (ed.), *New Perspectives for a Common Law of Europe* (London, 1978).

Rodríguez-Arana, 'De nuevo sobre la suspensión judicial del acto administrativo (1986–87)' (1989) REDA 639.

Roll (Lord of Ipsden), *The Mixed Economy* (London, 1982).

Roobeek, 'Telecommunications: an Industry in Transition' in de Jons (ed.), *The Structure of European Industry* (Dordrecht, 1988).

Roquette and Lefort, 'Implementation of the Public Procurement Directives in the 12 Member States of the EC' (1992) 1 PPLR 251.

Ross, 'Beyond Francovich' (1993) 56 MLR 55.

Ross, J. 'High-Speed Rail: Catalyst for European Integration?' (1994) 32 JCMS 91.

Rothwell, 'Le rôle des commandes publiques pour créer une infrastructure régionale innovante' (1984) 72 *Annales de l'Économie Publique, Sociale et Cooperative* 159.

Samaniego Bordiú, 'El control del derecho comunitario de los contratos publicos' (1990) RAP 401.

Samuel, 'Public and Private Law: a Private Lawyer's Response' (1983) 46 MLR 558.

Savy (ed.), *L'Intervention des Pouvoirs Publics dans la Vie Économique* (Limoges, 1978).

Scherer, 'Telecommunications and Public Procurement' paper presented at the *Europe-Japan Economic Research Center Seminar*, Brussels, 25/5/1988.

Schermers and Waelbroeck, *Judicial Protection in the European Communities*, 4th edn. (Deventer, 1987).

Scheuing, *Les Aides Financières Publiques aux Entreprises Privées en Droit Français et Européen* (Paris, 1974).

Schina, *State Aids under the EEC Treaty. Articles 92 to 94* (Oxford, 1987).

Schmitt von Sydow, 'The Basic Strategies of the Commission's White Paper' in Bieber, Dehousse, Pinder and Weiler (eds.), *1992: One European Market?* (Baden-Baden, 1988).

Schockweiler, 'La responsabilité de l'autorité nationale en cas de violation du droit communautaire' (1992) 28 RTDE 27.

Schockweiler, Wivenes and Godart, 'Le régime de la responsabilité extra-contractuelle du fait d'actes juridiques dans la Communauté européenne' (1990) 26 RTDE 27.

Schramme, 'Rapport entre les mesures d'effet équivalent à des restrictions quantitatives et les aides nationales' (1985) 21 RTDE 487.

Schwartz, *French Administrative Law and the Common Law World* (New York, 1954).

Schwarze, *Administrative Law* (London, 1992).

Scott, 'Standing in the Supreme Court: A Functional Analysis' (1973) 83 *Harvard Law Review* 645.

Seidel, 'Die Anwendung der EG—Richtlinien fur die öffentlichen Aufträge in der Bundesrepublik Deutschland' (1990) *Europarecht* 158.

Seidel, 'German Report to the 14th FIDE Conference' in FIDE *L'Application dans les États Membres des Directives sur les Marchés Publics* (Madrid, 1990).

Seidel, 'Implementation of the Public Procurement Directives in the 12 States of the EC' (1992) 1 PPLR 257.

Shanks, 'Introductory Article: the Social Policy of the European Communities' (1977) 14 CMLRev 375.

Shaw, 'Twin Track Social Europe. The Inside Track' in O'Keefe and Twomey (eds.), *Legal Issues of the Maastricht Treaty* (London, 1993) 295.

Siedentopf and Hauschild, 'La directive dans la Communauté Européene' in Siedentopf and Ziller (eds.), *L'Europe des Administrations? La Mise en Œuvre de la Législation Communautaire dans les États membres* (Maastricht, 1988).

Siedentopf and Ziller (eds.), *L'Europe des Administrations? La Mise en Ouvre de la Législation Communautaire dans les États membres* (Maastricht, 1988).

Simon and Barav, 'Le droit communautaire et la suspension provisoire des mesures nationales. Les enjeux de l'affaire Factortame' (1990) RMC 591.

Smith, 'The Francovich Case: State Liability and the Individual's Right to Damages' (1992) 13 ECLR 129.

Snyder (ed.), *European Community Law* (Aldershot, 1993).

Snyder, *New Directions in European Community Law* (London, 1990).

Snyder, 'The Effectiveness of European Community law: Institutions, Processes, Tools and Techniques' (1993) 56 MLR 19.

Söffner, *Awarding Building and Public Works Contracts in the EC*, IFO-Studien zur Bauwirtschaft 8/E, Institut fur Wirstchaftforschung a.v., Munich, 1984.

Söffner, 'Kleiner Aktionsradius der Bauunternehmen' in *IFO Schnelldienst* Nr. 15/ 1979.

Sohrab, 'The Single European Market and Public Procurement' (1990) 10 *Oxford Journal of Legal Studies* 522.

Soulié, 'La Passation des Marchés Publics en France et dans la Communauté Économique Européenne', Thèse (Paris, 1987).

Stein and Vining, 'Citizen Access to Judicial Review of Administrative Action in a Transnational and Federal Context' in Jacobs, F.G. (ed.), *European Law and the Individual* (Amsterdam, 1976).

Steiner, 'From Direct Effect to Francovich: Shifting Means of Enforcement of Community Law' (1993) 18 ELRev 3.

Steiner, 'How to Make the Action Suit the Case. Domestic Remedies for Breach of EEC Law' (1987) 12 ELRev 102.

Stigler and Becker, 'Law Enforcement, Malfeasance, and Compensation of Enforcers' (1974) 3 *The Journal of Legal Studies* 1.

Stigler, 'The Optimum Enforcement of Laws' (1970) 78 *Journal of Political Economics* 526.

Stockmann, 'L'abus de puissance d'achat de la part de la puissance publique en R.F.A.' (1987) 9 *Journées de la Société de Législation Comparée* 535.

Strange, 'A Dissident View' in Bieber, Dehousse, Pinder and Weiler (eds.), *1992: One European Market?* (Baden-Baden, 1988).

Street, *Government Liability* (London, 1953).

Struys, 'Questions choisies de procédure en matière d'aides d'État' (1993) 30 RTDE 17.

Stuyck and Wyttinck, note on Case C-106/89 *Marleasing* (1991) 28 CMLRev 205.

Sunkin, 'Judicial Review: Rights and Discretion in Public Law' (1983) 43 MLR 645.

Szyszczak, 'European Community Law: New remedies, New directions? Joined cases C-6/90 and C-9/90, *Francovich* and *Bonifaci* v. *Italy*' (1992) 55 MLR 690.

Szyszczak, 'Social Policy: A Happy Ending or a Reworking of a Fairy Tale?' in O'Keefe, and Twomey (eds.), *Legal Issues of the Maastricht Treaty* (London, 1993) 313.

Temple Lang, 'Community Constitutional Law: Article 5 EEC Treaty' (1990) 27 CMLRev 645.

Temple Lang, 'New Legal Effects Resulting From the Failure of States to Fulfil Obligations under European Community Law: the Francovich Judgment' (1992–1993) 16 *Fordham International Law Journal* 1.

Terneyre, 'Le droit des marchés publics dans la perspective de leur ouverture aux opérateurs communautaires' (1990) *Les Petites Affiches* no. 148, 13.

The Economist, Survey of Italy, 26 May 1990.

The Economist, 3 September 1994.

Thys and Henry, 'Government Procurement Regulations of the EEC' (1987) 21 *George Washington Journal of International Law & Economics* 445.

Torno Mas, 'La situación actual del proceso contencioso-administrativo' (1990) RAP 103.

Torno Mas, 'La suspensión judicial de la eficacia de los actos en la ley de la jurisdicción Contencioso-Administrativa' (1986) *Revista Jurídica de Cataluña* 77.

Toth, note on Case C-213/89, *R* v. *Secretary of State for Transport, ex parte Factortame Limited and Others* (1990) 27 CMLRev 573.

Toth, 'The Principle of Subsidiarity in the Maastricht Treaty' (1992) 29 CMLRev 1079.

Tovias, 'The Impact of Liberalizing Government Procurement Policies of Individual EC Countries on Trade with Non-Members' (1990) *Weltwirtschaftliches Archiv* 722.

Tullock, 'Two Kinds of Legal Efficiency' (1979–1980) 8 *Hofstra Law Review* 659.

Turpin, *Government Contracts* (Harmondsworth, 1972).

Turpin, *Government Procurement and Contracts* (Harlow, 1989).

Turpin, 'Public Contracts in the EEC' (1972) 9 CMLRev 411.

Uttley and Harper, 'The Political Economy of Competitive Tendering' in Clarke and Pitelis (eds.), *The Political Economy of Privatization* (London, 1993) 145.

Valadou, 'Enforcing the Public Procurement Rules in France' in Arrowsmith (ed.), *Remedies for Enforcing the Public Procurement Rules* (Winteringham, 1993).

Van Bael, 'Public Procurement and the Completion of the Internal Market: Law and Practice' (1989) LIEI 21.

Van de Meent, 'Enforcing the Public Procurement Rules in the Netherlands' in Arrowsmith (ed.), *Remedies for Enforcing the Public Procurement Rules* (Winteringham, 1993).

Van Gerven 'General Report presented to the 14th FIDE Conference' in FIDE *L'Application dans les États Membres des Directives sur les Marchés Publics,* Madrid 1990.

Van Miert, 'A Community Transport Policy Requires European Networks' (1992) 2 *EC Public Contract Law* 201.

Van Voorst tot Voorst and Van Dam, 'Europe 1992: Free Movement of Goods in the Wider Context of a Changing Europe' (1988) 25 CMLRev 693.

Veljanovski, *The Economics of Law. An Introductury Text* (London, 1990).

Vickerman, 'Transport Infrastructure and Region Building in the European Community' (1994) 32 JCMS 1.

Vogel-Polsky and Vogel, *L'Europe Sociale de 1993: Illusion, Alibi ou Réalité?* (Bruxelles, 1991).

Vogel-Polsky, 'L'Acte unique ouvre-t-il l'espace social européen' (1989) 2 *Droit Social* 177.

Wade and Forsyth, *Administrative Law,* 7th edn. (Oxford, 1994).

Wade, 'What Happened to the Sovereignty of Parliament?' (1991) 107 LQR 1.

Wainwright, 'Community Report to the 14th Fide Conference' in FIDE *L'Application dans les États Membres des Directives sur les Marchés Publics* (Madrid, 1990).

Wainwright, 'Legal Reforms in Public Procurement' (1990) 10 YEL 133.

Wareham, 'Subsidiarity: a Point of Principle' (1992) *Lawyer's Europe* 6.

Watson, 'Social Policy after Maastricht' (1993) 30 CMLR 481.

Weatherill, 'Enforcing the Public Procurement Directives in the United Kingdom' in Arrowsmith (ed.), *Remedies for Enforcing the Public Procurement Rules,* (Winteringham, 1993).

Weatherill, 'National Remedies and Equal Access to Public Procurement' (1990) 10 YEL 243.

Weil and Terré, *Droit Civil. Les Obligations*, 4ème edn. (Paris, 1986).

Weil, *Les Conséquences de l'Annulation d'un Acte Administratif pour Excès de Pouvoir* (Paris, 1952).

Weiler, 'The Community System: the Dual Character of Supranationalism' (1981) 1 YEL 267. Reprinted in Snyder (ed.), *European Community Law* (Aldershot, 1993).

Weiler, 'The Transformation of Europe' (1991) 100 *Yale Law Journal* 2403.

Weiler, 'The White Paper and the Application of Community law' in Bieber, Dehousse, Pinder and Weiler (eds.), *1992: One European Market?* (Baden-Baden, 1988).

Weiss, *Public Procurement in European Community Law* (London, 1993).

Weiss, 'Public Procurement in the EEC—Public Supply Contracts' (1988) 13 ELRev 318.

Weiss, 'The Law of Public Procurement in EFTA and the EEC: the Legal Framework and its Implementation' (1987) 7 YEL 59.

Wenzel, 'German Solution Not Likely to Last Long. Four Actions for Treaty Violation' (1993) 3 *EC Public Contracts* 11.

Wheaton, 'Defence Procurement and the European Community: the Legal Provisions' (1992) 1 PPLR 432.

White, 'In Search of the Limits to Article 30 of the EEC Treaty' (1989) 26 CMLRev 235.

Whiteford, 'Social Policy after Maastricht' (1993) 18 ELRev 202.

Wilke and Wallace, 'Subsidiarity: Approaches to Power-Sharing in the European Community' (1990) *R.I.I.A. Discussion Paper* no. 27.

Winkler, 'Law, State and Economy: the Industry Act 1975 in Context' (1975) 2 *British Journal of Law and Society* 103.

Winter, 'Direct Applicability and Direct Effect. Two Distinct and Different Concepts in Community Law' (1972) 9 CMLRev 425.

Winter, 'Public Procurement in the EEC' (1991) 28 CMLRev 741.

Winter, 'Supervision of State aid: Article 93 in the Court of Justice' (1993) 30 CMLRev 311.

Wishlade, 'Competition Policy, Cohesion and the Co-ordination of Regional Aids in the Community' (1993) 14 ECLR 143.

Index